The Artist as Professional in Japan

The Artist as Professional in Japan

Edited by

Melinda Takeuchi

STANFORD UNIVERSITY PRESS
Stanford, California

Stanford University Press
Stanford, California

Printed in the United States of America
on acid-free, archival-quality paper

Library of Congress Cataloging-in-Publication Data

The artist as professional in Japan / edited by Melinda Takeuchi.
p. cm.
ISBN 0-8047-4355-X (cloth : alk. paper)
1. Art, Japanese. 2. Artists—Japan—Social conditions—History.
3. Artists—Japan—Economic conditions—History. I. Takeuchi, Melinda.
N7353 .A75 2004
709'.2'252—dc22 2003024414

Original Printing 2004
Last figure below indicates year of this printing:
13 12 11 10 09 08 07 06 05 04

Designed by James P. Brommer
Typeset in 11/14.5 Bembo

This volume is dedicated to the memory of

Carolyn Wheelwright (1939–1989)

Contents

Editor's Note

When I embarked on this project, I never dreamed there existed so many variant, yet correct, methods of romanizing Japanese characters and transcribing dates. Our contributors seem to have found them all. Although measures worthy of a master sergeant were mustered to battle the demons of inconsistency, a few gremlins proved indefatigable. What to do, for example, when the same publisher lists itself as Shōgakkan in one publication and Shōgakukan in another? Some of us prefer to set off frequently found terminal characters like temple (*ji*) or painting (*e*) with hyphens so that readers unfamiliar with Japanese might begin to make sense of the language; others don't. In a similar vein, some contributors believe that in premodern times the surname Kanō was read with a short o, but not everyone agreed to this convention. I encountered the editor's classic dilemma between imposing my style on others and letting them speak with their own voice. One thing we did agree upon was to cite all Japanese names with the surname first. Consistency may be the hobgoblin of small minds, and while we recognize that it is also a mark of professionalism, there are times when absolute standardization eludes the grasp of mere mortals.

Several people deserve acknowledgment for shepherding this complicated project to fruition. We thank Muriel Bell for acquiring the manuscript and Mariana Raykov, whose efforts were as tactful as they were Herculean, for seeing it through. Tom Finnegan attacked sloppy prose with vigor and savvy. Mayu Tsuruya prepared the Glossary, and Carole Nowicke, librarian at Indiana University, gave up her Christmas holiday to create the index. Our gratitude to them all.

MELINDA TAKEUCHI

Illustrations

Contributors

KAREN L. BROCK, formerly associate professor of Japanese art history at Washington University in Saint Louis, is an independent scholar living in Red Lodge, Montana. Her published articles and ongoing research focus on Japanese picture scrolls from the twelfth through sixteenth centuries, and the literary and material culture of Kōzanji.

LOUISE ALLISON CORT is curator for ceramics at the Freer Gallery of Art and Arthur M. Sackler Gallery, Smithsonian Institution. Her interest in historical and contemporary Asian craft traditions grows out of periods of residence in Japan, India, and Thailand. She is the author of *A Basketmaker in Rural Japan* (Sackler Gallery, in association with Weatherhill, 1994), and her 1979 study of a Japanese ceramic-producing community (*Shigaraki, Potters' Valley*) was reprinted in 2000 by Weatherhill.

JULIE NELSON DAVIS, assistant professor of the history of art, the University of Pennsylvania, received her Ph.D. in Japanese art history from the University of Washington in 1997. She also studied at Gakushūin University (Peers' School) in Tokyo for two years (1992–94). A specialist in ukiyo-e prints, she has written several articles on that subject, and she is currently completing a book on Kitagawa Utamaro (1753?–1806).

CHRISTINE M. E. GUTH is an independent scholar. Her publications include *Art Tea and Industry: Masuda Takashi and the Mitsui Circle* (Princeton, 1993); *The Art of Edo Japan: The Artist and the City* (Abrams, 1996); "Charles Longfellow and Okakura Kakuzō: Cultural Cross-Dressing in the Colonial Context" (*Positions: East Asia Cultures Critique*, Winter 2000); and most recently *Longfellow's Tattoos: Tourism, Collecting, and Japan* (University of Washington Press, 2004).

DONALD F. MCCALLUM is an historian of Japanese art, with a particular interest in Buddhist sculpture. He has lived in Japan for a number of years and frequently returns for research. He is the author of *Zenkōji and Its Icon* (Princeton University Press, 1994) and numerous articles on a range of topics within Japanese art. He is currently working on a monograph, tentatively titled *The Four Great Temples of Seventh-Century Japan.*

JONATHAN M. REYNOLDS received his Ph.D. in art history from Stanford University in 1991. He has taught Japanese art history at University of Southern California since 2000 and has held research fellowships from the Japan Foundation, the Getty Foundation, the Center for Advanced Study in the Visual Arts, and the National Endowment for the Humanities. He is the author of *Maekawa Kunio and the Emergence of Japanese Modernist Architecture* (University of California Press, 2001).

MELINDA TAKEUCHI, professor of Japanese art at Stanford University and executive director of the Inter-University Center for Japanese Language Studies in Yokohama, is the author of *Taiga's True Views: The Language of Landscape Painting in Eighteenth-Century Japan* (Stanford University Press, 1992) and coauthor of *Worlds Seen and Imagined: Japanese Screen Paintings from the Idemitsu Museum of Art* (Asia Society, 1995). A specialist in Japanese painting and prints of early modern Japan, Takeuchi is currently working on a book on the horse in Japanese art and culture.

The Artist as Professional in Japan

Introduction

MELINDA TAKEUCHI

Japan! What romantic thoughts and memories arise at the name! Set uniquely along the coming paths of traffic between East and West, endowed by temperament to become the interpreter of East to West and of West to East, we have here an illuminated corner of history's scroll, a flash of human genius at highest tension. . . .

—*Ernest Fenollosa (1853–1908), early interpreter of Japanese culture in America*

When they had finished the main building and were working on the eastern wing, some carpenters squatted in a row to have their meal; I sat on the veranda and watched them. The moment the food was brought, they fell on the soup bowls and gulped down the contents. . . . They all behaved in exactly the same way, so I suppose this must be the custom of carpenters. I should not call it a very charming one.

—*Sei Shōnagōn, (eleventh century), court lady*

He [the potter Kyūemon] is handsome, intelligent, and so neatly dressed that he does not resemble an artisan (*shokunin*). On top of that, his work is excellent.

—*Sakai Uta-no-kami Tadakiyo, daimyo of the Umayabashi domain in Kōzuke, and senior councillor and great elder under the shogun Ietsuna (r. 1651–1680)*

Writing is unnecessary for a craftsman.

—*Takamura Tōun (1825–1879), sculptor and teacher of the sculptor Takamura Kōun (1852–1934)*

I am in search of absolute freedom in the artistic world.

—*Takamura Kōtarō (1883–1954), sculptor, grandson of Takamura Tōun, head of an Edo-period sculpture workshop*

Over a decade ago, the late Albert Elsen asked me to lead a session for his seminar "The History of the Artist from Ancient to Modern Times." It was thus by chance that I stumbled into the complex realm of the profession of the Japanese artist. As this panoply of remarks about Japanese artists reveals, the subject itself is so vast and riveting it was painful to hone it down to a two-hour class meeting; there was almost nothing I could assign the students to read. Without my realizing it, the seeds of this book were sown.

It was clear from the outset that this elephantine topic was too broad for one person to tackle. I decided to tap the resources of the field by organizing a panel for the College Art Association Meeting in 1990 on modes of artistic production in Japan. Three of the papers from that occasion, by Donald McCallum, Christine Guth, and Jonathan Reynolds, appear here with revisions.

This volume consists of individual case studies involving the professions of sculptor, painter, potter, printmaker, and architect; the span of time ranges from the seventh century to the twentieth. We regret that important media such as lacquer and textiles are not represented, but we set aside the unattainable goal of being comprehensive in favor of attempting to raise basic questions about what it meant (and still means) to be a Japanese artist. How did artists go about their business? What degree of control did they exercise over their métier? How were they viewed by society? What were some of the dynamics operating in the production, consumption, and evaluation of art and artist? How was the image of the artist "fashioned" during various periods?

HOW TO GRAPPLE WITH "ART" AND "ARTIST"?

If one ever doubted that "art" is a cultural construction, the smorgasbord of pronouncements offered at the beginning of this introduction, ranging from the eleventh to the nineteenth centuries, conveys a small glimpse of the terrible complexity of this contentious arena. What is taken for granted as the visual arts today clearly had a variety of meanings for different classes of people in different cultures at different times. Who decides? Serious study of Japanese culture began in the West during the ascendancy of the romantic notion of the artist in the late nineteenth century. This view not only informed early scholarly writings on Japanese art (witness the epigraph by Ernest Fenollosa at the beginning of this chapter), it has persisted with a sense of self-evident objectivity in the fabric of art-historical writing up to today. I recently polled the students in my lecture class about their notions of what the image of a "real artist" is. They enjoyed the discussion immensely, but I was astonished to discover that the overwhelming majority continues to line up on the side of the starving-in-the-garret, eccentric, loner-genius model, a paradigm that fits only a tiny percentage of the world's artmakers.

Thus an intractable conundrum manifests itself when we employ terminology and concepts that, although accepted as givens in the contemporary world, did not exist during the time under discussion. For most of East Asian history there was no word comparable to *art* in the Euro-American sense. If there was no such discursive realm as art, how can we properly characterize the material things we now anachronistically call "objects of art"? And if there were no *notions* of art or objects of art, is it even conceptually appropriate to speak of the makers of these objects as "artists"? If we cannot solve this problem satisfactorily—and we cannot—we should certainly be aware that at best we are doing an end run around it.

Satō Dōshin has traced, in abundant detail, the appearance, evolution, and nuances of the words *bijutsu* and *geijutsu*, the terms now used to designate "the arts" in contemporary Japan.[1] These compounds, along with terms such as *kaiga* (painting) and *chōkoku* (sculpture) were coined in the late nineteenth century as part of an ideological program to promulgate Western notions of the arts, and they represent a paradigm shift between two epochs.[2] As the title of Satō's book (*The Meiji State and Modern Art: The Politics of the Beautiful*) indicates, his interest lies in the relationship among art, politics, national identity, economics, and social class—the underpinnings of the modern art industry.

Tackling the problem of anachronism in employing Western notions of *art* for traditional Chinese visual culture, Lothar Ledderose points out that most of the people who produced China's bronzes, silks, lacquers, and statues were considered "workers—or at most, skilled artisans—who manufactured luxury goods."[3] Like the Japanese, the Chinese had no word for *art* until the late nineteenth century, when they borrowed the newly minted Japanese *bijutsu* (*meishu*). To reconstruct traditional Chinese parameters of "art," Ledderose turns to encyclopedias and lists of objects in collections, noting the inclusion or exclusion of various categories of objects.

In trying to characterize Japanese art and its makers in the context of this Introduction, I took a broader and simpler approach than either Satō or Ledderose. Upon reflection I realized that most of the material objects, even buildings, treated in these chapters were traditionally conceived within one of two (sometimes overlapping, sometimes distinct) existing epistemological purviews: *making* on the one hand, and *discussing* on the other—that is, purveyor versus consumer/connoisseur.

Making, which is covered by the ancient terms *gei* (mastery) and *kō* (fabrication), suggests hands-on construction, the mastery of a technique or a technology. It belongs to the preliterate, the physical, the immediate exigency of material "stuff." Techniques of making were typically passed down from generation to generation as closely guarded secrets, often transmitted orally. As the comment by Takamura Tōun at the beginning of this chapter shows, even up to the latter half of the nineteenth century fabrication could totally exclude the written word. Jōmon ceramics, predating writing, represent a kind of primordial *gei* or *kō*.

Discussion and criticism belong to the sphere of *bun*, literary achievement, or in the broadest sense to culture in general. *Bun* encompasses the cerebral world of language and writing. It is part of the apparatus for the construction of culture. It includes the literary arts and, of course, criticism and evaluation of the visual arts. It is as much about interpretive frames as it is about material things. When people talk today about "reading" a work of art, they are operating in the space between *gei/kō* and *bun*.[4]

As fabricators began to assume the dual roles of artist and commentator, or when literati created aesthetic objects as an avocation, the two realms drew closer. Guth's and Reynolds's chapters explore some of this territory. Throughout much of Japan's past, however, artists' thoughts toward their activities remained unrecorded. Others spoke for them; the pen was often sharper than the chisel, one might say. The chapters by McCallum and Brock reveal how the machine of political discourse worked to invent different views of the same individual over time. I explore a case of later artists manipulating the names of earlier ones for professional or cultural gain, while Cort's and Davis's chapters reconstruct some of the forces brought to bear on artistic reception by the makers' contemporaries. It was not until the second half of the nineteenth century that we get writings by artists on actual studio practice.[5]

I have been plagued throughout this volume by problems of nomenclature. Prior to the Meiji period, artists were described by the name of their medium, combined with the character for skill (*kō* or *takumi*, which can also mean skilled person); the medium could also be followed by the character for master (*shi*). None of the words in the modern arsenal of art criticism—*artist, artisan, fabricator*, the gendered term *craftsman* or its generic equivalent *craftsperson*—is a good translation for the traditional Japanese artist, although I use them more or less interchangeably, with the assumption that it is better to expand the conceptual borders of art making than to shrink them.[6]

SOMETHING BORROWED: CHINESE AND WESTERN INFLUENCE ON JAPANESE DISCOURSE

The collective realms of *gei/kō* and *bun* in Japan represent the intersection of various systems that often operated simultaneously. Japanese notions of the arts encompass strands from Chinese culture and, from the eighteenth century onward, European theories of the arts as well.

The Chinese offered the Japanese throughout their history various models for discussing visual culture and its makers. Chinese accounts of the earliest mythohistories, treating the preliterate age, ascribe to the great culture heroes the miraculous revelation of important technologies such as writing, divination, and sericulture. Many of these heroic deities were, in a sense, ur-craftspeople. Early Japanese conceptions of makers and critics undoubtedly originated in Chinese myths. As with Japanese Jōmon pottery, technological facility came first in China, then evaluation. Veneration of skill can be found, for example, in Zhuangzi's commendation of adroit tradespeople: the butcher so deft that his knife never dulled was held up as an exemplar of someone in tune with the Dao.

Although the Chinese who set the artistic standards may have relished the sophisticated bowls, cups, and plates produced by thousands of nameless potters, this does not mean they would have welcomed the creators of these marvels to their salons, any more than they would have invited to their tables the cooks who prepared the cuisine served on those extraordinary dishes. Artisans, those purveyors of necessities and luxuries that enriched the lives of people more powerful than themselves, ranked second from the bottom in the four-tier Chinese social scheme. This class was designated by the character *gong* (*kō* in Japanese). Chinese artisans occupied a position akin to Greek *banaussoi*, who were held in much lower esteem than poets and philosophers.[7]

It was within the realm of *wen*, culture, that the achievements deemed most profound took place. In hierarchical societies, the status of maker and product were often inseparable. It goes without saying that the so-called literati (in Chinese, *wenren*) were by definition those who abrogated for themselves the duty of setting forth the social norms in writing. One might say they were in charge of the "culture industry," to borrow Adorno's expression. The word *wenjen* could just as easily be translated "civilized or literate people," which of course says a great deal about those who did not fall into this category. These *belles lettrists* wrote prolifically about the criteria and standards of cultural production.

Painting and calligraphy were the two visual arts sanctioned by gentlemen for gentlemen that along with the attendant pastimes of music and a kind of strategic board game made up the four accomplishments of a cultivated individual. A painting by a literatus was deemed to possess an exponentially deeper order of profundity in China than a painting by an artisan, even though the artisan's work usually exhibited greater technical skill. This is not to imply that the literati never treated their products as commodities, because they did. Elaborate social rituals, however, neutralized the stigma of economic transactions. Such media as sculpture, ceramics, lacquer making or carpentry, which involved vigorous physical exertion—getting dirty or breaking one's fingernails—seem to have been off-limits to the Chinese gentleman. Upper-class Japanese appear to have been somewhat less reticent about tackling these more vigorous media; military aristocrats, for example, participated in hands-on pottery-making parties (see Chapter Five in this volume, by Cort).

Painters were the professionals most easily able to move between the worlds of artist and artisan in both China and Japan. Portraits of painters holding their brush could, after all, be mistaken for portraits of calligraphers or poets. The histories of both China and Japan are replete with individuals who took advantage of the ambiguity of this Chinese-delineated terrain (Tosa Mitsunobu and Kitagawa Utamaro being two examples explored herein).

The other great influence on Japanese thinking about art making came from the West. After the eighth Tokugawa shogun, Yoshimune (1684–1751), relaxed the censorship laws implemented by his predecessors, Western notions of art and the artist began trickling into Japan. By the end of the eighteenth century Shiba Kōkan (1747–1818) was able to pronounce, "Even though we often cannot read the descriptions written in the Dutch language, we still can get a thorough understanding of many of the things described merely by studying the pictures carefully. This fact alone proves the brilliance and superiority of Western [painting methods]."[8] Kōkan deliberately flew in the face of received wisdom from China asserting that deliberate awkwardness or amateurism takes precedence over verisimilitude. Kōkan's polemic was directed at the self-styled Japanese literati who espoused this Chinese attitude, and also at the Kano workshops that claimed to be the exclusive arbiters of painting theory, technique, and connoisseurship.

Kōkan was actually in a position to be possibly the first Japanese exposed to the contemporary notion of "art" as it was understood in eighteenth-century Europe. In his *Discussion of Western Painting* (*Seiyōga dan*), written in 1799, Kōkan refers (in Japanese phonetic katakana script) to a Dutch work in his possession. He transcribed it as "Konsuto shikirudobuuku."[9] This is the *Kunst Schilderboek* (Art picturebook), which employs the Dutch word for art, *kunst*. To my knowledge, Kōkan's use of *kunst* is the earliest appearance in Japan of a Western term for the generic category "art." What Kōkan made of it we are not in a position to say. He had no domestic concept with which to match it, and he did not elaborate on its meaning. Important as this discovery of the evidence for the word *kunst* in eighteenth-century Japan might be, it seems to have had no effect whatsoever on subsequent Japanese discourse during the Edo period, possibly because Japanese thinking was not ready for the epistemological category of "visual art."

Kōkan's work shows, though, that the Japanese were certainly aware of some of the Western criteria for vaunted painters. He copied from a Dutch book an image of the Greek Zeuxis, so celebrated for his realism that it was said that birds flew in the window of his studio and pecked at the grapes he had painted. Zeuxis' fruit exhibited the powers of mimesis that sat at the very pinnacle of Kōkan's desiderata for painting.[10] Kōkan also designed a copperplate engraving showing the (Western) painter in his studio, surrounded by globes, calipers, books, printing presses, eyeglasses, and other paraphernalia associated with scientific discovery.[11] During the late eighteenth century, Western and Chinese notions of empiricism converged to confer upon painters the presumed ability to explicate the natural sciences; this critical vision in turn was felt to unlock the secrets of the universe. The privileging of the painter's gaze was picked up and put to considerably more earthy uses by one of Kōkan's contemporaries, Utamaro (see Chapter Six in this book, by Davis).

After Japan opened its doors to the West upon the fall of the Tokugawa shogunate in 1868, disparate Western writings on art, aesthetics, and artists joined traditional practices and ideas. Although past protocols did not die out, another layer was added when the new Meiji government employed foreigners to teach art and encouraged Japan's sculptors, painters, and architects to study abroad. There they assimilated European theories of the arts and sought to incorporate these new ideas and practices into the Japanese social fabric upon their return. They then endeavored to present a newly retrofitted discursive concept, "Japanese art," to the West. In the drive to modernize the Japanese nation, Meiji bureaucrats promoted the production of industrial arts, the preservation of traditional arts as proof of Japan's past greatness, and the formal training of artists as part of university curriculum.

Guth's and Reynolds's chapters vividly portray aspects of the ensuing shakeup as it affected sculptors and builders. Now, with the advent of art schools, makers were formally instructed in the techniques of their profession, and they were compelled also to study such subjects as history, poetry, anatomy, and aesthetics.[12] The gap between maker and critic began to narrow. Besides eventually extirpating artists and their workshops from the communities in which they lived and worked, this curriculum gave the artist an incentive to produce other kinds of art (objects designed solely for exhibition, for example). It also provided them with the critical apparatus to write about it. New journals offered a forum for these emergent artist-critics from a variety of disciplines to define themselves. As a result, the advent of modernism in Japan provoked poignant intergenerational rifts (says Guth in Chapter Seven) as well as spirited dispute among contemporaries competing with each other to set forth the protocols of their burgeoning profession (see Reynolds's Chapter Eight). Such discussions often belonged to broader questions of redesigning and redefining the Japanese state, and their effects could be paralyzing to art production as well as catalyzing. Guth shows how the sculptor Takamura Kōtarō became so demoralized because he could not live up to the romanticized ideal of his idol, Auguste Rodin, that Kōtarō eventually devoted the bulk of his energies to writing about art rather than producing it.

ORIGIN MYTHS, TRADESPEOPLE, AND CANON FORMATION

It is no coincidence that the earliest surviving discourse on artistic production in Japan appeared also as a time when issues of emerging statehood and national identity drove the official rhetoric. The *Chronicles of Japan* (*Nihon shoki*, or *Nihongi*), completed in the early eighth century as an "official history" to legitimize the Yamato court, contain much that is of interest for establishing subsequent Japanese attitudes toward the artist. No one knows how ancient the stories related in the *Chronicles of Japan* really are, but this ideological document offers numerous fascinating parallels, brilliantly adapted, with the Chinese models that resemble it.

Just as the mythological culture-heroes of China invented and transferred the great technologies necessary to the world of human beings, so the divine ancestor of the Yamato clan, Amaterasu, the Sun Goddess, is associated with a number of crucial technologies of power. She herself mastered the art of weaving: seated in the Sacred Weaving Hall weaving garments for the gods she became so upset when her unruly nephew Susanoo threw a colt's skin through the roof that she hid in a cave and plunged the world into darkness.[13] According to one version offered in the *Chronicles*, the gods rallied by summoning craftspeople; they appointed various specialists to make the "sun-spear," the mirror, and the jewels required to lure her out.[14]

The text uses the Japanese word *be*, guilds specializing in crafts and services; the potters of the *haniwa* makers' guild furnishing the funerary sculpture for the great tumuli were distant ancestors of the ceramicist from Tosa sent to study Edo wares (see Cort's Chapter Five). Such guilds are the production structure discussed in McCallum's Chapter Two in this book. When Amaterasu subsequently sent the August Grandchild down to rule the earth, she delegated as his attendants the "first ancestors" of a number of such guilds, which included specialists in making hats, shields, metal objects, tree-fiber products (thought to be used in rituals), and jewels.[15] These primordial objects straddle two categories. There were technologies that yield items of value for conquest and temporal power: shields and metalwork. Others have to do with ritual and status objects. McCallum, for example, speaks of the "cap-ranks" of seventh-century society; hats clearly functioned more as semiotic markers of a person's importance than as simple protection for the head. Similarly, tree-fiber specialists and jewel makers created objects used in ritual propitiation of the gods. When Amaterasu sent her grandson down to rule the earth, she gave him mirror, sword, and jewel(s), a collection of paraphernalia reflecting this combination of bellicose and ceremonial.

The crafted objects named in the *Chronicles of Japan* were much more than inert lumps of fabricated wood, metal, and clay. They possessed magical powers of transformation. Mirrors, for example, could give birth to gods.[16] This conception of deities residing in or transmogrifying from inanimate objects is central to Japanese thought (as it is to many other religions). It gave rise to the enduring belief, shared by many cultures, that objects had a life of their own: the Western fairy tale of the red shoes, for example, or the popular notion that it was a bewitched kimono that burned down Edo in the great Furisode Fire of the Meireki era.[17] This principle of immanence is what gives icons and relics their power. It seems a logical extension of the concept of magical materiality that exceptional objects should be given names; this set up a resonance between named humans and named objects. It is perhaps no coincidence that both in the West and in Japan swords were among the earliest objects to receive names. Excalibur's counterpart, Kusanagi no tsurugi ("Grasscutter"), was discovered miraculously by Amaterasu's nephew in the tail of an eight-branched serpent.[18] Along with the mirror and jewel, it became one of the Three Imperial Regalia given to the first emperor.

We do not have accounts of the actual production of such hallowed objects, although we know that by the eighth century records indicate that in certain professions such as sutra copying ritual abstinence from polluting influences (garlic and onions, for instance) was essential to the magical efficacy of the final product; duties, salaries, and even meals were distributed according to finely cut distinctions in the ranking of the producers.[19] Temple ateliers (as discussed by Brock in Chapter Three) played a seminal role in the production and distribution of sacred objects. The elaborate purification rituals surrounding the rebuilding of the Ise Shrine still practiced in modern times are undoubtedly extremely ancient. The very body of the creator is a corollary to the sanctity of the product. Thus women were automatically banned from certain trades where the notion of pollution by blood would have been sacrilegious.

When material things can assume such power, it is a logical step from fetishizing an object to valorizing its maker. It is not surprising that the first "celebrity craftsmen" may have been swordsmiths, people literally on the cutting edge of matters of life or death. Swordsmiths were certainly among the earliest artisans to inscribe their own name on their works.[20] The name of the maker, along with the customary image of the deity Fudō often engraved into a sword, might have had an apotropaic function in warding off calamity. The presence of a noted fabricator's name on a piece (or the next best thing, attribution) might, among other things, serve to upgrade the object; confer dignity, authority, or protection on the owner; transform in some fashion those lucky enough to come into contact with it; or bolster subsequent ideological claims—not to mention enhance its value. The chapters by McCallum, Brock, and Davis as well as my own ruminate on the operations of associating objects and names.

One of the prominent features of the artists whose stories fill these pages is that their activities required the collaboration of numerous skilled colleagues, often deployed in the hierarchical structure of the hereditary workshop, organized like a family.[21] This was in effect a microcosm of a larger hierarchical social structure that usually placed purveyors of desirable items or skills considerably lower on the ladder than those who commanded their services. These purveyors often had little say in the selection of the theme or general style required for a given work.[22] Frequently—until the eighteenth century and the flourishing of bourgeois culture—their audience consisted of their social superiors. Sometimes, when the patron was extremely lofty, as with an emperor or a shogun, a go-between handled the commission; artists might never meet the client face to face. The maker's individual name, conferred by the head of the shop, usually included one of the characters from the head's own name. The individual's name was subsumed to a large degree by the house name. All these factors worked against the notion of savoring the artist's "individual touch."

As mentioned above, Japanese artists were traditionally categorized, and referred to in documents, by a vocational tag preceding their names. One finds numerous references to "master" (*shi*) coupled with the medium: "painter (*eshi*) so-and-so," "Buddhist sculptor (*busshi*) so-and-so." The less distinguished craftsmen were designated by the name of their medium plus the character *kō* (fabricator).

There was, however, a word that covered the collective artisanal class: *shokunin*. This two-character compound, of ancient vintage, appears in a Chinese text dating from the fifth to third centuries B.C.E.; there it is employed in the context of ox herders.[23] It later came to designate people who worked with their hands, although in China it was not as frequently used to denote artisans as it was in Japan.

Shokunin is a word with rich nuances in Japan. It means, simply, people (*nin*) with an occupation (*shoku*), but this covers a lot of ground. A fair translation of *shokunin* in its medieval sense might be "tradespeople," and that resonance continues to the present day. It must be noted that different occupations enjoyed varying status in various periods. Sculptors, for example, commanded greater respect in the Heian and Kamakura periods (Jōchō, for example, was a celebrated image maker) than they did in Muromachi. Conversely, potters, such as Nonomura Ninsei (ca. 1574–1660/6) or Ogata Kenzan (1663–1743) began to see their status rise during the Edo period.

There is something riveting about the voyeuristic activity of observing skilled people completely absorbed in their work, unaware that they are being watched. Laborers of all sorts seem to have fascinated aristocrats (those quintessential voyeurs) since Heian times, as the quote by Sei Shōnagon at the beginning of this chapter indicates. The polymath scholar Ōe Masafusa (1041–1111), for example, made a list of *shokunin* occupations that included "the imperial prince, high officials and advisors, aristocrats, literati, poets, painters (*gakō*), and warriors."[24] Focus soon shifted to the more plebeian end of this spectrum, and the word *shokunin* encompassed different kinds of occupations at different times.

Scholars have opined that the status of medieval *shokunin* was rather low.[25] This assessment, of course, depends on who is making the judgment; those in charge of *bun* by definition characterize what goes on within the sphere of *gei/kō*. The earliest depictions of workers, who emerge as a subject for painting in the Kamakura period (1185–1333), do indeed treat *shokunin* with little sympathy. The earliest surviving depiction of *shokunin* is a handscroll depicting the *Tōhokuin Poetry Contest Between Shokunin* (*Tōhokuin shokunin uta-awase*), purported to have been held in 1214 at the Tōhokuin villa, a residence formerly owned by the sister of the great Fujiwara Michinaga.[26] The representation is not just unsympathetic; it is ironic, in that it portrays five pairs of *shokunin* engaged in the unlikely act of conducting a fictive poetry contest. The occupations chosen for inclusion are a doctor paired with a fortune teller (first round); a carpenter and a blacksmith (second round); a sword sharpener and a metalworker (third round); a female shaman and a seedy gambler (forth round); and a fisherman and a peddler (fifth round). As is clear from the selection, which seems based on word plays and other intellectual considerations (*bun*), artisanal labor occupies only a corner of the rubric *shokunin*. Not only would many of these people have been marginally literate if at all; the conceit of a hairy naked gambler (who has literally lost his shirt, not to mention his loincloth) participating in an aristocratic activity such as court poetry stretches credulity almost as much as the suggestion that such a down-and-out might even be allowed within the gate of an important aristocratic mansion.

That a wide audience enjoyed depictions of *shokunin* is attested by the longevity of the theme. We reproduce here (Figures 1.1 through 1.3) sections

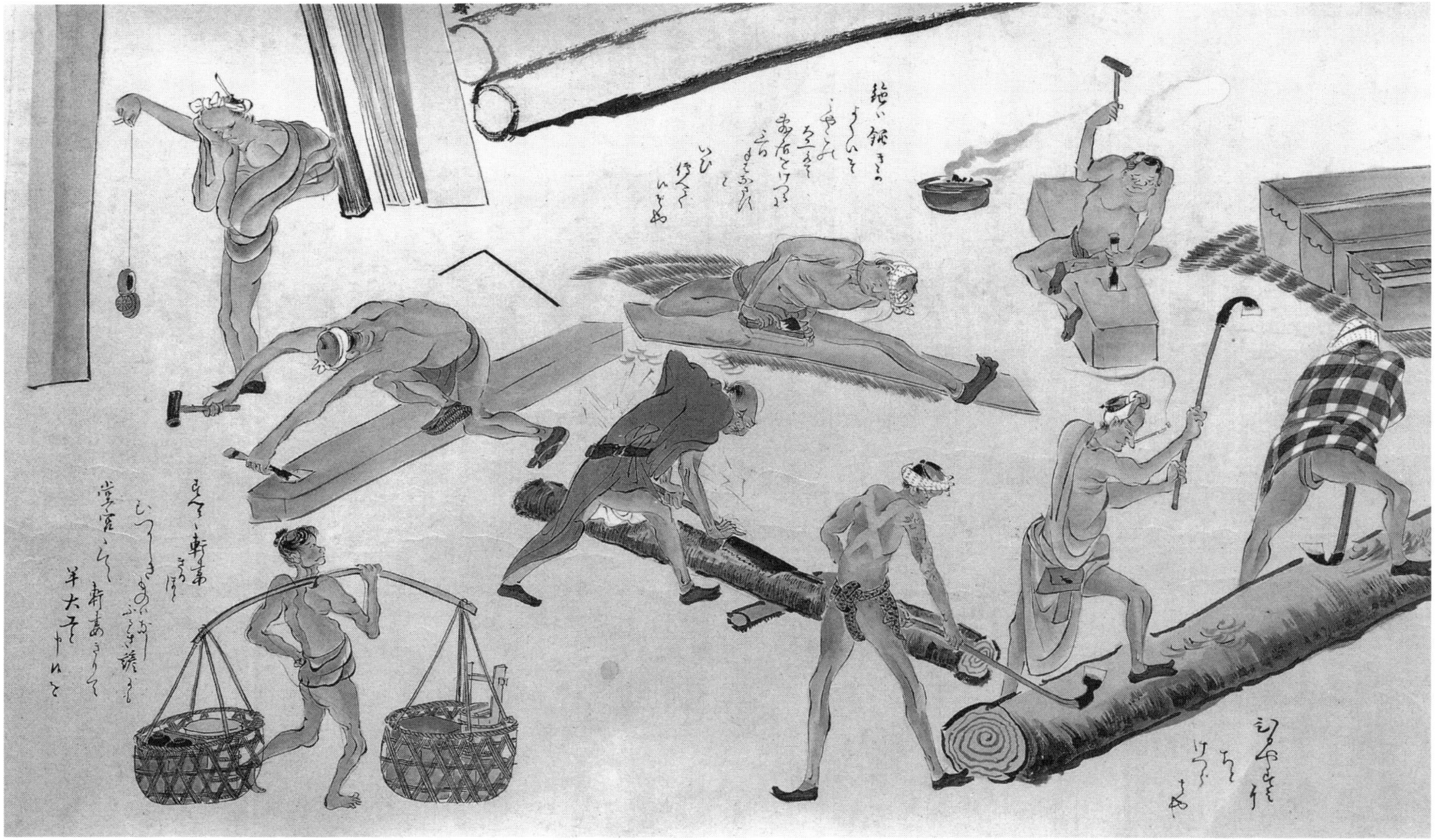

Figure 1.1 Kano Takanobu (1809–1892). Builders, from *Compendium of Edo Workers*, scroll 1, section 1. Handscroll, ink and color on paper, 36.2 cm x 1305 cm (entire scroll). Iris and B. Gerald Cantor Center for Visual Arts at Stanford University; gift of Dr. E. Nagura.

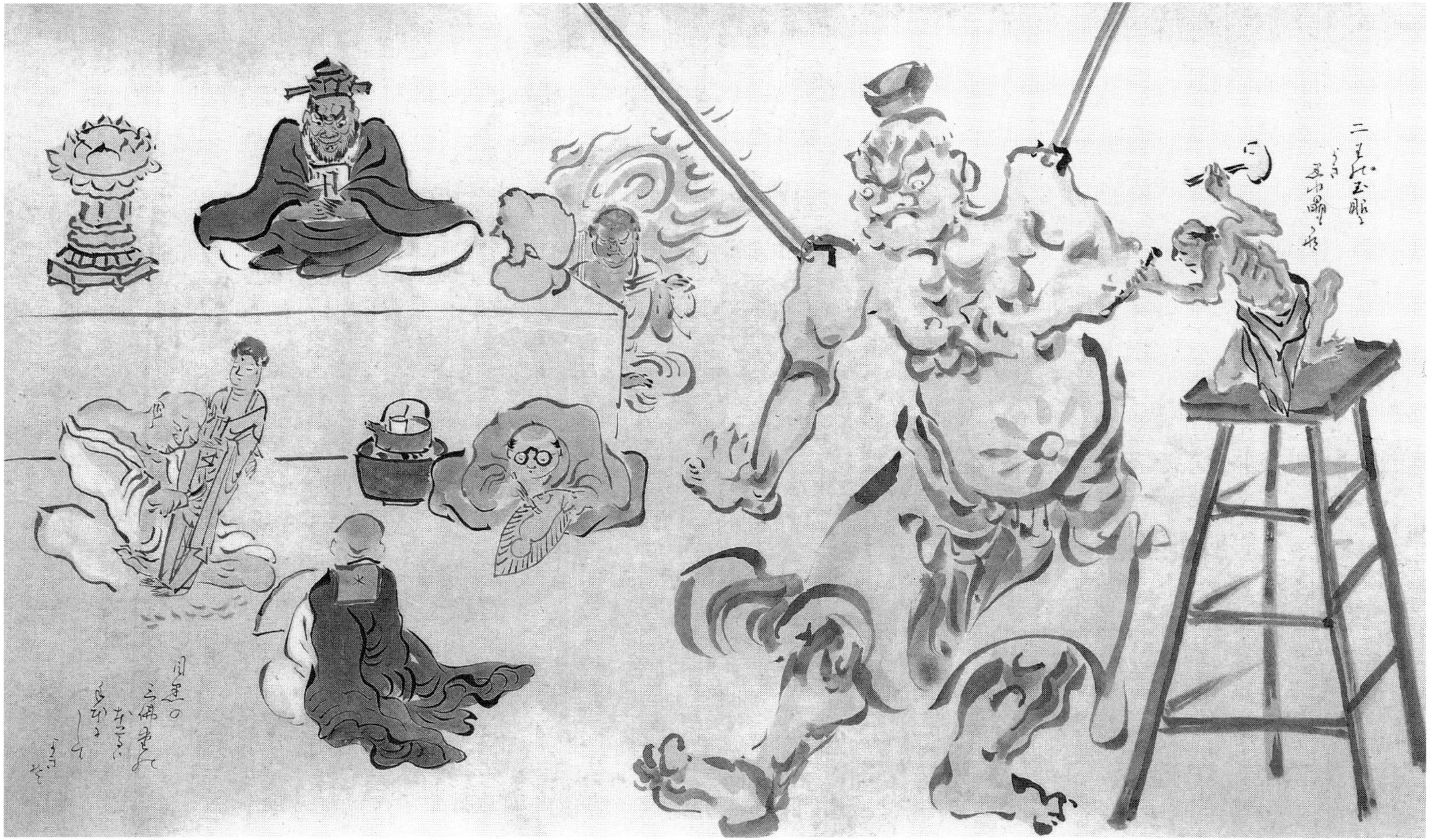

Figure 1.2 Kano Takanobu (1809–1892). Buddhist sculptor, from *Compendium of Edo Workers*, scroll 1, section 10. Handscroll, ink and color on paper, 36.2 cm x 1305 cm (entire scroll). Iris and B. Gerald Cantor Center for Visual Arts at Stanford University; gift of Dr. E. Nagura.

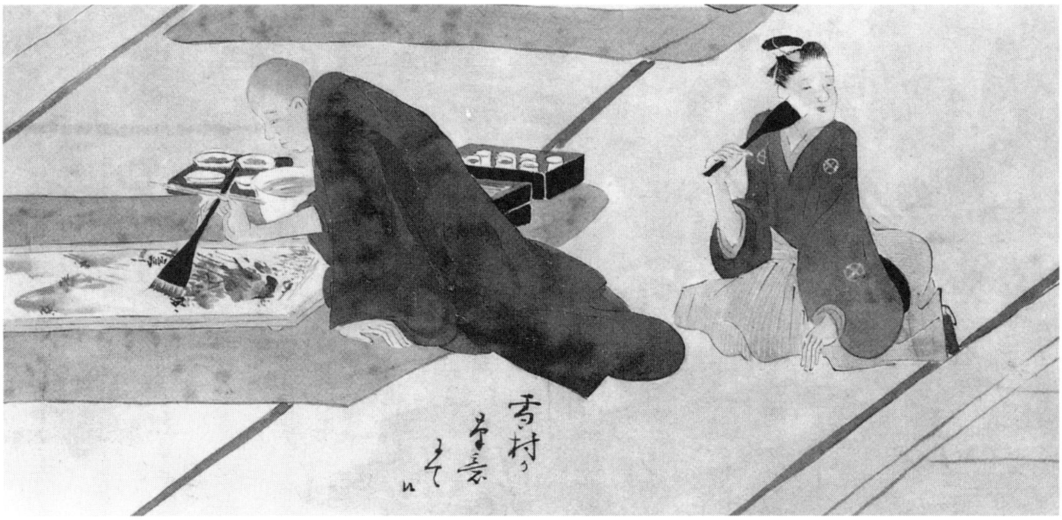

Figure 1.3 Kano Takanobu (1809–1892). Painter, from *Compendium of Edo Workers*, scroll 2, section 15 (detail). Handscroll, ink and color on paper, 36.2 cm x 996 cm (entire scroll). Iris and B. Gerald Cantor Center for Visual Arts at Stanford University; gift of Dr. E. Nagura.

from a set of three handscrolls copied by Kano Takanobu (1809–1892) from Kuwagata Keisai's celebrated *Assemblage of Edo Shokunin* (*Edo shokunin zukushi*); this scroll continued to be copied into the twentieth century.[27]

Although such pictures abound with fictions, they also furnish valuable documentation for the creation and distribution of objects. They consistently suggest, for example, the distribution of specific métiers on the basis of gender. Women's work in the artistic sphere included preparing *beni* (red dye); embroidery; dyeing; weaving; and selling painted fans, woven belts (*obi*), unpainted cotton cloth, and brocades.[28] It is possible to make out two of these traditional vocations, kimono and fan selling (along with prostitution) going on in shops in the detail of the screen illustrated in Figure 1.4. As would be expected, the trades relating to plastic art and building conducted by men were much more numerous: carpentry and building (Figure 1.1), roofing (two kinds: tile and shingle), plastering, lacquer making, sword polishing, making brushes for writing and painting, hat making, bow making, pottery, paper making, armory, sutra writing, carving of Buddhist sculptures (Figure 1.2), the work of painters (Figure 1.3), silversmiths, mirror makers, saddle makers, sword sheath makers; and several kinds of baskets (leather, wicker), quivers, arrows, riding apparel, and goldsmithing. Some of the *shokunin* are depicted wearing court clothing, others Buddhist garb. A diary entry from the Buddhist establishment Tōji, dated to the fourth month of 1364, refers to the carpenters, smiths, sculptors, and tatami makers working at that temple as

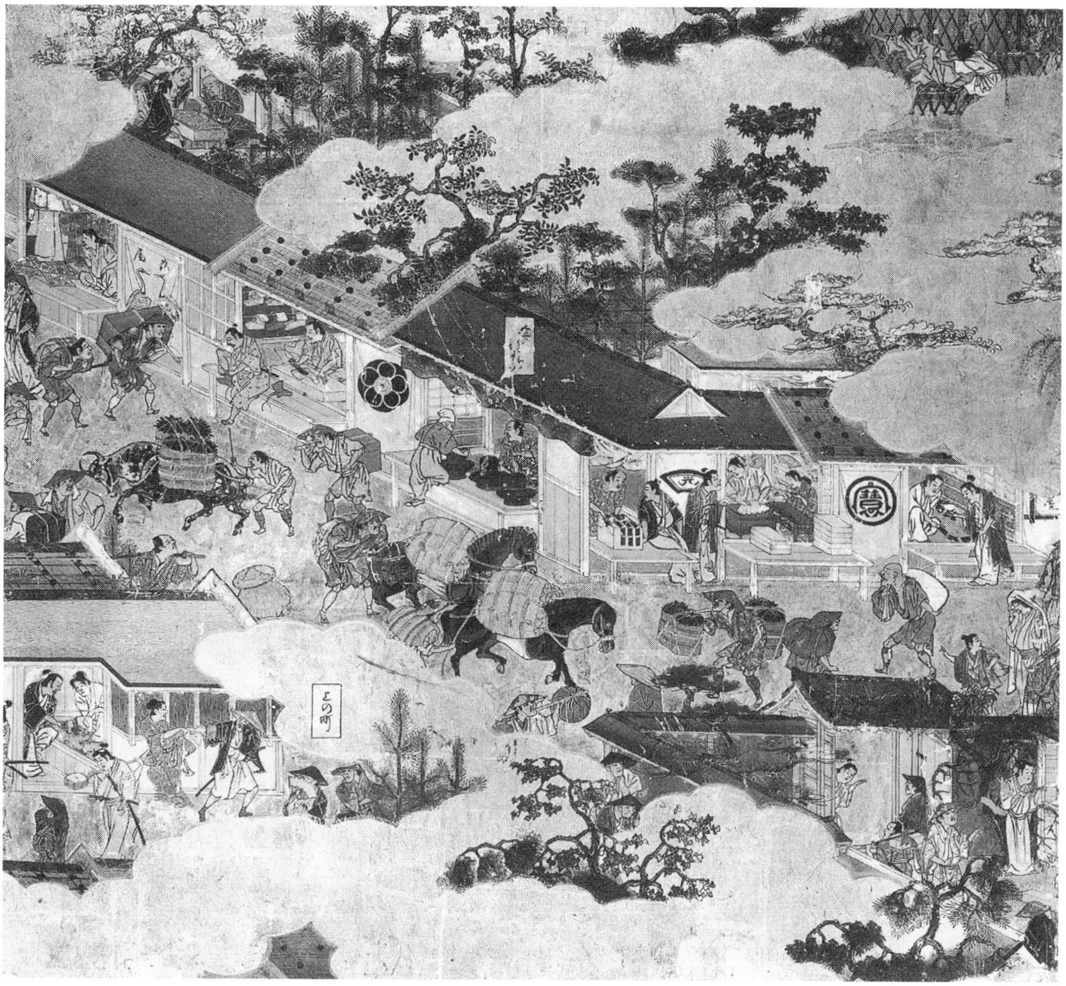

Figure 1.4 Anonymous. Fan shop, from *In and Out of the Capital* (so-called Funaki version). First half of the seventeenth century. Pair of six-panel screens, ink, color, and gold leaf on paper, 162 cm x 340 cm. Collection of the Tokyo National Museum. Detail of right screen, panel 6.

shokunin.[29] Some *shokunin* received honorific Buddhist titles.[30] Others were given court ranks, honorary governorships, and even stipends, as was the case with Tosa Mitsunobu (see Chapter Four). As is clear, *shokunin* collectively represent an enormous cross-section of the population.

Although many *shokunin* were evidently savvy entrepreneurs capable of furthering their interests, nonetheless the term *tradespeople* carried a stigma in upper-class society (as it still does in Great Britain). The word *shokunin* as a pejorative appears or is implicit in several of our chapters. As the epigraph at the beginning of this chapter about the potter Kyūemon shows, the speaker, a feudal lord, was pleasantly surprised that the individual who appeared before him did not resemble his stereotype of a *shokunin* (Cort, Chapter Five). Tosa Mitsunobu managed to exchange the tag "artisan painter" preceding his name during his early career for titles linking him to the imperial court in later life (Chapter Four). Kitagawa Utamaro and his publisher implicitly linked Chinese notions of the individual touch (associated with the literatus) and Western ideas of empiricism (the mark of a worthwhile artist) to add singularity to a professional whose product was part of an extensive division of labor (Davis, Chapter Six). When the sculptor Takamura Kōun was accepted into his master's workshop, he was told that the ability to read and write was unnecessary for a craftsman. Merely one generation later, Kōun's son wrote of his shame at his father for being a *shokunin* (Guth, Chapter Seven). Even though it is never explicitly mentioned, the specter of the scantily clothed *shokunin* carpenter (Figure 1.1) was undoubtedly among the images that the nascent professional architects who are discussed in Chapter Eight (the difference between white collar and blue collar) were trying to transcend.

Another leitmotif playing through this volume is the question of canon formation and makers' roles in it. By what complex processes are some artists and objects singled out to communicate rhetorical or aesthetic meaning, while others lapse into the background? What are the forces that shape art historical narratives? To what degree have artists themselves had a say in those narratives? How do some artists' names become invested with cachet, while others retreat into obscurity? Chapters Two and Three make clear how ideological and political exigencies filter the selection of canonical artists and works long after the maker's period of activity. Chapter Five reveals heroic attempts on the part of a potter and his ruler actively to join the aesthetic mainstream of their own day. Once makers join the ranks of the literate, they are able to have a say in the evaluative process. The case of Tosa Mitsunobu demonstrates this dynamic applied retroactively by his descendants, while Utamaro is made to speak for "himself" by a coterie of people skilled in manipulating text and image. The last two chapters reveal how sculptors and architects achieved the feat of placing themselves on equal footing with their critics, becoming simultaneously makers and interpreters of their art.

In the end, the pen proved mightier than the chisel. Although the great Buddhist monk Kūkai (774–835) declared that the power of the image exceeds the power of the word—and artists themselves by their aesthetic choices contributed the foundations of visual discourse—ultimately it was those controlling the written word who had the power to select, record, and perpetuate the names and works that form the backbone of the discourse. Without them, the discipline of art history would be very different today.

Chapter Two

Tori-busshi and the Production of Buddhist Icons in Asuka-Period Japan

DONALD F. MCCALLUM

The Shaka Triad (Figure 2.1) enshrined in the Golden Hall (Kondō) of Hōryūji is the most well-known member of a small group of superb images produced during the Asuka period (ca. 590–ca. 650).[1] Reproduced and discussed in virtually all general books dealing with Japanese art, the Shaka Triad is now such a familiar monument that we find difficulty in approaching it with fresh eyes, because we think that we have a firm grasp of its historical situation, including date, motivation for production, patronage circumstances, and even the name and title of the sculptor. In actuality, none of these factors is certain, and only a profoundly skeptical analysis of each offers the possibility of a fuller elucidation of the significance of the work. This type of analysis is of crucial significance for a study not just of the Shaka Triad but of Asuka sculpture as a whole, since there is a stylistically coherent category of about ten images that appear to have been produced in the same studio as the triad. The high quality of these sculptures has attracted a great deal of attention, especially because they were made at the initial stages of Buddhism in Japan.

In attempting to understand the significance of this group of sculptures, art historians have relied heavily on the inscription incised on the back of the mandorla of the Shaka Triad, which states that the image was made for the sake of an individual commonly identified as "Shōtoku Taishi," by a sculptor named "Tori-busshi."[2] Projecting from these details, scholars have usually labeled the entire group as belonging to the "Tori style" and tended to associate most or all of the images with the circle of Shōtoku Taishi. Because a full discussion of the putative role of Shōtoku Taishi in early Japanese Buddhism is not possible here, I concentrate on the Shaka Triad and related documen-

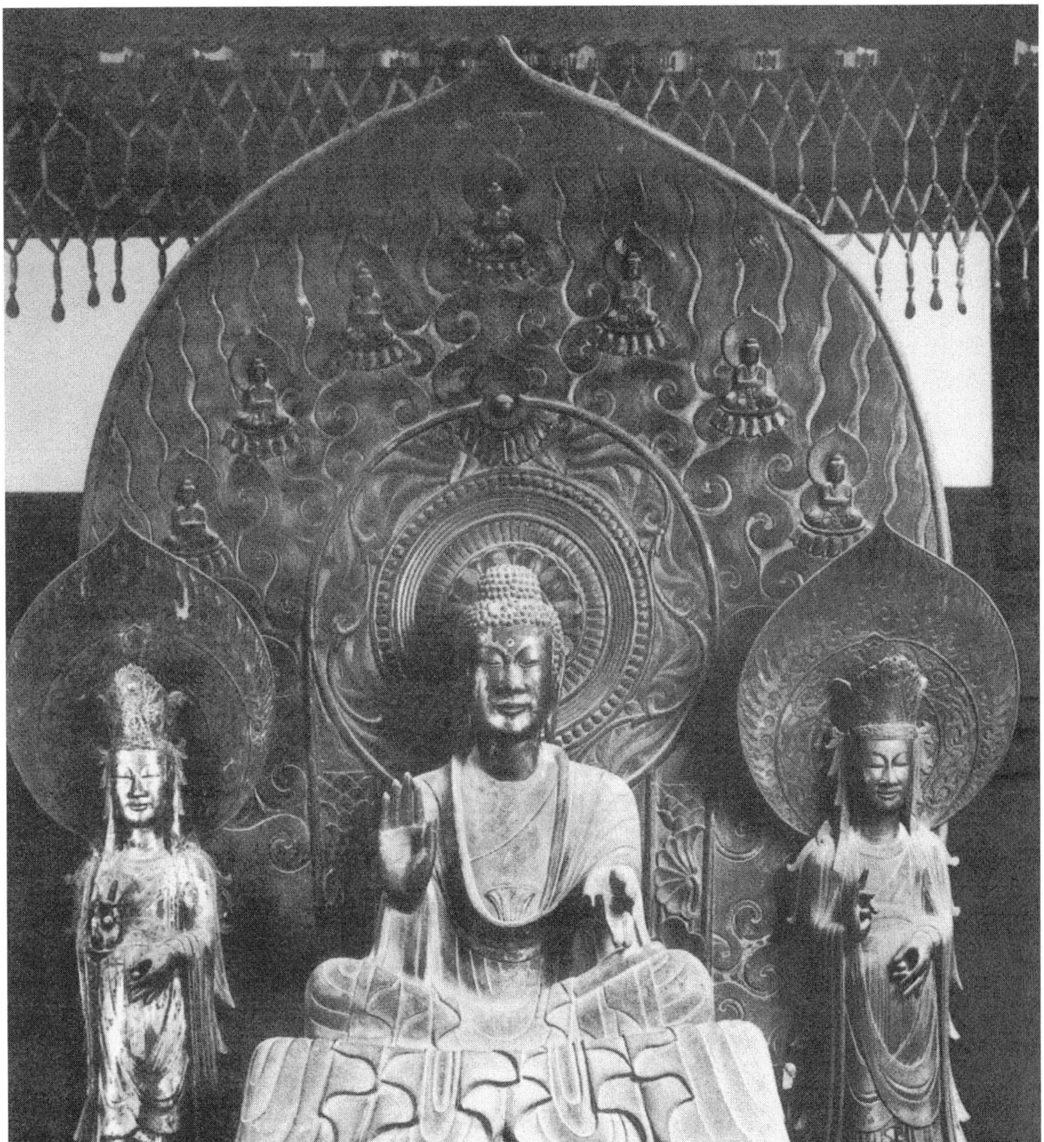

Figure 2.1 Shaka Triad, Hōryūji Kondō, Nara, Japan. Asuka period, gilt bronze, height of Shaka, 86.5 cm. Photo courtesy of Asuka Shiryōkan, Nara.

tary material, with the aim of elucidating the practice and politics of icon production at the initial stage of the tradition. Fundamental to my analysis is the contention that, contrary to orthodox opinion, Tori-busshi was not a hands-on sculptor, but rather a high-ranking individual who served as the supervisor of the principal studio active during the first decades of the Asuka period. Furthermore, I argue that the major patronage of this group of sculptural icons was not by the so-called imperial family, including Shōtoku Taishi, but instead by the Soga clan, the dominant political force of the time.

THE SHAKA TRIAD AND RELATED ICONS

As has just been noted, a large number of the extant Buddhist icons of the Asuka period have stylistic characteristics that are more or less closely connected to the Shaka Triad of the Hōryūji Kondō. Although there is some debate concerning the members of this group, the crucial monuments include these:

1. Asukadera Daibutsu (Figure 2.2)[3]
2. Hōryūji Kondō Yakushi[4]
3. Hōryūji Kondō Shaka Triad (Figure 2.1)
4. Hōryūji Yumedono Kannon[5]
5. Hōryūji Museum Shaka Triad[6]
6. Hōryūji Museum Standing Bodhisattva[7]
7. Seated Buddha no. 145, Tokyo National Museum (Figure 2.3)[8]
8. Standing Buddha no. 149, Tokyo National Museum (Figure 2.4)[9]
9. Meditating Bodhisattva no. 155, Tokyo National Museum[10]

This may not seem like a large corpus, but it does in fact constitute the majority of Asuka-period icons and certainly must be considered as the mainstream of early Japanese Buddhist sculpture.[11]

In studying the nine monuments just enumerated, we note several distinct patterns. Presumably a triad consisting of a seated Buddha flanked by standing bodhisattvas was the basic iconographic type. This can now be best seen in the Hōryūji Shaka Triad, but it was also the format of the Asuka Daibutsu, which displays holes at either side of the pedestal to accommodate the flanking bodhisattvas. Of course, the Hōryūji Museum Shaka Triad now lacks the right-side bodhisattva, although the original format is apparent. There is no way at present to determine if Seated Buddha no. 145 was always an independent icon or originally the central image of a triad, although the latter possibility seems more likely. The last of the seated Buddhas, the Hōryūji Kondō Yakushi, appears to have been made after 670 and thus should

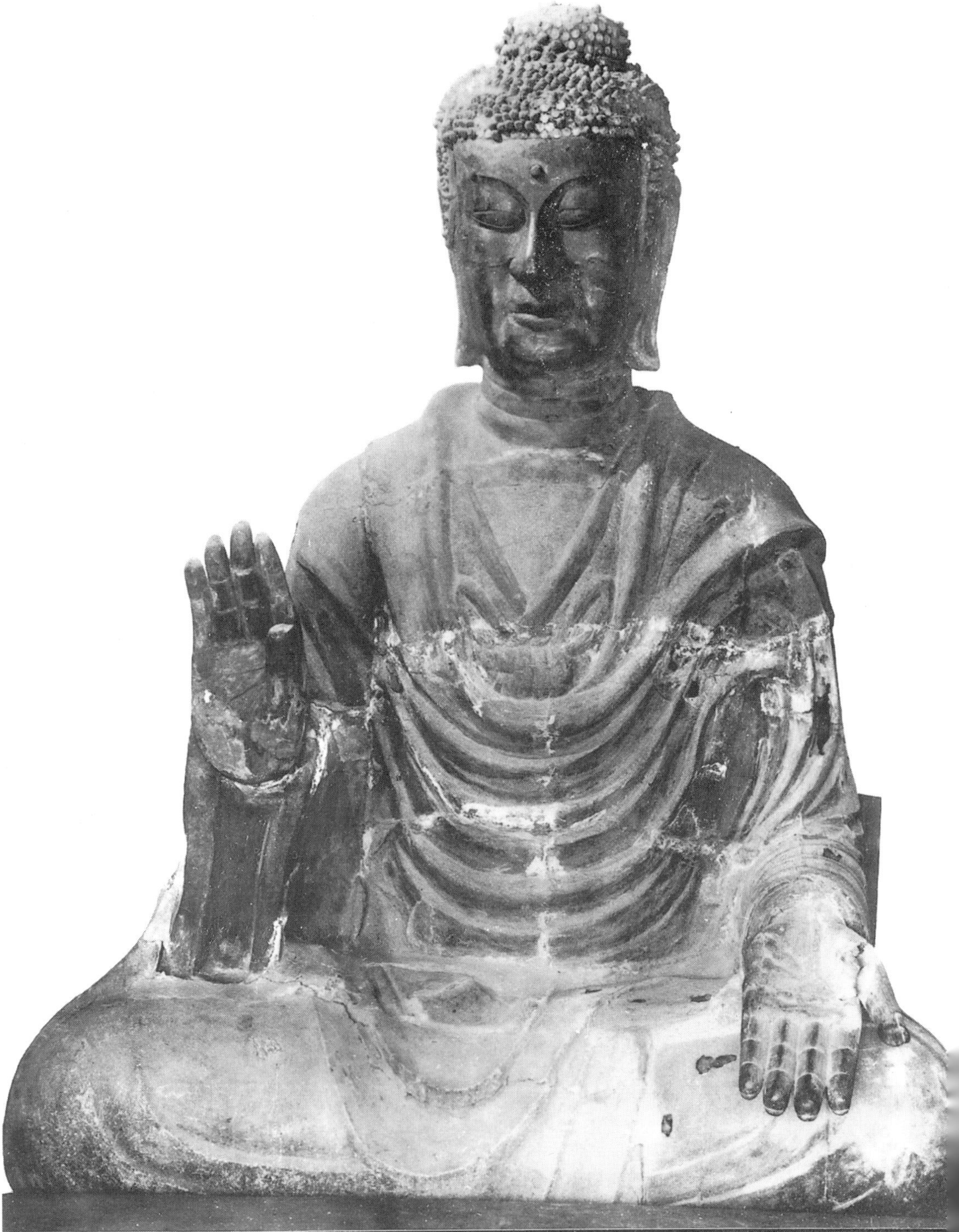

Figure 2.2 Daibutsu, Asukadera, Nara, Japan. Asuka period, gilt bronze, height 275.7 cm. Photo courtesy of the Nara Kokuritsu Bunkazai Kenkyūjo, Nara.

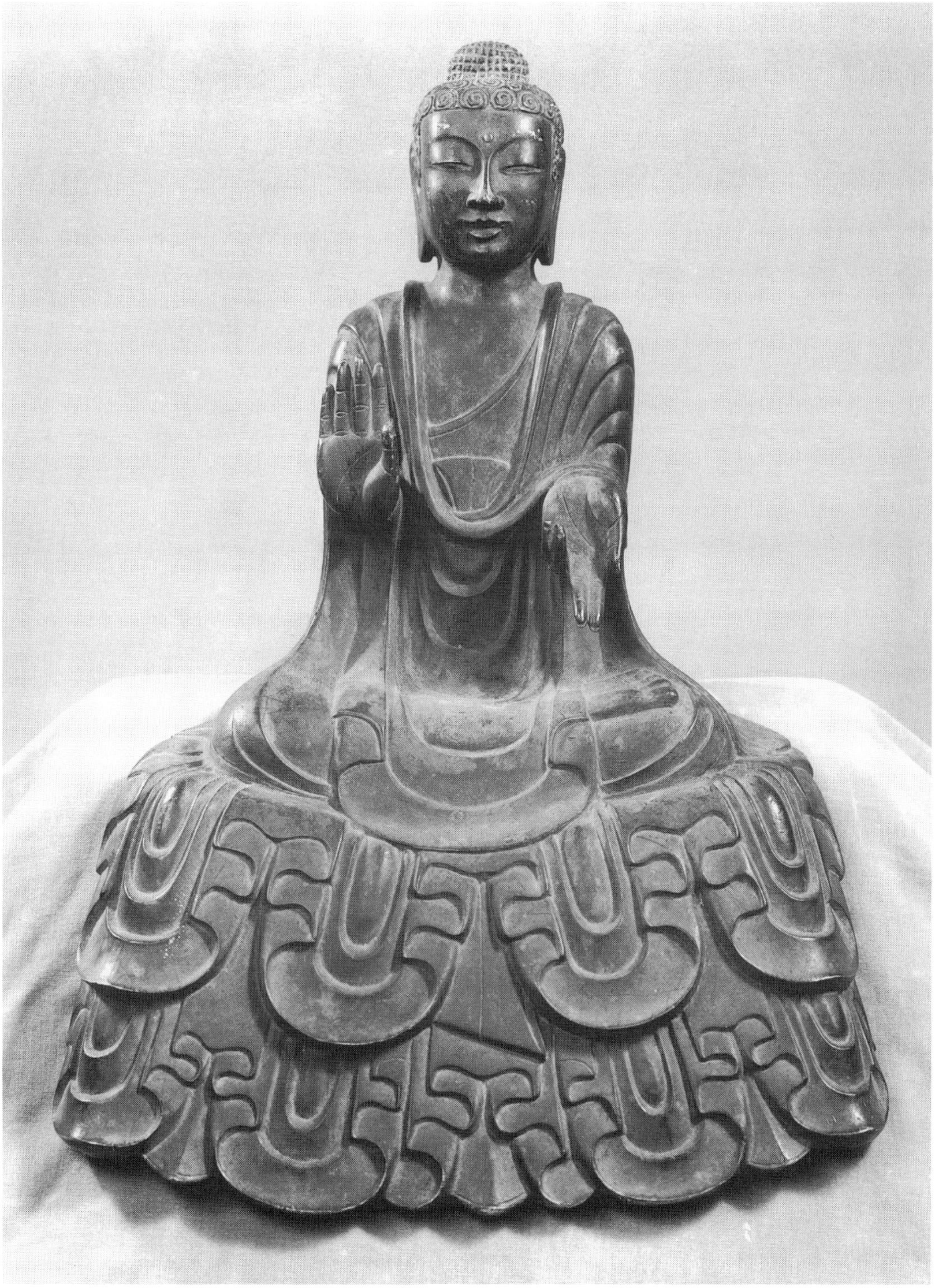

Figure 2.3 Seated Buddha no. 145, Hōryūji Treasure Hall, Tokyo National Museum. Asuka period, gilt bronze, height 27.9 cm. Courtesy of the Tokyo National Museum.

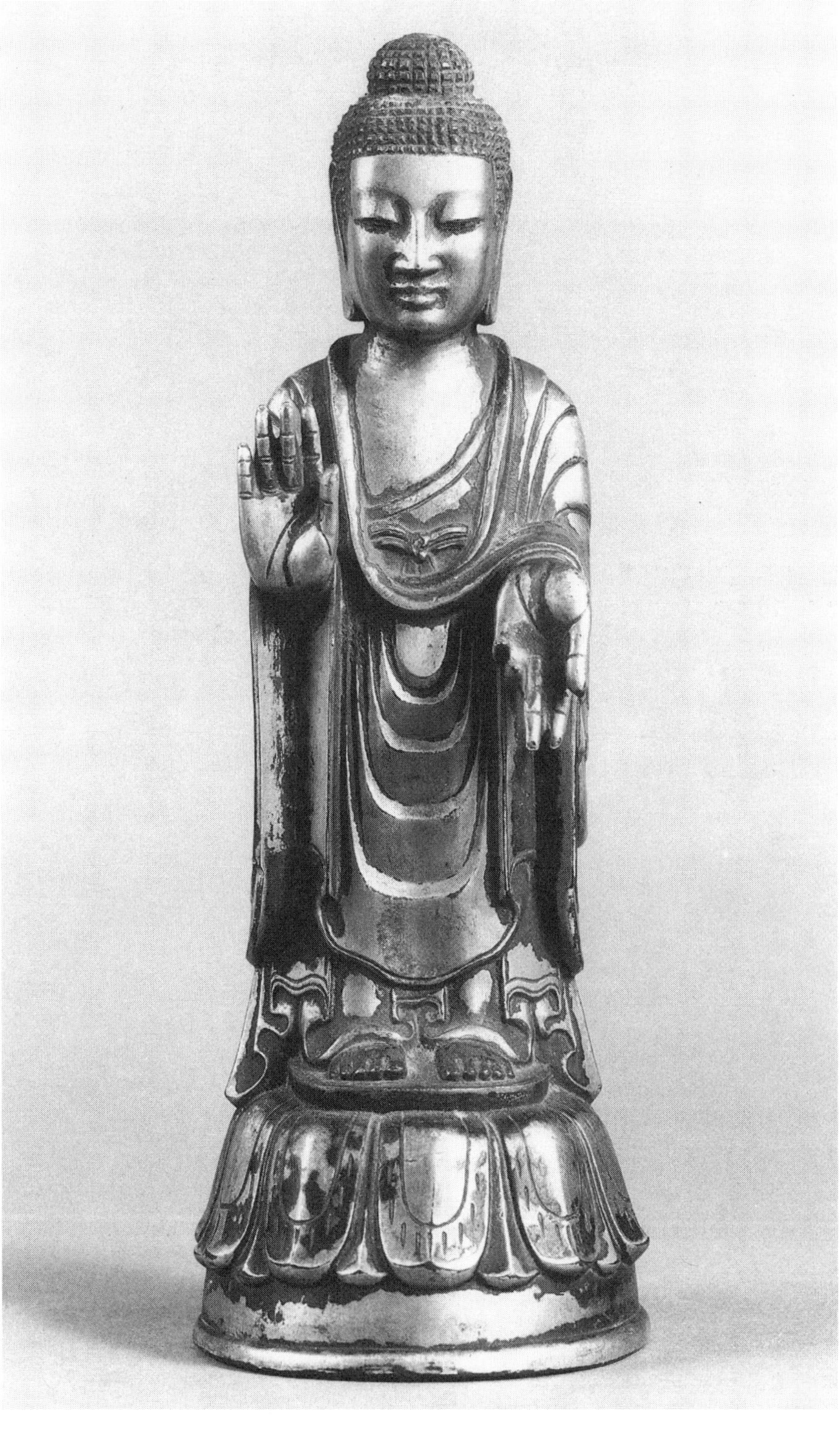

Figure 2.4 Standing Buddha no. 149, Hōryūji Treasure Hall, Tokyo National Museum. Asuka period, gilt bronze, height 27.4 cm. Courtesy of the Tokyo National Museum.

be considered an image related to the primary group rather than an original member.[12]

This triad format is obviously based on prototypes on the Korean peninsula; interestingly, among extant Three Kingdoms–period triads the most common type consists of all three figures in standing pose.[13] I suggest here that the Soga clan must have received a Shaka triad of the "seated Buddha, standing bodhisattvas" type that apparently assumed the role as the main model for many other images produced during the Asuka period. Consequently, Buddha no. 149 is a rather unusual example of a standing Buddha figure in this group.[14] Images such as the Hōryūji Yumedono Kannon and the Hōryūji Museum Standing Bodhisattva can be seen as independent figures closely related in style to the flanking bodhisattvas of the triads.[15]

Moving from iconographical to stylistic issues, we immediately see a high degree of consistency within the group. All of the Buddha figures are heavily draped, with precisely articulated folds; especially characteristic is the drapery overhang seen in monuments 3, 5, and 7 listed earlier. The emphasis is on frontality, and the images possess a dignified, rather remote demeanor. The bodhisattvas, both those that are parts of a triad and those that are independent icons, are closely related to each other in style and motif. Each has a prominent, mountain-shaped crown and quite similar arrangements of the drapery. As is the case with the Buddha figures, there is only a limited sense of bodily form under the robes.

THE MANDORLA INSCRIPTION AND ITS PROBLEMS

The Shaka Triad is backed by a very large mandorla that serves for all three figures, the central Buddha and the two flanking bodhisattvas. This mandorla has in its center the lotiform halo of Shaka, while the flanking bodhisattvas have their own separate halos. Other details of the mandorla include the Buddhas of the Past, floral decor, and the characteristic flame patterns symbolizing light. In its original configuration, the mandorla apparently had separately attached *apsaras* (flying figures) along the edges, since there are holes designed to accommodate these. The mandorla is a beautifully designed object, certainly well worth careful study in its own right. For the moment, however, we are concerned only with the undecorated back surface of the mandorla. Just above the middle is the inscription, incised into the surface of the bronze. One must keep in mind that this inscription was not cast with the mandorla proper and thus could have been added at any later date.

There are numerous problems connected with the Shaka Triad's inscription, several of which have thus far resisted all efforts at elucidation.[16] Here little more can be done than adumbrate some of the key issues and offer a summary of the narrative. The inscription consists of 196 characters, arranged in fourteen vertical columns of fourteen characters each. This degree of symmetry could not be coincidental, so one assumes that the author adjusted the text to fit the allocated format. This text includes these elements:

1. *What appears to be an era designation (nengō): Hōkō gan sanjūichi nen*

   There are serious difficulties associated with this part of the text, especially the fact that there is no evidence to indicate that *nengō* were used in Asuka-period Japan. If the first two characters, *Hōkō*, are taken to be the *nengō*, then the most logical interpretation of *gan* would be that it refers to the first year of the era. However, since *gan* is followed by characters that appear to read "thirty-first year," one has difficulty seeing how the two parts are related.

2. *Cyclical characters: kanoto-mi*

   These two characters probably correspond to the year 621. The text states that in the twelfth month of that year the previous "empress" died, and the usual assumption has been that this refers to Anahobe no Hashihito, the mother of Prince Shōtoku.

3. *Next year*

   In the first month, the twenty-second day of 622, the *Kamitsumiya Hōō* became ill.[17] Of course, this refers to Prince Shōtoku, but the title *Hōō*—"Dharma King"—seems totally impossible as a contemporaneous identification for the prince.

4. *Efforts on behalf of the sick prince*

   Various people, including his consort, princes, and ministers, prayed for his recovery and vowed to make a life-sized image of Shaka as an offering for his good health and long life. If Prince Shōtoku should not recover, they prayed that he be reborn in the Pure Land.

5. *Second month, twenty-first day*

   Prince Shōtoku's consort dies.

6. *Second month, twenty-second day*

   The "Dharma King" (Prince Shōtoku) dies.

7. *Completion of the Shaka Triad*

   This is recorded as taking place in the middle of the third month of 623, approximately one year after the death of the prince. Following is a long section of pious Buddhist sentiment.

8. Name and titles of Tori: Shiba Kuratsukuri Obito Tori-busshi

Translated, "The sculptor Tori of the Shiba family, Chief of the Saddlemakers' Guild."

Each of the five components of these eight characters is charged with meaning:

A. *Busshi*—a term used to identify the makers of Buddhist icons.
B. *Tori*—traditionally thought to be the personal name of the sculptor.
C. *Shiba*—one of the rare cases of a compound family name in China (Sima), here assumed to be the family name of Tori.
D. *Obito*—a title (*kabane*) given to the chief of a guild (*be*).
E. *Kuratsukuri*—identifies the guild associated with the making of saddles (*kura*) in early Japan.

Clearly, this text could not have been written in 623. The puzzling *nengō* (element 1) is very strange, and the way in which Prince Shōtoku is identified in elements 3 and 6 is impossible for such an early stage in Japanese history. Historical analysis indicates that the text was written after 670, as one component of the campaign to enhance the reputation of the prince.

Returning to our main theme, the career of "Tori-busshi," how should the designation referring to him be interpreted? The term *busshi* is not found elsewhere with reference to Tori, nor does it seem to have been employed as early as the Asuka period. Consequently, the occurrence here of *busshi* appears to be one more piece of evidence suggesting that the inscription was written later.[18]

THE KURATSUKURI-BE AND THE SHIBA

Perhaps the most effective point of entry into this aspect of the study is brief discussion of the "Saddlemakers' Guild" (Kuratsukuri-be). At first sight, it might appear strange that a member of the Saddlemakers' Guild was responsible for the production of Buddhist icons, although reasons for this association are presented later.

The processes whereby advanced technologies were transferred from the Asiatic continent to the Japanese islands are not fully understood. Traditionally, it has been asserted in Japan that craftsmen, often said to be from China but more likely from the Korean peninsula, "immigrated" to Japan, where they were employed by a native ruling class. More recent investigations have indicated that this distinction between immigrant craftsmen and native aristocracy is highly overdrawn, although such prejudices die hard and one still finds them lingering in general publications. Nevertheless, it now seems clear that settlers from the Korean peninsula occupied positions in all strata of society, including the governing elite. Members of the Saddlemakers' Guild would have provided an essential service to this elite, and thus they can be thought of as having had quite high status in contemporary society.[19]

Controversy has raged over the source of horse-riding warfare in Japan, with one camp seeing an invasion of the Japanese islands by a group of warriors from the Korean peninsula, while the other camp denies the historicity of such an invasion.[20] For our present purposes, we should note that both sides agree the prototypes for Japanese horse trappings of the Kofun period are to be found in Three Kingdoms Korea. Although some of the horse trappings excavated from Kofun-period tombs were undoubtedly imported from Three Kingdoms Korea, other examples must have been made in Japan by craftsmen who had come from the continent. It is, of course, within this latter context that the Saddlemakers' Guild belongs, because the documentary evidence strongly suggests that members of this guild came from Three Kingdoms Korea to work in Japan.[21]

Two types of evidence exist with regard to Kofun-period horse trappings: the archaeologically recovered objects and a number of references in early Japanese historical texts. Although these texts are notoriously unreliable, in the present context the existence of concrete objects allows one to be reasonably confident about the documentary sources. The earliest occurrence of the name Kuratsukuri in *Nihon shoki* (*Chronicles of Japan*), an entry dated Yūryaku 7 (traditionally believed to be equivalent to C.E. 463), appears in a rather complicated and bizarre story about the vicissitudes of a number of skilled artisans who were sent by Paekche to Japan. Reference is made to individuals of the guilds of potters, painters, brocade weavers, and saddlemakers, the latter person called Kuratsukuri Kenkui.[22] Deciding just how much weight to give this entry is difficult, since saddlemakers probably had come to Japan long before the 460s. Moreover, Kenkui's name is found within a group of fellow artisans in a context that suggests no special distinction accruing to the Kuratsukuri; I believe that the most appropriate assumption is that Kenkui was just one of a number of skilled craftsmen who came from the Korean peninsula to Japan, there to join the Saddlemakers' Guild.

What sorts of things did the members of the Saddlemakers' Guild make? As the radical "leather" of *kura* indicates, much of their work would have been with leather used for the harness and saddle. (Wood was also employed for the saddle tree.) In addition, elaborate metal fittings were applied to the saddle, and there were metal decorative elements in other parts of the horse trappings. These complex metal objects, often gilt bronze, would have been highly expensive, and one must assume that their production was one of the most important aspects of the work of the Saddlemakers' Guild. Probably the importance of horses and their equipment to the ruling class would have given the Saddlemakers' Guild a significant position in society, and this, combined with their knowledge of metalworking, made them likely candidates for the position of supervising the making of Buddhist icons when the need for such icons arose in Japan. One can imagine other possible craftsmen assuming this role, but the experience of the Saddlemakers' Guild working in bronze casting prepared them for this task.[23]

Most important for this chapter are three generations of the apparent leadership of the Kuratsukuri-be—(Shiba Tatto, Tasuna/Shima, and Tori-busshi)—who lived during the sixth century and early decades of the seventh. Before turning to these important individuals, however, a more fully articulated hypothesis as to the general nature of the Kuratsukuri-be must be proposed. Available evidence indicates that elaborate saddles were made prior to C.E. 500, and so *Nihon shoki*'s Kuratsukuri Kenkui was presumably a representative artisan attached to this guild. I argue that the leadership of the Kuratsukuri-be was assumed, in the later sixth century, by a family that called itself Shiba. Looked at from the perspective of dynamic processes, one imagines that there were significant transformations in the leadership structure of the Kuratsukuri-be from the fifth to the seventh centuries; that is to say, a conception based on an essentially unbroken hereditary line of leaders stretching over the centuries is no more plausible for a clan such as the Kuratsukuri than it is for the so-called imperial clan.[24] Presumably talented and ambitious individuals were consistently recruited on the Korean peninsula, and on occasion such individuals probably would rise through the ranks of the guild, succeeding to the headship at times when there was no heir, or no adequate successor to take over. Such a process goes a long way toward explaining the vigor and vitality of the Kuratsukuri in the centuries under consideration here.

In addition to those individuals I am referring to as members of the leadership group, there are several other people of Kuratsukuri lineage who occupied important positions in Asuka society. A brief consideration of their roles fills out our picture of the clan as a whole. *Gangōji engi* (747), which relates the history of Asukadera, refers to a man named Kuratsukuri no Obito Karami, who was one of four supervisors involved in certain aspects of the construction of the temple.[25] This reference, of course, places Karami at the center of Buddhist activity during the early Asuka period, although it is not clear exactly what work he was supervising. A few years later, there is a reference to a man called Kuratsukuri no Fukuri, who accompanied the envoy Ono no Imoko on the two well-known Japanese missions to the Sui court in 607 and 609 as a translator.[26] The question that immediately comes to mind is how Fukuri would have known Chinese. As has been suggested here, membership in the Kuratsukuri clan was not simply a matter of birth; presumably, entry was also available to those possessing special, needed talents. Since Fukuri was apparently skilled in Chinese, a reasonable assumption is that he was from the Korean peninsula, most likely Paekche, and perhaps he had even had previous experience in China itself.

The next member of the lineage to appear is Kuratsukuri no Tokushaku, who is said to have been appointed as one of the three supervisors of Buddhist monks and nuns in 624.[27] This important position in the Buddhist world suggests that members of the Kuratsukuri were centrally involved in the control and supervision of the Buddhist order.[28] Also interesting is a peculiar tale, given in a 645 entry, that has to do with one Kuratsukuri no Tokushi, a student who was purported to be friendly with a tiger.[29] His fellow Japanese students in Koryŏ (Koguryŏ) stated, when they returned home, that the tiger had taught Tokushi various magical arts, including what is apparently acupuncture. When the country of Koryŏ learned that Tokushi himself also wished to return home, they had him killed with poison. It is hard to know what to make of this story, but in the present context it places yet one more member of the Kuratsukuri lineage directly in the center of peninsular learning and culture.

Given the brevity of most *Nihon shoki* entries, it is striking that the various members of the Kuratsukuri lineage who are recorded emerge as an important if slightly odd group. The individuals just discussed—along with the detailed references to the three generations of the Shiba branch to be considered next—produce one of the most extended accounts of any of the ancient clan lineages. I believe this material leads to two important conclusions. First, obviously the Kuratsukuri clan was of considerable significance from at least the fifth century through the first half of the seventh. As is to be further elucidated, this importance was not limited to their activities in saddlemaking but extended to high political and religious roles. Second, the prominence of members of the Kuratsukuri lineage in *Nihon shoki* indicates that its editors drew extensively on Kuratsukuri sources in compiling their own book.

The preceding discussion was designed to be a general introduction to the Kuratsukuri clan, from its initial appearance in Japanese history through the first half of the seventh century. With this material in place, we must now consider the three generations who had the family name Shiba. This is the group that is supposed to have been intimately associated with the acceptance and early development of the Buddhist religion and, most importantly in the present context, with the production of Buddhist icons.

There is one important earlier occurrence of the name Shiba that may be relevant to the present discussion, although this occurrence is not in a Kuratsukuri context. During the period of the "Five Kings of Wa," roughly the fifth century, there are a number of records in the dynastic histories of the south Chinese states referring to relations with Wa (Japan).[30] Of interest here is an entry of C.E. 425 in *Songshu* stating that (King) San (of Wa) again sent as an envoy Shiba Sōtatsu, who presented tribute to the Song court.[31] The historiography of the "Five Kings of Wa" is so fraught with difficulties and problems that definitive claims here as to the identity and status of Shiba Sōtatsu are not prudent. Nevertheless, given the appearance of this name in the Song history we can reasonably assume that such an individual was involved in relationships between the Song court and Wa.

Some scholars have argued that Shiba Sōtatsu is an ancestor of Shiba Tatto (to be considered next). Machida Kōichi has emphasized the similarities of the two names, identical in three out of four characters (bold letters), in making his case:

Shiba Sō**tatsu**
Shiba Tatto.[32]

As will be seen presently, this hypothesis is plausible only if one accepts the idea that Shiba Tatto came from Southern Liang to Japan in 522, since that would yield a manageable gap of one hundred years between their respective appearances. I suspect, however, that there is no direct connection between the Shiba Sōtatsu mentioned in *Songshu* and the three generations of Shiba to be considered in a moment. More likely, in my view, is a situation whereby immigrants from the continent—China and the Korean peninsula—adopted as their own a prestigious Chinese surname such as Sima (Shiba), one of the most distinguished in Chinese history. Certainly the ideological implications of such a strategy are obvious, as an ambitious family strives to improve its position in society.[33]

There are four individuals recorded in the three generations of our Shiba lineage:

First generation	Shiba Tatto
Second generation	Tasuna and Shima
Third generation	Tori-busshi

Conflicting data exist for each of these people, necessitating a close, critical evaluation of the sources if one wishes to understand the status of each. Unfortunately, space does not allow a full analysis here, although some of the basic details concerning each must be considered.

Various efforts have been made to interpret Shiba Tatto as a sculptor from southern China who came to Japan in 522, bringing with him knowledge of Buddhism and Buddhist sculpture.[34] Before accepting this interpretation, we must recognize that it is based on twelfth-century and fourteenth-century texts and receives absolutely no support from the two texts written in the eighth century.[35] In fact, the earliest references to Shiba Tatto in the early texts correspond to the year 584 (Bidatsu 13), when Tatto was involved in the search for a Buddhist monk to worship the stone image of Maitreya brought to Japan from Paekche by Kafuka no Omi.[36] Historical credulity is stretched in the suggestion that Tatto came to Japan in 522 and was still active in 584. Moreover, as we shall see in a moment, he had a young daughter who, in 584, became the first nun. Some scholars have attempted to solve this chronological discrepancy by arguing that Tatto came to Japan one sixty-year cycle later, thus arriving in 582. Such errors in cycle do occur, but there are, in my view, other more reasonable interpretations that can be suggested for the career of Tatto.

An understanding of the activities of Tatto can only be achieved through an effort to delineate the context within which he worked. If the 522 arrival hypothesis is eliminated, one is left with a series of events that show Tatto closely associated with the leader of the Soga clan, Soga no Umako. Thus in 584 he responded to Umako's request to search for a Buddhist monk. Moreover, his daughter Shima became a nun at the request of Umako, while later another child, Tasuna, also entered the Buddhist order. All of this suggests that Tatto, as the leader of the Kuratsukuri-be, was closely associated with the Soga clan's pro-Buddhist policy during the crucial phase in which the supporters and opponents of the new religion were maneuvering for supremacy. Rather than considering Tatto as a craftsman, in my view he is better seen as an important retainer of the Soga clan, who had connections on the Korean Peninsula that enabled him to advance the cause of Buddhism as one aspect of the progressive policies of the clan.

Tasuna, who was the son of Tatto, is a somewhat enigmatic figure. He is discussed in a number of documentary sources, but in none of these cases is he given either of the titles—*suguri* or *obito*—that his father is said to have had, suggesting that he did not achieve a leadership role prior to entering the Buddhist order with the name Tokusai-hosshi.[37] Also, for some reason, the family name Shiba is never directly included in his designation.

The most detailed account of Tasuna's activities is in *Nihon shoki* under the year 587 (Yōmei 2):

> The Emperor's sores became worse and worse, and when the end was approaching, Tasuna of the Kuratsukuri-be [son of Shiba Tatto] came forward

> and addressed him, saying: "Thy servant, on behalf of the Emperor, will renounce the world and exercise religion. Moreover, he will make an image of Buddha sixteen feet high, and a temple." The Emperor was deeply moved. This is the sixteen-foot wooden image of Buddha that with its attendant Bosatsu now stands in the Temple of Sakata at Minabuchi.[38]

There are various important details in this entry. Although the Soga clan is not specifically mentioned, the events recorded must be understood as taking place within the context of Soga pro-Buddhist policy. Significantly, this entry precedes the decisive battle between the proponents and enemies of Buddhism by some months. Tasuna's vow to become a monk should be seen as another instance of a member of the Kuratsukuri-be engaging in an activity that furthered the cause of Buddhism, something that at this stage was associated with the circle of the Soga clan.

The reference to the making of a sixteen-foot wooden Buddha and its attendant bodhisattvas is difficult to explicate.[39] This seems like an extremely large image for such an early stage in the development of Buddhism in Japan, suggesting that "sixteen-foot" may be a conventional measurement that was inserted into the text at a later date. Of course, Sakatadera at Minabuchi was the family temple of the Kuratsukuri-be, leading to the suspicion that the reference to the icons included in *Nihon shoki* may have been retrospectively added to account for what existed there in the early eighth century.[40]

Some of the later texts refer to Tasuna as either a sculptor or a craftsman, and at least two of them explicitly identify him as a person from Paekche. Since I have strong doubts about the plausibility of the later textual strata's identification of Tatto as a person from China, it hardly seems appropriate now to accept this Paekche designation simply because it relates closely to a fundamental hypothesis of the present study: namely, that the Kuratsukuri-be had intimate connections with the Korean peninsula.[41] The argument has been advanced that the designation of Tasuna as a sculptor or craftsman in the later texts relates to the much earlier reference in *Nihon shoki* to the making of the "sixteen-foot Buddha" for Sakatadera. This is a plausible suggestion, but why would some of these later texts also refer to him as being from Paekche? Especially confusing is the fact that *Fusōryakki* calls Tatto a "Man of Han of Great Tang" while it refers to his son Tasuna as being from Paekche.

Shima, the daughter of Tatto and sister of Tasuna, is referred to in several ways, one by a Buddhist designation, Zenshin-ni (nun Zenshin). Like her brother Tasuna, Shima or Shimame is not specifically given the Shiba family name or a lay title. Rather, accounts of her life focus on her activities as a nun, with her religious name Zenshin.[42] She is the only member of this lineage who is given an age: *Nihon shoki* states that she was eleven years old in

584 when she became a nun, while *Gangōji engi* gives her age at that time as seventeen. The latter seems somewhat more plausible, but in either case we can assume that she was born in the later 560s or early 570s. This would indicate that her father, Tatto, was probably born some time between ca. 530 and ca. 550. Since it is not known if Tasuna was older or younger than Shima, we cannot be certain when he was born, but because Tori is described as Tasuna's son one suspects, on the basis of Tori's later activities, that Tori must have been born in about the 580s, which would push Tasuna's birth year back before about 560, and Tatto's back to before 540. Such speculation is highly imprecise, but I suggest tentatively the following chronology for the three generations:

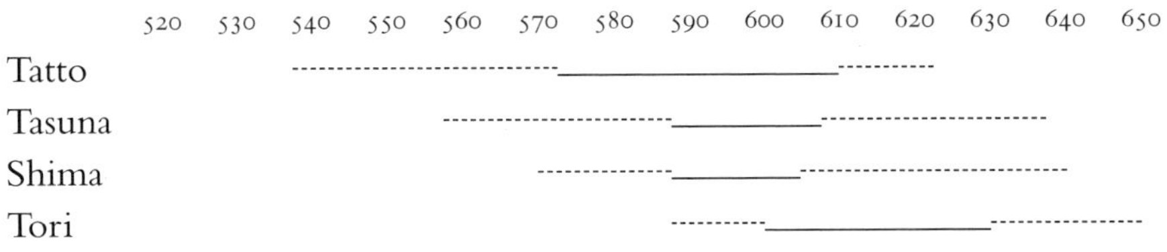

Somewhat surprisingly, both members of the second generation are recorded as entering the Buddhist order; also, as mentioned earlier, there are no indications of Tasuna assuming a leadership role. Since this seems to be a highly uncharacteristic situation for a politically ambitious family, we might suspect that the headship skipped one generation, passing from Tatto to Tori. This, of course, implies some overlap in their lives and careers.

In terms of relationship with the leaders of the Soga clan, apparently Tatto was somewhat younger than Soga no Iname (d. 570), Tasuna and Shima may have been about the same age as Soga no Umako (d. 626), and Tori may have been a contemporary of Soga no Emishi (d. 645).[43]

Full details of the career of Shima are not essential here. As is well known, shortly after she became a nun in 584 the anti-Buddhist forces led by the Mononobe arrested her and her fellow nuns and had them all flogged in the public marketplace as part of the persecution of the religion (585). Later in the same year, however, the nuns were returned to Umako, and he built a temple for them.[44] In 588, Zenshin and her companions traveled to Paekche to study Buddhism, returning to Japan two years later.[45] For our purposes, two aspects of the narrative are of importance: (1) the close connection between Shima/Zenshin and Soga no Umako and (2) her study in Paekche. This places her exactly in the center of the Soga clan/Paekche context that I have been striving to delineate.

With regard to the third-generation member, Tori-busshi, the available evidence suggests that he was also a close associate of the Soga clan, occupying a leadership position in the important Saddlemakers' Guild. The sources indicate that one of his responsibilities had to do with the making of Buddhist icons. Before considering exactly what that duty might have entailed, let us look at the rewards he is said to have received for his efforts with regard to icon making. Virtually all of the information concerning Tori-busshi is contained in three entries of *Nihon shoki* dating to 605 and 606. These entries deal, respectively, with (1) the commissioning of the two sixteen-foot icons for Asukadera to be made by Tori[46]; (2) the completion of the two icons in 606, with an interesting story of how Tori got the sculpture into the Golden Hall without breaking down the door[47]; and (3) a summary of the accomplishments of the three generations of the Shiba line, concluding with the rewards Empress Suiko granted to Tori for his services connected with the Asukadera icons.[48]

First he was granted the cap rank of *dainin*, the third highest level in the twelve-part scheme that was supposed to have been instituted in 603.[49] Although troubling questions remain as to the promulgation of the cap-rank system, for our purposes here the important detail is the extremely high level of cap rank that was supposed to have been conferred on Tori. By no stretch of the imagination can this be conceived of as an appropriate level for a craftsman, although it is certainly possible as a rank for the leader of a major group of retainers of the Soga clan, the Kuratsukuri-be. Similarly, Tori was granted twenty *chō* of water fields (more than forty-five acres) in the district of Sakata in the province of Afumi, a large amount that must be seen in the same context, as one of the rewards appropriate to the head of an important retainer group. I suggest that behind this story of the rewards by the empress to Tori recorded in *Nihon shoki* are circumstances of the rewards granted by the Soga clan to one of their principal followers.

What about the information recorded on the mandorla of the Hōryūji Kondō Shaka Triad? As we have seen, the mandorla inscription asserts that this icon was made by Tori-busshi for the sake of Shōtoku Taishi. This source and the detailed account in the 605–606 entries of *Nihon shoki* just cited constitute the pertinent data concerning Tori-busshi. Derived from these data is the orthodox account of Tori's patrons, who are all said to be immediate members of the so-called imperial family. I suspect that the mandorla inscription was written after 670 as one part of a broader campaign to shift credit for the patronage of Buddhism from the Soga clan to the "imperial" line. In this respect, I argue that this inscription is closely related to the 605 and 606 entries in *Nihon shoki* describing the making of the monumental gilt bronze image for Asukadera. Since those entries focused on the role of Kuratsukuri no Tori, we should not be surprised that when the Shaka Triad inscription was written Tori should be given the credit for its production. All of this being said, I hasten to add that I do not necessarily think Tori was completely uninvolved in the making of this icon. In fact, I believe the strongest likelihood is that he was the supervisor of *the* major studio making icons during the Asuka period. If such is the case, certainly an image as fine as the Hōryūji Kondō Shaka Triad could have emerged only from that studio.

I have made an effort to conduct an objective analysis of the evidence related to the status of "Tori-busshi." But it is appropriate here to step back for a moment and consider the historiographical issues from a wider perspective. Broadly speaking, there seem to be three basic approaches to Tori-busshi:

1. He did not exist.
2. He was an important person associated with the Soga clan who, among other tasks, supervised the production of Buddhist icons.
3. He was a hands-on sculptor who personally produced great works of art.

Logically, possibility one is of little significance, since if Tori-busshi did not exist somebody else had to have produced or supervised the production of gilt-bronze images, and because it is inconceivable that this mysterious person's name will ever be recovered we might just as well stick with the name of Tori-busshi as a label. Possibility two is the one I find convincing, since it seems to fit the evidence most completely. Nevertheless, I should add here that there are many proponents of the third possibility, who vigorously maintain that Tori-busshi was primarily a sculptor who devoted his entire career to the production of Buddhist icons.

A leading proponent of number three is Ōhashi Katsuaki, a scholar who has been cited frequently in this chapter. I should make it clear immediately that I have much respect for Ōhashi's scholarship, although I frequently find myself in fundamental disagreement with his conclusions. Basically, I see Ōhashi as an exemplar of what I would call the "imperialist" position, an approach that tends to take *Nihon shoki*, *Gangōji engi*, and other early texts quite literally, thereby seeing the so-called imperial family as primarily responsible for the early patronage of Buddhism and Buddhist icons in Japan. I hasten to add that I see Ōhashi as an "intelligent imperialist," since he clearly recognizes the importance of the Soga clan and makes efforts to factor their contributions into his overall narrative. Nevertheless, members of the imperial clan, such as Empress Regnant Suiko and Shōtoku Taishi, occupy a much larger role in his narrative than they do in mine.

Ōhashi has recently published a long article, with a title that can be rendered in English as "Concerning the Training of Kuratsukuri Tori as a Buddhist Sculptor," in which he argues that Tori-busshi began his studies of the process of icon making from his youth.[50] Specifically, he maintains that a sculptor who is said to have come from Paekche to Japan in 577,[51] as part of a mission to encourage Buddhism, opened a school to train young Japanese in the sculptor's art. Tori is said to have been a student in this school, and by the time the Great Buddha (Figure 2.2) of Asukadera was about to be produced Tori was a master craftsman, fully able to carry out the making of this enormous icon on his own. In fact, Ōhashi speculates that by this stage in his career Tori's skill would probably have exceeded that of his master from Paekche, which is why, in Ōhashi's view, only Tori's name is recorded in *Nihon shoki*. Ōhashi sees the Asukadera Great Buddha as a work of Tori's early years, and the Shaka Triad (Figure 2.1) of the Hōryūji Kondō as a work of his mature period. The result of this hypothesis, in my view, is that early Japanese Buddhist sculpture finds itself blessed with a great genius who produced some of the finest examples of Buddhist icons cast in bronze—certainly an appealing result for those seeking to aggrandize Japanese culture.

Ōhashi has, in my opinion, quite a rigid view concerning the movement of people and ideas from the peninsula to Japan. He imagines a sort of Meiji situation whereby foreign teachers provide young Japanese with the desired technology, and then, with this goal achieved, the teachers depart from the scene and the "Japanese" students take over.[52] But of course, the sixth-century situation was different from that of the nineteenth century, since in the earlier period large groups of people moved permanently from the peninsula to the islands. Moreover, these people were not humble immigrants subordinate to a native ruling class but were, rather, themselves of elite status. Within these groups there were individuals who specialized in all major arts and sciences, and when the need arose for their services they would be ready to act. (In some cases there were undoubtedly direct requests from Japan for specific workers.)

Considering all of this, it is unlikely that the sculptor, who is said to have come in 577, devoted himself to teaching young Japanese how to make images, since there was no demand for such things at that time. Only when there was a real need for such services would the demands be made, and it seems likely that at the initial stages, at least, craftsmen from the continent would have been able to satisfy the needs for specialized services.

There is not space in this chapter to present and analyze all of Ōhashi's arguments. As noted, his hypothesis is clearly and systematically developed, and if one is inclined to accept his premises the conclusions follow quite logically. The problem, of course, is with the premises. For those who doubt the centrality in early Japanese Buddhism of Empress Suiko and Shōtoku

Taishi, Ōhashi's focus on their roles, and his insistence on the validity of *Nihon shoki*'s account of "Tori-busshi" as working for the "imperial family" will not ring true.

CONCLUSIONS

Who, exactly, was Tori working for? As I have suggested, the available evidence indicates that the primary patrons of Buddhism and Buddhist icons during the early Asuka period were members of the Soga clan, especially Soga no Umako, who commissioned Asukadera and the related icons. However, in the early eighth century, when *Nihon shoki* was written, the Soga clan had long since been toppled and the ruling family wished to transfer credit for the establishment of the new state and the growth of Buddhism from the Soga, where it rightly belonged, to somebody in the so-called imperial line. This was when a relatively obscure prince, called "Prince Stable Door" (Umayado no ōji), was raised from obscurity and transformed into "Prince Saintly Virtue" (Shōtoku Taishi).[53] Together with his aunt, Empress Regnant Suiko, he is then described as being largely responsible for the patronage of Buddhism, going as far as suggesting that they were responsible for the donation of the principal icon of Soga no Umako's temple, Asukadera.

The Shaka Triad of the Hōryūji Kondō is crucially important for the development of this narrative, because if the claims made in its inscription can be validated we have strong evidence for the so-called imperial role. Careful analysis of the inscription, however, makes clear that this text could not have been written during the early Asuka period, since there are, as we saw, several instances of anachronistic chronological and personal terminology. The most likely possibility is that the inscription was incised on the mandorla of a triad moved into the new Hōryūji Kondō to replace a triad that was probably destroyed in the fire of 670.[54] Indeed, it was during the last decades of the seventh century that the first steps were being taken in the formation of the "Shōtoku Taishi myth," and thus this would have been an appropriate time to fabricate an inscription that was congruent with the newly developed imperial myth.[55] Similarly, the stories recounted in *Nihon shoki* cannot be thought of as based on "imperial" documents of the early Asuka period but were also modified to produce a pro-imperial narrative that met the needs of the current ruling house. With the mandorla inscription and *Nihon shoki* account, one sees a fully formulated narrative that convincingly transfers credit for the patronage of Buddhism from the Soga clan to the so-called imperial family.[56]

The motivations behind this procedure seem clear. By the end of the seventh century, the extraordinary accomplishments in the secular and religious spheres of the early Asuka period were generally recognized. Initial steps had been taken toward the establishment of a centralized state, while a great religion had been adopted; neither of these developments was without controversy at its beginning, but by the period under consideration here both were seen as completely natural and appropriate. The one remaining, somewhat uncomfortable, problem troubling the ruling faction was that the flourishing of early Asuka political and religious culture was essentially the result of activities carried out by the Soga clan and their allies. Some aspects of the Soga achievement could not be obscured, but there was an extensive campaign carried out by the imperialist ideologues to hide their role. As we have seen, the solution to this problem was to imply that Empress Suiko and Shōtoku Taishi were largely responsible for the new developments, although the activities of the Soga leaders could never be entirely hidden.

What, then, is the role of Tori-busshi in all of this? Although I believe it can be conclusively demonstrated he was the leader of a guild closely associated with the Soga clan, the standard sources imply that he was working for the imperial family, particularly for Empress Regnant Suiko. Since it was necessary to have *somebody* who was directly involved in the making of the early icons, the fabricators of the myth hit on the brilliant idea of using the leader of the Kuratsukuri-be, Tori-busshi; it was not too difficult to obscure his Soga connections and make him into an actual hands-on sculptor working for the imperial court. Significant problems arise with the latter interpretation, however, since the stylistic diversity among the images ordinarily associated with Tori is quite broad, making it unlikely that they are all the products of one designer. Efforts have been made to suggest that this diversity is a result in part of chronological evolution, although I propose an alternate source. The close connections of the Soga clan and the Kuratsukuri line with the Korean peninsula, especially Paekche, is well documented; I suggest that Tori-busshi, in his position as a supervisor of the production of Buddhist icons, would have recruited sculptors from the peninsula during the early Asuka period. As individual craftsmen they would have had slightly different styles, so it should not be surprising that variations are seen in the corpus described earlier. I propose that these important sculptures be referred to as the "Soga-Tori group," thereby giving appropriate credit to both the principal patrons and the supervisor of the studio that produced the images.[57]

Chapter Three

E'nichibō Jōnin, the Saint's Companion

KAREN L. BROCK

Being a santero is something that came from my ancestors.
—*Margarito R. Mondragon*[1]

How do we talk about painted-buddha masters?
—*Hirata Yutaka*[2]

In the preface to his painstaking study of painters of buddha images (*butsuzō*), Hirata Yutaka poses a challenge:

> . . . whenever we talk about the history of anonymous paintings, or about extant Buddhist paintings, we are speaking about painted-buddha masters (*ebusshi*). Even as we hope that a painting transcends its time period, it cannot escape the intentions of that period; and without documents we cannot know the historical character of such a painting.[3]

The names of painted-buddha masters are scattered throughout ninth- to fourteenth-century documents, but few extant Buddhist paintings can be linked definitively to individual painters, since signatures or seals do not appear until the middle of the thirteenth century.[4] Hirata's reading of both documents and paintings has illuminated the historical circumstances surrounding many painted-buddha masters: changes in their status and identity, their workshop practices, and patronage networks.[5] Even so, few works by named *ebusshi* will ever be folded into the "canon" of Japanese painting.[6]

This chapter revisits the case of E'nichibō Jōnin (active ca. 1211–ca. 1243), a painter of buddha images who *has* received notice. Two Japanese paintings bear attributions to Jōnin: the portrait *Saint Myōe Seated in Meditation in a Tree* (Figure 3.1) and a set of seven picture scrolls, known as *Kegon Origin Tales* (Figures 3.2 and 3.3).[7] Owned by the Kyoto temple Kōzanji since the mid-thirteenth century, both works have been the subject of much adulation and scholarly study for more than a hundred years. In fact, although Jōnin's name is frequently linked to these two paintings, claims for his authorship have

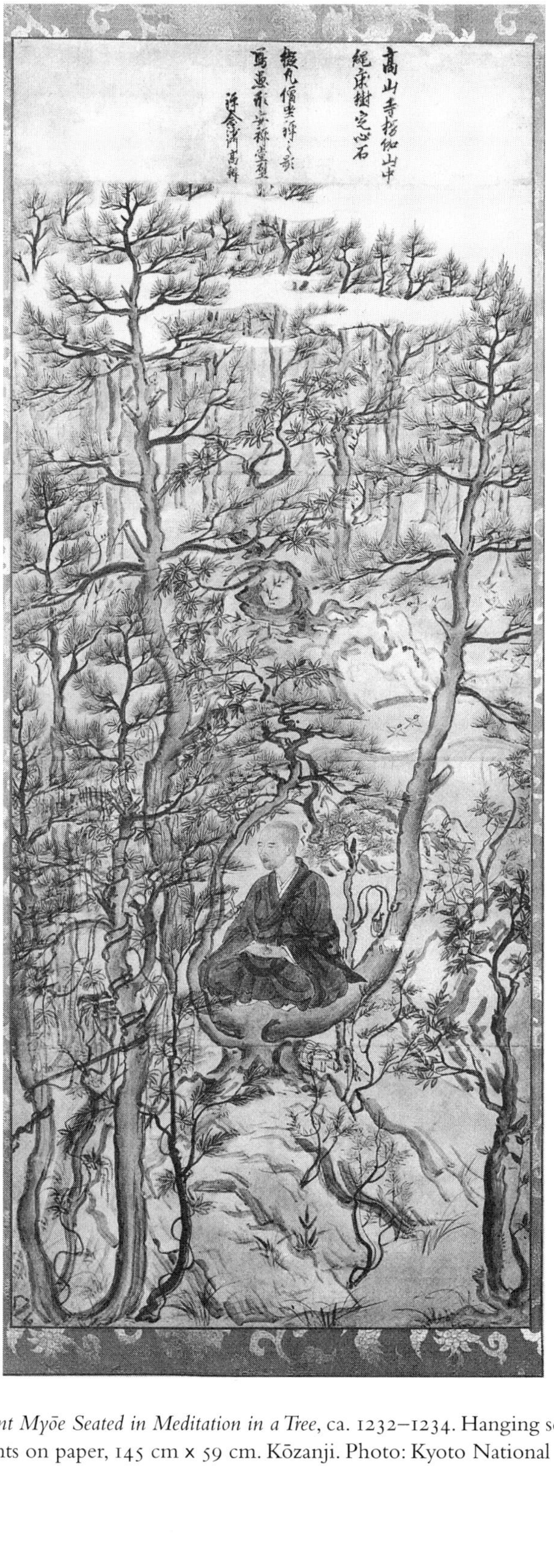

Figure 3.1 *Saint Myōe Seated in Meditation in a Tree*, ca. 1232–1234. Hanging scroll, ink and mineral pigments on paper, 145 cm x 59 cm. Kōzanji. Photo: Kyoto National Museum.

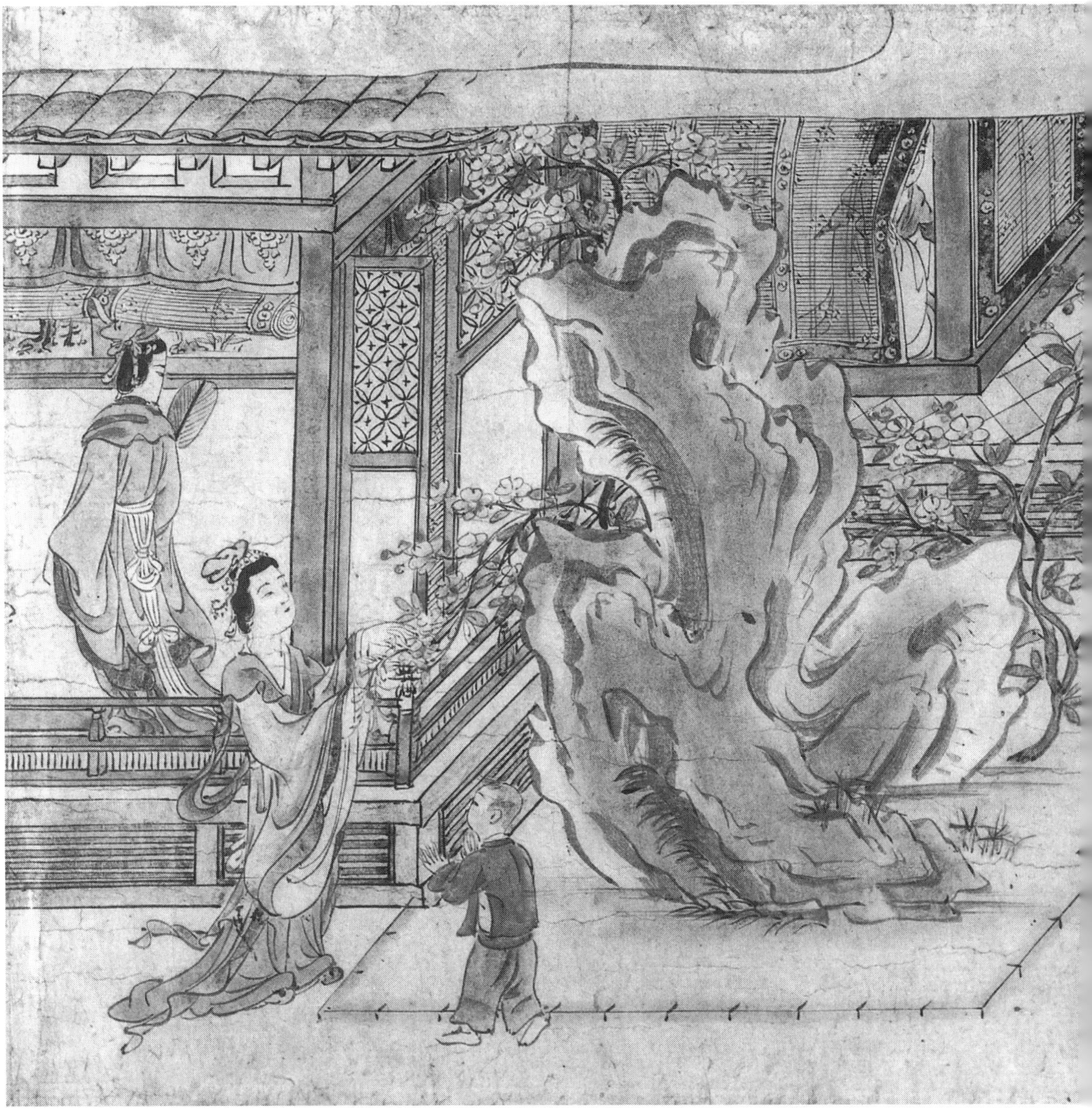

Figure 3.2 Gishō Meets Zenmyō. Detail from *Gishō* scrolls of *Kegon Origin Tales*, ca. 1219–1221. Handscroll, ink and color on paper, height 31.7 cm. Kōzanji. Photo: Kyoto National Museum.

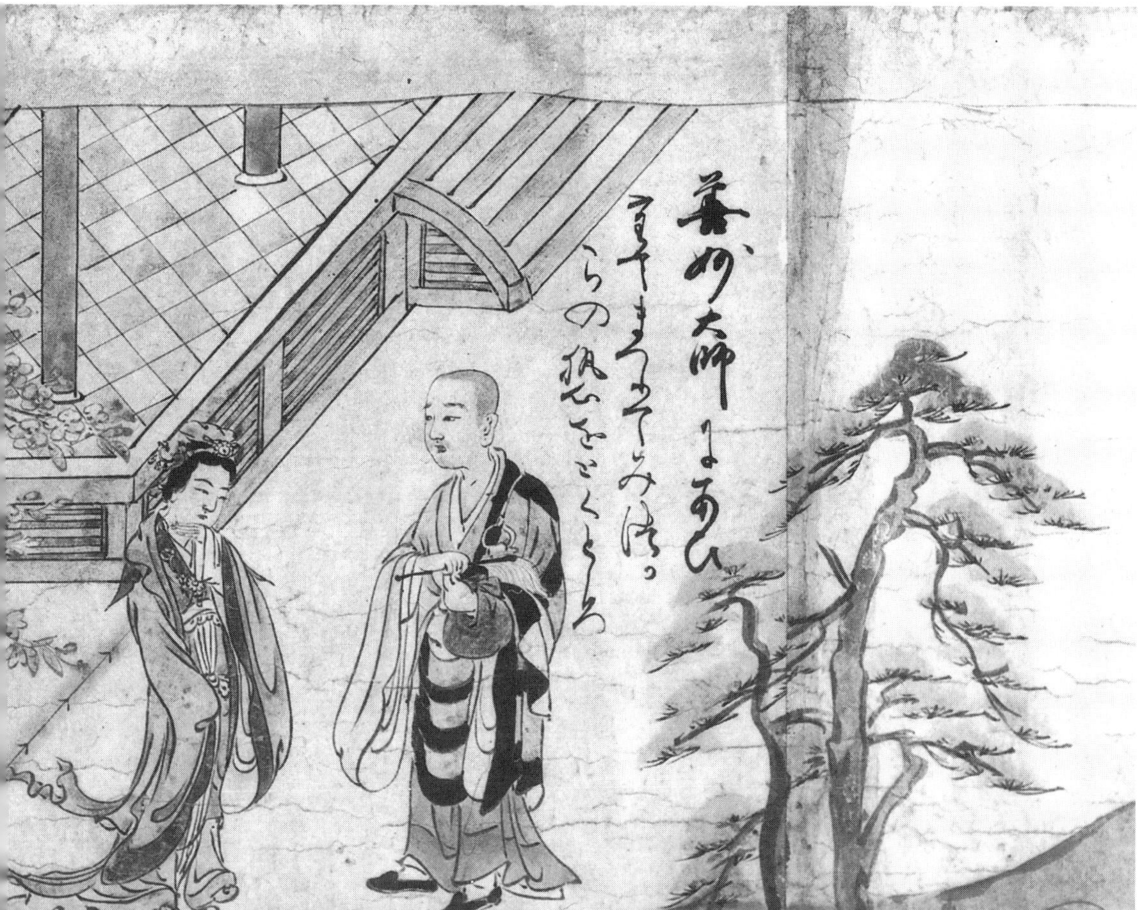
善妙大師にあひ

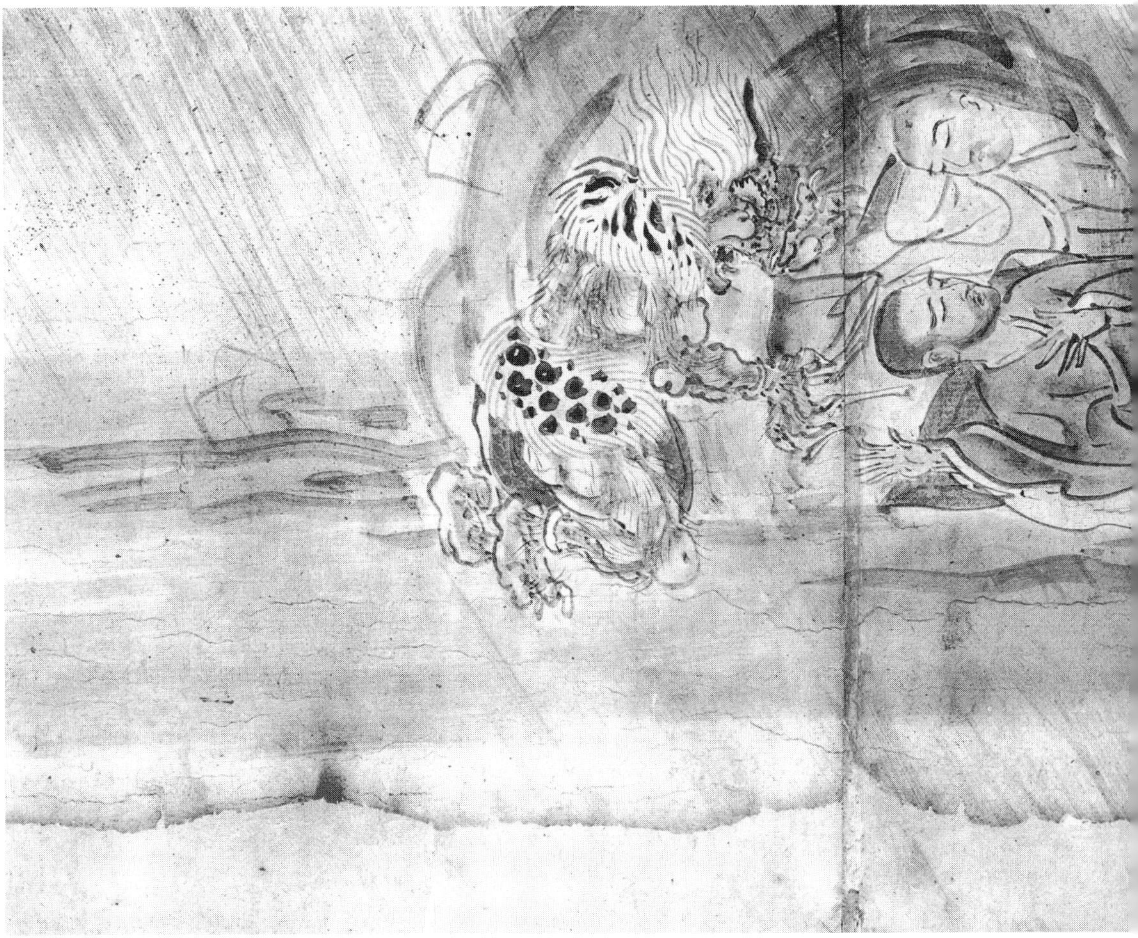

Figure 3.3 Gangyō Dreams of a Demon. Detail from *Gangyō* scrolls of *Kegon Origin Tales*, ca. 1233. Handscroll, ink and color on paper, height 31.7 cm. Kōzanji. Photo: Kyoto National Museum.

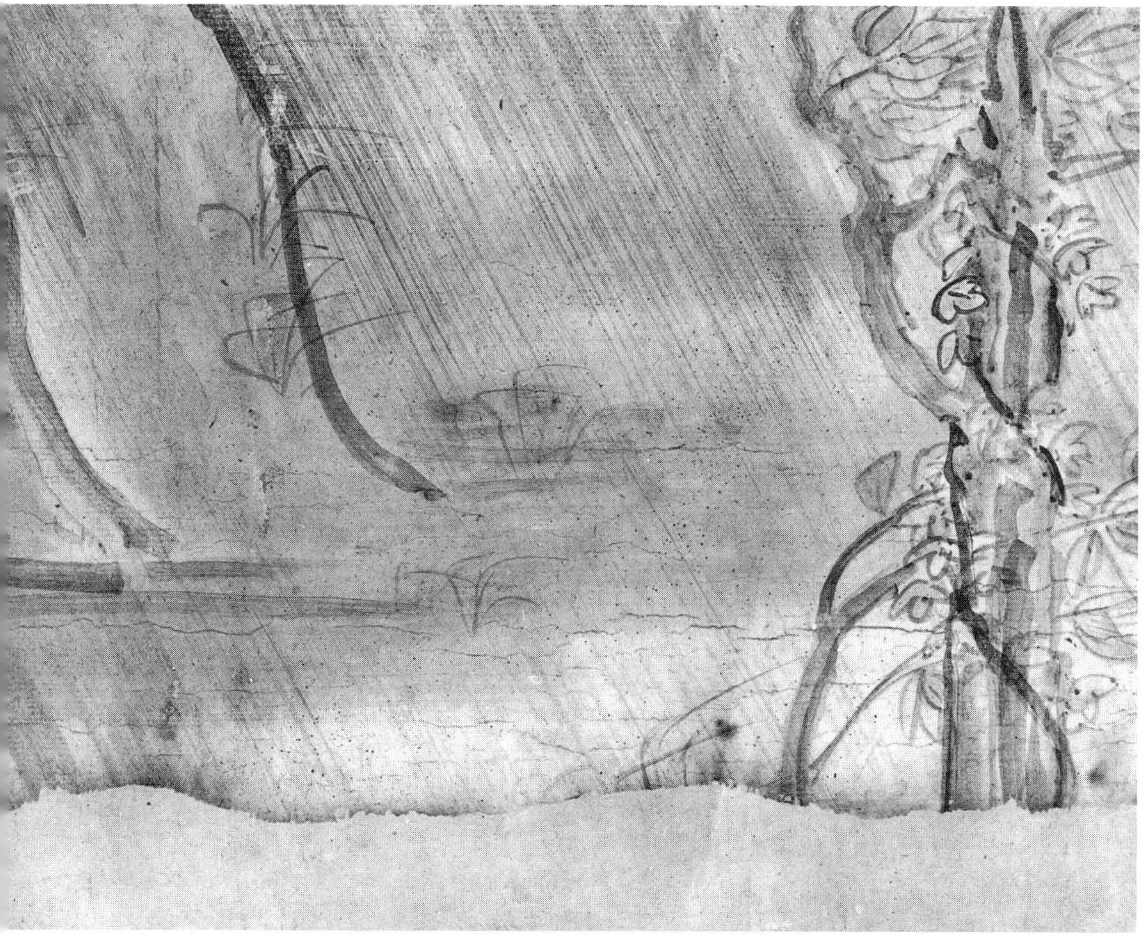

never been solid. They are not based on inscriptions or documentary evidence, or on the paintings' stylistic affinity with known works. The famous portrait of Myōe (1173–1232) is one of seven owned by Kōzanji, dating from the thirteenth to the nineteenth centuries, showing the monk in a variety of settings and poses.[8] As for the painter of *Kegon Origin Tales*, temple traditions in the Edo- and Meiji-period texts claimed either Tosa Mitsunobu (1434–1525) or Fujiwara Nobuzane (1177–1266/70). Early-twentieth-century writers discounted the Mitsunobu attribution as too late and dropped Nobuzane's name.[9]

Like the shifting attributions, since the seventeenth century Jōnin's artistic identity has undergone repeated transformations. The earliest discussion of Jōnin, by Kanō Einō (1631–97), placed him within an elusive lineage of painted-buddha masters known collectively by the name Takuma:

> The Monk Jōnin, sobriquet E'nichibō, was a disciple of Saint Myōe. By nature he loved to paint and he studied with Takuma *hōgen*. Some say he was Takuma's son. Therefore his paintings are in the treasure house of Kōzanji at Toganoo. His brushwork resembles that of Takuma. He exclusively worked on buddha images and miscellaneous paintings.[10]

Einō's association of Jōnin with the Takuma name apparently came from local legends about Takuma painters working at Kōzanji and neighboring Jingoji. In his biographies of Takuma painters, Einō recognized that all of them, including Jōnin, painted buddha and *kami* images. Several received honorary Buddhist ranks from the court, such as "Dharma-eye" (*hōgen*), as rewards for their service.[11] Yet by associating Jōnin with the otherwise unidentified Takuma *hōgen*, Einō characterized him as a minor painter in the "Yamato painting" (*Yamato-e*) lineage that stretched from Toba Sōjō (Kakuyū, 1053–1140) to Tosa Mitsunobu.[12] This dual image of Jōnin—as buddha image maker and "Yamato" painter—persisted well into the twentieth century.

The publication of a significant body of primary sources concerning Myōe and Kōzanji in the 1920s and 1930s finally enabled scholars to break free of traditional texts and attributions.[13] In his critical biography of Myōe (1929), Murakami Sōdō presented the first evidence that Jōnin *had* been a follower of Myōe and cited thirteenth-century records of Jōnin's paintings.[14] He began the task of sorting out the confused identities of Takuma painters to account for Jōnin's parentage. Murakami identified Shunga *hokkyō* ("Bridge of the Dharma") as a second painter who worked for Myōe and Kōzanji.[15] Murakami then made the controversial proposal that Shunga, Takuma Chōga, and Takuma Shōga were actually one person, and the father of Jōnin! Murakami's study revealed that thirteenth-century Kōzanji documents never use the "Takuma" label for Jōnin, Shunga, or anyone else.

The attribution to Jōnin of both *Saint Myōe Seated in Meditation in a Tree* and *Kegon Origin Tales* first appeared in the 1930s, when art historians recognized their stylistic affinities.[16] Jōnin's traditional association with the Takuma lineage was consciously downplayed to place both works within a newly defined canon of "Yamato painting" epitomized by *Origin Tales of Mt. Shigi*.[17] During the last fifty years, a consensus developed that *Saint Myōe Seated in Meditation in a Tree* and the *Gangyō* scrolls were painted by the same painter, presumably Jōnin, but no agreement has ever been reached about the identity of the *Gishō* scrolls painter.[18] Most studies conclude that the painter (or painters) of these works manifested a high degree of creativity and individuality, attributes not usually claimed for the anonymous makers of buddha images.

Do documentary evidence and the paintings themselves actually support Jōnin's authorship? This question lurks uncomfortably in the background of every study, precisely because there are obvious internal contradictions between documents and paintings. Even Hirata Yutaka struggles to explain the gap between documentary records of Jōnin as painter of buddha images and of the brilliantly conceived *Saint Myōe Seated in Meditation in a Tree*:

> In common practice, the reality of painted-buddha masters is illuminated by their painting lineage or by the techniques of their works. However, at the same time, it is also possible to explain them by considering the intentions of patrons who commissioned their works. . . . The existence of several outstanding works in Myōe's environment speaks of the existence of excellent painters. But the meaning of "excellence" is that, because of Myōe, they had opportunities to demonstrate their excellent painting skills.[19]

Hirata is not alone in crediting Myōe with the inspiration for these and many other Kōzanji objects.

Hirata's research contributed to one of the most oft-repeated myths about Kōzanji, that the temple was a center of artistic production during the first half of the thirteenth century. Some authors speak of "the prolific Kōzanji workshop" or "the Kōzanji atelier," claiming that Myōe himself directed a group of "artists" in fostering a "new painting movement."[20] Tanaka Ichimatsu viewed several Kōzanji paintings as thirteenth-century forerunners of Zen ink painting. He posited Myōe's connection to Zen by recounting the apocryphal tale of Myōe's encounter with Eisai (1141–1215), said to have given Myōe tea seeds and instruction in meditative practices.[21] Presumably Eisai also somehow introduced Myōe to new forms of painting. This so-called new movement was variously credited to the "Takuma School," to the importation of Zen paintings, or to Myōe himself.[22]

In my 1984 dissertation on *Kegon Origin Tales*, I found the collaborative processes involved in making picture scrolls, and issues of content and audience, far more compelling and rewarding avenues of inquiry.[23] By the summer of 1988, having viewed these several paintings on various occasions, I came to the startling conclusion that *Saint Myōe Seated in Meditation in a Tree* more closely resembled the *Gishō* scrolls than it did the *Gangyō* scrolls! Since I had already concluded that the *Gishō* scrolls could only have been made by a painter, or painters, thoroughly versed in picture scroll making, I realized the entire issue of Jōnin's participation in the making of both portrait and picture scrolls needs rethinking.[24] Other recent studies either question or ignore Jōnin's supposed contribution.[25]

In reexamining E'nichibō Jōnin, I do not start with the shaky premise that *Saint Myōe Seated in Meditation in a Tree* or *Kegon Origin Tales* were painted by him. Instead, I read documentary references to Jōnin within the larger context of contemporary hagiographical writings about "Saint" Myōe to understand him as a member of Myōe's monastic community. Then I look closely at three extant portraits of Myōe (Figures 3.1, 3.6, and 3.7), two of which I accept as authentic works made by Jōnin for Kōzanji. Further documentary evidence of Jōnin's other painting projects at Kōzanji considered thereafter shows him as a painter of buddha images, but not as a professional painted-buddha master.

JŌNIN, "THE BRUSH-WIELDING RENUNCIANT"

The intense focus on Myōe underestimates the importance of Kōzanji's larger community of monks and lay patrons. Several texts produced at Kōzanji during the first half of the thirteenth century document the painters (and carvers) whose buddha images and portraits were used by Myōe during lectures and ceremonies or installed in temple halls. Even a cursory reading of this material demonstrates that Myōe was not Jōnin's only patron, nor were all of the temple's treasures made by artisans in Kōzanji's employ or under Myōe's direction. In writing about Kōzanji painters, Murakami, Hirata, and others all excerpted the same primary documents but paid little attention to the documents themselves or the motives and relationships among *their* authors. These details directly affect our interpretation of the passages cited. Understanding the nature of "artistic production" for Kōzanji depends upon our recognizing who participated in the building of the temple and witnessed Jōnin, Shunga, and others at work. Isolating the few passages naming Jōnin is inadequate. He participated in many activities as an unnamed monk, and in some cases the deliberate *absence* of his name is significant.[26]

Had Myōe supervised a painting atelier at Kōzanji, some hint of that might surface in his own writings. A prolific interpreter and copyist of Buddhist texts, Myōe was equally adept in Chinese and Japanese and wrote both for monastic colleagues and aristocratic lay patrons. His *Dream Record*, compiled over forty years, serves in some degree as his autobiography, but it says little about Kōzanji or the painters he interacted with and does not name Jōnin.[27] However, one tantalizingly brief sentence does appear from 1205: "6/18: I earned 200 *sen*. I gave 100 to the buddha-master Satsuma and kept 100 for myself." This entry records Myōe's payment to Shunga for services performed before Kōzanji even existed.[28] In addition to *Dream Record*, Myōe frequently wrote liturgies for ceremonies and conducted lectures that used buddha or *kami* images as primary deities (*honzon*), but these texts omit details of paintings or their makers. Although Myōe's writings allow a rich interpretation of his spiritual life, they do not portray him as the actual supervisor of carpenters, carvers, and painters at Kōzanji.

Saint Making

Not long before his death, Myōe wrote three directives (*okibumi*) concerning his wishes for the future of Kōzanji. He acknowledged the efforts of his several closest followers, who had long since taken charge of temple matters, allowing him to fulfill his own desire for reclusion.[29] These several men left a significant body of original writings, as well as numerous hand-copied texts. Before and after Myōe's death in early 1232, they self-consciously endeavored to remember and record everything they had witnessed or heard during Myōe's conversations and lectures.[30] These writings created enduring images of Myōe, whom they regarded as Shōnin, translated here as "Saint."[31] Myōe never described *himself* as Shōnin; he always used self-deprecating phrases in his inscriptions on books and paintings.[32] In employing the word *Saint*, I seek to invoke the original implications of Shōnin, acknowledging that Myōe's sanctity derives from the commemorative activities of his many witnesses. Nearly all of the texts written by these "saint makers" are hagiographical in form and content.[33] A reference to a particular person—whether painter, patron, family member, or friend—should be considered in light of that person's spiritual and/or material relationship to Myōe or his temple. These elders mention Jōnin, either by name or indirectly through accounts of activities he participated in. Written after Myōe's death, these texts must all be read in conjunction with contemporary documents and inscriptions on Kōzanji manuscripts to recover missing details.[34]

Jōnin's name does not appear in Myōe's directives, nor in Kōzanji's several Shingon and Kegon lineage charts.[35] These charts differ in details, transcribed by later descendants with lineage or property claims of their own. They explain the overlapping connections between Myōe, his teachers, and his followers. Jōnin's absence reveals that he was not one of Myōe's primary followers in either Shingon or Kegon doctrine, that he did not head any of Kōzanji's subtemples, and that he did not have followers. Yet since Jōnin interacted with the senior monks, the charts present a frame for assessing Jōnin's status.

Myōe's three most prominent followers began their monastic careers at Jingoji, where they first made Myōe's acquaintance. The eldest, Jōshin (1174–1250), appears exclusively in Shingon lineage charts, first as a follower of Gyōji (1148–1226), Myōe's uncle, and later of Myōe.[36] From 1216, he became involved at Kōzanji, officially a separate precinct of Jingoji. In 1229, Myōe persuaded Jōshin to remain permanently at Kōzanji, and Jōshin in turn brought with him a large library of Shingon texts.[37] In his final directive, Myōe installed Jōshin as head of Kōzanji, even though he was a relative outsider compared to other temple elders. Jōshin's saint-making activities consist of compilations of his recollections of Myōe and a detailed record of the events surrounding Myōe's death.[38]

Jōshin mentions "Jōnin E'nichibō" *once* in his account of Myōe's final days, the first month of 1232. During this period, many followers and patrons of Myōe sent inquiries or condolences, and some experienced auspicious dreams or other unusual events dutifully recorded by Jōshin. Around noon on the eighteenth, the day before Myōe died, Jōnin E'nichibō dozed off and dreamed that "a solemn and delicate heavenly child, alone, and with great dignity and presence, walked into the abbot's thatched hut."[39] The child in this dream might be Zenzai, the young boy whose pilgrimage to fifty-five "good friends" in the final chapters of the *Flower Garland Sutra* appears repeatedly in Myōe's own dreams, practices, and imagery.[40] Jōnin's dream and the other auspicious events recorded by Jōshin all offer evidence of Myōe's "saintliness."

Jōshin was the eldest of Kōzanji's senior monks, but Kikai (1178–1250) was closest to Myōe. He appears in Shingon lineages because of his time at Jingoji, but his name figures more prominently in Kegon lineages, as Myōe's chief follower.[41] Kikai left Jingoji in 1198 to live and study with Myōe and remained with him until the saint's death. Throughout their more than three decades together, Kikai served Myōe in a variety of roles, especially as perennial witness and go-between with those who would distract the saint. At the end of his life, Myōe expressed profound appreciation for Kikai. Instead of burdening his dharma-companion with the headship of Kōzanji, he placed Kikai in charge of scholarship. Upon Myōe's death, Kikai wrote *Life of Saint Myōe*, incorporating Myōe's own accounts of his early life and his own recollections of their time together.[42] Throughout this text, Kikai writes of events Jōnin participated in but never mentions him by name. For instance, in describing Myōe's final days, Kikai emphasizes Myōe's appearance, activities, words, and visions. The assembled monks, presumably including Jōnin, continuously chanted dharani for several days and also meditated, while five (unnamed) monks waited on the dying saint.[43]

The third of Myōe's closest followers, Ryōten (1180–1255), also studied Shingon at Jingoji and joined Myōe in 1198.[44] In his final directive, Myōe placed Ryōten in charge of economic matters, precisely because Ryōten (along with Kikai) had played the critical role in the building of the temple. Since Ryōten outlived both Jōshin and Kikai by five years, he must have shared his memories of Myōe with members of the next generation. Around 1250, Ryōten completed *Catalogue of Kōzanji's Sacred Sutras*, to document the astounding book collecting and copying activities of the entire community.[45] *Catalogue* lists the titles of manuscripts copied by Jōnin, although it does not name him. Ryōten's *Catalogue* is the only contemporary document to mention *Tales of Gishō and Gangyō* (aka *Kegon Origin Tales*), but without any further detail.[46]

Sutra Copying

While Jōshin, Kikai, and Ryōten managed Kōzanji's affairs, Myōe *did* play a guiding role in one enterprise: the borrowing, copying, studying, and lecturing on Buddhist texts. The Kōzanji storehouse still contains hundreds of manuscripts copied by Myōe, his close followers, and numerous lesser-known monks and nuns. From inscriptions on extant manuscripts, we know that Jōnin copied or corrected sutras from 1211 to 1229. Murakami first published a few of these examples, and subsequent writers have filled out the list.[47] These manuscripts are more than mere dates in Jōnin's chronology; they reveal much about his identity and status within the Kōzanji community.

Over a period of six months in 1211, Jōnin joined at least seven other monks in writing the entire eighty–fascicle *Flower Garland Sutra* in forty small paste-bound books (Figure 3.4).[48] Jōnin wrote ten of these books, fascicles forty-one through sixty, inscribing his name in each volume. In the first six books, he identifies himself as "The unlearned Kegon renunciant Jōnin."[49] A lengthy dedicatory inscription in the seventh volume explains that Myōe raised the funds for this project:

> Due to Myōebō's fundraising, from among the eight parts of a set of the eighty-fascicle *Flower Garland Sutra*, I write this with the dedicated heart of a believer for the sake of joining vows with all living beings in all generations. By dwelling in and holding fast to this merit, the dharma-eye, that faultless torchlight of wisdom, shines brightly. How much more so whenever there is one reading or one hearing, one's inner fragrance will spread outward, gradually deepening. And in the future I must see the Fifty-five Saints of the

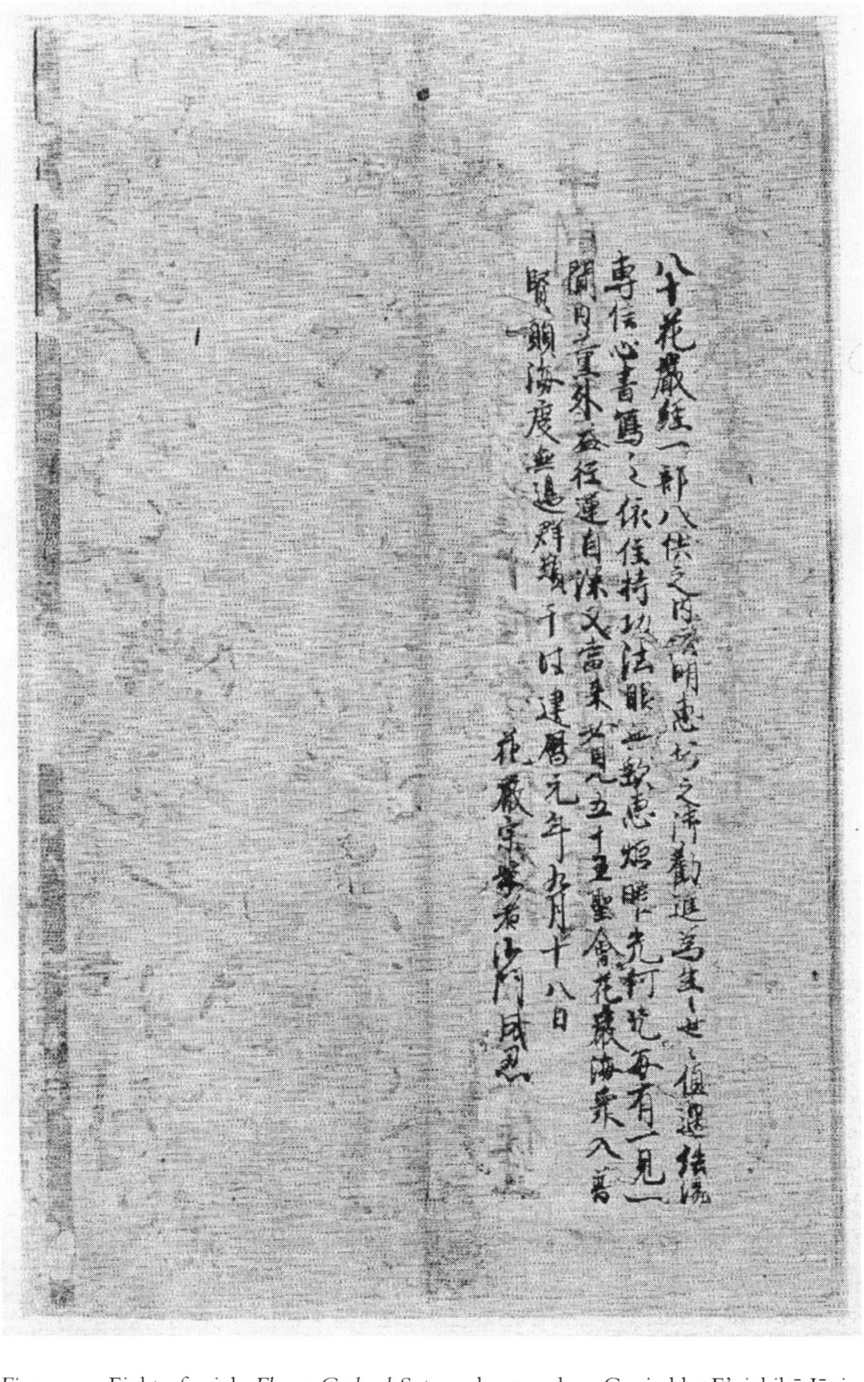

Figure 3.4 Eighty-fascicle *Flower Garland Sutra*, vols. 53 and 54. Copied by E'nichibō Jōnin in 1211. Book, ink on paper. Kōzanji. Photo: Kōzanji Team.

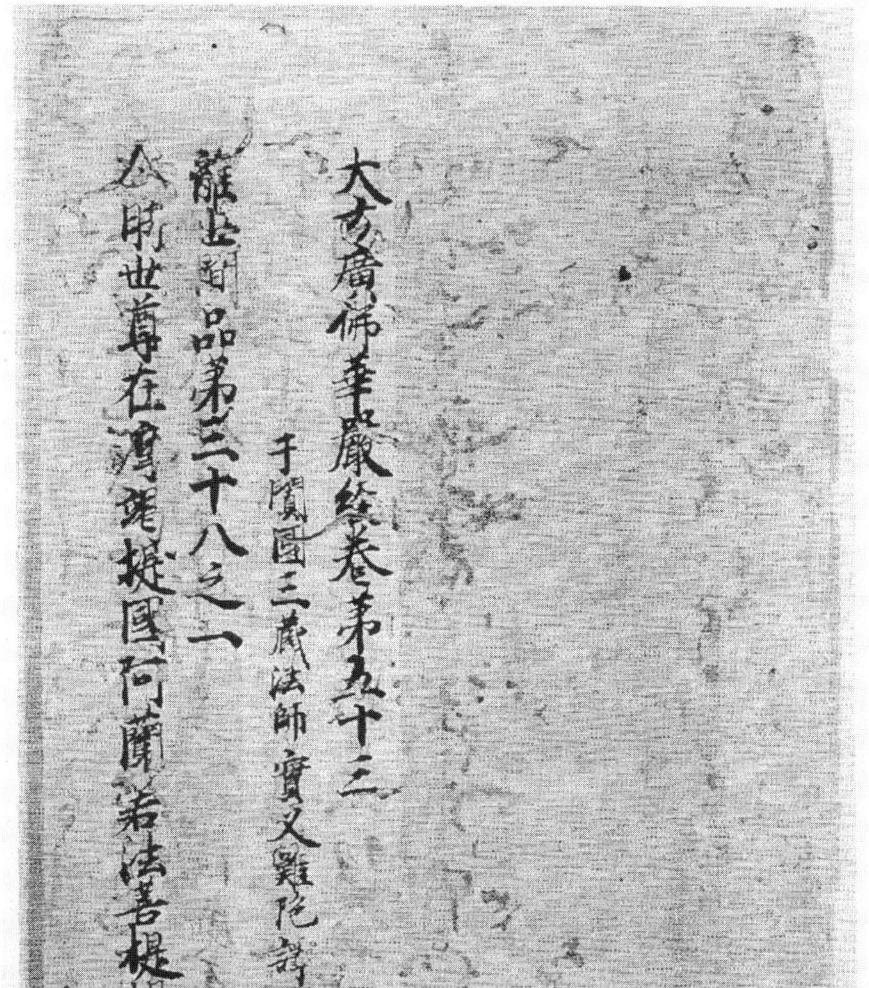
大方廣佛華嚴經卷第五十三
于闐國三藏法師實叉難陀譯
離世間品第三十八之一
爾時世尊在摩竭提國阿蘭若法菩提場中普光

> Flower Garland Ocean Assembly and enter the vow of Fugen to cross the ocean to the infinite multitudes. The time is Kenryaku 1/9/18. Jōnin, the renunciant studying Kegon.[50]

The wording of the long inscription is not unique to Jōnin's colophons, but his signatures show a self-awareness of his progress in studying the content of the sutra. In his final three books, he becomes "the renunciant seeking dharma."[51] In addition to his role as fundraiser for this project, Myōe wrote a few lines at the beginning of the first book.[52]

Jōnin was one of the three primary participants in this project, all of whom signed themselves "renunciants." Gyōben (active 1191–1256) also wrote ten books, and Ryōten wrote eight. Ryōten was already thirty-two when he took up this copying project. Gyōben copied texts at Jingoji as early as 1191, and he may have been older than Ryōten.[53] Myōe praised Gyōben in his final directives as someone who had been with him from the beginning at Jingoji and resided at Kōzanji for a long time.[54] During the Kennin era (1201–4), Gyōben made a trip to south China (modern-day Fujian Province). He returned with a complete Song printed edition of the Buddhist Canon (Tripitaka), perhaps the source for this copying project.[55] Because the "renunciants" Ryōten and Gyōben were already mature men in 1211, Jōnin's claim of being "unlearned" does not necessarily indicate youth; he could have begun his Kegon studies late in life.[56]

Inscriptions by Jōnin on later manuscripts show a continued rise in his self-esteem. Less than a year after he was "unlearned," he signed himself "writer-monk" (*shuppitsu sō*).[57] The shift from "renunciant" to "monk" could indicate that he received ordination during that year, or it may mark a change in his relative status within the community.

Jōnin accompanied Myōe when the latter moved away from Kōzanji in 1218. According to Kikai, in the autumn of that year Myōe and all but two or three of his followers took up residence in the hills behind Kamo Shrine. The move resulted from retired emperor Gotoba's (1180–1239) appointment of a new superintendent at Jingoji. Gotoba in turn directed the head of Kamo shrine, Nobuhisa (1171–1223), to build four or five monks' residences as well as a sutra storehouse for their use.[58] For the next few years, Myōe and his followers went back and forth from Kōzanji to Kamo. This unsettled period saw the initial building phase at Kōzanji, the tensions resulting in the Shōkyū War of 1221, and its sad aftermath.[59] Since the Jingoji-Kōzanji area became a refuge for family members of Gotoba's losing faction, Myōe's move to Kamo appears in retrospect to have been prudent. Given Myōe's penchant for study and meditation, the Kamo retreat functioned as a safe haven from upheaval.

Toward the end of their stay at Kamo, in 1222, Jōnin and several other monks participated in a lavish project to copy the forty-fascicle *Flower Garland Sutra*. Over a period of six days, Jōnin wrote four fascicles in four scrolls.[60] His signatures all refer to himself as "brush-wielding monk" (*shuppitsu biku*) and state that he copied the texts while at the Kamo retreat. Only half of the extant thirty-eight scrolls were inscribed, but Jōnin may have been the most senior of the five monks who signed their names. One scroll bears an explanatory colophon, written by "unlearned in Kegon doctrine, the monk Shōjō, age 29."[61] According to Shōjō, in the previous spring Myōe and the assembled monks took turns reading this sutra before a set of images of *Sixteen Rakan*. As the nun Jū'nenbō listened to them, her heart filled with affection and she vowed to commission a copy of the sutra written according to the "prescribed method" (*nyohō*). Throughout the summer, she pressed Myōe about the project and by fall he relented, allowing ten monks to carry out this special practice over a period of seventeen days. The work was divided, four scrolls per copyist, and the task was accomplished with great care and ceremony. Shōjō ended his dedication with the wish that the patron and all the copyists would benefit from the merit of the project and the joining of their vows.

The nun's desire for a copy of the *Flower Garland Sutra* written according to the "prescribed method" refers to a set of solemn procedures followed by the copyists, but also to the quality of the materials.[62] The resulting scrolls are of much finer quality than the norm among Kōzanji's manuscripts. Every scroll has a wrapper and frontispiece of dyed indigo paper, decorated with cloud patterns of gold and silver dust, threads, and cut flakes of several sizes. The sutra text is carefully written within gold-ruled lines, attached to a black sandalwood roller and hand-woven tie. Such expensive materials alone hint at Jū'nenbō's wealth. Since she had access to Myōe's community from the spring through the fall of 1222, I suspect she was closely related to Nobuhisa, and that the project was carried out on behalf of their entire family.[63]

In *Life of Myōe*, Kikai described the impact of this project on Myōe:

> In autumn of the same year this person, a nun, made a great vow. She directed ten monks at that mountain temple to begin a practice of copying a complete set of the 40–fascicle *Flower Garland Sutra* according to the prescribed method. When the copying was finished, Shōnin spoke. The previous night he had a dream in which ten or more cloaked monks come, their joy following as they listened. The prescribed method of copying the *Lotus Sutra* has been carried out from ancient times to the present, but in Japan I have never heard of anyone copying the *Flower Garland Sutra* according to the prescribed method. In the biographies of Great Tang, there are many examples. . . . I wonder if this dream of those some ten cloaked monks coming to follow their joy, is a sign that the assembly of the Sixteen Rakan and other dharma-protecting saints will come to follow their joy at the copying of this sutra.[64]

As always, Kikai focuses on Myōe's powerful dreams and words, rather than the mundane details of the participants. Kikai witnessed the project, but he did not collaborate, perhaps because he held too senior a position to copy sutras on demand.

After the move back to Kōzanji, Jōnin continued to copy sutras on a much smaller scale. In the late summer and fall of 1224, a nun named Kinbutsu sponsored another "prescribed method" copy of the same sutra, to which Jōnin contributed one scroll, signing himself "the brush-wielding renunciant, the lion Jōnin." Jōnin probably reverted to the humble term "renunciant" in response to Myōe's own frequent use of the same term, but the self-appellation "lion" seems curiously boastful.[65] This is Jōnin's last-known sutra-copying project, but in 1227 and 1229 he checked others' work for errors. Since the 1220s and 1230s were the period in which Kōzanji's several halls were built and outfitted, the attention of Kōzanji monks, including Jōnin, must have been diverted to that larger task.

Vow Taking

Jōnin's participation in sutra-copying projects does not suggest any particular closeness to Myōe, although his activities place him securely within Kegon practice at the temple. One final reference to Jōnin further situates him among his peers. From 1225 until a few months before he died, Myōe held public lectures and vow-taking meetings (*sekkai*) twice a month at Kōzanji's Golden Hall.[66] A diary of meetings held over eight months in 1230–31 records the names of Kōzanji monks who participated. "E'nichibō" occurs ninth in a list of eighteen names that is organized by the monks' seniority and status at Kōzanji.[67] Not all of the monks have been identified, nor are their dates known. Jōnin is listed third after Ryōten (born in 1180) and immediately before Kōshin (born in 1192), suggesting a birth date for Jōnin in the late 1180s. Jōnin would thus have been in his early twenties when he first copied out the *Flower Garland Sutra* as an "unlearned Kegon renunciant" in 1211.

These vow-taking meetings became Kōzanji's principal venue for interaction with the broader public, and they drew in crowds of people, aristocratic and common. In 1229, Fujiwara Teika (1162–1242) wrote a vivid yet unsentimental picture of one of these meetings in his diary:

> Today my wife and daughter went secretly to Toganoo. Myōebō administers vows every month on the fifteenth and the last day. People say that everyone in the realm gathers there as if he were Śākyamuni himself. Even though it is important to join others in making vows, I hate following the crowds. I find myself filled with pity at the sight of poor beggars wallowing in their conversion. . . . Being compressed in a crowd is like entering a small bottle, you can't see anything. . . . [68]

In *Life of Myōe*, Kikai wrote extensively about the visions and miracles experienced by Myōe and others on these occasions. He noted that all of the monks sat in a row and chanted together.[69] Myōe stressed the importance of these meetings in his final directives, when he appointed two elders to take charge of them after his death: the aged Shōjitsu (1152–1234) for whom the appointment must have been purely honorary; and Shinkei (1177–1258), the Jingoji monk who sent Gyōben to China some thirty years earlier. In his directive, Myōe distinguished the monks in his community by the terms "elders" (*rōsō*), "dharma-companions" (*dōbō*), attendants (*jija*), and lower-ranking monks (*gesō*).[70] Jōnin, the "brush-wielding renunciant" who copied sutras and chanted during vow-taking meetings, was considered one of Myōe's "dharma-companions."

JŌNIN, "PAINTED FROM HIS HEART"

The only text discussing Jōnin's paintings at Kōzanji is the official temple "history," *Kōzanji Origin Tales*, produced in 1253 by Kōshin (1192–1255).[71] Kōshin appears in both Shingon and Kegon lineage charts as a follower of Myōe, and his name immediately follows Jōnin in the diary of vow-making meetings. But Kōshin was not a long-term resident of Kōzanji either before or after Myōe's death. Members of the temple community nonetheless recognized his formidable literary and scholarly abilities. They enlisted Kōshin to compile the temple history, to collate Myōe's poems, and to correct the Chinese version of Kikai's *Life of Saint Myōe*; Kōshin also recorded Myōe's lectures and other sayings.[72] All of these projects vouchsafe Kōshin's extraordinary access to temple elders and their written records.

Kōzanji Origin Tales transmits an "official" point of view, and Kōshin must have relied heavily upon the recollections of Kikai, Ryōten, and Shinkei to write it. At its most basic level, the text functions as a registry of the several temple buildings and their contents; it records the names of prominent imperial and aristocratic patrons, as well as the makers of the majority of Kōzanji's carved and painted icons and portraits. Throughout the text, "origin tales" (*engi*) explain the vicissitudes of halls or icons and the locations where Myōe experienced dreams or auspicious events. These tales frequently echo Myōe's *Dream Record*, Kikai's *Life of Saint Myōe*, and various other sources.[73] Kōshin describes the appearance and contents of buildings as of 1253. With the exception of Myōe's several residences, none of the buildings housing the elder monks or their possessions are mentioned. Thus Kōshin's *Kōzanji Origin Tales* is by no means a complete account of what actually existed at Kōzanji.

Kōshin mentions paintings by Jōnin, Shunga, and Kaneyasu (active 1207–

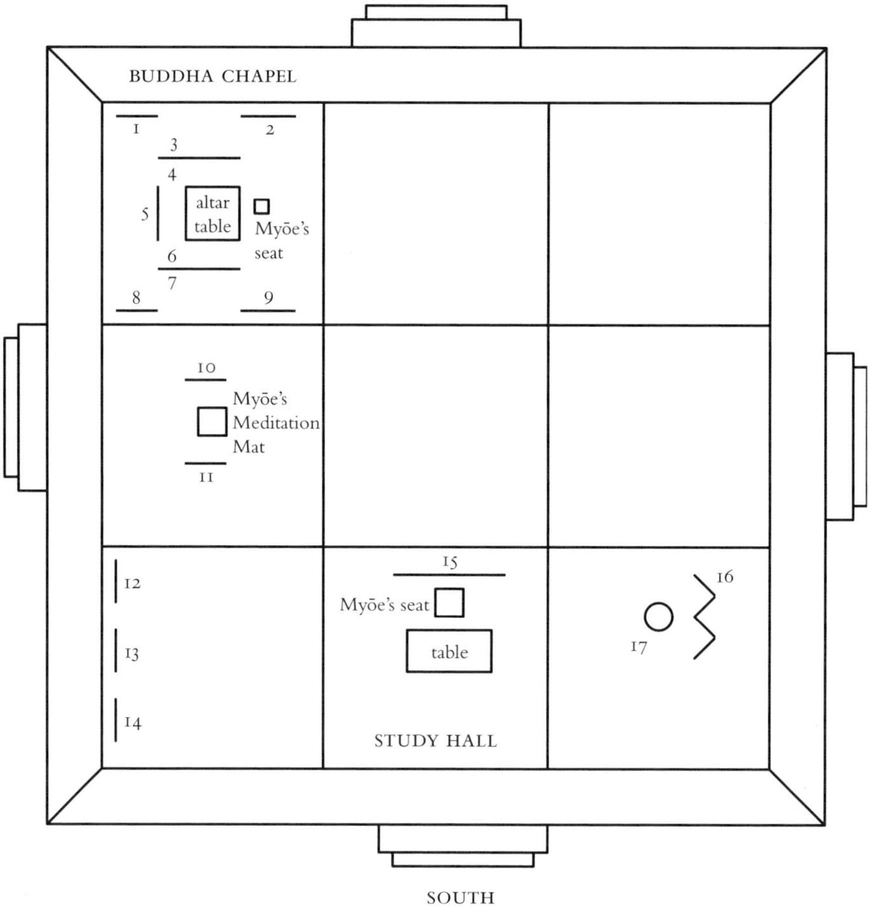

1 Kaneyasu's Bishamon
2 Zenzai and the Fifty-five Good Friends
3 Fazang portrait
4 Womb World Mandara
5 Five Mysteries
6 Diamond World Mandara
7 Kōbō Daishi portrait
8 Gotoba's Amida Triad
9 Kegon Ocean Assembly
10 Jōnin's Nagafusa portrait
11 Jōnin's "True Reflection of the Saint"
12 Jōnin's Five Saints Mandara
13 Jōnin's Aji Palace
14 Jōnin's Bishamon Auspicious Dream Image
15 Jōnin's "True Reflection of the Saint"
16 Jōnin's Bonten, Taishakuten, Bishamonten, and Idaten screen
17 Zenzai sculpture

Figure 3.5 Meditation Hall Precinct, ca. 1253. Hypothetical plan based upon description in *Kōzanji Origin Tales*. Drawn by Karen L. Brock.

ca. 1233), as well as several more lacking their makers' names (Tables 3.1 and 3.2). In 1253, the majority of these paintings were on display in a single building, a three-bay, four-entrance hall at the center of the Meditation Hall Precinct (Zendōin) (Figure 3.5).[74] Kamo Nobuhisa originally built this building for Myōe's Kamo retreat but moved it back to Kōzanji in 1222. During Myōe's final years, the building served as his living quarters, private buddha

Table 3.1 Paintings by E'nichibō Jōnin

Date	*Subject*	*Patron*	*Location*
1224/4	Ananda	Nuns?	Zenmyōji Golden Hall
1227	Jizaiten	Myōe	Worship Hall, Kōzanji Golden Hall
Before 1232	True Reflection of the Saint	Myōe?	Meditation Hall Precinct, Buddha chapel
	True Reflection of Kakushin (Fujiwara Nagafusa)	Myōe?	Meditation Hall Precinct, Buddha chapel
	Rushana Five Saints Mandara	Myōe	Meditation Hall Precinct, study
	Aji Palace Dharma gate	Myōe	Meditation Hall Precinct, study
	Bishamon Auspicious Dream Image	Myōe	Meditation Hall Precinct, study
After 1232	True Reflection of the Saint	Kōzanji monks	Meditation Hall Precinct, study
	Screen with paintings of Bonten, Taishakuten, Bishamonten, and Idaten	Shinkei	Meditation Hall Precinct, study
1243	Kasuga Daimyōjin, copied after Shunga's painting	Kujō Michiie	Tōfukuji Kasuga Shrine

chapel (*jibutsudō*), meditation cell, and study (*gakumonsho*). In addition to all of the buddha images in Myōe's private chapel, Myōe cherished a portrait of his first patron and Kōzanji's earliest benefactor, Fujiwara Nagafusa (1170–1243), brushed by Jōnin. According to Kōshin, Myōe spoke to Nagafusa's portrait; hence it too must have been painted while its subject was alive.[75]

In his study Myōe received and lectured his fellow monks and visitors from outside, and there he spent his final days of illness with the temple elders. Upon the Saint's death, his followers buried him on a terrace just above the Meditation Hall Precinct.[76] They then set aside Myōe's private buddha chapel and his study as memorial halls (Figure 3.5). By 1253, the Meditation Hall Precinct included four additional buildings, among them a thirteen-story pagoda filled with carved and painted images, added in 1236–37.

In the main building, Myōe's private buddha chapel, facing west, contained eleven hanging scrolls set up on stands and hung on the walls (Table 3.2). The larger south-facing study had three hanging scrolls on one wall, and a four-fold screen surrounding a wood-carved image of Zenzai. The

Table 3.2 Painted-Buddha Images at Kōzanji

Date	*Subject*	*Painter*	*Patron*	*Location*
1203–4	Kasuga and Sumiyoshi	Shunga	Myōe	
1235	(same paintings)	(same)	Konoe family	Eastern Sutra Repository
1224	Chinese version, Sixteen Rakan			Zenmyōji Golden Hall
1225	Sixteen Rakan	Shunga	Shunga	Rakan Hall
1227	Sixteen Rakan		E'nōbō of Ninnaji	Rakan Hall
Between 1225 and 1241	Chinese painting of Śākyamuni Triad		Shinkei	Rakan Hall
	Twenty Ten in one painting		Shinkei	Rakan Hall
	Chinese painting of Amida		Shinkei	Rakan Hall
1227–32	Five Mysteries	Shunga	Myōe	Three-Story Pagoda
	Zenzai and Fifty-five Good Friends	Shunga	Myōe	Three-Story Pagoda
	Kegon Ocean Assembly	Shunga	Myōe	Three-Story Pagoda
	Six Ten	Shunga	Myōe	Three-Story Pagoda
Before 1232	Five Mysteries			Meditation Hall Precinct, Buddha chapel
	Two-World Mandara			Meditation Hall Precinct, Buddha chapel
	Portraits of Fazang and Kūkai			Meditation Hall Precinct, Buddha chapel
	Kegon Ocean Assembly			Meditation Hall Precinct, Buddha chapel
	Zenzai and Fifty-five Good Friends			Meditation Hall Precinct, Buddha chapel
	Amida triad in gold characters	Gotoba	Gotoba	Meditation Hall Precinct, Buddha chapel
	Bishamon	Kaneyasu		Meditation Hall Precinct, Buddha chapel
1236–37	Jeweked Tower Mandara		Kakugon *hōgen*	Thirteen-Story Pagoda
	Sixteen Rakan		Kakugon *hōgen*	Thirteen-Story Pagoda
	Eight Shingon Patriarchs		Dōshin of Ninnaji	Thirteen-Story Pagoda

paintings represented an extraordinary mixture of subject matter: *Two-World Mandara*, hanging scrolls of Rushana and the myriad deities of the *Flower Garland Sutra*, portraits of Shingon and Kegon patriarchs, the Five Mysteries (*Gohimitsu*), and a host of protective deities (*ten*). A "True Reflection of the Saint" (*Shōnin shin'ei*) painted by Jōnin became the central object of devotion in each of these spaces and the focus of separate memorial services sponsored by various patrons.

Seated on a Rope-mat

Kōshin first discusses Jōnin's "True Reflection" in Myōe's meditation cell.

> In the second bay to the south of the buddha chapel he [the Saint] established a place for meditation on a single platform with a rope-mat. On a screen to the left of this rope-mat is affixed a true reflection of Shōnin seated in meditation in his rope-mat tree. This was here even while Shōnin was still alive. The inscription in Shōnin's own writing says: "Imitating the reflection of an ordinary monk in seated meditation." It was brushed by E'nichibō Jōnin and the inscription is from Shōnin's own brush.[77]

The extant painting, which exactly matches Kōshin's description, is today known either as *Portrait of Saint Myōe* or *Seated on a Rope-mat* (Figure 3.6).[78] Painted on two pieces of silk of differing widths joined horizontally, it measures just under thirty-six centimeters wide by forty-five centimeters tall. The inscription on paper adds another sixteen centimeters to its height. The painting's tattered and patched condition makes it difficult to identify original silk and drawing. The shadowy figure of Myōe in the center is about thirteen or fourteen centimeters in height. He sits in meditation with his head turned to his right, hiding his famously mutilated ear. The surroundings appear to be a forest; a few lines of a tree trunk are barely visible on Myōe's left. The large empty area below Myōe is entirely replacement silk. Myōe's position in relation to the tree trunk and lost silk suggest that the composition resembles *Saint Myōe Seated in Meditation in a Tree* (Figure 3.1). Perhaps the painting has been cut down. The inscription above the painting implies this may be the case:

> My stupid form, seated in meditation in the Rope-mat Tree on Mt. Ryōga, is placed on the wall where I meditate.
> Imitating the reflection of an ordinary monk seated in meditation.
> The renunciant concentrating on meditation, Kōben
> Painted by E'nichibō Jōnin, who lives together with the renunciant on Mt. Ryōga.

This inscription says the painting hung on a "wall" (*heki*), while Kōshin used the word "screen" (*shōji*) in *Kōzanji Origin Tales*. If *wall* and *screen* are not

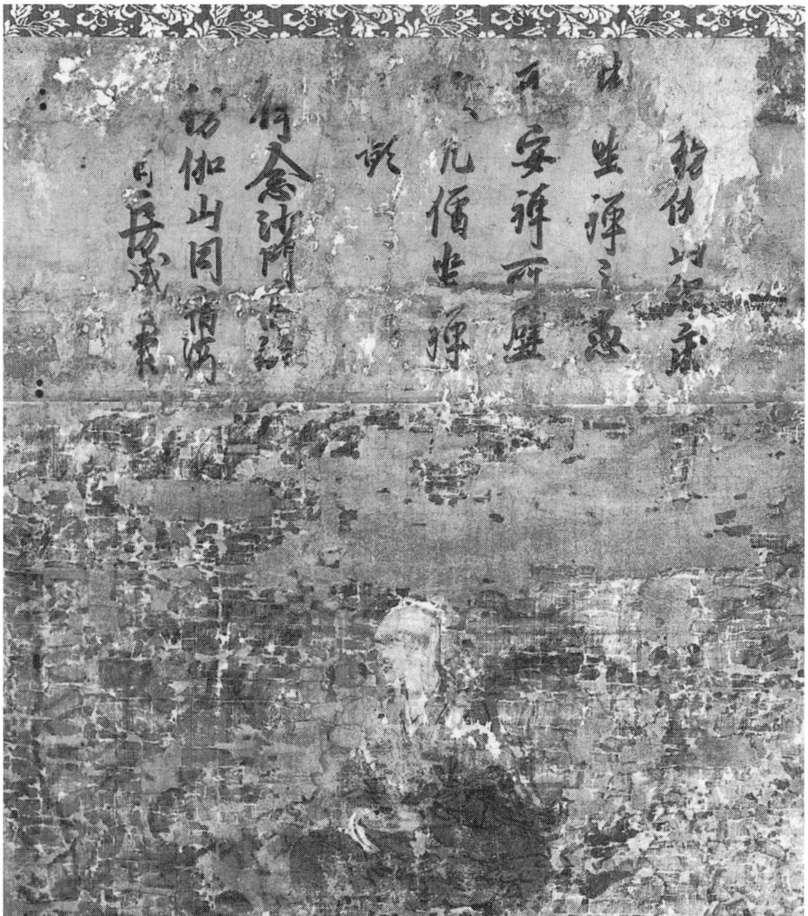

Figure 3.6 *Saint Myōe Seated on a Rope-mat.* Painted by E'nichibō Jōnin, ca. 1224–1226. Hanging scroll, ink and color on silk, 60.9 cm x 35.8 cm. Kōzanji. Photo: Kyoto National Museum.

interchangeable words, then the difference in wording suggests that the painting changed formats.[79] Perhaps the painting *was* originally taller, made to hang on the back wall of Myōe's meditation cell, but after Myōe's death his followers cut it down to fit the more intimate format of a screen placed beside the saint's meditation mat. This may account for the loss of the upper trees, and for the fact that the two pieces of painting silk differ so oddly in width. Certainly the painting's terrible condition is consistent with the kind of damage it would have received if attached to a small screen left on display for a long time.

Because this inscription is written on a separate sheet of paper rather than on the painting silk, a skeptic might question whether it has always belonged with the painting and whether it is in fact in Myōe's own hand or a close copy added during a later remounting. Most writers accept the inscription at face value, on the basis of the calligraphic style and the comparable damage found throughout the silk and the paper. Indeed, the extraordinary effort made to patch and repair this painting—on several occasions—attests to the charismatic power of this "true reflection" for successive generations. Why go to such trouble unless both inscription and painting were in fact original? The content of the inscription should have been written by Myōe himself, as only he would have used the expressions "stupid form" and "renunciant" in addition to his formal name Kōben.

The inscription further explains that the subject is Myōe seated in his "Rope-mat Tree" (*Jōshōju*). This tree actually existed behind the temple on the mountain, which was named Mt. Ryōga by Myōe after the Mt. Laṅkā of the *Laṅkāvatara Sutra*. According to this text, it was from Mt. Laṅkā that King Ravana sent a flower chariot to bring back Śākyamuni and have him preach. George Tanabe sums up Myōe's curious appropriation this way:

> At his Mt. Laṅkā, Myōe re-created the world of Śākyamuni. Upon being unable to go to India, he had taken meditative journeys but now he did not even have to depart in trance. He did not bother with the mythic vision of importing holy sites from India through the air to become holy spots in Japan. He simply took the ordinary surroundings and refashioned them by force of imagination and the power of naming.[80]

The viewer of this painting, then, *could* interpret it simultaneously as Myōe meditating on Mt. Ryōga or even Myōe as Śākyamuni on the real Mt. Laṅkā. Myōe began using the name Mt. Ryōga in 1223 or 1224, as he spent more time there away from temple construction.

The most intriguing detail of Kōshin's account in *Kōzanji Origin Tales* is the statement that this "true reflection" was already on display in Myōe's buddha chapel while the saint was alive. Myōe's inscription, naming Jōnin as his live-in companion on Mt. Ryōga, further verifies the "authenticity" of Myōe's meditative practice, as witnessed by Jōnin. Whether hung on the wall or affixed to a screen, this "true reflection" intentionally served as a substitute (*katami*) for Myōe when he and Jōnin were on Mt. Ryōga.[81] Myōe also made several trips away from Kōzanji in his last years, even going so far as his native Kii province just months before he died. Perhaps Jōnin also made this "true reflection" as a precaution. If Myōe died unexpectedly, the temple would already have a true-to-life memorial portrait.[82] After Myōe died, the portrait served as the focus of ceremonies funded by one of Kōzanji's most prominent lay patrons, Fujiwara Morikane (1191–1245).

According to an inscription on the back of this painting, it was last remounted in 1762. In that year, several of Kōzanji's most treasured paintings were remounted, and a few copied, although not this portrait.[83] Given the remarkable veneration Jōnin's worn-out painting received in the centuries after Myōe's death, this is probably one of the several Myōe portraits seen and recorded by temple visitors during the Edo period.

Holding His Rosary

Following his detailed description of Myōe's buddha chapel and meditation cell Kōshin moves on to Myōe's study in the same building. In 1253, Myōe's "everyday seat" occupied the center of the space, and behind it stood a single-panel screen.

> Hanging from this [screen] is a true reflection of Shōnin, a hanging scroll, painted by the same. For this image, Shōnin's longtime dharma-companion, E'nichibō Jōnin, personally measured the length of his eyes and ears. His appearance was not at all different.[84]

A small-character note in the text says that Jōnin exhausted his talents in reverently painting this image from his heart. Kōshin's words stress Jōnin's extraordinary closeness to Myōe, which allowed him to create a life-size representation.

Jōnin's painting, conventionally labeled *Holding His Rosary*, is quite large, at 111 cm. in height and 80.5 cm. in width (Figure 3.7).[85] Three lengths of silk joined vertically form the painting surface. Unlike the previous painting, there is no inscription. The provisional title comes from Myōe's active pose, and although the beads have almost disappeared their shadow remains. Myōe's head and hands are largely redrawn; the only original lines define the folds of his robe, and one black line defines his surplice. The ghostly white horizontal lines at the bottom of the painting indicate that he is sitting on a tatami mat. Myōe's life size and wide-open eyes correspond to Kōshin's description, and the scale and details of the painting resemble other

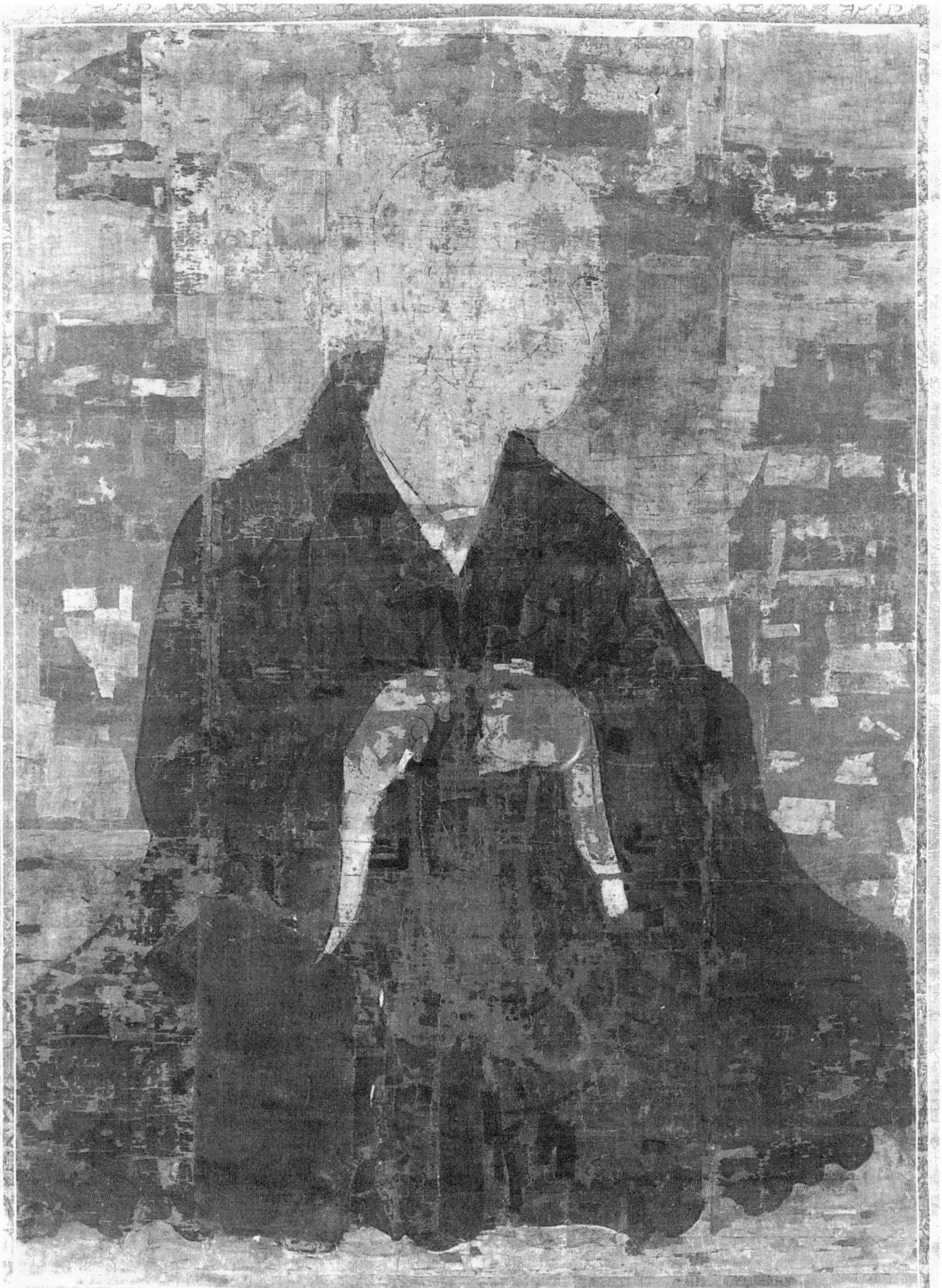

Figure 3.7 *Saint Myōe Holding His Rosary*. Painted by E'nichibō Jōnin, ca. 1232–1233. Hanging scroll, ink and color on silk, 111.5 cm x 80.5 cm. Kōzanji. Photo: Kyoto National Museum.

formal portraits of monks in this period.[86] The painting's tattered condition, like that of *Seated on a Rope-mat*, also attests to a long history of use and display. To accommodate this painting, the screen behind Myōe's everyday seat in the study hall had to be considerably larger than the one placed by his mat in the meditation cell.

Although the outlines of Myōe's features and open eyes are redrawn, he is positioned so that his mutilated right ear is visible. According to Kikai's *Life of Saint Myōe*, during a period of profound despair in 1196, when the solitary Myōe was living in reclusion in Kii province, he endeavored to rid himself of pride in his appearance by cutting his ear with a knife.[87] In *Kōzanji Origin Tales*, Kōshin wrote that when Myōe cut his ear the blood splattered everywhere, including all over the ritual implements then placed on the altar table in Myōe's private buddha chapel. That is why his followers treasured them all the more and why the implements remained in place after the saint's death. In the smaller *Seated on a Rope-mat*, Myōe faces in the opposite direction, as if to hide the damaged ear. The change in orientation may signify a difference between how Myōe allowed himself to be portrayed and how his followers pictured the saint. In other words, this large formal painting was probably made upon Myōe's death for memorial purposes.

Kōzanji Origin Tales explains that this study was the place where Myōe instructed his followers in life, but it later became his sickroom. As discussed above, the days leading up to Myōe's death were vividly described by both Jōshin and Kikai. As he lay dying in his study, Myōe directed the hanging of two paintings on opposite walls to either side of the mat where he reclined.[88] A *Five Saints Mandara* hung on the east wall behind Myōe, who faced an image of Miroku on the northwest.[89] On his final morning, Myōe washed his hands, put on his surplice, grasped his beads, and sat up to face his followers and deliver his final instructions. He spoke in a strong voice as he led them in paying homage to Miroku. This large portrait thus may capture Myōe's final moments with his followers.

When Myōe's study was transformed into his memorial chapel, a table set up in front of this "true reflection" held several items formerly used by Myōe: his sutra box, incense burner, bell, inkstone, fan, lamp, and water jar, positioned "just as they had been during his lifetime." Three of Myōe's followers treated his "true reflection" as if it were alive, daily serving him food, hot water, and medicine, and lighting the lamp. Nuns, monks, and lay followers all contributed the funds for these daily offerings and the services of three monks. Among the patrons were Kamo Nobuhisa's older and younger sisters, both of whom had become nuns. Given Kōshin's account of Jōnin measuring Myōe's features, and the detailed descriptions of this room both during Myōe's final illness and after his death, the conclusion that this large formal portrait was indeed painted for memorial use by his followers and patrons seems warranted. Unlike *Seated on a Rope-mat, Holding His Rosary* does not now have any inscription naming Jōnin as the painter. It was not remounted or copied in 1762, but it was certainly among the several Myōe portraits seen by temple visitors during the Edo and Meiji periods.

Saint Myōe Seated in Meditation in a Tree

Previous writers about *Saint Myōe Seated in Meditation in a Tree* (Figure 3.1) have cited the aforementioned records in *Kōzanji Origin Tales* to make their case for Jōnin's authorship of this famous portrait. Most of them knew of the two worn-out portraits when they were writing, although the paintings were not published until 1971.[90] In his article describing thirteen portraits of Myōe, seven at Kōzanji, Mori Tōru declined to make the definitive attributions to Jōnin now claimed. For Mori and others, the fact that Jōnin painted two other portraits of Myōe in use at Kōzanji sufficed to make the case for Jōnin as painter of *Seated in Meditation in a Tree*. However, there appears to be considerable hesitancy in stating the obvious: that the painting *does not* correspond to either of the two "true reflections" described in *Kōzanji Origin Tales*, and comparisons to the two extant Jōnin portraits, admittedly difficult, do not support the attribution.

Furthermore, *Seated in Meditation in a Tree* represents a major departure from the more typical, formal monk's portrait such as *Holding His Rosary*. The medium is paper rather than silk, consisting of five sheets pasted edge to edge vertically, all 59 centimeters wide. The height of the bottom four sheets is 32–33.2 centimeters. The inscribed paper is 15.9 centimeters, exactly half the size of the other four. These sheets of paper are a standard size commonly found in horizontal picture scrolls; echoing common practice in that format, they must have been pasted together before painting.

By contrast, *Seated in Meditation in a Tree* has been well cared for throughout its history and was last restored in 1956. The paper is in very good condition, indicating that the painting could never have been hung for long periods, or subjected to the darkening of incense or lamp smoke. Despite the paper's condition, the present coloring departs considerably from its original appearance. All of the light yellowish-brown areas of earth, the shadows behind the pine needles, and the areas within outlined leaves represent the ghostly traces of malachite green pigment, which has worn off. Traces of azurite blue, lead white, and faded organic earth tones appear under magnification. Only the black and gray ink lines and washes, the brown pigment on the trees, and the flesh tones of Myōe's face and hands have not changed significantly. Instead of the subtle, almost monochromatic painting, celebrated by many writers, the original image would have been predominantly green in color.

Something of this original color scheme may be recaptured through comparison to the best preserved areas of *Kegon Origin Tales* (Figures 3.2 and 3.3). In depictions of rocks in the *Gishō* scrolls, for instance, opaque green pigment apparently thinned out to unpainted areas, where gray wash lines outline and sculpt the rocks.[91] Quite possibly both paintings made use of more than one shade of green, differences being achieved by the coarseness or fineness of the ground pigment or through the addition of white. Traces of azurite are also found on the rocks in both paintings, although most of the blue color in *Kegon Origin Tales* is indigo. The reddish-brown color of the tree trunks in the *Gishō* scrolls is generally darker than their counterparts in the portrait. Here and there the trees are also dotted with green and white moss, a feature not now visible in the Myōe portrait. Although the pine needles in the portrait are clearly a variety other than those in the *Gishō* scrolls, they were both painted with ink lines under the now lost green pigment. Many of the gray lines in the portrait might have been concealed by pigment, but the original balance of color to ink cannot now be reconstructed.

As for Myōe, he sits with his eyes closed in meditation in his Rope-mat Tree with a bifurcated trunk. His left ear is exposed to the viewer, his hands clasped in meditation. This view of the monk closely matches his appearance in *Seated on a Rope-mat*, although the figure of Myōe here is actually some seven centimeters taller. He wears a surplice over his gray robe and sits on a white cloth that peeks out from under his robe. Myōe has neatly placed his tall wooden clogs just below and behind the tree trunk. His rosary and an incense burner emitting smoke hang behind on a convenient branch. A walking stick with its forked handle is barely visible leaning against a tree branch to his right.

The dense forest is filled mostly with pine, although a few deciduous trees can be seen. Several large rocks dot the forest floor; the largest one below the tree could be Myōe's so-called Calm-mind Rock (*jōshin seki*). Blooming wisteria vines encircle the tree to Myōe's right, although the flowers have faded over time. Wisteria defines the scene as the fourth month, early summer, and it even suggests a connection between Myōe and the Fujiwara family. Apparently wisteria actually grew on Mt. Ryōga; one of Myōe's poems refers to "purple clouds of wisteria" near his mountain hermitage.[92] In many ways, this is an intensely sensuous painting. Imagine sitting in Myōe's tree with your eyes closed. Hear the wind blowing among the pines, the several birds calling overhead, or the chittering squirrel high up in the branches. Smell the incense and the fragrant wisteria. Feel the early summer dampness drying from your clothes as the sun begins to warm you. Did all this rich detail exist in Jōnin's *Seated on a Rope-mat*, or was that simpler composition improved upon here by another painter with an eye for such details?

The inscription on *Seated in Meditation in a Tree* differs slightly, but significantly, from that on *Seated on a Rope-mat*:

> On Mt. Ryōga at Kōzanji, are the Rope-mat Tree and the Calm-mind Rock.
>
> Imitating the reflection of this ordinary monk seated in meditation,
>
> a copy (*sha*) of my humble form that hangs on the wall of the Meditation Hall.
> The renunciant concentrating on meditation, Kōben.

The mention of "Kōzanji" and "Meditation Hall" both indicate this painting's *distance* from the place where Jōnin's painting was hanging. The phrase "Rope-mat Tree" appears in both inscriptions, but here it is used differently. In the inscription on Jōnin's "true reflection" it denotes where Myōe is sitting; here it is paired with "Calm-mind Rock" as if to explain the two sacred sites on Mt. Ryōga depicted in the painting. Use of the word *copy* (*sha*) also suggests that this painting is based on the one in Myōe's Meditation Hall.[93] If Myōe wrote this inscription (there is some debate about this), then *Seated in Meditation in a Tree* could be an "authorized" copy of Jōnin's original made for a place and person located *outside* of Kōzanji. Finally, the inscription does not mention Jōnin's name, which looms large in Myōe's inscription for *Seated on a Rope-mat* (Figure 3.6) and *Kōzanji Origin Tales*. The complete lack of any mention of Jōnin here makes a compelling case against attributing this painting to Jōnin, even though his "true reflection of the Saint" was obviously consulted in its making.

MORIKANE, THE "SAINT'S LONGTIME PATRON"

Kōshin briefly mentions a third "reflection of the Saint" in *Kōzanji Origin Tales*, one located outside the temple grounds proper. In this case, he offers no details about the maker or format, nor does he claim true-to-life authenticity for this image. This vagueness probably derives from the fact that this "reflection" was privately owned by Fujiwara Morikane, the man who sponsored memorial ceremonies in front of Jōnin's *Seated on a Rope-mat* in Myōe's meditation cell. Morikane was a member of the Senior Nobles and one of Kōzanji's most important benefactors both before and after Myōe's death. Details of Morikane's relationship to Myōe and his activities at Kōzanji are scattered throughout texts and documents in the Kōzanji archive.

In his account of Myōe's last days, Jōshin says that upon Myōe's death

Morikane gave up his official duties for a month so that he could go into deep mourning at his "Garden of Happiness" (*Kangien*) retreat. There Morikane conducted private ceremonies, employing four senior monks to chant the forty-fascicle *Flower Garland Sutra* before a painting of Śākyamuni.[94] Writing in 1232, just two months after Myōe's death, Jōshin does not mention an image of Myōe at Kangien. But in 1253, Kōshin extensively describes Morikane's patronage of Kōzanji, his devotion to Myōe, and his Garden of Happiness retreat. Morikane dedicated a small buddha hall there in 1234, where he installed a three-foot carved image of Śākyamuni with Kikai as officiant.[95] Morikane supported three Kōzanji monks who took turns carrying out daily devotional practices. According to Kōshin, when Morikane died there (in 1245), he obtained nirvana as a result of his devotion to the Saint.

Most important, Morikane's retreat included "a place for the Saint's reflection" (*Shōnin eidokoro*). Kōshin appears familiar both with the material setting for the image and the chanting carried out there: three rounds of the Sonshō dharani, and one hundred repetitions of the Bright Light mantra (*Kōmyō shingon*). In 1239, Morikane dedicated, again with Kikai officiating, a stone stupa containing Myōe's hair and fingernails. This was placed either before his "reflection of the Saint" or elsewhere at Kangien. *Kōzanji Origin Tales* describes this stone stupa as a "King Asoka stupa" type. The small old-style King Asoka stupa now located directly in front Myōe's own tomb is possibly the one originally dedicated by Morikane at Kangien (Figure 3.8).[96]

The most tangible link among Myōe, Kōshin, Morikane, and the "Saint's reflection" is a small stone called "Stupa-stone" (*Soba-ishi*, Figure 3.9), a mere three centimeters long. Myōe acquired this stone in the late 1190s, on the rocky beach of an island located in Yuasa Bay in his native Kii province. At that time, Myōe was preoccupied with making a journey to India to visit Śākyamuni's sacred sites. Although Myōe never realized his goal, he cherished this small stone, which became his lifelong substitute for those sacred sites. Myōe kept it with him when he retreated to Mt. Ryōga, where he built a special pedestal for it.[97] Before he died, Myōe gave his Stupa-stone to Kōshin, who in turn gave it to Morikane to assuage his grief. For Myōe the stone had been a substitute for Śākyamuni; now it took on a second identity as Morikane's surrogate for Myōe. Just as Myōe's followers kept their teacher's personal effects on display before Jōnin's formal memorial portrait of Myōe in the saint's former study, so Morikane placed this treasured memento before his own "reflection of the Saint."

Myōe's poetry anthology (also compiled by Kōshin) explains Morikane's special attachment to Myōe. A poetic exchange between Morikane and Myōe from 1226 has a particularly long headnote.[98] In Myōe's words:

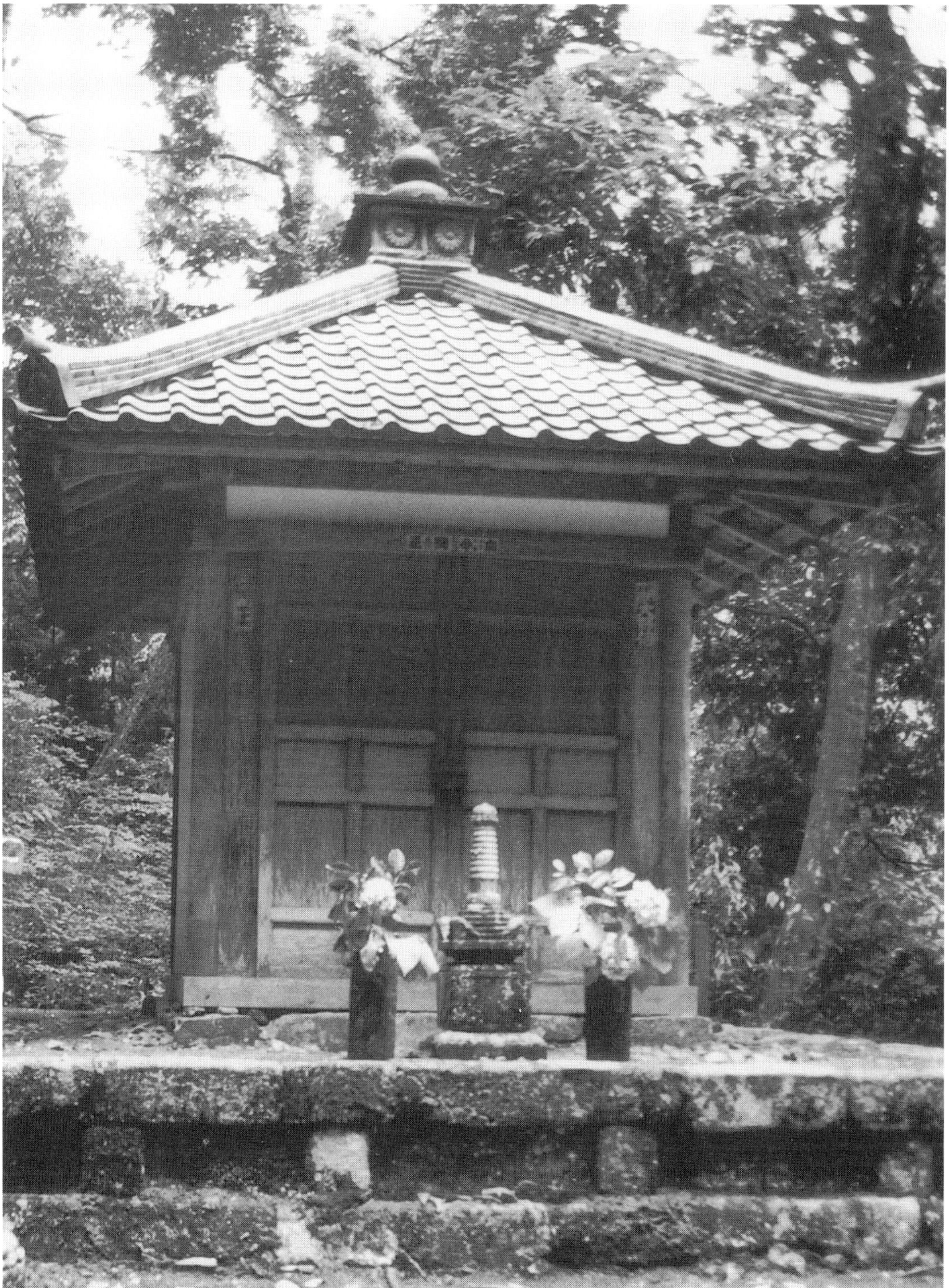

Figure 3.8 King Asoka style stupa. Stone. 1239. Originally commissioned by Fujiwara Morikane for Kangien. Now located in front of Myōe's tomb. Kōzanji. Photo: Karen L. Brock.

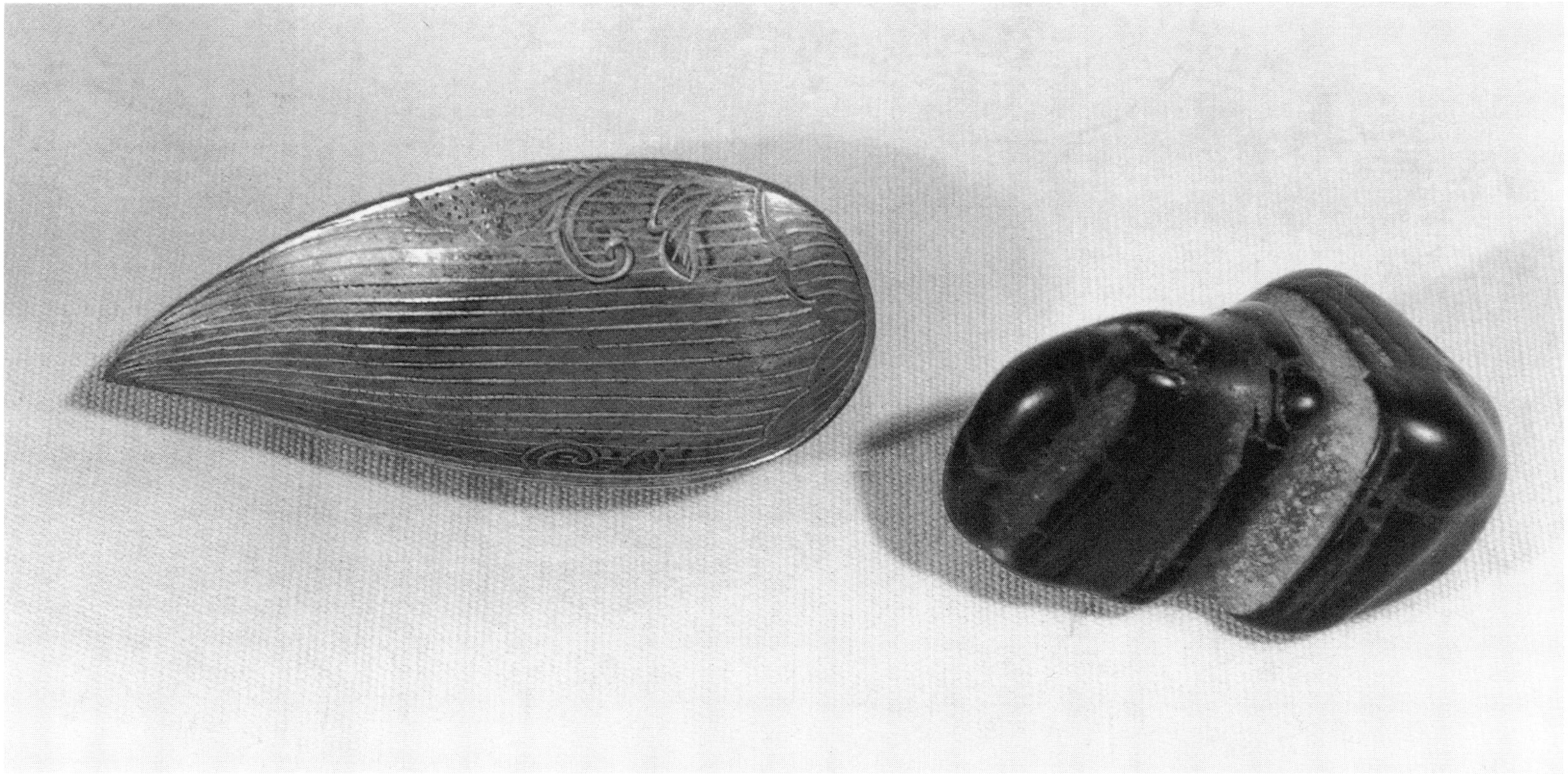

Figure 3.9 Stupa-stone and its platform. Found by Myōe on the beach at Takashima in Yuasa Bay. Given to Fujiwara Morikane ca. 1232. Height 3 cm. Kōzanji. Photo: Kyoto National Museum.

> On 8/9 ōmiya Saishō Middle Captain Morikane came to my retreat asking to receive the "Eight Fasting Precepts." On the next day, the tenth, just as the sun rose I administered these fasting precepts to him according to the rules, in my private buddha-chapel. This humble monk sat facing the vow-taker's seat and one by one he received the transmission. I had him read my own text on the self-pledging of vows and he promised to keep this method of self-pledging every month. We emerged at about four o'clock on the tenth. The next day he sent a letter which said many things, such as "how this matter makes me realize that I am caught in the wheel of rebirth," and "here on my pillow in a euphoria of five desires, I suddenly feel intoxicated. Now it is difficult to hold on to happiness."

Wasureji yo	I have not forgotten
Yatsu no koto no ha	Those eight words
Onozukara	Although I still
Mutsu no michi ni wa	Return to
Nao kaeru to mo.	the Six Realms.
Yatsu no chikai	As long as you do not
Mutsu no chimata ni	Forget the eight vows or
Wasurezu wa	the Six Worlds,
Sue wa hotoke no	In the end you will leave
Michi e idenamu.	On the path to buddhahood.

E'nichibō Jōnin's "true reflection of the Saint" could have been hanging on the wall of Myōe's meditation cell by 1226. Since Morikane pledged his vows with Myōe in this room, one can appreciate the special resonance place and memory held for him.

Morikane also frequented Myōe's twice-monthly vow-taking meetings and no doubt became well-acquainted with all of Kōzanji's residents. Fujiwara Teika's description of one such meeting in 1229 concludes with a reference to Morikane: "I hear that the two Senior Nobles Morikane and Sadataka always attend and join in with the beggars."[99] Judging from these two references, as well as the records in *Kōzanji Origin Tales* and Jōshin and Kōshin's accounts of Morikane's grief, Morikane viewed Myōe and his teachings as his personal guide to salvation. In recognition of such dedication, Morikane's name appears after those of Kujō Michiie (1193–1252) and Saionji Kintsune (1171–1244) in the draft of a letter written by Myōe in 1231, a few months before the latter's death. In the letter Myōe requests that these three men, along with two Ninnaji prelates, be granted responsibility for the continued support and success of Kōzanji.[100] Myōe's trust in Morikane was rewarded by the latter's considerable support of the temple after Myōe's death.

Morikane's Kangien served as more than a mountain retreat for this retired court official. It functioned as a second memorial chapel to Myōe in imitation of the Meditation Hall Precinct at Kōzanji. Thus Morikane's extensive material support of Kōzanji, his building a private memorial chapel, and his devotion to sites sacred to Myōe's memory demonstrate a level of veneration unmatched by any other lay patron. Furthermore, Morikane's acquisition of Myōe's Stupa-stone and making of a stone stupa containing bodily relics of Myōe also reveal the high regard of Myōe's followers for this Senior Noble. Kōshin's detailed recording of Morikane's beneficence in *Kōzanji Origin Tales* documents their collaboration.

Thus a strong circumstantial case can be made for identifying *Seated in Meditation in a Tree* (Figure 3.1) as Morikane's "Saint's reflection" at Kangien. The inscription hints that the painting was made for a location outside of Kōzanji, and it suggests this "reflection" is a "copy" of Jōnin's "true reflection of the Saint" in the Meditation Hall Precinct. Morikane sponsored memorial ceremonies in that location, precisely because he himself cherished memories of visiting Myōe there. Morikane could not have had this precious portrait made without the gratitude, support, and consent of Kōzanji's elders.

If Morikane had *Seated in Meditation in a Tree* made for Kangien, would Jōnin have received the commission? Surely Jōnin knew of Morikane's support of Kōzanji, just as Morikane knew that Jōnin had painted the two "true reflections of the Saint" in the Meditation Hall Precinct. One might expect Morikane to have eagerly sought Jōnin's participation, since Jōnin is repeatedly characterized as Myōe's "companion" and reputedly captured his authentic likeness. But the omission of Jōnin's name from the inscription, the word "copy," and Kōshin's lack of specificity, taken together with the unusual format, coloring, and brushwork of *Seated in Meditation in a Tree*, all argue instead for a painter from outside the Kōzanji community. The inscription, whether brushed by Myōe or not, could have been prepared separately from, or even in advance of, the painting.[101] If Jōnin was primarily a monk who served Myōe, who copied out sutras, and who made painted buddha images on a small scale for temple use, perhaps he was not Senior Noble Morikane's first choice. Instead, I suspect that Morikane would have commissioned a member of the court painting bureau to make this lively copy of Jōnin's "true reflection." Sometime after Morikane died, both the Stupa-stone and the portrait were turned over to Kōzanji's storehouse.

"BRUSHED BY JŌNIN"

Jōnin's image-making activities for the Kōzanji community were not limited to his two "True Reflections of the Saint." Kōshin records seven other projects "brushed by Jōnin," all of them buddha images painted for devotional use by Myōe or others in the community (Table 3.1). In all of these references, Kōshin never once calls Jōnin a "painter"; nor did Jōnin use that appellation in his own inscriptions on sutras. He is a "renunciant," a "dharma-companion," or simply a "monk." By contrast, Kikai and Kōshin both identify Shunga as a "painter" (*eshi*), "buddha-master" (*busshi*), or "Bridge of the Dharma" (*hokkyō*), all contemporary terms denoting professional painter status. Kaneyasu, who painted a single buddha image at Kōzanji and headed the court painting bureau by 1224, was also indisputably a professional painter.[102]

Hirata Yutaka and others who have written about Jōnin, Shunga, and Kaneyasu isolate references to each of them, in order to characterize their lives and works individually. However, when the references to paintings in *Kōzanji Origin Tales* are matched to numerous passages in Kikai's *Life of Myōe* and other Kōzanji manuscripts, a much richer picture of Jōnin's paintings emerges. With the exception of the two "true reflections of the Saint," Jōnin, Shunga, and Kaneyasu all painted overlapping subjects developed by Myōe from his Shingon and Kegon doctrines and practices (Table 3.2). Many of these buddha images or assemblies of deities derived from imported printed books, woodcut prints, or even paintings. Still more paintings of the same subjects, whose painters' names were not recorded, were donated to Kōzanji by a variety of monastic and aristocratic patrons from outside.

The actual practice of painting buddha images has been well explained by Hirata, using documents, extant paintings, iconographic drawings, and full-scale preparatory drawings.[103] In general, painted-buddha makers adhered to long-standing traditions of iconography, style, and composition so that their images would be accurate representations based on authoritative models of the past. Thus they consulted drawings in iconographic manuals and received direction from learned monks. Innovation in the making of buddha images, whether painted or carved, came about through the importation of new models or, not infrequently, was based on an auspicious vision or dream by a prominent monk. Full-scale preparatory drawings (*kamigata*) were submitted to monks and patrons before the final project began, and some extant preparatory drawings bear notations of colors or needed corrections. These preparatory drawings would be the foundation for the underdrawing rendered in light ink on silk, probably by the most experienced painter in a workshop. Mineral pigments were built up on both sides of the silk, but only the front was finished with final outlines, gold, and other touches.

For Jōnin to have painted buddha images and portraits for Kōzainji, he must have received some basic training in their making. Jōshin, Myōe, and some of the other elders had themselves undergone Shingon training with a prominent iconographer of the period, Kōzen (1120–1203).[104] Jōnin could have received similar training, but he must also have learned the complex techniques for handling silk, mixing pigments and glue, and perhaps even mounting. If we consider Myōe's relatively narrow circle of acquaintances before the 1206 founding of Kōzanji, the most logical conclusion is that Jōnin learned to paint from Shunga, through whom he came into contact with Myōe. Myōe commissioned paintings from Shunga as early as 1201, and at that time Shunga had apprentice painters in his household.[105] Whether or not Jōnin was Shunga's son, or the son of someone named Takuma, he probably trained in such an environment. If he was born in the late 1180s, Jōnin would have been the right age to have been apprenticed to Shunga before signing himself "unlearned Kegon renunciant" at Kōzanji in 1211.

Many of Jōnin's subjects overlapped with those painted by Shunga, Kaneyasu, and other unnamed painters, suggesting that Jōnin either collaborated with them or used the same models for his own paintings. The Sixteen Rakan theme, for instance, captured Myōe's imagination as early as 1198, when he obtained a Chinese printed version.[106] Myōe employed a set of *Sixteen Rakan* as the focus of the *Flower Garland Sutra* readings at the Kamo retreat in 1222. Jōnin's painting of *Ananda*, dedicated to Zenmyōji's Golden Hall in 1224, and Shunga's complete set of *Sixteen Rakan* dedicated to Kōzanji the following year, could have been copied from Myōe's prints at approximately the same time.[107] Another example of potential overlap is Jōnin's "auspicious dream image" of Bishamon, on display in Myōe's study and memorial chapel. If we assume a dream of Myōe's as the source for the image, then it may date to 1218, when Myōe was engaged as a healer.[108] Whether Myōe made sketches of the deity or merely described it to Jōnin, Kaneyasu's painting of Bishamon in Myōe's buddha chapel could have been a professionally finished version later made for worship. Since Myōe already had one image made by Jōnin, I suspect Kaneyasu's Bishamon was made as a gift to Myōe, perhaps by the woman whose daughter he healed in 1218.[109] At Myōe's death, one of these two Bishamon images was found in his sutra bag, along with various texts and *Dream Record* fragments.[110]

A more concrete example of Jōnin copying Shunga, not described in *Kōzanji Origin Tales*, is Kōzanji's unique image of the Kasuga deity.[111] In 1203–5, Myōe received several oracles from the Kasuga deity that prompted him to make sketches. Myōe sent these to Shunga, who made a pair of hanging scroll paintings of Kasuga and Sumiyoshi. In 1235, Shunga's paintings were enshrined in Kōzanji's Eastern Sutra Repository, where ceremonies were sponsored by members of the Konoe branch of the Fujiwara family. In 1243, Kikai wrote a note describing *six* paintings of the Kasuga-Sumiyoshi subject at

Kōzanji, and an additional painting of Kasuga painted by Jōnin for Kujō Michiie, to be enshrined at the latter's newly built Tōfukuji.

The oldest of Kōzanji's extant paintings of Kasuga and Sumiyoshi (Figure 3.10) could be the two small "cut-out" paintings, then kept separately at Kōzanji, as described by Kikai in 1243. A remounting inscription on the back of this painting, dated 1762, says it was done by E'nichibō Jōnin, and that the two halves of the painting had been handed down in two separate locations before being reunited in this single painting. The two deities were remounted together on the same occasion as *Seated on a Rope-mat,* but a copy was made to be hung in its place during temple icon displays (*kaichō*) in the late Edo period. An intriguing contrast exists in the fate of these two paintings. Jōnin's original "True Reflection of the Saint" was patched and remounted, to remain a devotional icon precisely because of its authenticity. The paintings of the Kasuga and Sumiyoshi deities, on the other hand, could be recopied many times over for public display, even while the older versions were repaired and stored away.

To return to Jōnin's artistic identity, Kanō Einō and other early writers claimed, on the basis of temple traditions, that E'nichibō Jōnin was the true son of Takuma *hōgen.* We don't know who Kanō Einō meant by "Takuma *hōgen,*" but in all likelihood Jōnin was the son of a "painted-buddha master" before joining the Kōzanji community and becoming a monk. Given Myōe's enduring patron-painter relationship with Shunga *hōkkyo* (from 1201 to 1232), Shunga is a likely candidate for Jōnin's teacher, if not also his father. During the 1220s and 1230s, both responded to Myōe's need for buddha images, and they probably collaborated on some projects. Of the two, Shunga's projects were more numerous, demanding, and time-consuming, especially his extensive paintings for the interior of the three-storied pagoda. Shunga lived outside Kōzanji and had apprentices; Jōnin worked on a more modest scale while going about his duties as "dharma-companion."

Jōnin, Shunga, Kaneyasu, and a host of unnamed painters from outside the Kōzanji community all had some access to imported Chinese printed books and paintings. Gyōben, Jōnin's fellow renunciant who copied sutras in 1211, probably brought back many such paintings, perhaps the very ones donated by Shinkei to the Rakan Hall. All of the documentary references to these painters or to paintings given to Kōzanji fall within the subjects produced by painted-buddha masters of the period, and by members of the so-called Takuma School in particular. Some of them no doubt preserved earlier iconography and style, while others must have responded to fresh stimuli from abroad or from Myōe's imagination.

The characterizations of Kōzanji as a center of "artistic production," of

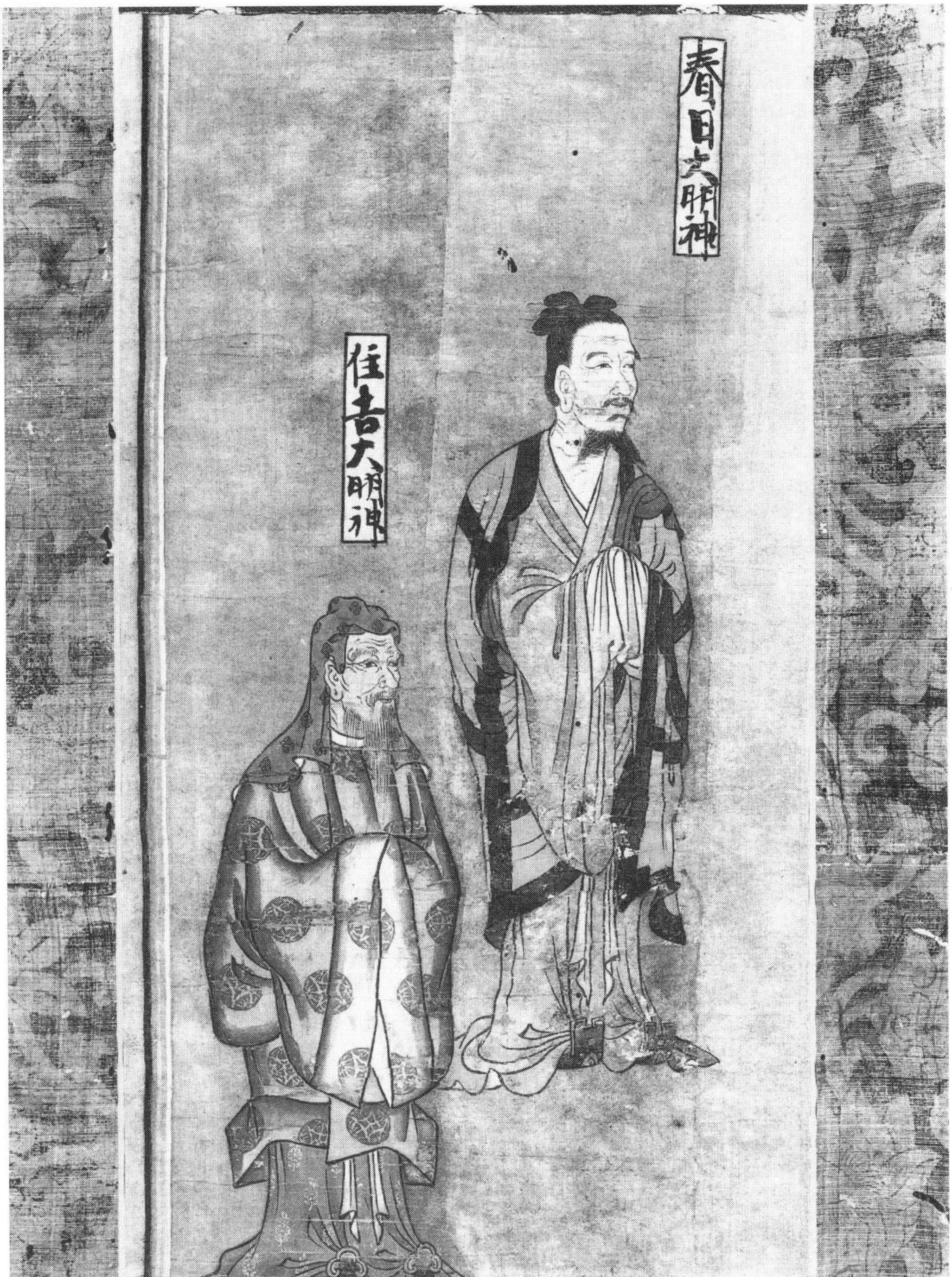

Figure 3.10 Kasuga Daimyōjin (right) and Sumiyoshi Daimyōjin (left). Attributed by 1762 inscription to E'nichibō Jōnin. First half of thirteenth century? Hanging scroll, ink and color on silk, 38.7 cm x 20.2 cm. Kōzanji. Photo: Kyoto National Museum.

Kōzanji paintings as representing a "new painting movement," or Myōe as a supervisor of a "painting atelier" all stem from an anachronistic view of how painted-buddha masters worked in tandem with their monastic and lay patrons. During the 1220s and 1230s, Kōzanji bustled with visiting carpenters, carvers, and painters who worked on several projects at once, no doubt thoroughly disturbing Myōe's meditations. Myōe directed Jōnin and Shunga's efforts, but as a practitioner of Shingon and Kegon who insisted on the correct representation of iconographical details.

Finally, none of the many references to Jōnin or Shunga support their involvement in making picture scrolls with the landscapes, buildings, secular figures, and lengthy compositions as found throughout *Kegon Origin Tales*. Rather, the absence of painters' names associated with *Saint Myōe Seated in Meditation in a Tree* and the *Gishō* and *Gangyō* scrolls in thirteenth-century Kōzanji documents supports my contention that they were made outside of Kōzanji initially for aristocratic patrons whose families in turn later donated them to the temple. This conclusion does not exclude the possibility that Myōe, Jōnin, or Shunga were involved in the making of these several paintings, at least on an iconographical level.

Everyone who affixes Jōnin's name to these "masterpieces of Japanese painting" credits him with a remarkable degree of talent, creativity, and personal style, qualities monks of his status at Kōzanji probably did not possess. Neither the Kōzanji elders nor Jōnin himself used the word *painter* to describe his identity or status. Although Jōnin did not write any hagiographies of his temple's founder, his two "true reflections of Saint Myōe" in the Meditation Hall Precinct became a real focus for Kōzanji's ongoing task of preserving Myōe's memory and garnering financial backing. If Jōnin's standing as an "artist" recedes as a result of my exploration of his less famous or lost images, nonetheless he emerged as Kōzanji's most successful saint maker. The names of Jōshin, Kikai, Ryōten, and the other Kōzanji elders have consistently been downplayed in the literature on Myōe. The names of the painters of Morikane's "reflection of the Saint," the extant *Saint Myōe Seated in Meditation in a Tree*, and *Kegon Origin Tales* have been lost since the mid-thirteenth century. But thanks to Myōe's inscription naming Jōnin as the painter of *Saint Myōe Seated on a Rope-mat*, and Kōshin's brief descriptions in *Kōzanji Origin Tales*, Jōnin's name has outlasted them all. Jōnin and his beloved Saint Myōe remain dharma-companions for eternity.

Chapter Four

Signed, Sealed, and Delivered: Tosa Mitsunobu (1434–ca. 1523) and the Afterlife of a Name

MELINDA TAKEUCHI

> The quasi-magical potency of the signature is nothing other than the power, bestowed on certain individuals, to mobilize the symbolic energy produced by the functioning of the whole field, i.e. the faith in the game and its stakes that is produced by the game itself.[1]
>
> —*Pierre Bourdieu*

A name can work magic. It transforms something from unsettling anonymity into comfortable familiarity ("Ah, so that is a work of so-and-so. I know that name!"). Under the spell of the name, an object takes on the qualities of its maker—a madonna becomes "a Leonardo." Owners and connoisseurs go to absurd lengths to assign names to objects: "The Painter of the Louvre Gigantomachy," "The Kiss Painter," or "The Painter of Acropolis 606." A name has the power to organize bodies of discursive knowledge, where, as Derrida puts it, it "risks to bind, . . . to link the called" into a *de facto* group.[2] Names encompass time, place, and agency. Issues of monetary value, cultural capital, and ideological authority also accrue around the name. The cult of the name can take on a life of its own, quite independent of the individual it appears to designate. This afterlife, moreover, shifts according to historical circumstance.

I became aware of the fascinating fluidity of the relationship between an artist's name and a body of work that might be attached to it when I began to study Tosa Mitsunobu (1434–ca. 1523), a painter active in Kyoto court circles. I stumbled upon the curious phenomenon of "Mitsunobu" being linked to a significant, but diverse, group of beautiful anonymous screens, most of which have no demonstrable link with the artist.[3] Many of these attributions, dating from the early Edo period on, were made by the most eminent connoisseurs of the day. Lacking signatures, the screens stood mute while Mitsunobu's name was made by others to speak for them, thus binding the objects with an authoritative—if fictitious—link to this head of a medieval workshop.

I offer four examples, all probably dating from the late sixteenth or early seventeenth century. Figures 4.1a and 4.1b show a pair of six-panel screens depicting *Trees and Plants of the Four Seasons.* A traditional theme, they are executed with color, fine lineament, and gold and silver dust; they display a flat pictorial space, meticulous attention to small detail, and a proliferation of such details.[4] The set bears an inscription by that lion of the seventeenth-century Kano studio, Tan'yū (1602–74), announcing that they are by the brush of Tosa Mitsunobu.

Figure 4.2, *Pine Tree,* a single six-panel screen, has an inscription attributing it to the brush of "Sakon Shōgen Fujiwara Ason Mitsunobu"—a more grandiloquent evocation of Mitsunobu's name, which now includes his court ranks and thus links him with the nobility.[5] This was written by Mitsunobu's great-great-great grandson Tosa Mitsunari (1646–1710), who was understandably more deeply invested than the rival Kano were in underscoring Mitsunobu's noble associations. Although also decorative in style, it clearly differs from the preceding example: it uses gold leaf; bolder and more simplified forms; and a much shallower, more steeply inclined, and more abstractly decorative picture space.

Figure 4.3, another six-panel single screen of *Pines,* treats the same theme. Although the sense of design is quite different—pines extend from top to bottom of the picture surface in a less abstract setting—it too bears an inscription on its surface, this one by a leading painter of the Tosa school, Tosa Mitsuoki (1617–91), attributing it to Mitsunobu.[6]

Figure 4.4 is a single screen, *Pine Trees and Chinese Black Pine,* attributed to Mitsunobu, again by Tosa Mitsunari.[7] It deploys a more elaborate pictorial space, with layers overlapped like stage scrim, as well as an entirely different way of using gold: gold paint, gold particles, gold ground, gold mist, scalloped golden clouds, a golden sky, and an attached metallic disk representing the sun.

What the four complete or partial sets of screens have in common is that they belong to the visual rhetoric known as the courtly, or native. Japanese connoisseurs used the term *Yamato-e* to distinguish the national tradition from the Chinese-inspired mode of painting (alternatively called Kara-e, Suiboku, or Kanga in different epochs).[8] These paintings all belong to the realm of the abstract, gilded, elaborate, and sensual. They treat themes considered to be traditionally Japanese. We know from paintings and documents that there were many Yamato-e workshops active during the late fifteenth and early

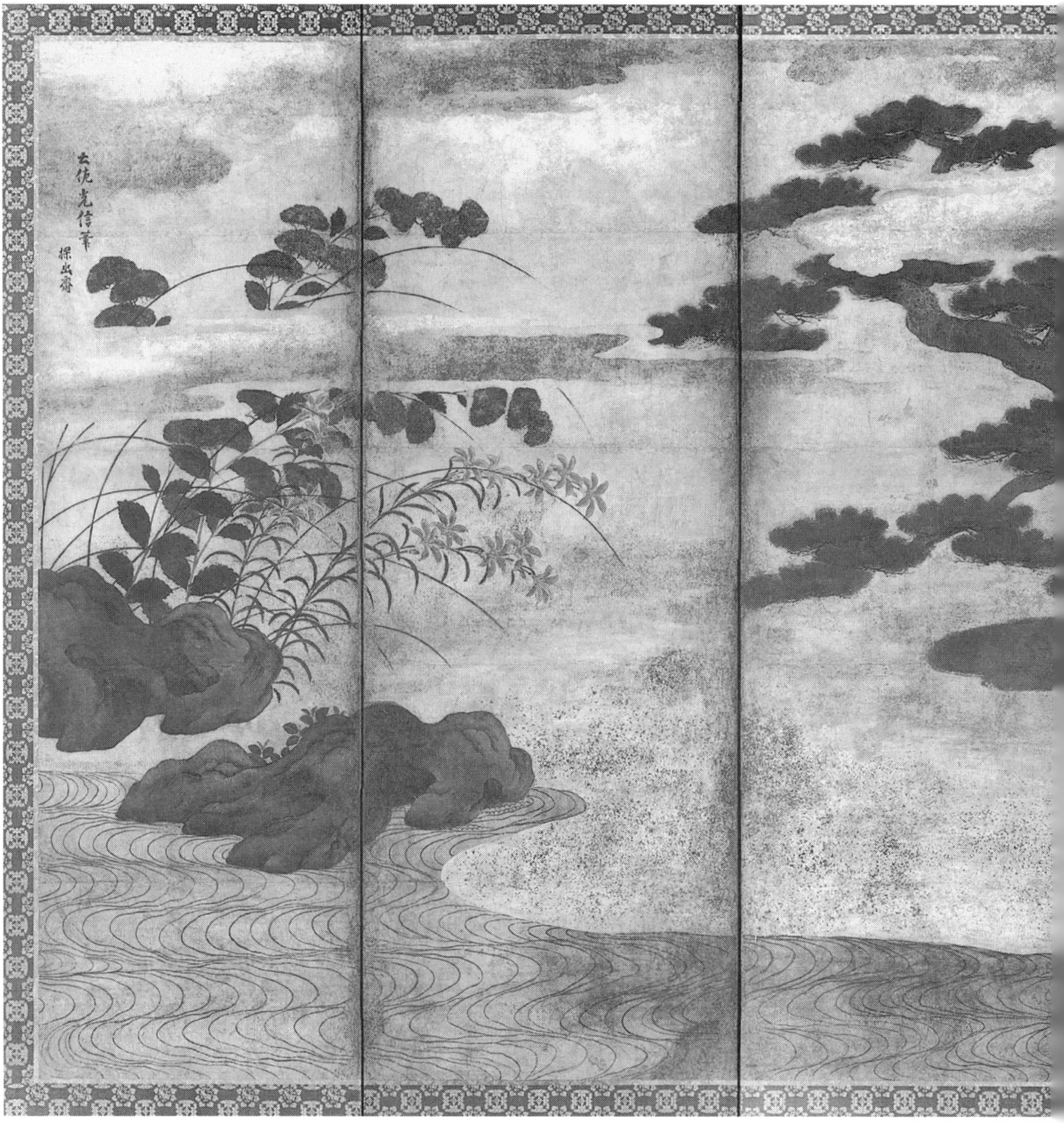

Figure 4.1a Anonymous (attributed to Tosa Mitsunobu by Kano Tan'yū). *Trees and Plants of the Four Seasons*. Muromachi period, about 1500. Pair of six-panel screens, ink, color, and gold on paper, each screen 166.8 cm x 327 cm. Courtesy of the Idemitsu Museum of Art, Tokyo.

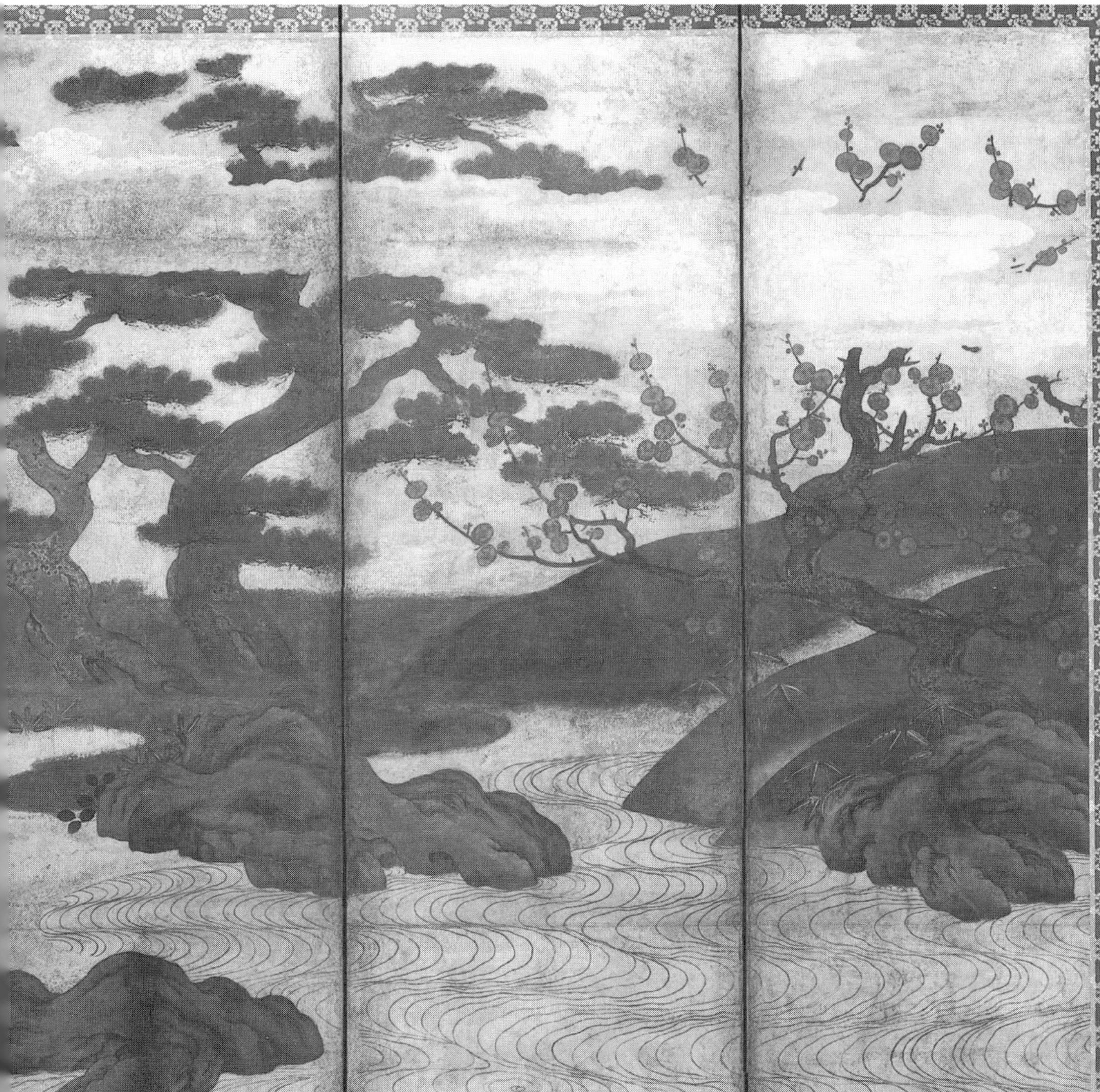

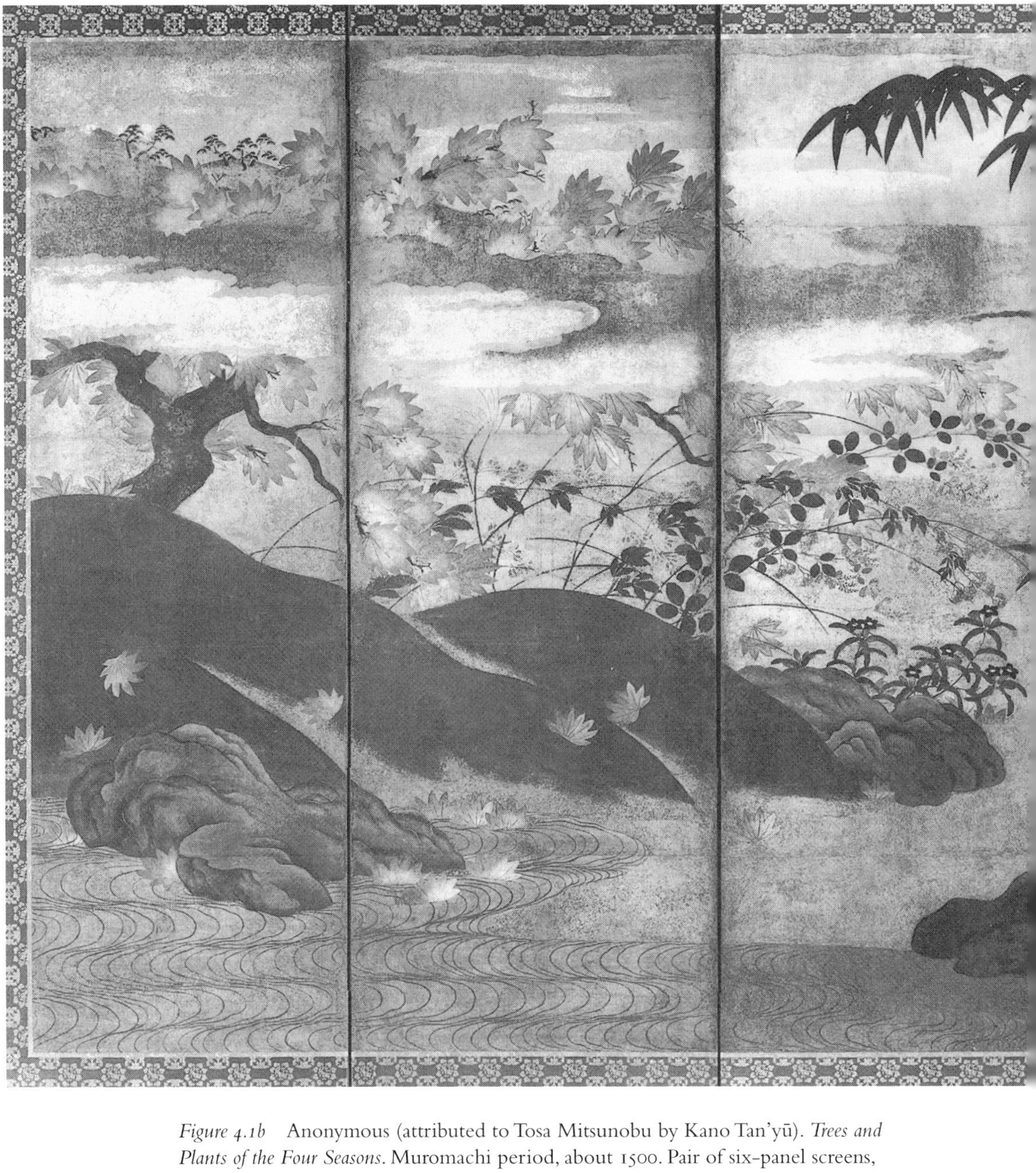

Figure 4.1b Anonymous (attributed to Tosa Mitsunobu by Kano Tan'yū). *Trees and Plants of the Four Seasons.* Muromachi period, about 1500. Pair of six-panel screens, ink, color, and gold on paper, each screen 166.8 cm x 327 cm. Courtesy of the Idemitsu Museum of Art, Tokyo.

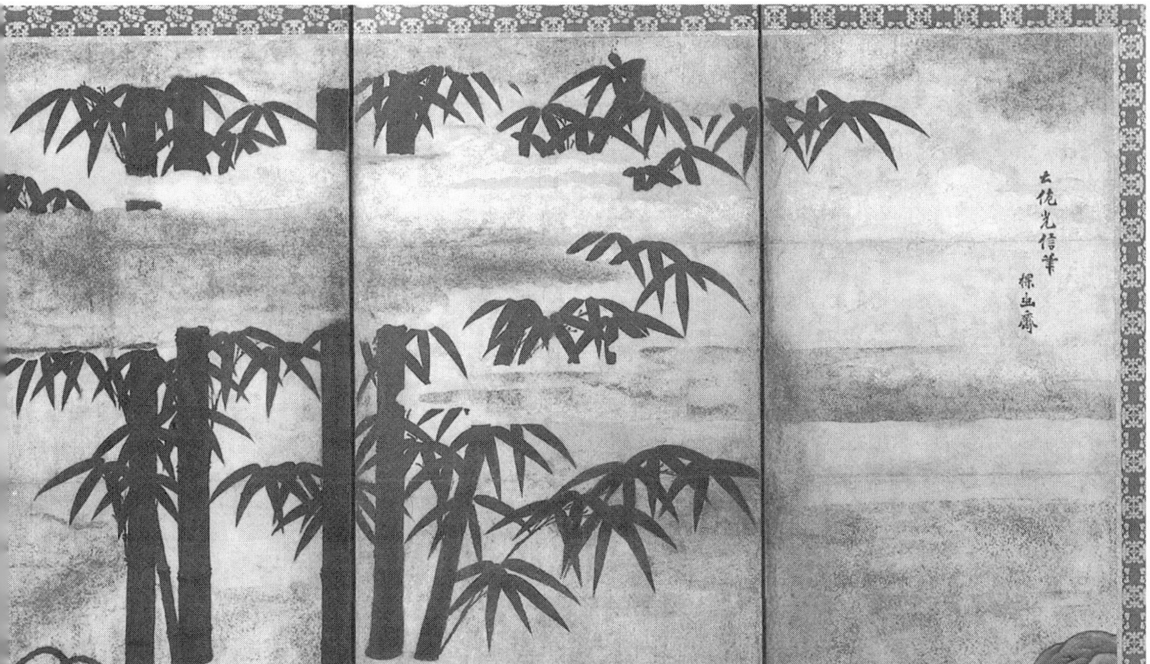

土佐光信筆
探幽齋

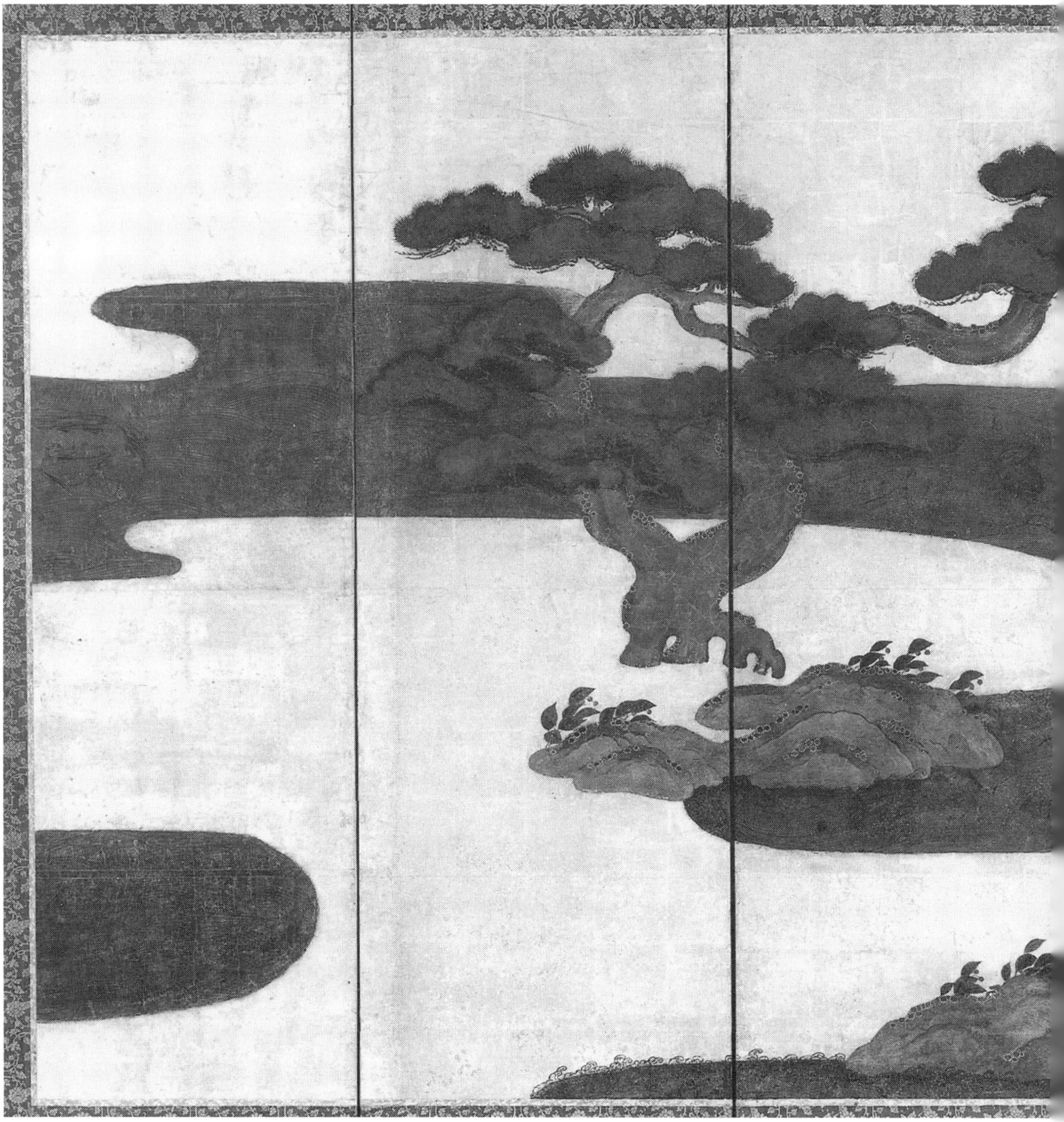

Figure 4.2 Anonymous (attributed to Tosa Mitsunobu by Tosa Mitsunari). *Pine Tree.* Muromachi period, early sixteenth century. Single six-panel screen, ink, color, and gold leaf on paper, 143.8 cm x 278.4 cm. Courtesy of the Idemitsu Museum of Art, Tokyo.

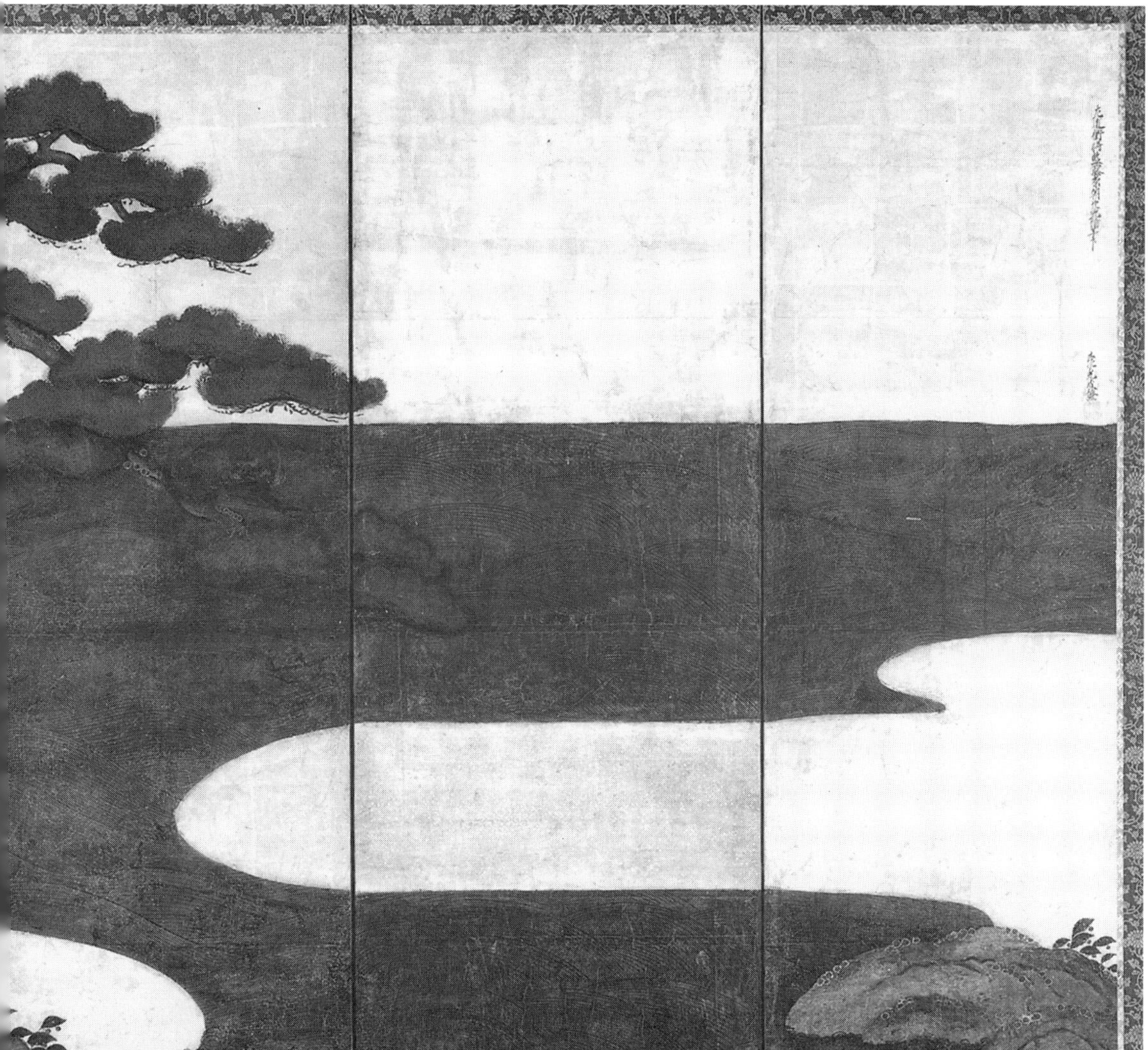

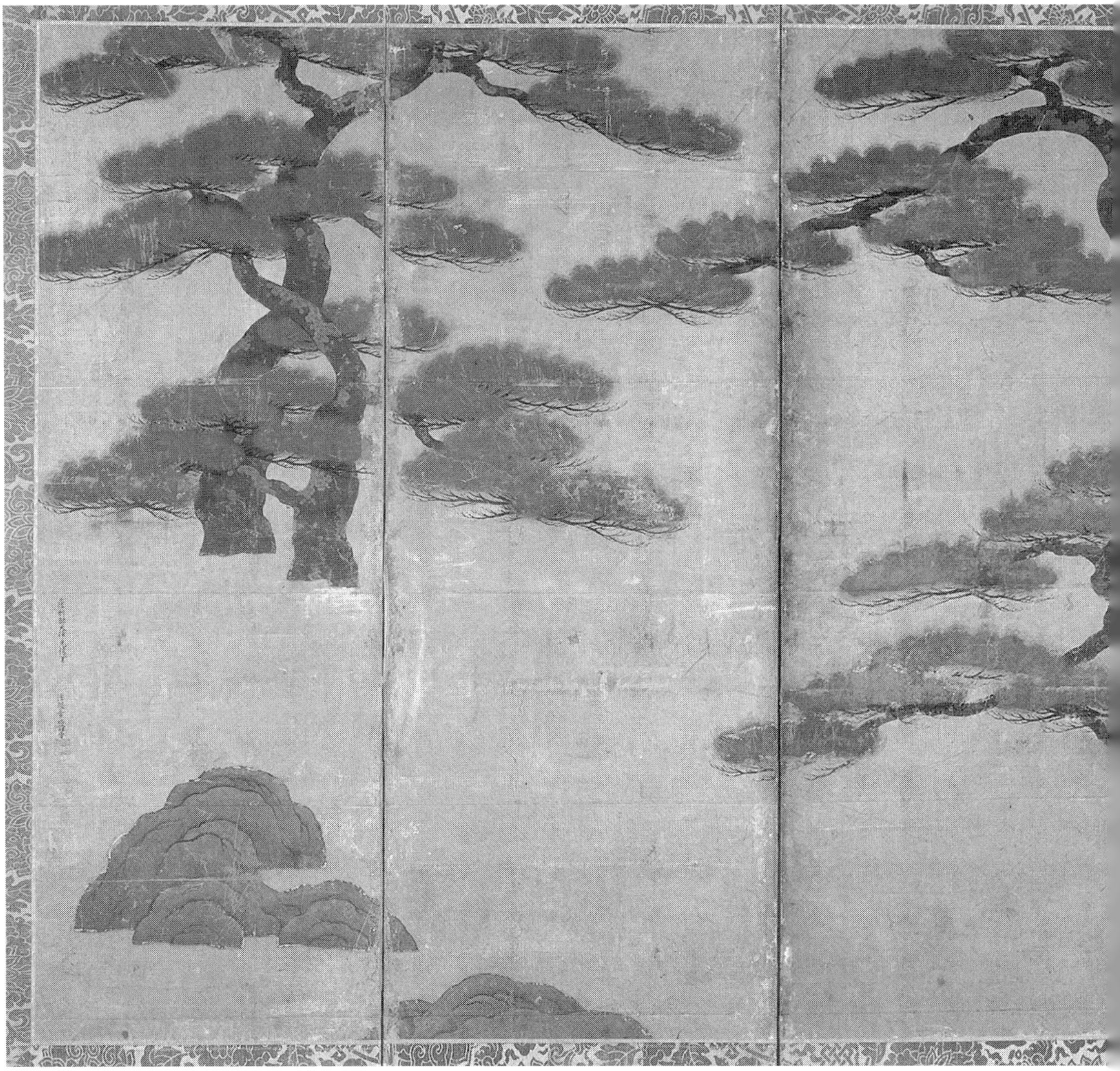

Figure 4.3 Anonymous (attributed to Tosa Mitsunobu by Tosa Mitsuoki). *Pines*. Muromachi period, sixteenth century. Six-panel screen, ink, color, and gold leaf on paper, 153.5 cm x 345 cm. Courtesy of the Tokyo National Museum.

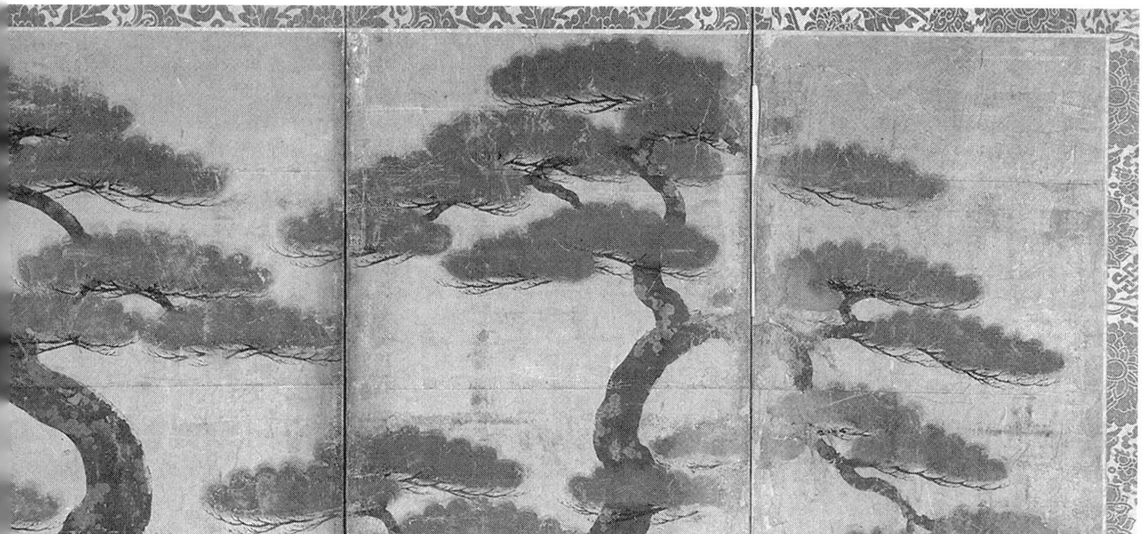

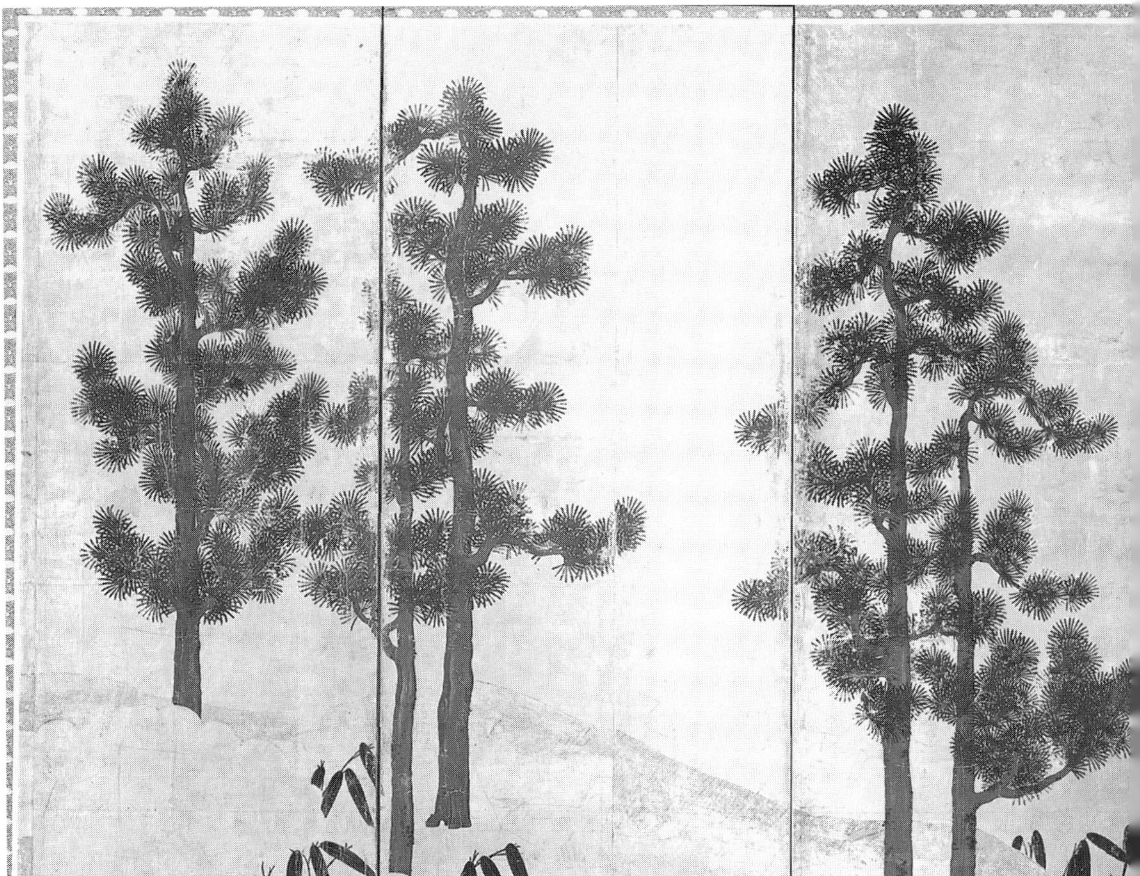

Figure 4.4 Anonymous (attributed to Tosa Mitsunobu by Tosa Mitsunari). *Pine Trees and Chinese Black Pine.* Muromachi to Momoyama period, possibly mid-sixteenth century. Six-panel screen, ink, color, and gold leaf on paper, 164.9 cm x 367.6 cm. Courtesy of the Idemitsu Museum of Art, Tokyo.

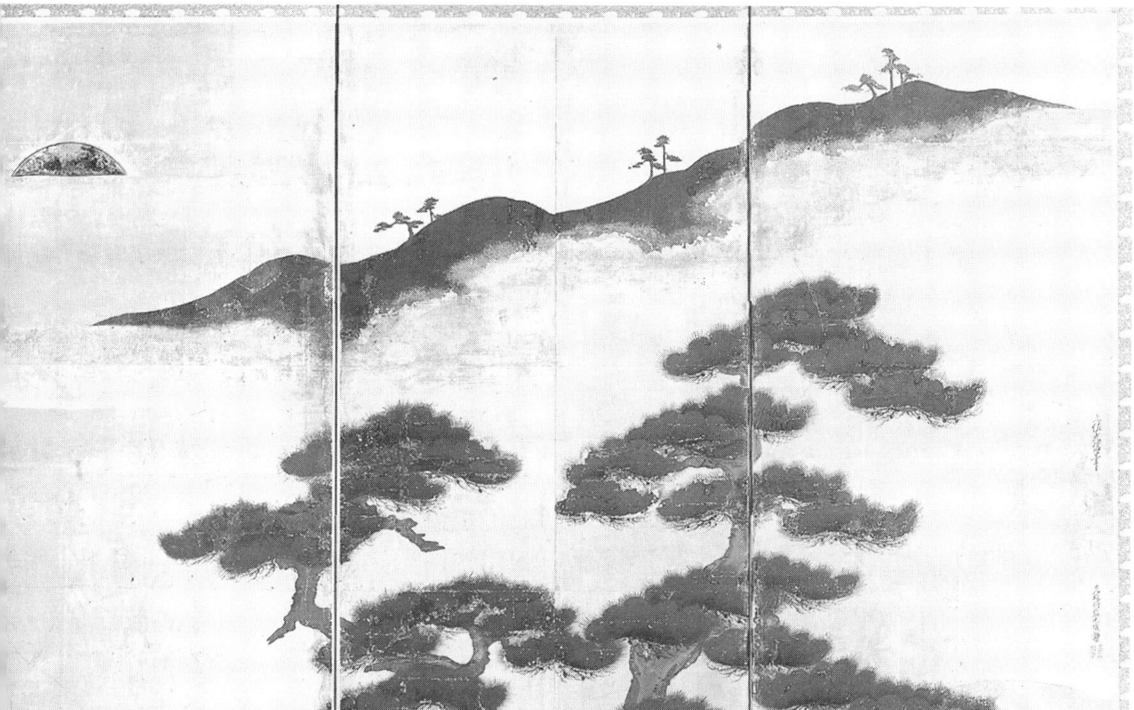

sixteenth centuries. So why, we might ask, has Tosa Mitsunobu's name been selected as the matrix that "risks to bind" this unlikely conglomerate together?

At issue, of course, are the assumptions and agendas brought by the viewer to the subjectivity of an artist and the legacy he or she leaves to us. What is involved in the processes of selection, criticism, evaluation, and connoisseurship? How—and why—do standards change over the ages? Answers to these questions are related to society's perceptions of both painter and painting.

MITSUNOBU THE MAN

For me as a specialist in painting of the Edo (1615–1868) period, the dearth of information on sixteenth-century artists came as a shock, because the painters of "my" period are so richly documented. There are abundant corpora of paintings, seals, signatures, contemporary connoisseurial judgments, and arresting biographical anecdotes. Pre-Edo Yamato-e paintings usually lack signatures, making it extremely difficult to arrange and discuss them (although they may have colophons written by others, mentioning the artist). This phenomenon even elicited comment in twelfth-century China, where authorship was a central cataloguing tool, and theories about artists and their status constituted part of a developed critical apparatus. The cataloguer of the emperor Huizong's (r. 1101–26) collection laments plaintively, "There are painters in Japan but we do not know their names."[9]

Not a single accepted extant painting bears the signature of Tosa Mitsunobu, although there are works inscribed by his contemporaries as being from his workshop.[10] It has been suggested that this absence of signatures has to do with the inappropriateness of placing one's personal name on an object designed to be seen by an emperor or by clients of status far superior to the artist—which in itself speaks reams about society's perception of the court painter.[11] In fact, the appearance of seals and signatures on Tosa paintings coincides with the social shifts that signal changing artist-patron relationships in the late sixteenth and early seventeenth centuries.

Thus the absence of Mitsunobu's own mark on the product presents enormous problems in trying to reconstruct his oeuvre (or more correctly, the products of his workshop). At present there are only nine paintings associated with Mitsunobu, none of them screens.[12] Understanding of Mitsunobu's career is possible through abundant but laconic references to him scattered throughout aristocratic, military, and temple documents; letters and diaries; through the archive of Tosa family documents (*Tosa Documents*, or *Tosa monjo*); and through notations of his participation in certain projects, including colophons on handscrolls themselves.[13] Biographies of him (and of Japanese painters in general) did not appear until more than a century after his death.

Mitsunobu the man presents numerous problems to later generations desiring to know him. Where did he come from? Who were his artistic forbears? How did he get his name? Thanks to the complexity of medieval names, kin and service group relationships, and social protocols, much of the record is probably ultimately irretrievable.[14]

The earliest item in the *Tosa Documents*, the largest collection of material pertaining to Tosa painters, bears a date of the first year of Genkyū (1204).[15] The recipient is unclear, but it emanates from the Kamakura shogun Minamoto Sanetomo (1192–1219) and concerns an income property in the province of Settsu. Its inclusion in the group of Tosa documents implies an ancient pedigree for the Tosa. The first artist actually to be associated with that name, however, did not arrive on the scene until two hundred years later: Yukihiro (fl. 1406–34 or 1443).[16] The Tosa name makes its appearance in the context of an honorary governorship ("Kami") of Tosa province; the full reference to this individual is "Gakō [skilled painter] Tosa no Kami Fujiwara Yukihiro."[17] The appointment of these honorary governorships—as empty and yet as charged as the title of Prince of Wales—appears as part of the honorific arsenal of epithets attached to a number of painters listed in the *Tosa Documents*; for example, Yukimitsu (fl. 1352–89), who directed the Palace Painting Office and is sometimes considered the founder of the Tosa line, is addressed as "Edokoro Echizen no Kami Yukimitsu" in a *Tosa monjo* document of 1360.[18] The Tosa family might just as well have ended up as the Echizen family, since these governorships were wholly fictitious (and probably not heritable) anyway. To make matters even more complicated, Yukimitsu was described by one of Mitsunobu's noble contemporaries as "Kasuga [Edokoro] Yukimitsu" (Yukimitsu of the Kasuga Atelier) as well.[19]

If the reader is thoroughly confused by all this, it is useful simply to recognize that these interchangeable medieval forenames are filiational tags rather than indications of consanguinity. The grand name of Fujiwara—the greatest clan, but not the only one, that traditionally served the imperial house—keeps cropping up in conjunction with Tosa painters. To work at court, one needed affiliation with an official service clan.[20] This accounts for the enormous number of painters, sculptors, lacquerers, and potters throughout Japanese history whose names include the characters Fujiwara.[21] In such cases Fujiwara is not a surname—the artists most likely had no Fujiwara blood flowing through their veins—but it is a special clan name (*ujina*) meeting an indispensable precondition for service. In many cases, perhaps, the name Fujiwara was taken only *after* the bearer went to work for the court. This helps explain why the courtiers Nakanomikado Nobutane (1442–1525) and Sanjōnishi Sanetaka (1455–1537), probably following the representation of Mitsunobu himself, were at pains to designate Fujiwara Yukimitsu as an ancestor (*senzo*) of Tosa Mitsunobu.[22] The link would not necessarily, however, have been that of blood. Additionally, artists—such as those with Kasuga, Rokkaku, or Awataguchi "surnames"—were frequently known by the location of their workshop, as must have been the case with the aforementioned Kasuga Fujiwara Echizen no Kami Yukimitsu.

To enter the world of Mitsunobu is to embark on an odyssey into a dense thicket of court ranks, land grants, formal contracts, and cryptic observations made in passing. Here is the general picture that can be gleaned from contemporary documents, which seems more like a curriculum vitae than a biography. In 1469, he was appointed director of the Palace Painting Bureau. By the early sixteenth century, he was receiving income from at least five estates throughout Japan, much of this provided by the military government as well as the court (as indeed the first document in the *Tosa monjo*, a deed from Hōjō Tokimasa on behalf of the underage shogun, indicates). He attained a court rank a little more than halfway up the ladder, the highest yet acquired by a professional artist: Fourth Rank (of nine), Junior Grade (*jushi ige*). Mitsunobu's workshop produced portraits, narrative picture scrolls, Buddhist icons, screens, and fans. We do not know for certain the year of either his birth or his death: he just ceases appearing in documents after 1521, although Edo-period sources round off his age to the tidy—and unsubstantiated—figure of ninety years of age.

Nor have we any contemporary biographies of or anecdotes about him, as exist in abundance for so many Edo-period artists. A sketch portrait (*funpon*) of him, preserved in the collection of Tosa family sketches, has recently come to light (Figure 4.5). It shows him seated cross-legged and erect, in voluminous formal court robes and hat, wearing a sword and holding a *shaku* (an implement carried by courtiers in China and Japan, originating, it is said, to keep one's breath from drifting toward the emperor). Although the portrait exudes an aura of dignity, the heavily wrinkled face, given in conventional three-quarters view toward our left, betrays little about the individual except for his advanced age. Any physical deformities, if they existed, have been edited out. In facial type, the portrait resembles the many other Tosa sketches in the archive of elderly venerables, especially pictures of the legendary poet Kakinomoto Hitomaro (fl. ca. 680–700).[23]

It is a matter of extreme good fortune to pick up little tidbits about Mitsunobu from aristocratic diaries: his participation in linked-verse contests at the courtier Nakanomikado Nobutane's mansion, his attending a lecture on the *Tale of Genji*, or an invitation for him to partake of a New Year's breakfast at the courtier Kanroji Motonaga's house.[24] But his reconstructed biography lacks a shaped narrative, with peaks and troughs of a life, the little sparks of human interest that turn dry facts into the stuff of stories and legends.

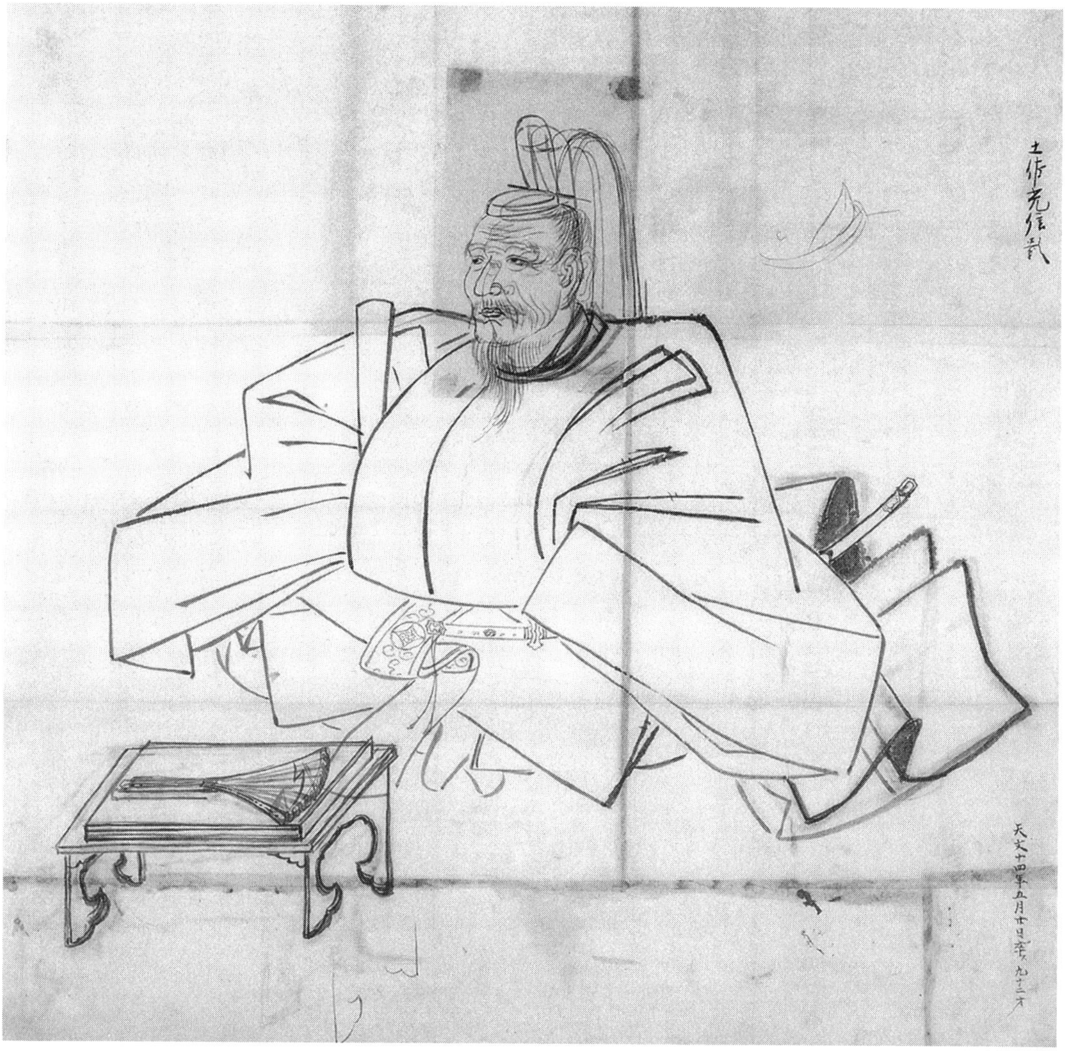

Figure 4.5 Anonymous. *Sketch of Tosa Mitsunobu.* Muromachi period, dated 1545 (Tenmon 14), fifth month, twentieth day, at the age of ninety-two (Japanese count). Single-sheet, ink on paper, 49.3 cm x 47.2 cm. Courtesy of the Archives of the Kyoto University of Arts.

This relative scarcity is not simply a function of the greater distance in time, or of documents being lost. It represents a different view of the medieval business of painting, centered on the workshop and run according to the model of the family.

There is a theory that the structure of the traditional medieval Japanese family business (*kagyō*), or house (*ie*), originated in the various offices and bureaus of the ancient imperial court: families of archive keepers, sake brewers, metal casters, cooks, or poem reciters.[25] These workers gradually assumed hereditary rights to their offices, on the basis of their accumulated skills, and they passed down these techniques, often kept secret, from generation to generation to perpetuate the rights and rewards accompanying such privileged employment. Tangible benefits appeared in the form of income and gifts, while the intangible boon of such patronage included connection to powerful supporters. The appearance of Japanese family names may have resulted from the necessity to prove affiliation with one's "skill group" before partaking legitimately of the security that it offered.

Medieval painting workshops (along with organizations of blacksmiths, carpenters, sculptors, potters, noh dramatists, tea ceremony specialists, lacquerers, gamblers, and even prostitutes) were organized according to the principle of the *ie*, whether they served temples, shrines, powerful private aristocratic or military families, the shogunate, or the court.[26] The head of the workshop, by custom male, made the economic decisions, determined and enforced house policy, dealt with patrons, oversaw the grand design of commissions, attended to the most important particulars (including the fine drawing), and distributed the details of execution to the various assistants. Assistants, often but not always family members, worked their way through various tasks as part of their training: they copied models, saw to the sizing of the paper or silk support, prepared and applied coloring. Some even subspecialized in the application of heavy mineral pigments, others in light vegetable tones.

The degree to which the maker has control over his or her final product is one mark of the difference between today's concepts of "artist" and "artisan." The head of a medieval workshop was obliged to carry out commissions from powerful superiors with scrupulous attention to the demands such people placed on them. The vision was largely that of the patron, often dictated by unalterable precedents, the flouting of which would be wholly unthinkable.[27] In many cases, go-betweens such as Sanetaka acted as middlemen between workshop heads and high-court nobles, and especially the emperor, in a role not unlike what Donald McCallum ascribes to Tori-busshi (Chapter Two). The success of the project thus rested heavily on the go-between's head as well. To say something produced in Mitsunobu's workshop is "by" Mitsunobu is stretching the concept of authorship to the limit. It ignores the difference in status between producer and client and erases the participation of a large number of collaborators.

A certain tension thus arose when professionals such as Mitsunobu obtained employment and its attendant benefits at court. Professional tradespeople never attained sufficient rank to be able to appear in the presence of the emperor.[28] The great social divide was drawn between the courtiers of the first three ranks and those, like Mitsunobu, of Fourth Rank and less, who constituted the fringes of the nobility and were not permitted to enter the Courtiers' Hall.[29] When noblemen such as Nobutane or Sanetaka wrote about Mitsunobu, they usually preceded his name with honorific (if by then thoroughly atrophied) titles: "Shōgen" (Lieutenant of the Bodyguards—subdivided, in descending order, into "Sakon," the Left, and "Ukon," the Right); "Tayū" (Senior Assistant Head) and "Shōyū (Junior Assistant Head); or "Gyōbu" (member of the Punishments Ministry). Additionally one finds contemporaries attaching to his name such generic epithets as "Kami" (Governor); "Daibu" ("grandee," the same terminology used of the Chinese gentry class); and "Ason" (courtier). These same inflated titles continue to appear in the seventeenth-century attributions inscribed on Figure 1.4. Only rarely was the occupational designation gakō ("[a person with] painting skill") affixed to Mitsunobu's name. Affiliation with the imperial court allowed painters to shift their cultural identity from occupation or livelihood to social status—a major redefinition of an individual's relationship with the world.[30]

Despite the rosy picture of this prodigy of Yamato-e that emerges in the later narratives, a look at Mitsunobu's times, known as the "Country at War" (*Sengoku jidai*), confirms that he must have faced numerous difficulties that did not make it into his personal history. For one thing, leadership of the Palace Painting Bureau was not hereditary. Records of the heads of the bureau from the fourteenth century on indicate a relatively rapid turnover of the families of directors, which usually changed upon the ascension of a new emperor.[31] It has even been suggested that by the Muromachi period (1333–1575) the Palace Painting Bureau as an official bureaucratic entity no longer existed, and that when the emperor needed something painted, the job was contracted out to various local workshops.[32] The issue cannot be resolved here, but we can verify that competition was fierce. There were a number of rival, well-connected ateliers recorded in the literature of the period.[33] It is generally accepted that Mitsunobu managed to wrest the directorship of the Palace Painting Bureau (in whatever form it existed) away from the Rokkaku workshop and pass the position to his son Mitsushige (otherwise known as Mitsumochi, 1496–ca. 1572); and that the premature death in battle of Mitsunobu's grandson Mitsumoto (fl. 1530, d. 1569) ended for a hundred years the Tosa family's grip on the directorship of the Palace Painting Bureau. Furthermore Mitsunobu himself had problems, as did so many during the turmoil of his era, in collecting the income from some of his provincial properties.[34] Fifty years after Mitsunobu's death, not only did the Tosa family lose their imperial employment, they seem even to have lost their ability to eke out a livelihood in the ruined capital. They quit Kyoto altogether in search of richer pecuniary pastures—namely, the wealthy merchants of the port city of Sakai.

What happens to titled craftspeople when they lose their association with the imperial court? Do they become once again common artisans? Even though the aura of their connection with the court followed the Tosa to Sakai, I think their status in the world must have sunk somewhat. It is significant that, during this interlude of exile, seals with their individual names start appearing on (actually on the verso of) their paintings. This represents a major shift in the relative positions of artist and client: the once-courtly Tosa are no longer working for their superiors, they are in the employ of merchants—and the former cachet of their house name becomes part of the cultural capital of their work, acting like a poultice to draw upward in capillary fashion the standing of their new patrons.

MITSUNOBU THE CONSTRUCT

The first recorded evaluation of Tosa Mitsunobu after his death occurs in a judgment by Hasegawa Tōhaku (1539–1610) in *Tōhaku's Explanations of Painting* (*Tōhaku gasetsu*). It gives no inkling of the retrospective fame that was to come. Tōhaku, evidently unimpressed by Mitsunobu, offers the cryptic observation that the painter Kubota Shōgen is just as good.[35] Tōhaku is probably talking about Kubota Tōbei (fl. late fifteenth century), who, like Mitsunobu, headed an atelier in Kyoto. Tōbei is, at least today, considered a minor figure. It is a mark of the degeneration of courtly titles in the late sixteenth century that Tōhaku refers to Kubota as Shōgen, lieutenant of the bodyguards, even though there is no evidence that Kubota served the court. Tōhaku's remarks reveal two important representations. The first is that before the early seventeenth century, Mitsunobu's name had not yet become synonymous with Yamato-e. The second is that the tendency to inflate Yamato-e painters by identifying them with empty court ranks had appeared by Tōhaku's time.

How, then, did the Tosa come to rise from almost refugee status to become the index of the court style? How did a new, more stylistically diverse Tosa Mitsunobu get superimposed over the old one? Lying behind these questions is another: Why did connoisseurs become increasingly interested in notions of authorship in this notoriously anonymous Yamato-e lineage of painting?

A primary factor in the rise of Mitsunobu's reputation was the return of the Tosa family to Kyoto in 1634. Under the aggressive leadership of Tosa Mitsuoki, the Tosa worked hard to regain the directorship of the Palace Painting Bureau in 1654, almost one hundred years after they had lost it. They were not about to lose it again, and indeed they retained it through the nineteenth century. It is significant that Mitsuoki now for the first time places signatures and seals on his paintings, which suggests a transformation in the status of Tosa artists. Laura Allen has suggested that he did this in competitive response to the Kano studio's practice of signing their works.[36] Painters of the Chinese lineage had been signing their works ever since the fourteenth century; many of the new maverick urban painters, such as Tawaraya Sōtatsu (d. ca. 1643) followed suit. Mitsuoki not only displayed his name on his own works, he included it prominently on the attributions he inscribed on old unsigned paintings, such as the screen reproduced in Figure 4.3.

Economic, political, and sociological factors coalesced to create what we might call the Mitsunobu construct. For example, there is considerable evidence for the increasing availability of painting to a mass urban audience, seen, for example, in a comparison of the famous screens depicting the city of Kyoto called *In and Around the Capital* (*Rakuchū Rakugai-zu*). The so-called Machida screens, painted in the early sixteenth century, do not show any painting establishments among their myriad shops.[37] This is not to imply that such enterprises did not exist in early sixteenth-century Kyoto—we know from literary evidence that they did—but it does show that they were not considered among the indexical sights of the city. The Uesugi version of *In and Around Kyoto*, showing the city in the later sixteenth century, does, on the other hand, include what appears to be a paint-to-order children's portrait shop (right screen, panel 4, center). Painters were clearly featured among the human resource assets of the city. The Funaki *In and Around the Capital* screens, dating to the beginning of the seventeenth century, include two hanging scroll establishments and two fan shops (Figure 4.6). The section reproduced here shows a fan shop at the intersection of Gojō and Teramachi, surrounded to our right by a money-changer's and to the left by a millstone purveyor, a footwear shop, and an establishment selling kimonos. The appreciation of marvelous objects spilled beyond the purview of high culture to become available to common townspeople who could afford such things. Numerous artisans rushed in to take advantage of this new market. Diversity of products gave rise to the impulse to identify and categorize them.

In tandem with this came an increased emphasis on provenance—or, to put it in modern terms, brand names. The names and logos of the shops are proudly displayed on signs and curtains in Figure 4.6. In emulation of the Ashikaga shoguns' aesthetic advisors (*dōbōshū*) of the Ami family, the warlord Toyotomi Hideyoshi established the Kohitsu line of hereditary connoisseurs of calligraphy in the late sixteenth century.[38] Around the same time, Hon'ami Kōetsu (1558–1637) became famous for his expertise in evaluating swords.

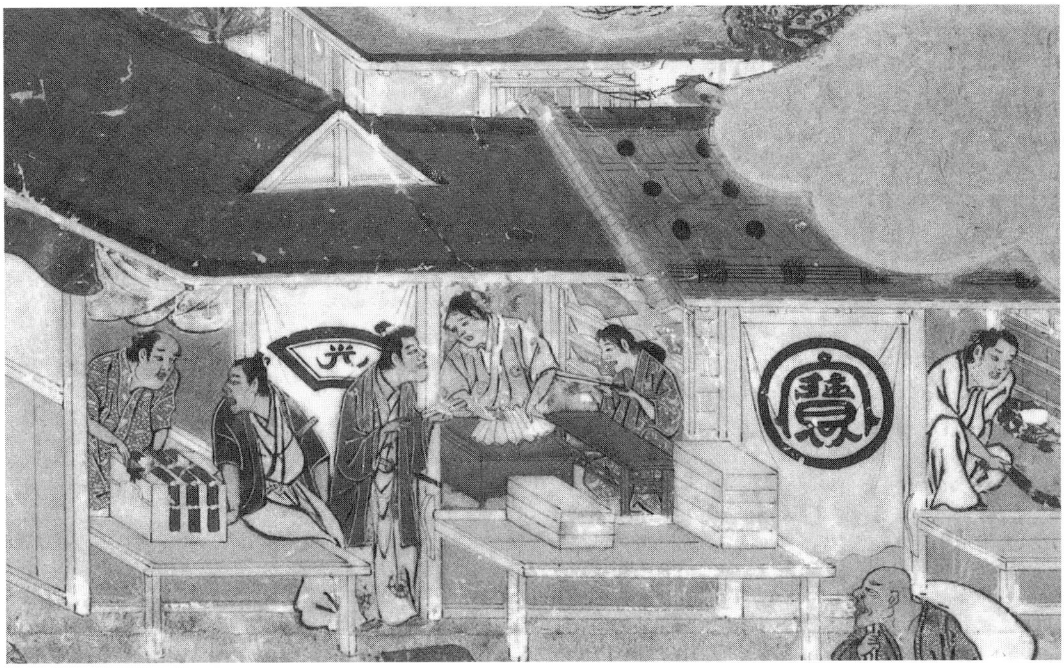

Figure 4.6 Anonymous. Fan shop, from *In and Out of the Capital* (so-called Funaki version). First half of the seventeenth century. Pair of six-panel screens, ink, color, and gold leaf on paper, 162 cm x 340 cm. Courtesy of the Tokyo National Museum. Detail of right screen, panel 6.

Clearly, the New Age of the Commodity had dawned. The developing enterprise of naming, acquiring, verifying, and celebrating fine things in turn contributed to the emergence of guidebooks such as *The Dappled Cloth of Edo* (*Edo kanoko*), which tells who the famous artisans and wholesalers were, and where one could find their shops.[39] In the eighteenth century, these expanded into regular publications such as *Who's Who in Kyoto* (*Heian jinbutsu shi*).

It was the first Tokugawa shogun, Ieyasu (1542–1616), who set the stage for the seventeenth century's subsequent preoccupation with "correct" lineages and official histories. Ieyasu went to considerable pains, including outright fabrication, to demonstrate that his house was related to the Minamoto so he could assume the mantle of shogun legitimately.[40] We find this preoccupation with lineage and history mirrored in Confucian scholarship, in noh, in tea, and in painting, to name a few areas.

The impulse for sanctification by lineage generated the beginnings of a formal art-historical discourse in Japan. As would be expected, the prime movers behind it were the elite old-guard workshops, among them the self-proclaimed Chinese lineage of Kano and their Japanese-style counterparts, the Tosa. Both groups responded to the threat of stylistic dilution from the plethora of freelancing parvenus, and both, in different ways, seized the opportunity to advance the fame and interests of their own family.

In 1623, Kano Ikkei published *Kōsōshū*, which was based on Chinese painting ideology but revolutionary in the Japanese context; this was followed by his *Tansei jakuboku shū*, which included biographies of Japanese artists. Needless to say, it granted pride of place to the Kano painters. Throughout the seventeenth century, Kano artists produced numerous treatises. The Kano family's lionizing of their predecessor Motonobu may have supplied the motivation for the Tosa family's corresponding celebration of Motonobu's older contemporary, Mitsunobu. In speaking of the Tosa school, Kano Einō (1631–97) damned them with faint praise in *The History of Our Country's Painting* (*Honchō gashi*, 1678); he suggested that they were good at what they did, but that this was limited, rigid, and effeminate.[41]

Certainly the Tosa could not permit Kano attacks on their house to go unrebutted. Tosa Mitsuoki wrote *The Great Account of Our Country's Painting Methods* (*Honchō gahō taiden*) in 1690—relatively late in the game compared to the Kano—to counter with a defense of his own camp.[42] He criticized the Kano painters on various technical points, which today seem relatively petty. The framing of his treatise, however, was motivated by the same classifying and legitimizing impulses—and indeed the same sinological terms of engagement—that inspired the Kano.

In addition to members of the established Kano and Tosa workshops, Confucian scholars too adopted the Chinese literati custom of writing about painting and painters during the seventeenth century. Kurokawa Dōyū (d. 1691), a Confucian doctor from Hiroshima and the author of a miscellany of works including botanical studies, local histories, and poetry, was a friend of both Kano Einō and Tosa Mitsuoki. Dōyū's work *Record of Enpeki Studio* (*Enpekiken ki*) of 1675 is an example of the kind of writing by general *belles lettrists* that follows the times in promoting the Tosa as synonymous with Yamato-e and connects legitimacy in painting with the old establishment lineages.[43]

As part of this new art-historical enterprise, signatures, seals, and connoisseurship became important tools of both Tosa and Kano practice. Kano and Tosa painters alike were called to authenticate paintings for a burgeoning group of collectors. It was at this point that many old, unsigned paintings in the Yamato-e style that no one knew what to do with came to be attributed to Mitsunobu (and to other early Tosa family artists), as is the case with the four examples given at the beginning of this chapter.

Connoisseurship and collecting are sisters. The increase of connoisseurial activity is symptomatic of the expansion of collecting into the realm of the commoner during the Edo period. The legendary collections of the past—

notably the Shōsōin, reflecting the Chinese notion that the treasures protect the realm; or the Ashikaga collection, which affirmed the rights of the medieval shoguns to participate politically because of their position culturally—found prosaic reflections during the Edo era in the simple pleasure of a townsperson's "finding a bargain at an [antique] shop" to add to his or her collection.[44] Echoes of the original talismanic nature of possessions are to be found in such Edo popular notions as the one that owning paintings by a given artist could help one's family flourish, or that erotic pictures might protect the house from fire.[45] The rise of interest in individual artists is connected also to the new notions of biography, personality, and subjectivity that emerged during the Edo period. We begin to see a plethora of nonaffiliated painters with individualistic styles. They were a diverse group, including dropouts from Kano studios, among them Kusumi Morikage (c. 1620–90) and Hanabusa Itchō (1652–1724), both painters reveling in iconoclastic attitudes toward Kano-school orthodoxy. Iwasa Matabei (1578–1650) must also be counted in this number; in inventing artistic legitimacy for himself, Matabei proclaimed himself to be the "last in the line of Tosa Mitsunobu"—a preposterous declaration charged with the sort of overt defiance of the establishment that drove Kano and Tosa painters to defend their turf. Of course, there was also the great Tawaraya Sōtatsu and his workshop, who might be seen as horning in on commissions from the court at Tosa expense. It was precisely in the environment of conflicting systems of canonization that the name of Tosa Mitsunobu began to assume such a multiplicity of meanings.

MITSUNOBU THE PROBLEM

Let us return to Derrida's anxieties about the properties of the name (that "risks . . . to link the called"). There exist questions from the very beginning about the "nameable" (for example, should works by Mitsunobu's atelier be known under Mitsunobu's name? Who decides? Upon what criteria?) as well as about the related notion of "authorship."

The proper name, Tosa Mitsunobu, has come to preside over (at least) three entirely different discursive domains, coinciding with the three historical epistemes through which it has passed. These transformations can also be characterized as the broad "paradigm shifts" encompassed by the changes in social structure, from the medieval to the premodern and to the postmodern periods.

During the medieval period, Mitsunobu's name was synonymous with a production unit, the *ie*. Its products were the result of collective labor; the house was structured so that its products could be perpetuated by trained interchangeable individuals with access to closely guarded secret techniques. The patriarch of the workshop, one of a number of contenders for lucrative commissions, had to bow to the demands of elevated patrons very much his social superiors. At the mercy of court politics, professional Yamato-e painters fought fiercely—and quite frequently unsuccessfully—for that ultimate reward, the privilege of working for the emperor. The real payoff took the form of (often devalued) court ranks, stipends from fiefs whose income was sometimes not available, the honor of being allowed to circulate on the fringes of the courtly nobility, and the use of the lofty-sounding titles that came with this territory.

In the Early Modern, or Kinsei, period, a host of nonaffiliated "urban painters" (*machi-eshi*) emerged to serve a clientele consisting largely of their peers. Modernity and commodity are related phenomena. Often trained in the classical workshops but lacking loyalty to the dogmatic approach demanded by the *iemoto* system, these urban painters experimented with innovative themes and styles. With their "modern look" and independence of production, they posed a real threat to Kano and Tosa orthodoxy. Around the time that townspeople's self-awareness began to coalesce into a celebration of their own culture, biographies, anecdotes, and legends concerning their own world—including artists and craftspeople—heralded the awakening of a new kind of subjectivity. Julie Davis's chapter on Utamaro examines in detail how this translated into a manufactured persona for artists. Many of the human-interest anecdotes set forth during the Edo period about contemporary Japanese painters bear an uncanny resemblance to archetypal stories about artists related by Kris and Kurz in their classic study *Legend, Myth, and Magic in the Image of the Artist.*[46] In addition, creative "biographers" adopted stories about artists wholesale from Chinese accounts.

Kano and Tosa painters reacted by creating discursive domains of their own. They wrote histories of painting placing their respective schools at the center. Delving into Chinese sources, they too found anecdotes and legends to retrofit their predecessors. The assertion in *The History of Our Country's Painting* (*Honchō gashi*) that Kano Motonobu (the quintessential savvy businessman) disdained wealth and fame, refused to curry favor with his superiors, and loved to travel about the countryside sketching (a story lifted verbatim from a Chinese biography of the literati artist Huang Gongwang), is probably the most jarringly anachronistic, not to mention self-serving.[47] It is a forerunner of the paradigm of the independent artist (see Christine Guth's chapter in this volume) applied retroactively to the workshop situation.

During the Edo period, the number of paintings attributed to Tosa Mitsunobu ballooned to an estimated one hundred pieces—even as other connoisseurs unrelated to the established schools lamented that Muromachi paintings by the Tosa were truly rare.[48] The visual and thematic system of Yamato-e, in its medieval heyday a pluralistic enterprise consisting of a host of competing workshops, was conflated primarily into one unit under the Tosa name. Mitsunobu himself, a vacuum by virtue of the paucity of actual information known about him, became the perfect vehicle for these accretions—the proverbial empty signifier with only the slightest whisper of a signified. Mitsunobu's name became synonymous with "Kyoto," "courtly," and "old."

Contemporary theorists have had much to say about the notion of the author or artist's existence as a discursive construct. With the advent of deconstruction and its skepticism, it is no coincidence that Mitsunobu's accepted "oeuvre" has now dwindled from the one hundred works of the Edo period to a mere nine. This is more than a matter of mere physical attrition of objects. Mitsunobu's biographical deposit in the form of an established oeuvre consists of the constant addition and removal of paintings-as-texts, rotating in and out of his orbit, putting new spin on the meaning of his name. Art historians' careers have been made and broken during the slippage of the boundaries of an oeuvre.

In his essay "What Is an Author?" Michel Foucault demonstrates how an author's name serves an organizing or classifying function to link a series of texts, establishing among them a "relationship of homogeneity, filiation, authentication of some texts by the use of others," and using these classifications to set one group apart from other groups of texts.[49] These observations are particularly apposite to the case of the medieval Japanese painter, and indeed they seem tailor-made for a "painting subject" such as Mitsunobu, although they also have implications for any author who ever created anything.

Every era reinvents its cognitive strategies as new "givens," and sloughs off, like old skin, any representation falling out of step with the times. Even in an era such as ours, where people can claim to speak seriously about the "end of history," one perversely yearns to know what the name "Tosa Mitsunobu" will mean—and what shape will be taken by the "relationship of homogeneity, filiation, [and] authentication of some texts by the use of others" used to establish his oeuvre—a hundred years from now. In the end, the name of an artist transcends time, space, materiality, and ultimately discourse itself.

A Tosa Potter in Edo

LOUISE ALLISON CORT

In the seventh month of the year 1678 (Empō 6), a samurai of the Tosa domain named Morita Kyūemon, age thirty-eight, accompanied by two servants, set sail from the main Tosa harbor on the southern coast of Shikoku on a ship bound for Osaka. From Osaka he took a boat up the Yodo River via Fushimi to Kyoto; from Kyoto he traversed the Tōkaidō trunk road by palanquin and on horseback all the way to the capital city of Edo, where he remained through the fifth month of the following year. Although a warrior, Morita Kyūemon had been trained as a potter, and he ran the Odo pottery, a small enterprise comprising two workshops located close by the castle in Kōchi, headquarters of the Tosa domain. His journey and sojourn in the capital were conceived and managed by domain officials for the express purpose of improving the quality of Odo pottery.

The pottery's products encompassed utilitarian and ornamental wares used by Tosa citizens as well as by the ruling Yamauchi house within its own residences in Kōchi and Edo. The desired transformation of a modest local product into refined and stylish pottery worthy of formal presentation to other domain rulers (daimyo), to government officials, and perhaps even to the shogun could only be accomplished in Edo. The Tosa domain's goal was a ceramic gift that matched the exacting aesthetic and technical standards of Edo warrior culture and competed with the nationally recognized ceramic wares from Kyoto and Seto yet conveyed an unmistakable Tosa origin, just like the dried bonito (*katsuobushi*) that was already a sought-after presentation from the domain. This chapter explores that difficult mission, the motivations that generated it, how the officials of the Tosa domain sought to accomplish it, and how well it ultimately succeeded.

The key source is Kyūemon's own record of the eleven months, which survives in the original and has been published (Figure 5.1).[1] Although classified as a diary (*nikki*), it more truly resembles notes taken for a report on the official mission. (The final report, if prepared, has not survived.) Written with brush and ink in a notebook of bound Tosa mulberry paper, the document rarely notes the author's personal thoughts. In unembellished, businesslike prose, it records what Kyūemon did day by day in connection with his assignment—where he went, whom he met, what he did, and occasionally even what he said. Juxtaposed to other domain documents, including genealogies of Tosa warrior families and daily records of domain activities, it allows us to witness the events in which Kyūemon played a key role. Indeed, the sequence of events related in the document reads like a drama whose key scenes take place within the reception rooms, offices, and living quarters of the Tosa *yashiki* and other warrior residences in Edo, where Kyūemon performed according to the precise instructions of his supervisors.

Before we go on to examine the events and their meanings in detail, it is useful to characterize the nature of daimyo-sponsored ceramic production within Japan as of 1678. Until recently, Japanese ceramics of the Edo period have been studied chiefly in their aspect as an art form, giving the mistaken impression that most ceramics were tea bowls or vases and that pottery was associated primarily with aesthetic expression or leisure-time amusement of cultivated daimyo and merchants. Current studies have begun to address the nature of pottery as a commodity, making use of archives and archaeological material excavated from sites of daimyo mansions, temples, and merchant compounds.[2] Widespread daimyo engagement in the sponsorship of ceramic production coincided with the arrival of Korean potters in Japan in the aftermath of the Bunroku and Keichō military campaigns (1592–98) and was encouraged by the reallocation of domains under the new Tokugawa government. It is becoming clear that, from the outset, pottery's primary importance to most daimyo sponsors was as a source of revenue. Production of ceramics for the sake of presentation or personal cultivation, when it did take place, was an added embellishment to a sound base of commercial products such as rice bowls, sake bottles, or storage jars.

As is well known, the Japanese campaigns in Korea in the last decade of the sixteenth century, whatever their military outcome, had the energizing effect of introducing new repertories of Korean technology, including refined glazed ceramics, into Japan. Korean ceramic technology not only revitalized existing production centers such as Mino but also was the basis for establishing new industries, especially in Kyushu and western Honshu. The most successful of those enterprises still flourish today, notably in Arita,

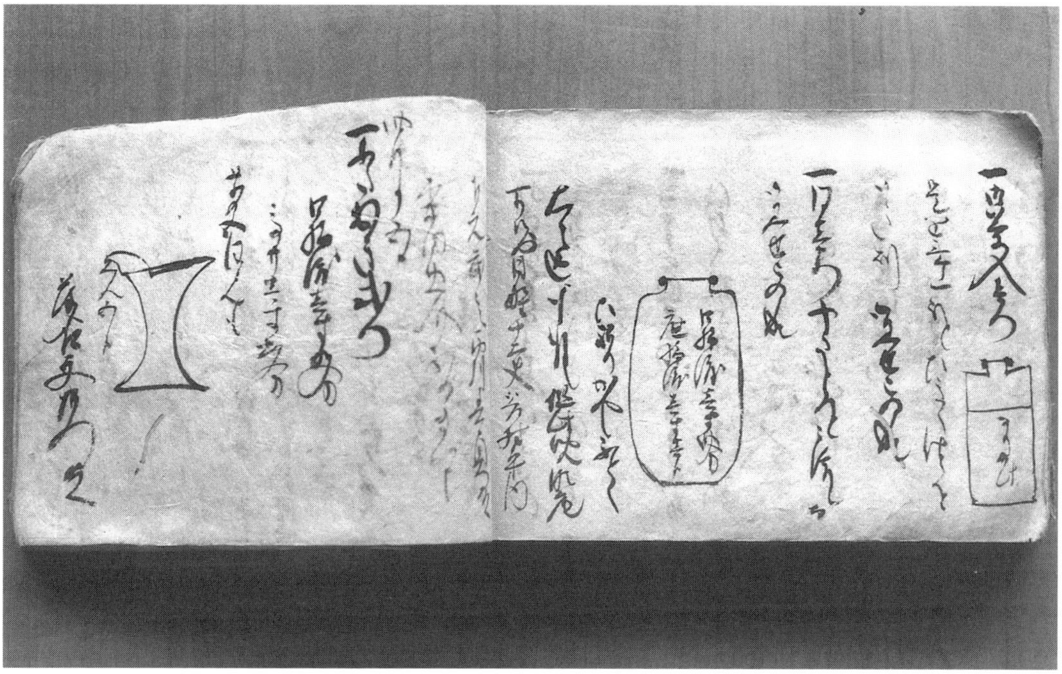

Figure 5.1 Double page from Morita Kyūemon's diary (1679, fourth month, days four and five), showing sketches of two tea caddies and a tea-kettle lid rest for which he received commissions, with notes on details of shape and glaze. Courtesy of the Morita family, Kōchi.

Karatsu, and Hagi. What is not generally understood is how many fledgling domain-based ceramics industries did not take hold. Some were cut short by the major reorganization of landholding in 1600, after the Tokugawa victory at Sekigahara, when some would-be patrons on the losing side were dispossessed of their land. Such may have been the case with the Chōsokabe house, which lost its base in Tosa to the Yamauchi clan and with it a pottery production said to have been started by a Korean potter. (This local lore was formerly discounted, but archaeological evidence of Korean-style ash-glazed pottery in the lowest level of one Tosa kiln site now seems to support it.) Other potteries floundered during the first several decades of the seventeenth century, when the Edo government continued to shift daimyo from domain to domain in search of a perfect balance of allies and former opponents. During those decades, even certain settled domains found their economies unable to support overly ambitious production of would-be luxury ceramics that could not match the quality and prestige of Kyoto wares from commercial kilns in the old capital, Seto products backed by the Owari branch of the Tokugawa house, or Chinese imports. Still other domains succeeded so well that they exhausted their resources, especially timber to fuel the kilns.

A decisive moment in the emergence of the Japanese ceramics industry took place in 1637, when the Saga domain thoroughly reorganized the structure of porcelain production at Arita, limiting the number of workshops and controlling access to raw materials with the goal of stable, regulated growth. Enterprising Osaka merchants stepped in to distribute Arita's products domestically, while the Dutch East India Company transported the wares overseas to an eager new market. By the 1660s, the revenues of this flourishing industry could support the establishment of a separate workshop to produce the luxury porcelain that we know as Nabeshima ware, for private use by the Nabeshima house.

In Tosa, by 1653, the unwelcome impact on local markets of ceramics from Hizen province—Karatsu stoneware as well as Arita porcelain—was the impetus for the Yamauchi house to consider financing the establishment of its own pottery workshop. This pragmatic decision was typical of actions taken by the second head of the domain, Tadayoshi, to create a secure base for the Tosa economy. "If Tosa too has good clay that can be made into pottery," he wrote in the document authorizing the project, "the clay will prove to be a treasure; moreover it will provide everyday crockery for the warriors in our service and the humblest inhabitants of our domain."[3]

Domain officers contacted an Osaka potter named Kuno Shōhaku, who agreed to take on the project and—most agreeably—did not contest the modest stipend proposed by the parsimonious Tadayoshi. Shōhaku located clay suitable for making glazed pottery within Tosa, although he dashed one of Tadayoshi's hopes by failing to find raw materials for porcelain that might have competed with Arita's wares. During his five-year stay in Tosa, Shōhaku built kilns both in Kōchi and in the Nakamura branch domain, and he trained two local youths, both sons of low-ranking samurai, as his successors. Morita Kyūemon was one of those boys.[4]

In his practical way, Tadayoshi conceived that a domain-sponsored pottery should yield both utilitarian crockery and refined pieces suitable for dining, display in formal reception rooms, temple use, or presentation. (In this he followed the precedent of potteries established earlier in other domains, where in some cases two separate workshops operated to produce distinct types of ware; such was the practice in Satsuma, for example, one of the domains that received immigrant Korean potters. Kilns in the village of Naeshirogawa made black-glazed utilitarian pottery, while a workshop close by the domain's castle produced white-bodied ceramics for *chanoyu* or tea ceremony use.) Local records suggest that the Odo pottery was modestly successful on both accounts during its first twenty years of activity. Shōhaku's first firing contained assorted ceramic shapes for *chanoyu*, display, and dining—"tea caddies, tea bowls, tea-ceremony water jars, vases, incense burners, and dishes."[5] After the devastating Meireki fire of 1657 in Edo destroyed many warrior residences, Odo pottery was sent to restock the Tosa establishment.[6] But domain documents do not record any presentations of Odo ware to other daimyo, suggesting that domain officials judged that the products were not yet worthy of wider distribution.

The man who became the fourth head of the Yamauchi house in 1669 brought a different outlook to domain affairs, and he began to use the revenues of the strong economy that Tadayoshi had established to raise Tosa's cultural reputation. Toyomasa himself enjoyed activities typical of cultivated and prosperous daimyo: he practiced Nō-drama chanting (*utai*), built a flower garden in Kōchi Castle, and socialized with Uji tea merchants and other representatives of culture from Kamigata (the Osaka-Kyoto region). Not surprisingly, he also turned his attention toward more aggressive development of Odo pottery as a presentation ware. Acutely aware of Edo tastes and standards, Toyomasa realized that Odo products needed to be polished and updated. He and his advisors planned the sequence of events recorded in Morita Kyūemon's diary to which we now turn.

Improvement of the Odo repertory depended upon the pottery master's detailed knowledge of current daimyo taste as reflected in the products of other daimyo-sponsored kilns as well as in wares from kilns in Kyoto. That knowledge was to be sought by firsthand visits to the sources of such pottery, not simply by examination of the finished products, which had already taken place in Kōchi. Kyūemon followed the usual route from Tosa to Edo (Map 5.1), but conveniently that route allowed him to visit all the key ceramic production centers located between Osaka and Edo.

Among commercially sponsored kilns, Kyūemon visited Takahara and Naniwa in Osaka, Asahi in Uji, and six workshops within Kyoto, beginning with the famed Omuro kiln operated by Nonomura Ninsei.[7] In Kyoto, Kyūemon observed that, although the techniques used by capital potters were familiar, the products were innovative, departing from the orthodox wheel-thrown forms that he had learned from Kuno Shōhaku. Kyūemon noted hanging vases in the shape of bamboo flutes; incense burners shaped like shrimps, mandarin ducks, and pheasants; and plates formed like abalone shells. His later records of the pots he made in Edo show that he attempted deer-shaped incense burners, molded plates, and other complex sculptural forms representing the height of Kyoto fashion.

Kyūemon's guide to Omuro was the merchant Izutsuya Han'emon, whose

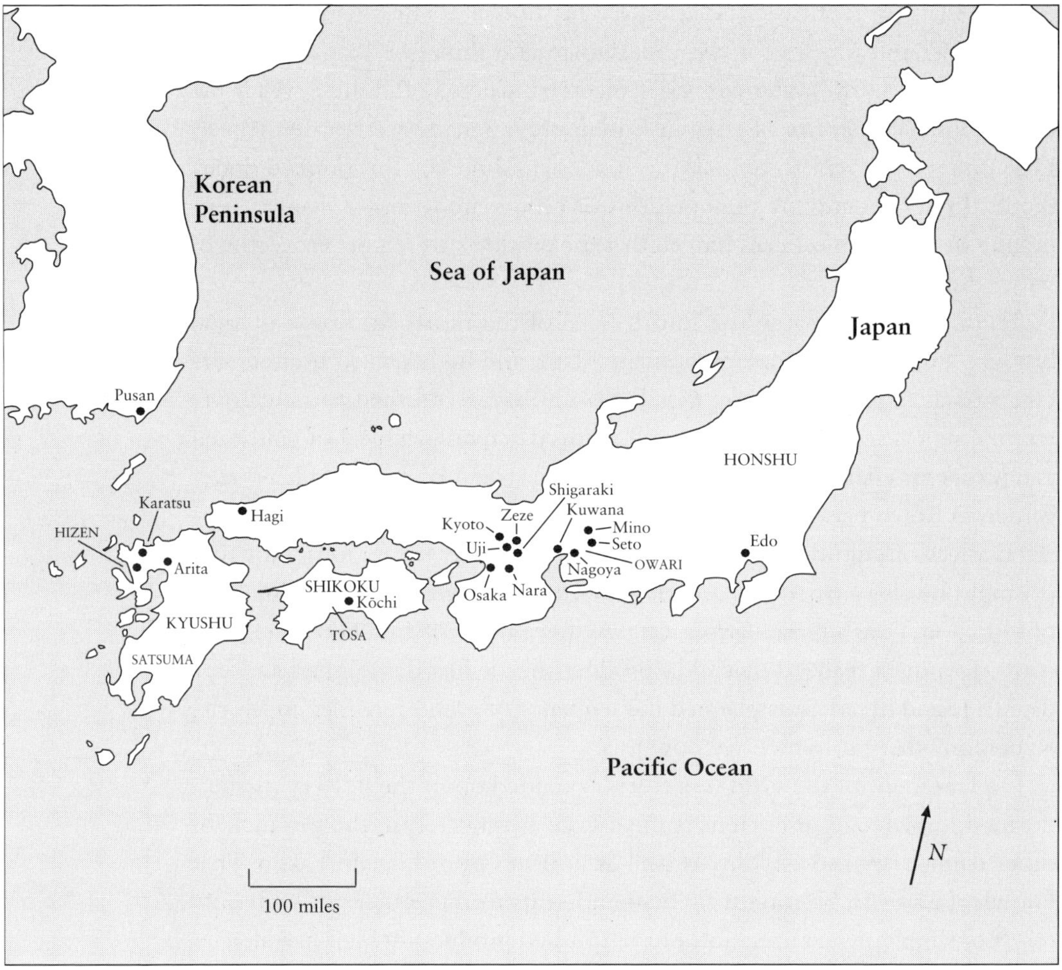

Map 5.1 Map of Morita Kyūemon's Journey from Tosa to Edo, 1678.

dry-goods firm served the Tosa domain and whose pedigree included an ancestor who had been a *chanoyu* disciple of the influential tea master Sen no Rikyū (1522–91). Supported by such credentials of Kyoto good taste, Han'emon's diverse services to the Tosa domain included advising on the acquisition of gifts to be presented to the shogun and on the purchase of antiques for the domain collection. Kyūemon records that he asked the merchant whether there wasn't a system for learning connoisseurship (*mekiki*) of ceramics. Han'emon (who must have been amused at the rustic potter's naïve expectation) responded that experience was the only teacher. Once in Edo, Kyūemon must frequent antique dealers' shops to study old pieces. This procedure suggested by the cultivated Kyoto merchant does not seem to have been part of the original plan devised by the domain officers. Immediately upon reaching Edo, Kyūemon therefore sought approval for, and subsequently made, regular visits to shops of dealers, known as *karamonoya*, where he handled Chinese tea caddies and Korean tea bowls, even borrowing some to make copies.

Kyūemon's visits to daimyo-sponsored kilns at Zeze, Kuwana, and Seto and to the kilns in Shigaraki, a domain directly administered by the Tokugawa government, required elaborate arrangements that were coordinated by Tosa domain officers based in Kyoto and Edo.[8] Production at Zeze, Kuwana, and Seto centered on Chinese-style tea caddies, which numbered among the essential possessions of a warrior. The brown-glazed jarlets were part of the equipment for customary socializing and entertainment in the form of *chanoyu*; upon the owner's death, they passed in sets along with swords as heirlooms to male relatives and colleagues. Accordingly, daimyo kilns placed emphasis on the pedigree of their wares. The officer of the Zeze domain who received Kyūemon spoke proudly of Zeze tea caddies that had been presented to Tokugawa Ieyasu (1542–1616), founder of the Tokugawa government. Still more impressively, the three "official" (*goyō*) potters in Seto, who worked directly for the Owari branch of the Tokugawa house (within whose domain Seto lay), boasted of their ancestor who had traveled to China 450 years earlier to study Chinese ceramics at the source. As the result of this illustrious founder, Seto tea caddies held pride of place in warrior collections, second only to Chinese pieces.[9]

Once in Edo, Kyūemon's principal activity—the key element of the domain's strategy for Odo pottery—was an innovative form of direct marketing that also served as a means of obtaining firsthand knowledge of the individual tastes of respected daimyo connoisseurs. Using a portable potter's wheel and clay brought from Tosa, Kyūemon conducted demonstrations of throwing and trimming ceramic forms in various warrior reception rooms. In a carefully orchestrated series of thirty demonstrations presented before Toyomasa, other members of the Yamauchi house, other daimyo, *dōbōshū* (cultural advisors in the service of the shogunal government), and high-ranking government administrators, Kyūemon advertised the Odo product at the same time as he received direct instruction for refinement of form and execution.[10]

The most remarkable aspect of the instruction is that it extended beyond verbal commands to direct manipulation of the freshly thrown clay form by Toyomasa and other distinguished warriors. Kyūemon's diary describes this hands-on procedure as "adding irregularity (*ifū*)." That this procedure took Kyūemon by surprise is evident from his record of seeking clarification after its first occurrence (when Toyomasa bent the rim of a tea bowl). Nishikawa Shuntei, who served the Tosa establishment in Edo as *sadō* or specialist in *chanoyu* and related social skills, explained to the potter that *ifū* (usually an indentation in the rim) defined the "front" of a tea bowl. Japanese connoisseurs had long admired distortion of the regular, wheel-thrown ceramic form, particularly in tea bowls. Such irregularities originated as accidents of handling or firing, but beginning in the late sixteenth century Japanese potters added the distortions intentionally. In the course of Kyūemon's demonstrations, adding *ifū* became the prerogative of the daimyo who literally left his mark on the vessel made to his order before his eyes.

The concept of pottery making as performance that Kyūemon's demonstrations embodied underlay a special form of ceramic production called *niwayaki*, which emerged in the early seventeenth century. In this "garden pottery," the entire process of making and firing pots was conducted using small kilns built within the private estates of wealthy sponsors, who amused themselves as amateur potters while professionals oversaw the technical aspects of preparing the raw materials, glazing, and firing. In Nagoya, Kyūemon heard about the earliest known daimyo-sponsored garden kiln, located within Nagoya Castle and operated by the Seto "official" potters.[11] But the most prestigious garden kiln of the day operated on the premises of the Shugakuin Detached Palace in Kyoto, abode of retired emperor Gomizuno'o (1596–1680). Kyūemon delayed his departure from Kyoto by several days while waiting—unsuccessfully, as it turned out—for permission to visit that elite workshop, which may have served as Toyomasa's chief inspiration.

Kyūemon's first Edo demonstrations were trial runs that took place within the Tosa residence before an audience of Toyomasa and his guests. Finally Toyomasa felt sufficient confidence in the procedure to authorize the potter's demonstration at a banquet whose chief guest was Sakai Uta-no-kami Tadakiyo (1624–81), a relative of Toyomasa by marriage but also the *tairō* or Great Elder at the apex of the Tokugawa administrative structure. Toyomasa was delighted when Uta-no-kami gave his blessing to the project by praising Kyūemon as "handsome, intelligent, and so neatly dressed that he does not resemble an artisan. On top of that, his work is excellent." Clearly, as a criterion for a drawing-room demonstration of pottery, the potter's appearance superseded mere skill.

Four days later, Uta-no-kami commanded a demonstration by Kyūemon at his own residence. In preparation, Kyūemon received explicit instructions from the domain officials that, if asked whether the pieces he threw for Uta-no-kami could be fired in Edo, he was to reply that they would have to be taken back to Tosa to be fired in the Odo kiln. Indeed, that very question was posed to Kyūemon, and he replied exactly as instructed. Why was the issue of firing in Tosa so important? Should Toyomasa have wished, it would have been possible for Kyūemon to fire pieces in Edo; Kyūemon visited two thriving commercial kilns in Edo and even bought samples from them.[12] Moreover, by that time a garden kiln staffed by the three official potters from Seto is believed to have been operating occasionally within the Toyama detached residence of the Owari Tokugawa domain.[13] Firing in the Toyama kiln (provided it were not forbidden to an outside potter) or in one of the commercial kilns, however, could have revealed to rivals the shapes that Toyomasa hoped to develop as trademark pieces of the Odo kiln. Conversely, firing in the Odo kiln would firmly establish the Tosa identity of those special pieces destined for presentation to the warriors who had helped design them.

Once Kyūemon's demonstration for Uta-no-kami had been completed successfully, Toyomasa could send the potter out to mansions of other government officials. After each demonstration, Kyūemon repeated the procedure piece by piece for Toyomasa and received instructions on which shapes to "take back to Tosa to serve as models." In particular, Toyomasa requested four government officials, all known for their connoisseurship and their family collections of antique *chanoyu* ceramics, and all with close ties to the Yamauchi house, to serve as Kyūemon's aesthetic advisors. To those men Kyūemon made repeated visits to receive orders for specific pieces as well as criticism of his execution of those pieces.

When Kyūemon left Edo in the fifth month of 1679 to return to Tosa, he carried back a wealth of clay and paper models, verbal instruction, and experience. He bore orders from various well-placed officials, foremost of whom was Uta-no-kami. Toyomasa undoubtedly looked forward to a successful expansion of the Odo pottery production, on the basis of Kyoto forms, Edo polish, and Tosa flavor. But that expansion never took place. In 1680, upon the installation of the new shogun, Tsunayoshi, the once all-powerful Sakai Uta-no-kami Tadakiyo, implicated by his advocacy of an alternate successor, was removed from office, and his mansion where Kyūemon had demonstrated was confiscated; he died the following year. With the downfall of Uta-no-kami, several other men on whom Toyomasa had pinned his hopes also fell from power.

How those political events in Edo affected the reputation of the pottery from Tosa is not entirely clear. Other factors influencing the development of Odo ware included the skills of Kyūemon and his successors and market conditions, notably the continuing rise in status of Arita porcelain. Tosa domain records extending into the first several decades of the eighteenth century do show that gifts of Odo pottery were given on a regular basis to

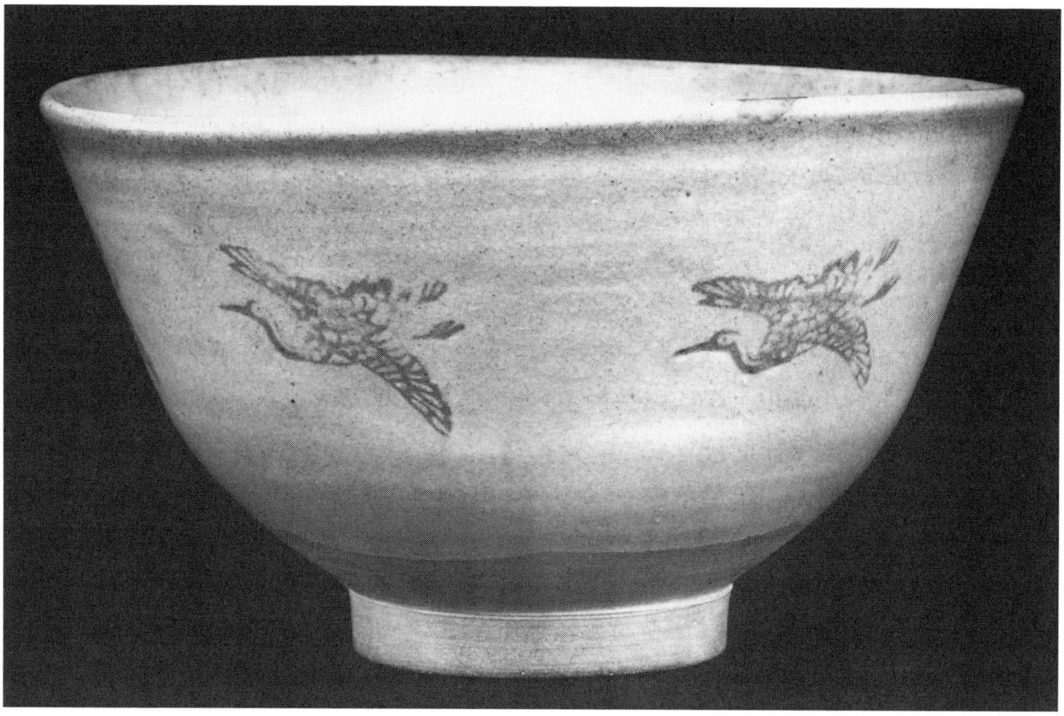

Figure 5.2 Odo ware tea bowl with stamped and inlaid design of six flying cranes. Shape of bowl closely follows a sixteenth-century Korean bowl form. Possibly seventeenth century. Courtesy of the Trustees of The British Museum, accession number 2084.

friendly daimyo and officials (Figure 5.2). Yet the ware never attained the reputation that would have qualified it for presentation to the shogun. In that sense, at least, Toyomasa's ambition was never realized. In the nineteenth century, domain policy shifted toward active encouragement of utilitarian pottery, while the Odo potters received explicit orders to cease production of luxury wares. Today Odo pottery is scarcely known outside the former Tosa domain, modern Kōchi prefecture. Only the chance survival of Morita Kyūemon's diary preserves the record of a bid for national fame by an ambitious daimyo with cultural aspirations.

Chapter Six

Artistic Identity and Ukiyo-e Prints: The Representation of Kitagawa Utamaro to the Edo Public

JULIE NELSON DAVIS

Her head resting on her hand, her brush wet with ink, the courtesan Hanaōgi of the Ōgiya house muses over the words she will use to begin a letter to her now absent lover (Figure 6.1). The artist, Kitagawa Utamaro (1753?–1806), has drawn her as though he had viewed this moment firsthand and "captured" it in this print. The composition implies that Utamaro was an intimate of the private world of the high-ranking courtesan, allowed to witness a part of her life not normally accessible to the outside observer. Any man knowledgeable in the pleasure district's mores would have considered himself fortunate to be received by her, but he likely would not have been present during a moment as private as this.

Indeed, the average visitor to the Yoshiwara pleasure district would have felt lucky just to witness the parade of a high-ranking courtesan in the company of her full entourage—a scene that, by this time, had become a standby in ukiyo-e. By contrast, Figure 6.1 illustrates Hanaōgi in a private reverie. The close-up view of her face suggests that Hanaōgi, even though beautifully dressed and with her hair in a perfect coiffure, may be unaware that she is the object of voyeuristic inquiry. Or perhaps she has allowed herself to be observed in her private occupations for the purpose of portraiture. Nevertheless, both narratives, which presuppose that this is the "real" Hanaōgi, are generated by the visual effects of the print itself. To take Utamaro's image for the real thing, as though it renders an individualized portrait of the actual person, however, is to consume the image as well as its rhetorical structures whole.

I propose an alternative reading: that these prints used text and image in a strategy to persuade their audience of their "reality," and as such they

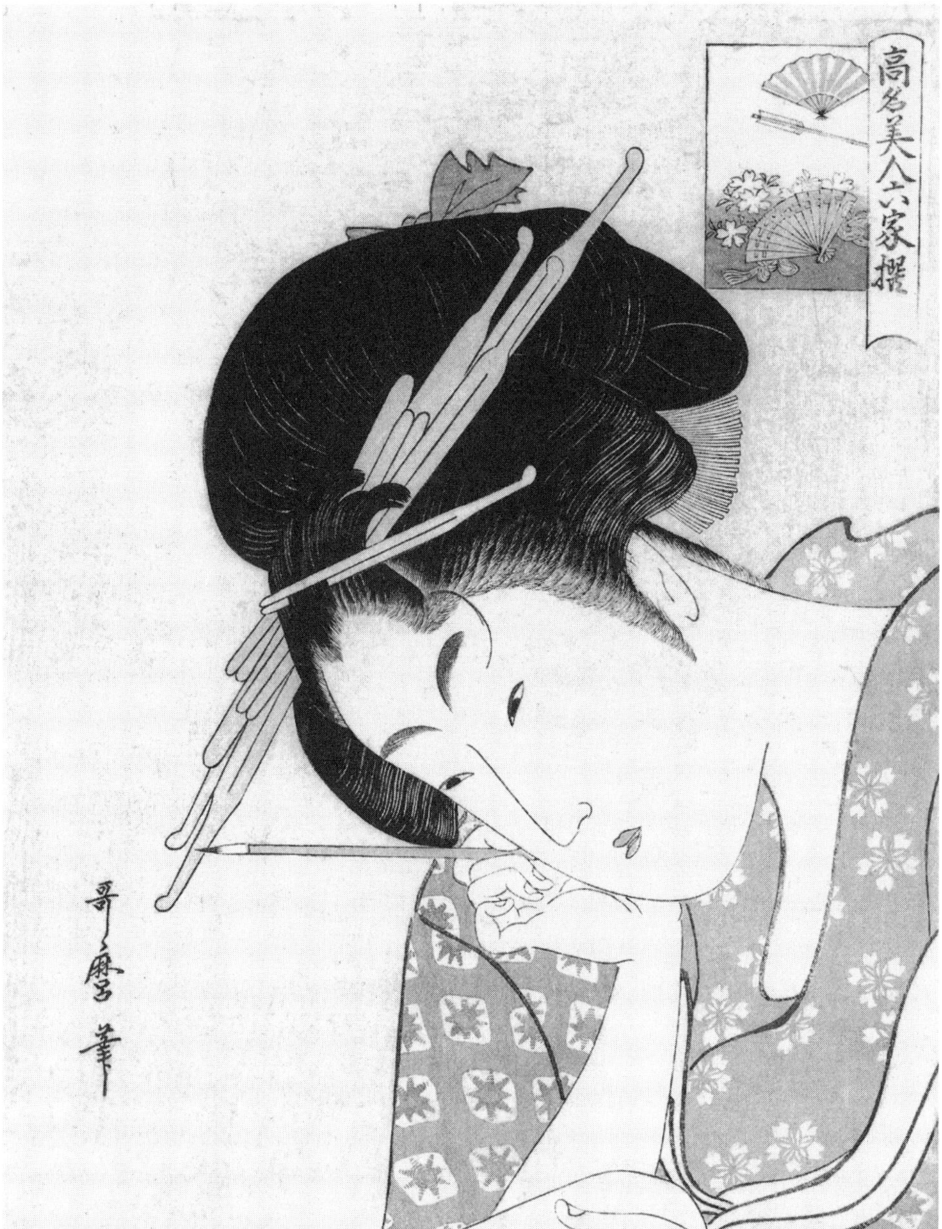

Figure 6.1 Kitagawa Utamaro (1754–1806). *Kōmei bijin rokkasen: Ōgiya Hanaōgi (Famous Beauties Likened to the Six Immortal Poets: Hanaōgi of the Ōgiya)*, ca. 1798. Ink and color on paper, 38.6 cm x 26.2 cm. Clarence Buckingham Collection, 1925.3824. Photograph courtesy of the Art Institute of Chicago.

operated with the purpose of promoting the artist along paradigmatic lines.[1] Ingenious publishers used a strategy of discursive replication to influence audience interpretation. Reciprocally, viewer response would have affected the success or failure of their enterprise, as well as the selection of successive subjects and modes of representation. Ukiyo-e images were constructed both for and by their audience in a coordinated interplay of supply and demand. Utamaro's images therefore played with the ukiyo-e "codes" understood by audience, artists, and publishers. That the operations of his images in this manner have frequently been interpreted as revealing Utamaro's ability to portray the "psychological" state of his subjects, based on an inferred direct observation, proves the efficacy of this strategy.

Utamaro is rightly recognized as one of the most important figures in the history of ukiyo-e. His body of documented work numbers well over two thousand designs in paintings, prints, and illustrated books.[2] Their production testifies to an ukiyo-e market that embraced the pleasures and leisure activities of late-eighteenth-century Edo (present-day Tokyo). But to read his designs as transparently representative of his personal experience is to believe that he observed women such as Hanaōgi, and others, in their natural environments. This chapter argues that the Utamaro we seem to know from his art is a carefully constructed personality expressed through the objects bearing his signature.

Three established paradigms for artistic excellence were manipulated in the description of the artist known as "Utamaro." All three are present in the depiction of Hanaōgi. These concepts were expressed in the rendering of the subjects as well as in the texts associated with the images. First, Utamaro was delineated as a "naturalist," an expert in drawing all forms of living beings. He was an artist who was able to turn that talent toward all that he observed, even Hanaōgi herself. Second, Utamaro was presented as a true "artist." This is evidenced in the rendering of Hanaōgi that seems to preserve Utamaro's hand, just as it is also reinforced in the signature, "from the brush of Utamaro," a phrase linking concepts of artistic mastery with his name. Third is the implied appearance of an intimacy with his subjects. Not only does Utamaro seem to have gained privileged access into the inner zones of the Yoshiwara, but he even appears to understand the very thoughts of his subjects. Other rhetorical paradigms can be linked to the name of Utamaro, but these three—naturalism, talent, sophistication—are primary signifiers of genius used in the strategy of promoting Utamaro as an artist of merit. Before launching into a discussion of these artistic paradigms, it would be helpful to set the background within which they occurred.

THE UKIYO-E MARKET AND BRAND NAMES

The marketing of Utamaro manipulated period concepts of merit that were more commonly used in other established artistic traditions. This was not a new strategy in ukiyo-e publishing. Prints and illustrated books were part of a consumer culture, and their makers—designers, writers, and publishers—became associated with specific genres and talents. Ukiyo-e lineages, such as the Katsukawa, Torii, or Kitao "schools," were expected to make images in a certain style or genre, and their school affiliation functioned as a "brand name" in the ukiyo-e market. Those outside established lineages, such as Okumura Masanobu (ca. 1686–1764) and Suzuki Harunobu (1724–70), were defined through other means, but their names too became linked with their images in a similar fashion.[3] Writers of popular fiction also became brand names and employed strategies of authorship familiar in literary theory. For example, Santō Kyōden (1761–1823) was a master at manipulating authorial guises.[4] That writers and print designers, like Kyōden and Utamaro, could achieve name-brand status should not be unexpected, however, in an urban culture where Kabuki actors and courtesans achieved celebrity status.

The production of cultural fame took advantage of the growth of wealth and leisure in eighteenth-century Edo. Tokugawa society in Utamaro's day was nominally organized according to a Neo-Confucian order that stressed appropriate behavior according to social class and status.[5] A significant military population was necessary in the city of Edo for the operation of the Tokugawa shogunal government (*bakufu*), which paid strict attention to perceived incursions of its rule. The large population of merchants and artisans, the suppliers of the city's goods and services, responded to shogunal control with practices that flouted restrictions without actually contravening them. This community was the target audience for ukiyo-e, and they supported an extensive publishing industry that included ukiyo-e prints and an array of literary genres from light fiction to serious works.

Concrete information about the cost of ukiyo-e prints does not survive to this day. Prints do, however, appear to have been relatively inexpensive within the broader publishing industry. The frequently cited comment by writer Santō Kyōden that a single sheet print was sold for about 20 *mon*—about the same price as a bowl of noodles—indicates that at least some prints were not costly.[6] Unfortunately, Kyōden does not describe what kind of print that was, and it seems likely that the prices for prints ranged from the expensive to the inexpensive, depending on quality, format, size, and special effects. Also unknown is the number of sheets constituting a print "run," but in Utamaro's lifetime it seems likely that an edition would be on the order of several thousand.

In the mid-eighteenth century, the population of the shogunal capital of Edo exceeded one million.[7] The sale of prints and other published material at the end of the eighteenth century would have benefited greatly from a culture of capitalistic enterprise where marketing products, and celebrity, were widely understood. Ukiyo-e prints were increasingly regarded as Edo specialties; already by the mid-eighteenth century prints were called "*Azuma nishiki-e*," or "brocade pictures of the East." This term suggests that prints could compete with the famous brocade fabrics of the imperial capital, Kyoto.[8] Perhaps prints were one additional aspect of a rivalry that sometimes defined Edo as "up-to-date" and Kyoto as "traditional," and to define ukiyo-e prints as specialties of Edo also promoted them beyond its borders. In such an environment, the marketing of an artistic persona for someone like Utamaro may be regarded as complicit in ongoing contests of the zones of "culture" and regional identities.

Ukiyo-e prints were made in a collaborative process. The designer (the "artist") submitted a drawing to the publisher, the producer of the project. In the case of the print of Hanaōgi (see Figure 6.1), this was Ōmiya Gonkurō, and he, like other publishers, is identified by the crest included on the print. The publisher also hired or kept on staff block carvers, printers, and shop assistants who produced the work from the artist's drawing. Artists may have been consulted during the process, but exactly how much someone like Utamaro contributed to the final appearance of the print, beyond the submission of the drawing, is unknown. In the later eighteenth and early nineteenth centuries, the names of shop artisans (that is, carvers and printers) are infrequently included on single-sheet prints, in contrast to book colophons, which often named them. When required by the *bakufu*, approval by the publishing guild is seen in the inclusion of the *kiwame* (guarantee) seal, otherwise known as the censor's seal.

In spite of the collaborative nature of the venture, however, prints seem to have been called in their day, as they are now, by the name of the designer whose signature is prominently displayed on the final print.[9] The signature designates authorship of the image: the name Utamaro becomes synonymous with it as a brand name.[10] As a result, the authorial function in prints also works in the same way as in literature: being engaged in an imagined Utamaro scene is to be transported into a world associated with that author, with all that Utamaro represented. The manipulation of the semiotic associations surrounding the name Utamaro indicate that the authorial function was understood, and exploited for particular effects.

THE HISTORICAL PERSON VERSUS THE UTAMARO PERSONA

Writing a biography for Utamaro is difficult. The facts that remain must be evaluated by the status they occupy as evidence. Distinctions between records that served state or official purposes and those that served as reportage must be maintained, and evidence must also be critiqued according to the purpose it served at the time. In Utamaro's case, documents that may be considered to have official status are scarce. This complicates the question of separating the historical person from the Utamaro persona. Records regarding the date or place of his birth, his family lineage, his possible marriage or children, or other activities are no longer extant.[11] The most secure of his dates, that of his death in Bunka 3 (1806), comes from his grave site. But the stele is a modern reconstruction from records that are long destroyed, hindering the assessment of their authenticity (Figure 6.2).[12]

The next level of evidence, that of personal effects, such as letters and diaries, does not remain. Notations found in period books by friends and acquaintances point to Utamaro's alliances with the *au courant*, establishing him as one of their own. These and other citations are valuable indications of the regard Utamaro received in poetry and ukiyo-e circles. However, since they were included in books intended to inform their audiences that these were the names worth knowing, their status as facts must be regarded with an eye to their ambition of promoting their own reputation.[13]

What may be regarded as the first canon of ukiyo-e, the *Ukiyo-e ruikō*, was being compiled during Utamaro's lifetime, and it remains the most important text for ukiyo-e history in the premodern period. Versions survive in manuscript, with apparent variations. *Ukiyo-e ruikō* was not circulated in printed form during the Edo period (1615–1868). It was begun by Ōta Nanpo (1749–1823) in 1790, and additions continued to be made into the nineteenth century.[14] Modern Japanese historians have published analyses of the text, but a complete English translation has yet to be published.

The earliest extant copy, called the *Ukiyo-e kōshō*, is dated to 1802. Period aficionados Sasaya Shishichi Kuninori, Santō Kyōden, and Shikitei Sanba (1776–1822) updated Nanpo's text. The son of an impoverished samurai and scholar of Chinese classics, Nanpo was a leading literary figure in Edo. Along with the popular writers Kyōden and Sanba, he traveled in many of the same circles as Utamaro; their understanding of ukiyo-e would probably have been based upon personal interactions and information then available in the publishing shops. Information about earlier ukiyo-e figures may have come from writings then available, from prints and illustrated books, or from oral accounts. The *Ukiyo-e kōshō* edition is limited mainly to painters and the ma-

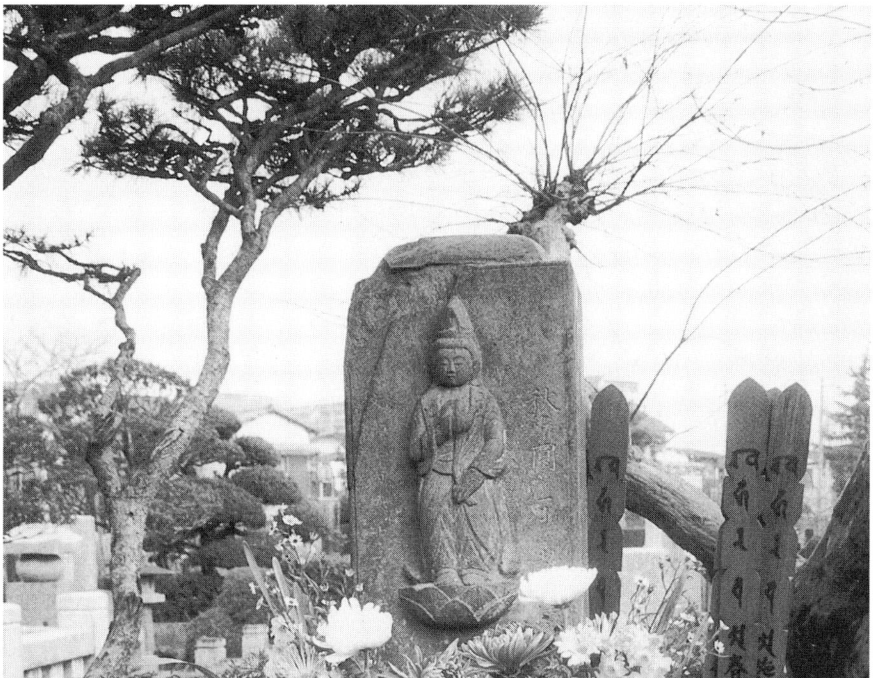

Figure 6.2 Utamaro's grave stele at Senkōji. Julie Nelson Davis photograph.

jor designers, while later versions of the *Ukiyo-e ruikō* include more names and works. Distinctions made in the text between painters and designers of various print types indicate an active hierarchy of discrimination between makers and their type of object.

The entry on Utamaro included in the *Ukiyo-e kōshō* is brief:

> Kitagawa Utamaro, personal name Yūsuke.
>
> At the start entered the studio of Toriyama Sekien and studied pictures in the Kano school [style]. Later [he] drew pictures of the styles and manners of men and women and resided temporarily with *ezōshiya* [picture-bookseller] Tsutaya Jūzaburō. Now lives in Benkeibashi [Edo]. Many *nishiki-e* [full-color prints].[15]

With the exception of his personal name and place of residence, this entry tells us little more about Utamaro's biography than could be gleaned from his extant oeuvre. It does suggest, however, that the associations between Utamaro and such figures as his teacher, Toriyama Sekien, and his publisher, Tsutaya Jūzaburō, were significant. It also points to their status as two names in the ukiyo-e world. The Kano school name would have imparted prestige, as would the reference that he was a designer of the *nishiki-e* (a more prestigious and costly technique than others). As this version was written by those most familiar with Utamaro, it is among the most useful for biographical purposes.

A more important form of evidence is Utamaro's oeuvre. Utamaro's paintings, prints, illustrated books, and other works have been organized in a chronology constructed through using dates, when available in the works themselves or determined through associations with events, and through a charting of stylistic transformations.[16] A few drawings attributed to Utamaro remain, but they do not reveal much about his artistic process. Analysis of patterns of production, such as shifts from designing modest illustrated books to full-color poetry albums, is important in establishing movements from one medium to another as it also verifies shifts in relationships between the designer, his publisher(s), and his audience(s). Much can be derived from careful examination of Utamaro's body of work.

Within this corpus of work are Utamaro-signed prints and illustrated books that include texts appearing to reveal his artistry and personality. Unfortunately, the authorship of these texts is unknown. Texts appearing on Utamaro materials seem to suggest they were written by Utamaro himself, but it seems worthwhile to recognize that these may not have been written by the artist. Their authorship should, I suggest, be regarded as uncertain. Likewise, texts written by authors that take Utamaro as their subject and that appear in objects illustrated by Utamaro should also not be taken as documentary in intent. These texts were more than merely historical accounts. Instead, they function more to promote Utamaro than to divulge him to the audience.

Such texts would be better understood as information deliberately delivered to a public conditioned to interpret it in a conventionalized manner. Like the details revealed about the private lives of courtesans and Kabuki actors, these notations functioned to attract the attention of an audience interested in celebrities. The task of promoting Utamaro would not have been borne entirely by the text. The image too would have added its own reifying power. The manipulation of information combined through text and image to the audience was meant to perpetuate and produce celebrity. This approach influenced the audience of the day, and it continues to have an impact today.[17]

As Roland Barthes (1915–80) pointed out, texts and images of this kind cannot be read as "the voice of a single person, the author 'confiding' in us," but must be read as illusionistic elements that function to construct the author (artist) in the mind of the reader (viewer).[18] This idea can be applied to our understanding of Utamaro and taken beyond reading the texts to considering how the "language" of painting also transmitted concepts of artistic authority. Like text, images manipulate the interpretive response, and formal elements confer meanings that influence the viewer's understanding. Line, texture, and color, along with other formal elements, function as signifiers in a larger visual language. Even a single brush stroke may refer to an entire artistic and critical tradition.[19] In China and Japan, the marks left by the brush worked within an economy of signification and reception, in a "cultured sensitivity to brush dynamics,"[20] that was the very foundation of painting.

Painting seems to have been the standard against which ukiyo-e was measured. The *Ukiyo-e ruikō* makes this clear in how artists are described: those who are noted as painters are accorded higher status than those who remained associated with prints. For example, Hishikawa Moronobu (ca. 1618–94) is described as a master of both *Yamato-e*, construed there as a reference to classical painting, and of *Japanese* painting, the latter category encompassing all forms of painting practiced in Japan at the time.[21] Harunobu, likewise, is noted as the innovator of the *nishiki-e* and elevated by the designation "Yamato-eshi," or master painter of *Yamato-e*.[22]

These and other period comments attest to the degree to which the art of the brush held a higher place than that of the print. Evidence of that attitude is also seen in the way that the "painterly line" is often preserved in ukiyo-e prints. The act of reproducing the line signifies that the brush movements of the hand of the painter were deemed essential. Duplicating the shape of the line from the preparatory drawing as it was carved into the woodblock is evidence that the line was charged with significance: it preserved the "hand" of the "artist." This suggests that for both producers and viewers the reproduction of the "mark of the artist" demonstrating a high level of technical facility signified the artistic value of painting. Combined with the right kind of text too, the discursive effects of the brush could associate the designer with *painting* in a move that would serve to elevate him, along with his viewers, to a new level.

THE MAKING OF THE UTAMARO PERSONA: THE PUBLISHER TSUTAYA JŪZABURŌ AND THE ARTIST UTAMARO

Prior to his first publication with Tsutaya Jūzaburō (1750–97) in 1782, Utamaro studied painting and drawing with Toriyama Sekien (1712–88). Sekien is best known today for his illustrated books on ghosts and demons. He was a pupil under the Kano school artist Kano Gyokuen (1683–1727), a painter in the employ of the Tokugawa shogunate and the head of the Okachimachi branch of the Kano school. Sekien transmitted his knowledge of traditional painting to his students, who included Koikawa Harumachi (1744–89), Momokawa Chōki (fl. late eighteenth to early nineteenth century), the woman print designer Toriyama Sekiryū, Utamaro, and possibly Utagawa Toyoharu (1735–1814).[23] Sekien's role in transmitting the Kano school style, as well as his mastery of tea ceremony, flower arranging, and *haikai* poetry, to his students was significant.[24]

Some of Utamaro's earliest known images, produced under his first artistic nom de plume Toyoaki, appear in books published with Sekien as lead artist, including *Eternal Spring* (*Chiyo no haru*) of 1770. Utamaro also produced numerous illustrations for *kibyōshi* (yellow-backed novelettes) and other book formats during this early period, presumably under the supervision of Sekien. In the 1780s, Sekien frequented a circle that included *kyōka* ("crazy verse") poet Hōseidō Kisanji (1735–1813) and print designer Kitao Shigemasa (1739–1820). Kisanji and Shigemasa were working with publisher Tsutaya Jūzaburō at the time. It is undoubtedly through this circle that Utamaro became acquainted with the master publisher.[25]

It is probably no coincidence that the formation of the Utamaro persona follows the same pattern as did the career of his publisher, Tsutaya Jūzaburō.[26] Also known as Tsutajū, the publisher sponsored many popular writers and ukiyo-e print designers of the last quarter of the eighteenth century. By the time Tsutaya is said to have taken Utamaro into his shop, about 1782, he had published works of fiction by the aforementioned Harumachi and Kisanji, as well as produced technically and artistically fine printed albums by ukiyo-e designers. Nanpo wrote that he regarded Tsutaya's 1781 publication of one of

Kisanji's novelettes, *Virtue Seen like a Fleeting Dream* (*Miru ga toku issui no yume*), as the best of its class.[27] Such praise would no doubt boost Tsutaya's reputation. Tsutaya and Utamaro participated in Nanpo's poetry group under the pseudonyms "The Ivy That Clings" (*Tsuta no karamaru*) and "The Brush That Slips" (*Fude no ayamaru*), respectively. Their affiliation with Nanpo opened up possibilities for further collaboration, while such proclamations of quality surely brought recognition of Tsutaya and his stable to those who valued Nanpo's admiration.

The formation of the Utamaro persona began during the period of the artist's association with Tsutaya. Tsutaya's promotion of Utamaro was probably related to his own position as a relative newcomer to the field of full-color prints after having achieved success in other aspects of publishing in the 1770s. Operating from 1773 in a shop located outside the main gate of the Yoshiwara, Tsutaya had made his name as a publisher of guidebooks (*saiken*) that detailed information about the brothels, teahouses, and courtesans of Edo's Yoshiwara pleasure district. These guidebooks, and particularly those illustrated by Kitao Shigemasa bearing commentary by Nanpo, seem to have been extremely popular.[28]

Tsutaya's apparent financial success as a publisher of guidebooks enabled him to take risks, notably when he decided to break into the full-color print market. His publication of the *A Mirror of Comparisons of Beauties of the "Blue Towers"* (*Seirō bijin awase sugata kagami*, 1776), a luxuriously printed album of the famous courtesans of the quarter illustrated by Kitao Shigemasa and Katsukawa Shunshō (1726–92), appears to have been a coup in the publishing world.[29] Shigemasa and Shunshō were prominent artists of the 1770s, and the work represents the extent to which Tsutaya was willing to dedicate resources to high-quality productions in his attempt to outshine his rivals.

But a move into the field of full-color prints would have set Tsutaya against such well-established rivals as Nishimuraya Yōhachi and Tsuruya Kiemon, both of whom had shops in the heart of the publishing district of Toriabura-chō in Edo's Nihonbashi neighborhood. Tsutaya thus expanded his "stable" and astutely identified his niche in the market by gathering around him ukiyo-e figures such as Shigemasa, Shunshō, and their students, and many writers who frequented the Yoshiwara. In 1783 Tsutaya bought out the publisher Moriya Kohei and moved into the Toriabura-chō neighborhood, within close proximity of his rivals. Thereafter, there was no question of Tsutaya's intention to take over a part of the market for single-sheet prints.

Toyoaki changed his name to Utamaro in about 1781–82. This corresponds roughly to the beginning of his association with Tsutaya. A simple black and white print, dating to about 1782, pasted into Ōta Nanpo's sketch-

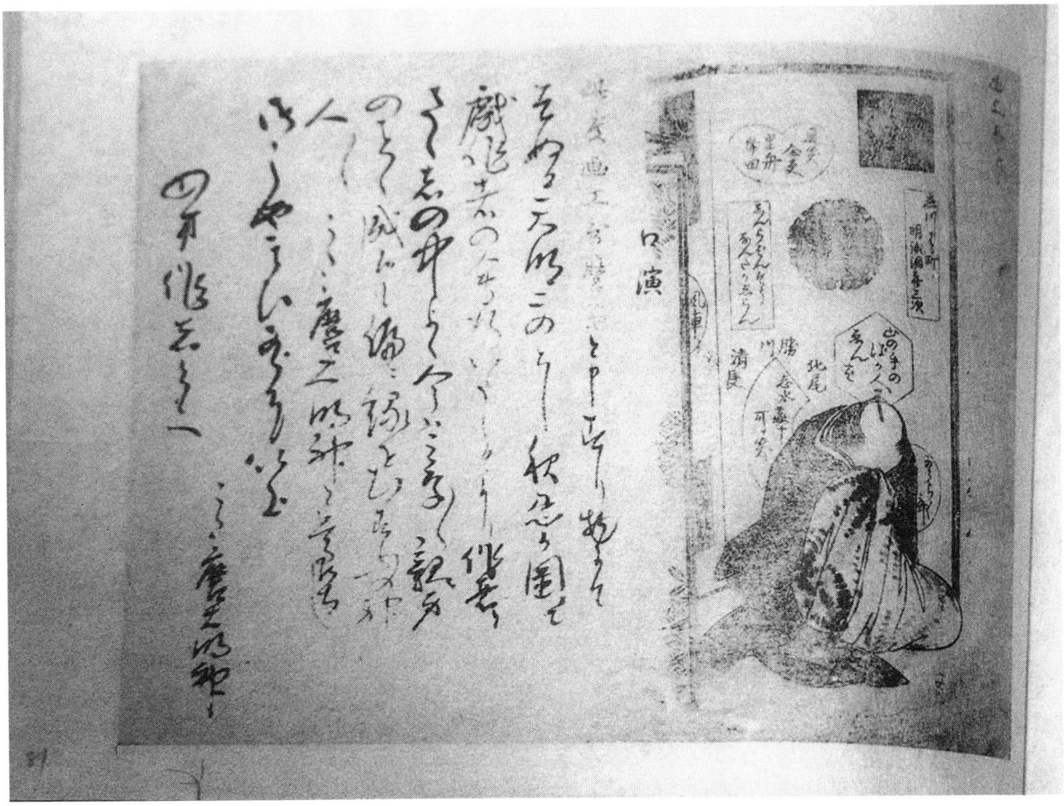

Figure 6.3 Utamaro. "The great god Utamaro," from *Ōta Nanpo's scrapbook* (*Shokusanjin hantori-cho*), assembled ca. 1783. Fragment of surimono woodblock print on right, notes by Nanpo on left. Photograph, facsimile edition of *Shokusanjin hantori-chō*, Beisandō, 1931 (original now missing).

book is one of the first indications of how this "new Utamaro" may have been launched into the world of ukiyo-e. Under the art name "Utamaro," the artist is shown bowing toward the viewer during what may have been his formal presentation to the artists and writers named on the print. These glitterati included the poets Nanpo and Akera Kanko (1740–99), the writers Harumachi and Kisanji, and the ukiyo-e masters Shigemasa, Shunshō, and Torii Kiyonaga (1752–1815; Figure 6.3). The short speech reproduced along the left is signed "the great god Utamaro," and his position before the names of these *ukiyo* cognoscenti suggests that he will soon join this elite rank.[30]

Tsutaya's familiarity with the Yoshiwara is manifest in his role as publisher of guidebooks for it. By contrast, Utamaro's connection to the Yoshiwara is uncertain, at least until his name appeared in 1783 on the roster of members of the Yoshiwara group for a "Who's Who" listing of *kyōka* groups.[31] Yet the precise nature of Utamaro's relationship with these poets (and with the courtesans of the Yoshiwara), and the role he may have played there, is largely unknown. Extant publications related to the poetry groups suggest he may have had close contact with the poets and their world.[32] These publications and his images have led us to presume a high degree of intimacy between Utamaro and the women of the quarters. Given the information that is presented in the prints, such a reading of intimacy seems quite natural. But in actual fact, the images have been contrived to appear so. Their purpose in promoting these celebrities must be taken into account when reviewing these texts.

Utamaro worked exclusively with Tsutaya until the mid-1790s. One of the images produced from their collaboration is in Figure 6.4; it dates to 1783 and portrays geisha preparing for the annual Niwaka festival. Its style imitates that of Torii Kiyonaga; it shows how much Utamaro, like other contemporaries, modeled his work on Kiyonaga at that time. Stylistic appropriation in ukiyo-e, and in Japanese art generally, is not unusual. It might have been seen as sincere flattery, but it also borrows from something proven to sell.

Utamaro's signature is displayed prominently on the left-hand side. Tsutaya's characteristic ivy-leaf crest, however, is not visible. Instead, the publisher's name appears on the book on the floor, which happens to be one of his Yoshiwara guidebooks. This not only renders Tsutaya's name synonymous with these publications, it also underscores his expertise on the pleasure quarter. Additionally, it makes the innuendo of how necessary Tsutaya's guidebooks were to be in-the-know about the Yoshiwara. By extension, Utamaro is tagged as having access to the Yoshiwara. But to assume that he did is to believe those codes as though they were representing the real. Instead, it is worth pointing out that the image does not inherently give the kind of information that would be useful evidence of his having been present at the scene. The women here, in their costumes, conform to set types; for all we know, the guidebook may be the source of Utamaro's information. The carefully placed details and the seemingly informal poses are meant to assert that Utamaro observed the scene.

"NATURAL TALENT": REGARDING INSECTS AND OTHERS

In 1788 Tsutaya published the anthology *Illustrated Book: Selected Insects* (*Ehon mushi erabi*) as a commission for a poetry group. It was illustrated by Utamaro and includes a postscript written by his teacher, Sekien (Figure 6.5). The depiction of the natural world in this manner is not one of the major genres in ukiyo-e. Rather, it is connected to *painting* traditions. Utamaro's album mimics painting through the "painterly" execution of the images, the swells and curves of the line of the brush and the gradation of tones and vivid color.

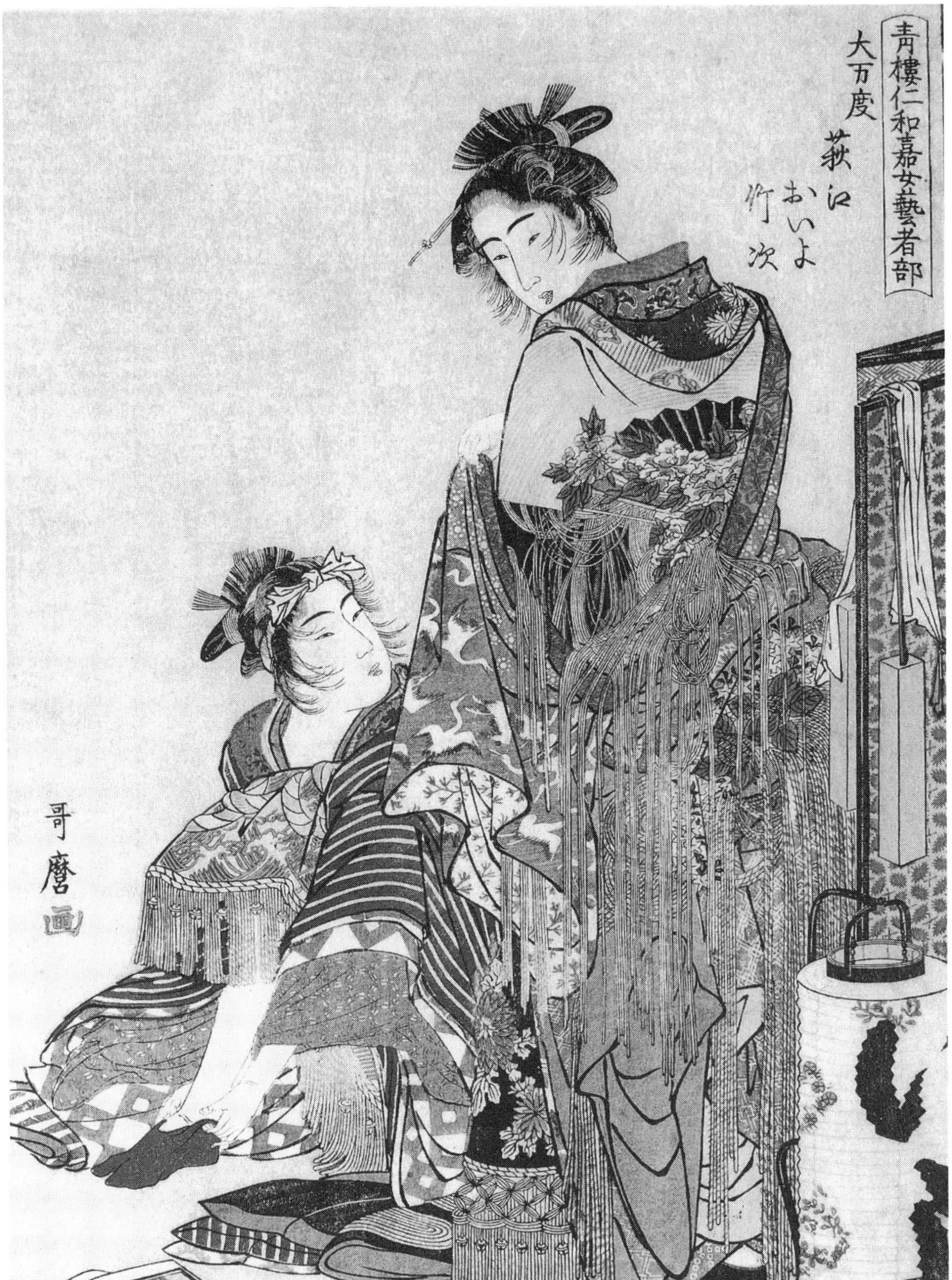

Figure 6.4 Utamaro. *Female geisha in the Niwaka Festival of the "Blue Towers": Oiyo and Takeji of the Ogie School in Ōmando Performance* (*Seirō niwaka onna geisha no bu: Ōmando: Ogie Oiyo, Takeji*), 1783. Nishiki-e, ōban format. Collection of the Tokyo National Museum.

Utamaro's play on painting genres is paralleled by the poets' verses that allude to poetic traditions. The appropriation of such legacies was intended to invoke high culture.

Utamaro's insects and amphibians in *Selected Insects* are arranged among flowers and plants in compositions that seem to have been drawn from life. Yet the images are clearly based upon previous codified traditions, namely, flowers-and-birds and fur-and-feathers. Utamaro learned how to paint in this manner from the Kano-trained Sekien, whose own woodblock printed *Sekien Painting-style* (*Sekien gafu*), published in 1774, used similar compositions and techniques. Sekien's postscript in Utamaro's work drew attention to Utamaro's special talent as well as his knowledge, claiming them as true to both tradition and nature:

> These are true pictures from the heart—my student Utamaro captures the life expressed in the being of the insects, and he follows the laws of painting in pictures and abides by the rules of the brush to draw life in its heart and spirit. Long ago, as a child, Mr. Uta, who cares for the details of things, was even in amusing himself someone who studied intently while playing with a dragonfly tied by a string (flap-flap) and by carrying crickets and grasshoppers in his palm. And I warned him often, fearful for that life (likeness) that so he deeply desired [to understand]. But now in the means of his brush, in truth and sincerity he has burnished the virtue of his deeds. He puts to shame old painting—stealing the luster of the jewel beetle, rashly borrowing the scythe of the praying mantis and digging into the earth with the worms, to return in pictures directly buoyant with mosquito larvae. In the dark origins his way is illuminated by the glow of firefly lights and he loosens the thread of the spider's cobweb, in line with the collected poetry by these gentlemen, while the engraver Fuji Kazumune uses his knife to set it to the cherry-wood, and it is left to me to pray to the truth of its origins.
>
> Tenmei 7 the year of the Sheep—written by Toriyama Sekien[33]

In this passage Sekien describes Utamaro as having penetrated the world of insects, even borrowing their own distinct features to draw their forms. Utamaro is thus responsible for their brilliance in the final image; the engraver is delineated as only the vehicle of transference to the woodblock.

Sekien praises Utamaro with familiar tropes for talent—from the "true pictures from the heart" to following "the laws of painting" and "the rules of the brush." Utamaro is shown in a classic construction, in the trope of capturing the life spirit as a child in close observation of living things. These are time-honored set phrases for genius in Chinese and Japanese painting.[34] They were not, however, commonly used for ukiyo-e artists. In fact, no ukiyo-e artists prior to Utamaro had had their artistry proclaimed in a printed text like this.

Such set markers of genius were gleaned from a long textual tradition

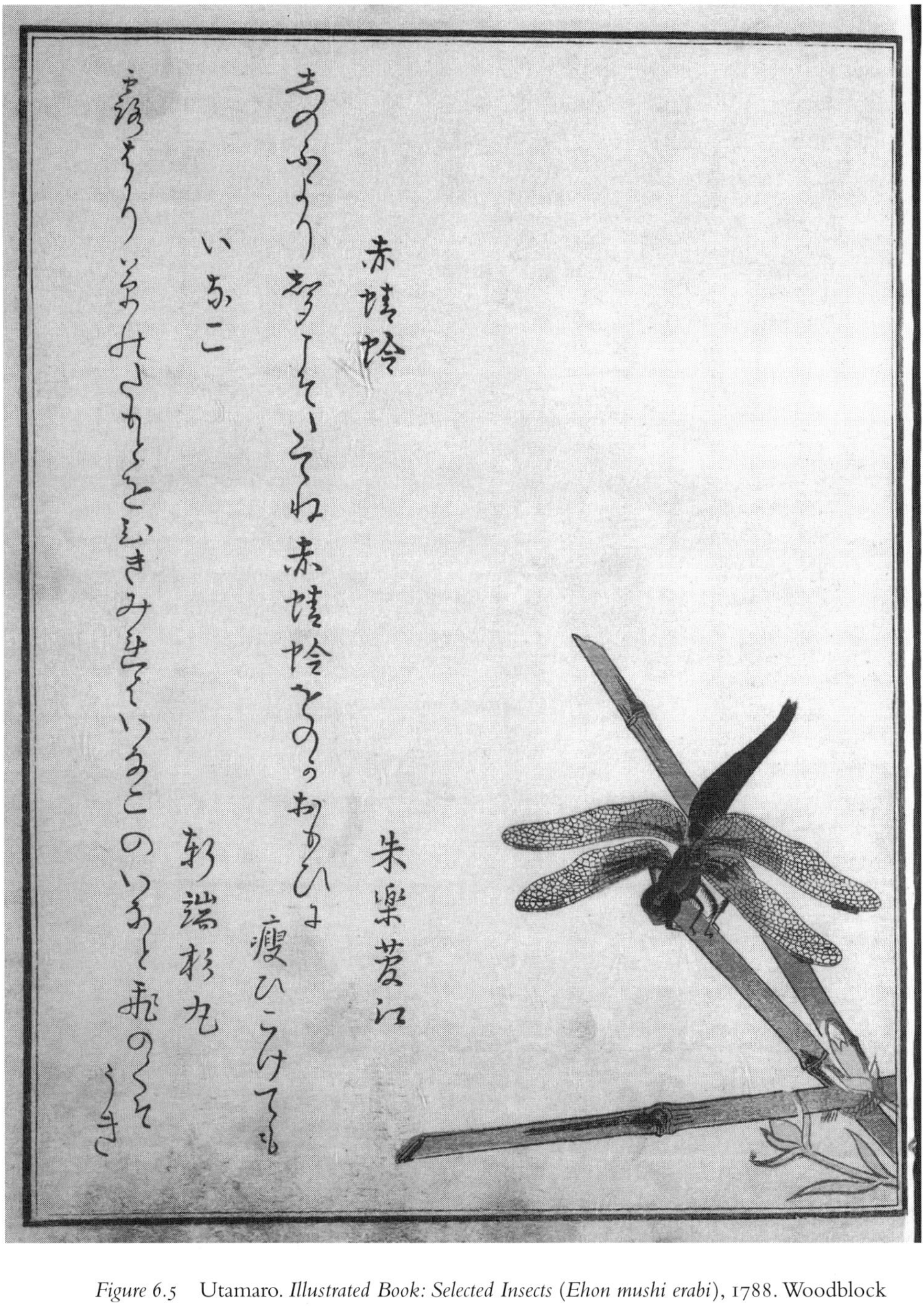

Figure 6.5 Utamaro. *Illustrated Book: Selected Insects* (*Ehon mushi erabi*), 1788. Woodblock printed album, 27 cm x 18.2 cm. Martin Ryerson Collection, photograph by Greg Williams. Photograph courtesy of the Art Institute of Chicago.

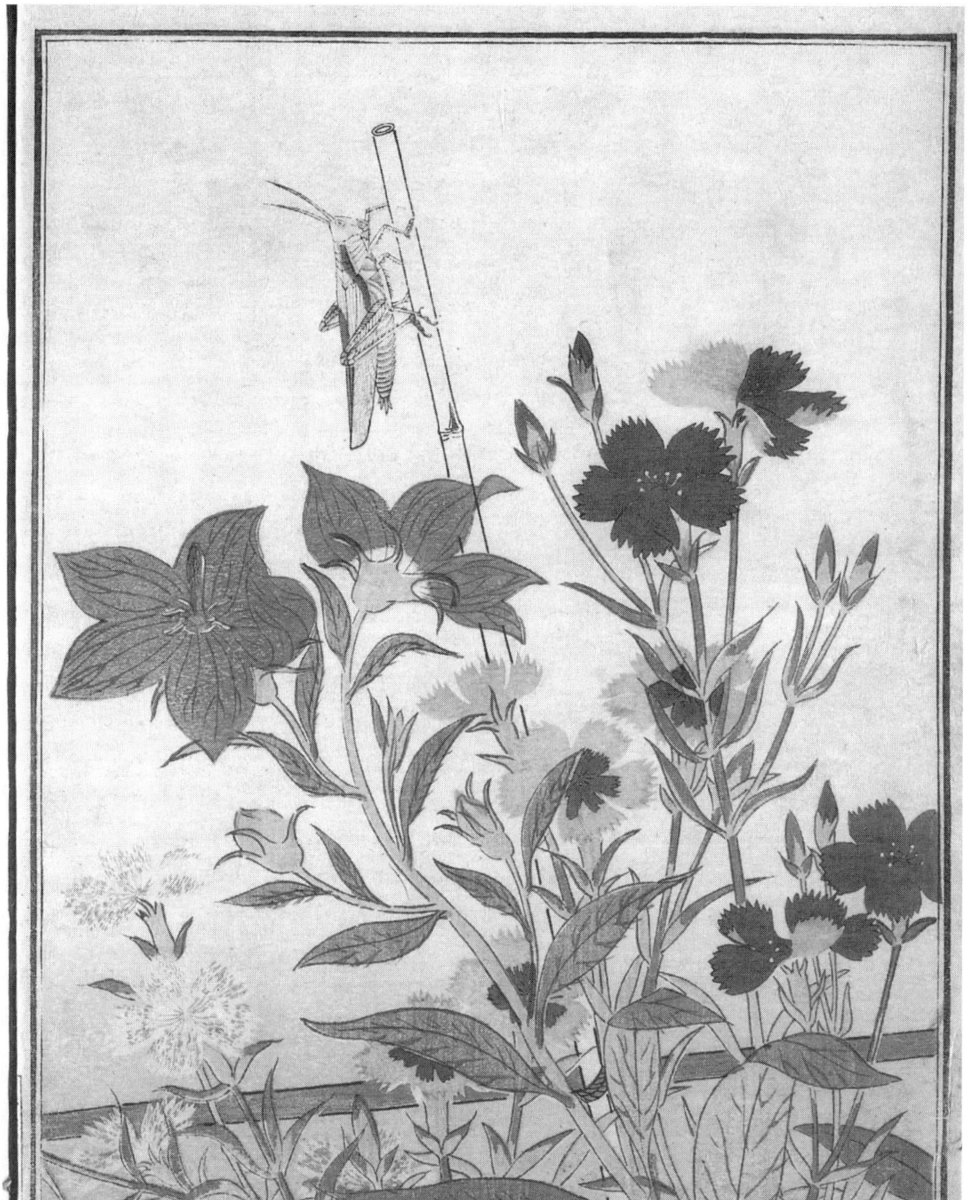

originating in China. Japanese theorists prioritized hierarchies of technique and style, as well as painters and schools, which they combined with traditional aesthetics and theories of artistic practice (see Chapter Four). The Kano and Tosa schools participated in this painterly discourse, and many other painters and critics joined in throughout the Edo period.[35] Sekien's text transfers elements of these discussions to Utamaro.

After having replicated the world of insects in print, Tsutaya and Utamaro appear to have turned next to capturing the life expressed in the human being. In another deluxe edition issued in the same year as *Selected Insects*, Utamaro applies his newly constructed "naturalistic gaze" to the human figure in the production of the *Erotic Book: The Poem of the Pillow* (*Ehon Utamakura*; Figure 6.6). Although the book is unsigned, as is typical of prints and books of erotica at this time, the connection with Tsutaya and Utamaro would not have been difficult to draw: the ivy-leaf crest on the man's kimono mimics Tsutaya's own ivy-leaf crest, while the name of the book, *Utamakura*, plays on the name of Utamaro together with an array of highbrow references to classical literature.

In the most famous image in *The Poem of the Pillow*, the sumptuous color and description of textures—light gauzy material, thick shiny hair, and smooth white skin—exhibit the same attention to detail as if it had been a study from nature. Even though the image has been reproduced by the woodblock carver, Utamaro's mark has been tellingly preserved in the painterly lines of the kimono, the delicate description of the grasping hands, the sensitive delineation of the man's eye, and the fine lines of the woman's hair. These lines refer to the traditions of painting and calligraphy, and in being so self-consciously reproduced assert Utamaro as the author of this image. The poem on the fan by a *kyōka* poet with the pseudonym Yadoya no Meshimori[36] puns on the configuration of human anatomy and the problem faced by a snipe that has caught its beak in the mouth of a clam:

In the clamshell	Hamaguri ni
Its beak firmly caught	hashi o shikka to
The snipe	hasamarete
Cannot fly away	shigi tachi-kanuru
The autumn dusk	aki no yūgure
Meshimori	Meshimori

The preface to *The Poem of the Pillow* is unsigned, but as it speaks of Utamaro in the third person, it has a tone suggestive of the connoisseur reporting on the status of things as they are. Like the preface of the *Selected Insects*, that of *The Poem of the Pillow* is designed to manipulate the reader's interpretation of the images in the book, and of its artist Utamaro:

> Untying the obi of the Yoshino River, exposing Mount Tsukuba from the trailing hem of a robe, forming the connection between the lovers like the Imo and Se mountains, the lovers forge their bond. So do we print in these Azuma brocades [brocades of the East]—that place from where the bird cries—a coverlet of pillow pictures in a bed of flowers, secluded by a standing screen of mist. At one glance the eye is startled. So too the heart throbs, and the spirit flies, stopping below the undersash of Ide, pressing, and entangling the legs [like the reeds] of Naniwa, toward the jewel-comb box of Hakone—it is like using the hips. Ah! More than one who is unskilled in drawing pictures, he who has skill in the art of love, without pressing too hard, moves the hearts of everyone. And, so, what shall we call this volume? Ah! That's it. To compare this to the poems of Henjō and to borrow from the title of the writings of Lady Sei, and even coming close to the name of the painter, I call it *Ehon Utamakura, Erotic Book: The Poem of the Pillow*—a companion to the awakening of spring perhaps.[37]

Utamaro is characterized, through both text and image, as a master of the arts of the brush and of sex. His skill as a painter and a lover is reinforced by the similarity between his name and the title. The association between his art and his life is made all the more concrete by the innuendos that these images are derived from his own experience.

Text and images employ the same tropes used with such success in *Selected Insects*. As Utamaro described the insects in their "natural" state, so has he portrayed the lovers in theirs. References to Abbot Henjō (816–890), one of the six immortal poets, and to Sei Shōnagon (fl. late tenth century), author of *The Pillow Book* (*Makura sōshi*), along with other poetic allusions, invest the work with classical flavor. They serve to connect the text to literary sources educated readers would have been expected to know, and in so doing they elevate the makers' and readers' cultural stature. Such metonymic linkage with the "artist" is promotion masquerading as revelation: a strategy for representing the public identity of the artist according to the familiar paradigms of naturalism and artistic skill. The new element is the notion of Utamaro's sexual prowess, manifest in the symbolic connection between the phallus and the brush. These devices reappear in nearly all of Utamaro's later works, implying that they remained indispensable components in the imaging of artistic talent.

REVEALING PERSONALITIES: "UTAMARO THE PHYSIOGNOMIST"

In the following decade, the "artist known as Utamaro" continued to be linked with the female form. From about 1792, Tsutaya and Utamaro concentrated on the undoubtedly lucrative market of prints of beautiful women (*bijinga*). This shift may have been in response to the Kansei reforms, which

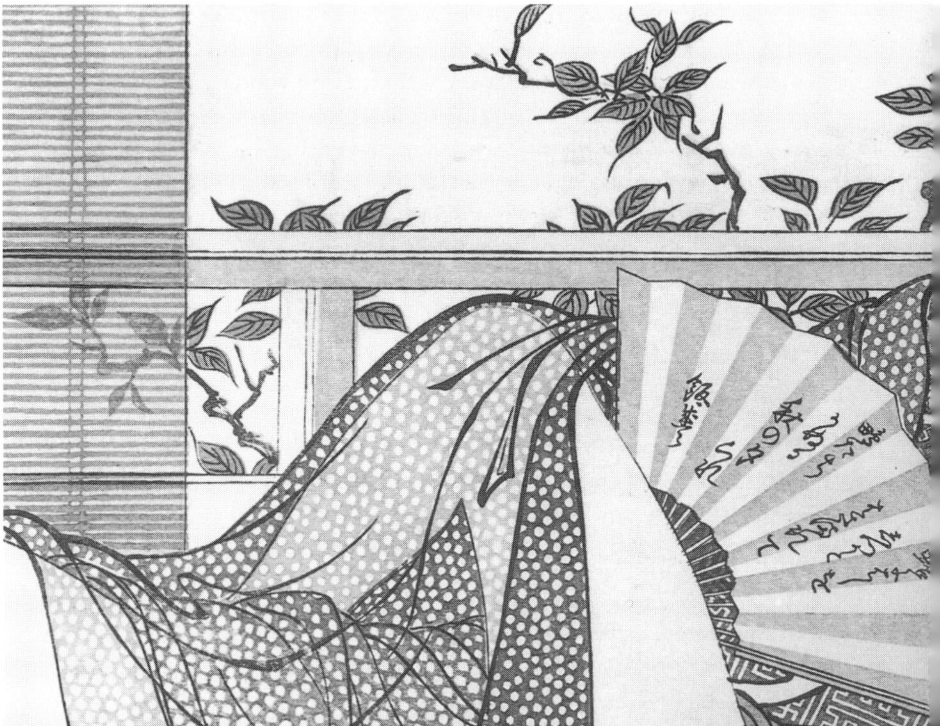

Figure 6.6 Utamaro. *Erotic Book: The Poem of the Pillow* (*Ehon Utamakura*), 1788. Nishiki-e, ōban format. Copyright © The British Museum.

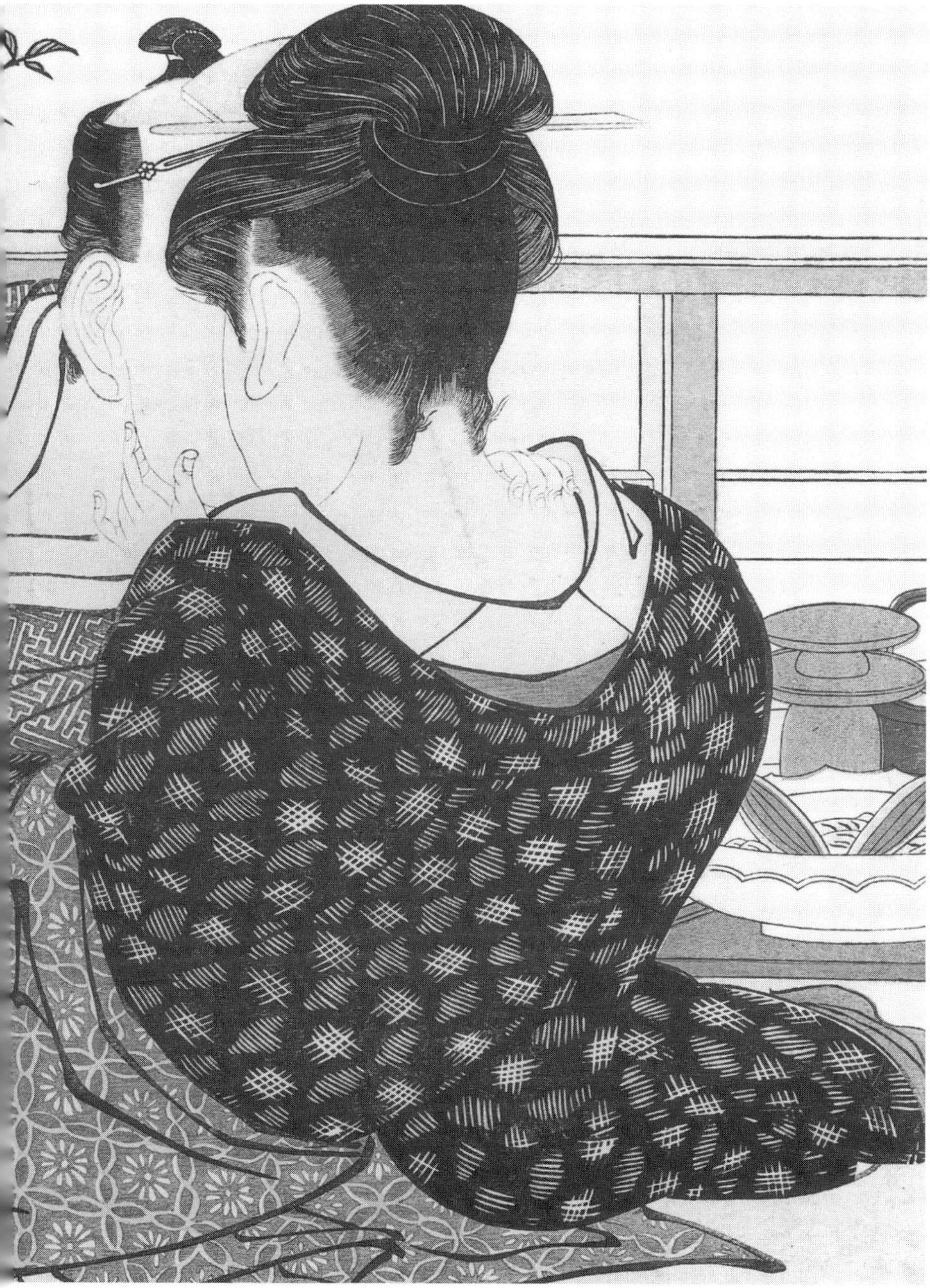

were promulgated in the fifth month of 1790 to regulate publishing. The edicts targeted items that were broadly conceived of as morally suspect or wasteful. Almost replicating the earlier Kyōhō reforms (1716–35), the Kansei reforms banned books that contained unorthodox ideas, were signed with pseudonyms, or were written in Japanese syllabary (kana) and founded on "baseless rumors."[38] The Kyōhō injunction against books and prints that represented current events in the guise of ancient ones was reissued. Another significant element was added to the Kansei reforms: the prohibition of extravagant objects with "rhetorical flourishes."[39] Was this last aimed directly at the sumptuous poetry albums published by Tsutaya and illustrated by Utamaro, as has been suggested?[40]

Similar edicts were reissued in the tenth month of the same year,[41] a sure sign that the first round of edicts had little effect. A mechanism of control became necessary. Representatives from the guild of booksellers were now required to inspect and register publications while still in draft form.[42] For prints, this meant that after 1791 the approval seal had to be included in the final state of the image, together with the signature of the designer and the seal of the publisher.

The Kansei reforms, which directly affected Tsutaya, had an impact on the prints issued with the Utamaro signature. Tsutaya had crossed the authorities before with the publication of books in the 1780s by Koikawa Harumachi that poked fun at the shogunal administration. He was not severely punished for this offense, but in 1791 he was dealt a serious blow after publishing three *sharebon* ("witty books") by Santō Kyōden. Although these three works were initially approved and placed on sale, they were later considered depraved and injurious to public morals. Both author and publisher were prosecuted and disciplined—Tsutaya paid a heavy fine, Kyōden was sentenced to fifty days in manacles—and even Kyōden's father was severely reprimanded. The guild representatives who had acted as censors were banished to the provinces.[43]

It is not surprising that with the subsequent decline of his fortunes Tsutaya turned to publications with a wide appeal, or that Utamaro became associated with the depiction of attractive women, an ukiyo-e genre that had long been profitable. Beautiful women were depicted using the same strategies for representation seen in *Selected Insects* and *The Poem of the Pillow*; they were structured to suggest that Utamaro was as expert at depicting the natural form and spirit of his female subjects as he was at rendering the mysteries of insects and sexuality.

The "Utamaro gaze" incorporates more here than was usual in ukiyo-e. The objects of his inquiry are not just the kinds of "public" women already familiar in ukiyo-e prints, such as courtesans, teahouse girls, and geisha. They also include "private" women, mothers, wives, and daughters, who hitherto were less frequently seen in ukiyo-e. Private women, whose lives were demarcated by the domestic sphere, became a familiar subject in later Utamaro prints. This shift in the portrayal of women opened up the realm of the "ukiyo-e gaze," extending it beyond the sphere of public pleasures into the zone of the private.

Two examples from the first important series of the Tsutaya-Utamaro collaboration in this area, the *Ten Types in the Physiognomic Study of Women* (*Fujin sōgaku juttai*, ca. 1792–93), demonstrate how the Utamaro gaze delineated women, for the public view (Figures 6.7 and 6.8). These women have not shaved their eyebrows, as was customary for wives in this period. Married women of the time also blackened their teeth, as did courtesans, a custom that is seen in one of these prints. Formally, the figures are composed in a manner similar to the animals in *Selected Insects*: each figure is caught in a natural moment, as though this is the most revealing pose for her personality type.

Seemingly frozen in time, the figure is also removed from a specific place. The use of the mica background to mimic a polished mirror or the precious gold or silver background used in screen painting creates the impression that the figure is floating on the picture plane, effectively abstracting her from her real world surroundings. As with Utamaro's insects, the impression created is of an empirical study of a category of things, arranged by typologies and delivered up for consumption as though it were a study in naturalism.

Both prints include texts that define the subjects as particular types of Edo women. The first line of the cartouche informs the reader of the purpose of the series—"ten examples of physiognomies of women"—while the second line names the so-called type. The positioning of each figure, along with her gesture and expression, is designed to expose her physiognomic type. Text and image collaborate to construct each according to normative designations, while reinforcing the concept of Utamaro as the kind of man who could "read" personality from physical likeness.

In Figure 6.7, the woman turns as though engaged in conversation. She wipes her hands with a small towel. Her simple hairstyle and garment seem to have been perfunctorily arranged. The comb slips from her coiffure and tiny errant, untrimmed hairs erupt at the nape of her neck; her robe drifts off her shoulder. These things suggest that she is the type who is neither fussy nor tidy but does things without particular regard for propriety. The second line of the cartouche on the print states that she is the physiognomic type with a "floating spirit" (*uwaki no sō*), the light-hearted type.[44] The text

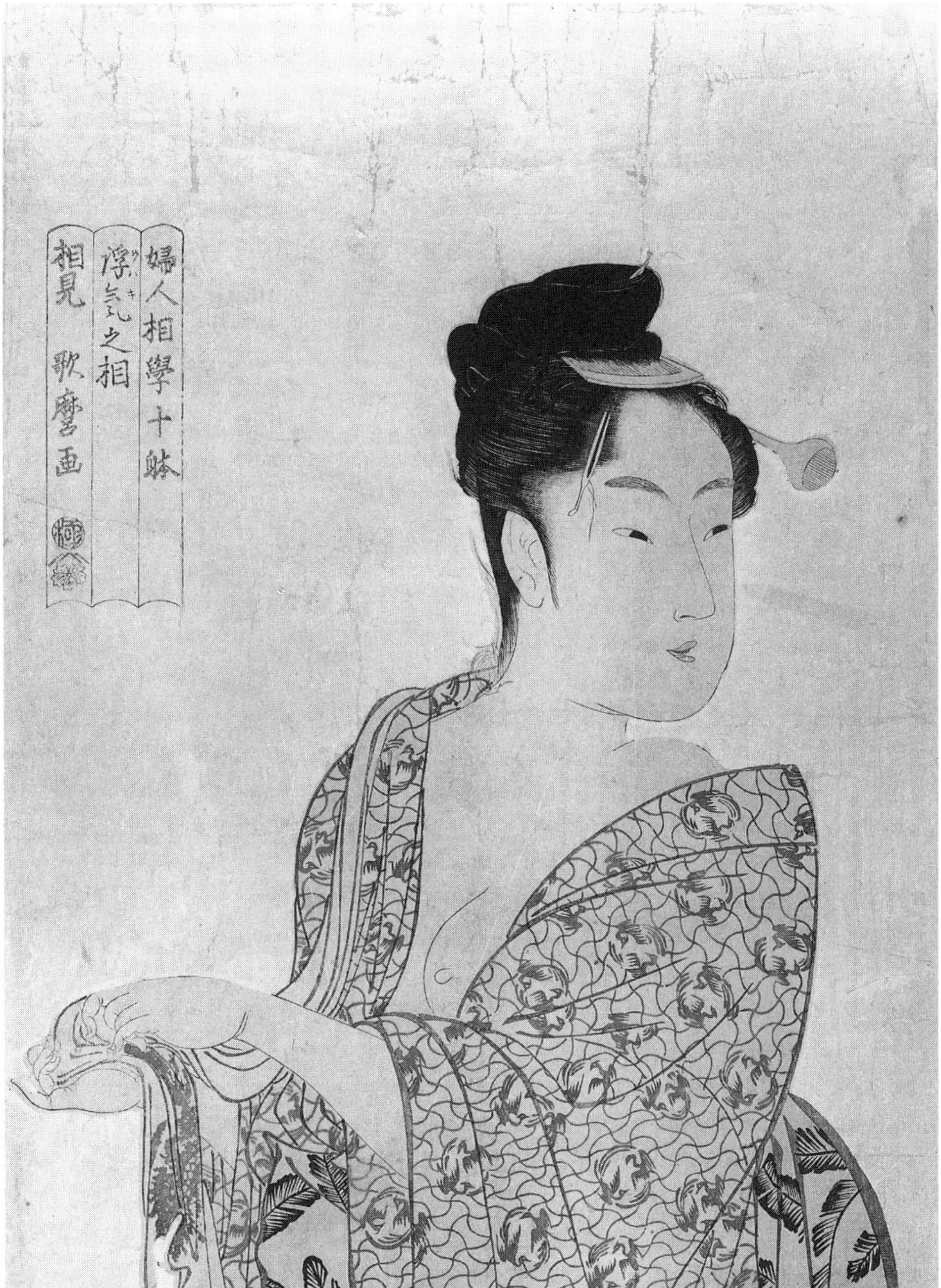

Figure 6.7 Utamaro. *Ten Types in the Physiognomic Study of Women: The Lighthearted Type* (*Fujin sōgaku juttai: Uwaki no sō*), ca. 1792–1793. Nishiki-e, ōban format. Collection of the Tokyo National Museum.

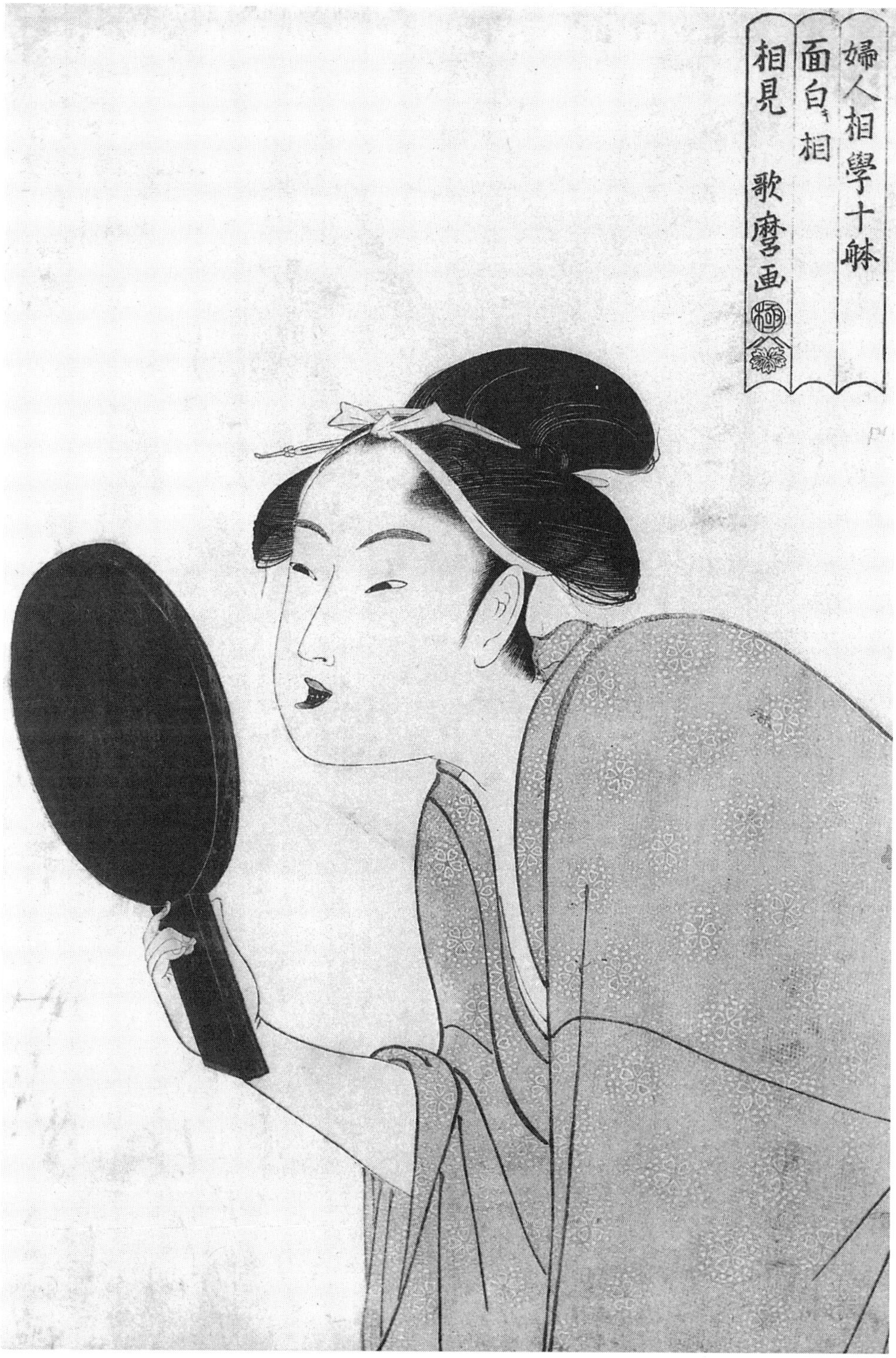

Figure 6.8 Utamaro. *Ten Types in the Physiognomic Study of Women: The "Engaging" Type* (*Fujin sōgaku juttai: Omoshirokisō*), ca. 1792–1793. Nishiki-e, ōban format. Copyright © Allen Memorial Art Museum, Oberlin College, Oberlin, Ohio; Mary A. Ainsworth bequest, 1950.

implies that she is prone to be fickle and capricious in her duties, a reading reinforced by Utamaro's description of her slapdash appearance. She also wears a glass *poppen* in her hair, a toy that made a sound like a trumpet when blown. Like that toy, she is transparent; more accurately, her "true" character has been rendered transparent by the gaze of "Utamaro the physiognomist," as Utamaro's signature on the third line of the cartouche reads.[45]

As in Figure 6.7, the far-right line in Figure 6.8 records the same series title. The inscription in the far left repeats the signature "drawn by Utamaro the physiognomist," followed by the guild seal and Tsutaya's trademark crest. The middle line of the cartouche labels the woman as the "*omoshiroki*" type, a title that evokes the classical use of *omoshiroshi* as "charming" or "engaging," as well as perhaps the modern "interesting" and "fun." It may be hard for us today to understand how this woman might be characterized as charming. As she checks the appearance of her blackened teeth in the mirror before her, she seems more engaged in her outward countenance than the measure of her character. Perhaps this image plays upon the Confucian admonishment to pay more attention to one's moral fiber than to one's outer appearance. If so, the contrast between her charming appearance to the outside, public world and her true, private self is shown by Utamaro. Thanks to his vision, we are let in on the secrets that physiognomic studies may reveal.

The formal study of physiognomy had been introduced to Japan from China in the early Edo period.[46] Chinese physiognomic practice was based on the "reading" of an individual's face to interpret the pattern of Heaven in an earthly object; it was employed by portrait painters.[47] Japanese painters also made use of physiognomic studies, Maruyama Ōkyo (1733–95) and Tani Bunchō (1763–1840) in particular are known to have been interested in physiognomy. Although the extent to which Utamaro relied upon published physiognomic studies is not the subject of this article, it seems clear that he was familiar with the regard paid to physiognomy. He does not appear occupied with the kind of careful diagnosis of individual facial features that professional physiognomists would have shown. By the middle of the eighteenth century, many books had been published on physiognomy in Japan, among them one by the ukiyo-e artist Okumura Masanobu.[48] The interest in physiognomy extended beyond interpretation of personality into reading of the amorous characteristics of types.[49] Physiognomy was also parodied in smart literary circles,[50] suggesting a likely point of departure for Utamaro and his publisher. In fact, Tsutaya himself is sometimes credited with the idea of producing the series of physiognomic studies of women.[51]

The signature "drawn by Utamaro the physiognomist" declares Utamaro to be equipped with the power to measure appearance, interpret its meaning, and present it to the viewer's inquiring gaze. The innuendo of Utamaro's direct observation and deep intimacy may even imply that he might have known these women more intimately than did any others.

BEAUTY IN DISARRAY AND OTHER YOSHIWARA NARRATIVES

It also seems to have been important to Utamaro's producers to present him as being a *tsū* (literally, a connoisseur), as one of those sophisticated male *bons viveurs* who had mastered the art of gentlemanly cool. Acclaimed in popular literature and ukiyo-e prints as the epitome of the Edo man about town, the *tsū* had expertise in the ways of the pleasure districts; he would have been permitted entry denied to the average man. Utamaro's images of the Yoshiwara present a familiarity with the ways and world of the Edo *tsū*; they imply privileged access into the inner realms of the pleasure quarters (Figures 6.9 and 6.10).

The prints in *The Twelve Hours of the "Blue Towers" Series* (*Seirō jūni toki tsuzuki*), dated to around 1794–95, depict the full period of a day and night in the houses of the pleasure district. Like Kyōden's novel *The Other Side of the Brocade* (*Nishiki no ura*), one of the troublesome three published by Tsutaya in 1791, *The Twelve Hours* includes hours that were strictly off-limits to visitors. It seems likely that Kyōden's novel inspired Utamaro's series,[52] although the two works differ significantly in the how they mapped that terrain.

Kyōden's story discusses only the daytime hours, while Utamaro's series of twelve images portrays a view from each of the approximately two-hour periods that made up the twelve "hours" of the cycle of day and night.[53] Utamaro's prints include scenes taking place when the district was officially open as well as those after public hours. Some daytime hours described by Kyōden, and repeated in six of Utamaro's prints, may have been available to intimate male guests with a privileged status in the brothel. For the man who considered himself a *tsū*, remaining late marked his status and status within the Yoshiwara.[54] Clients who remained through the morning hours (and were charged exorbitant rates for the pleasure of doing so) were seen as tiresome distractions. The privilege was apparently worth the price, however; it established the client as one of the Yoshiwara cognoscenti. Kyōden's text and Utamaro's images are designed to have the quality of being eyewitness accounts. Surely, these narratives proclaim, those personages counted among the great *tsū*, worthy of envy by those less fortunate.

Kyōden's approach to the daytime hours was to unveil unseen moments. His prose parodies situations rather than striving for documentary realism.

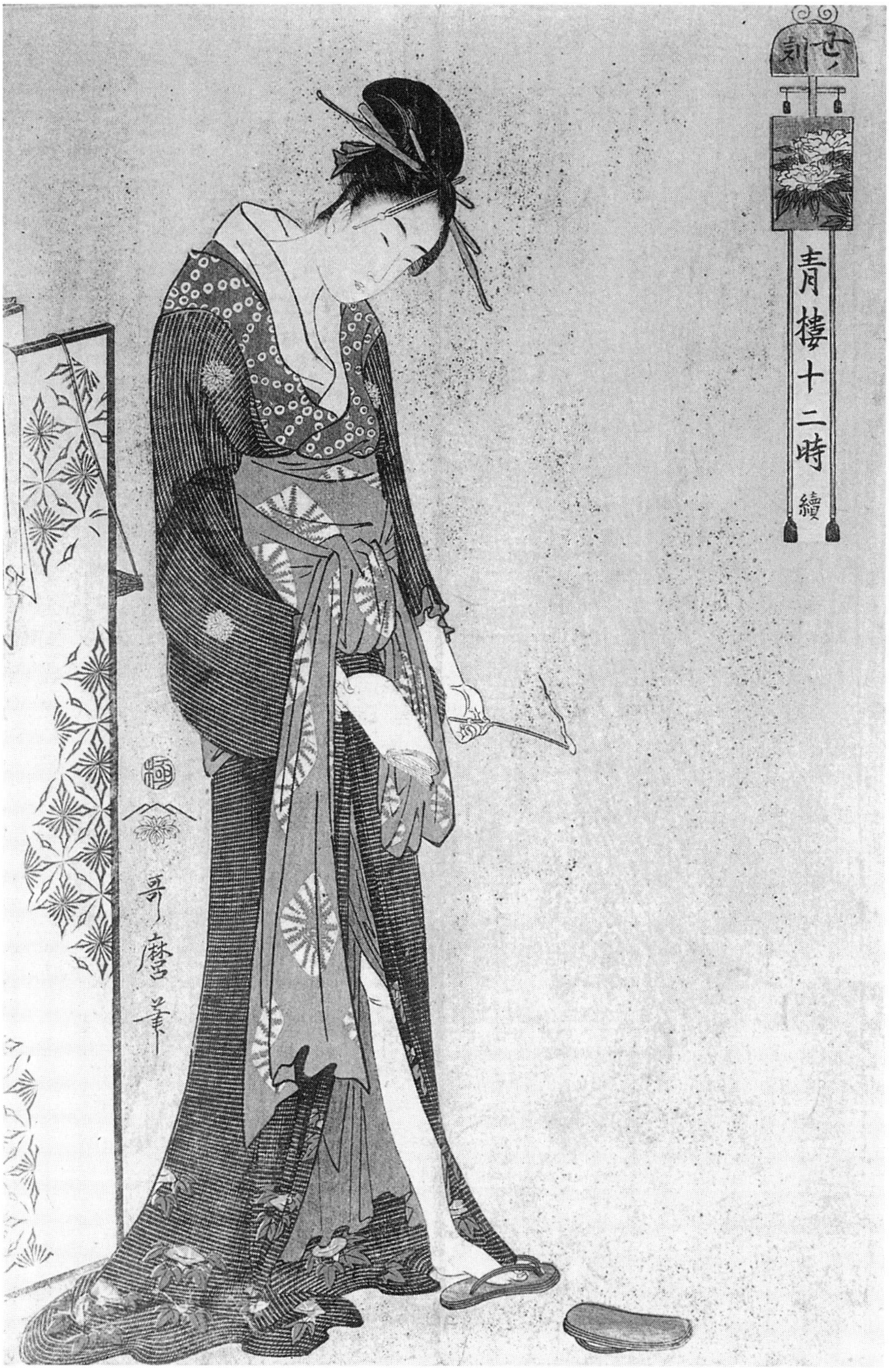

Figure 6.9 Utamaro. *The Twelve Hours of the "Blue Towers" Series: The Hour of the Ox (Seirō jūni toki tsuzuki: Ushi no koku)*, ca. 1796. Woodblock, 38.1 cm x 25.4 cm. Gift of Miss Katherine S. Buckingham to the Clarence L. Buckingham Collection, 1925.3051. Photograph courtesy of the Art Institute of Chicago.

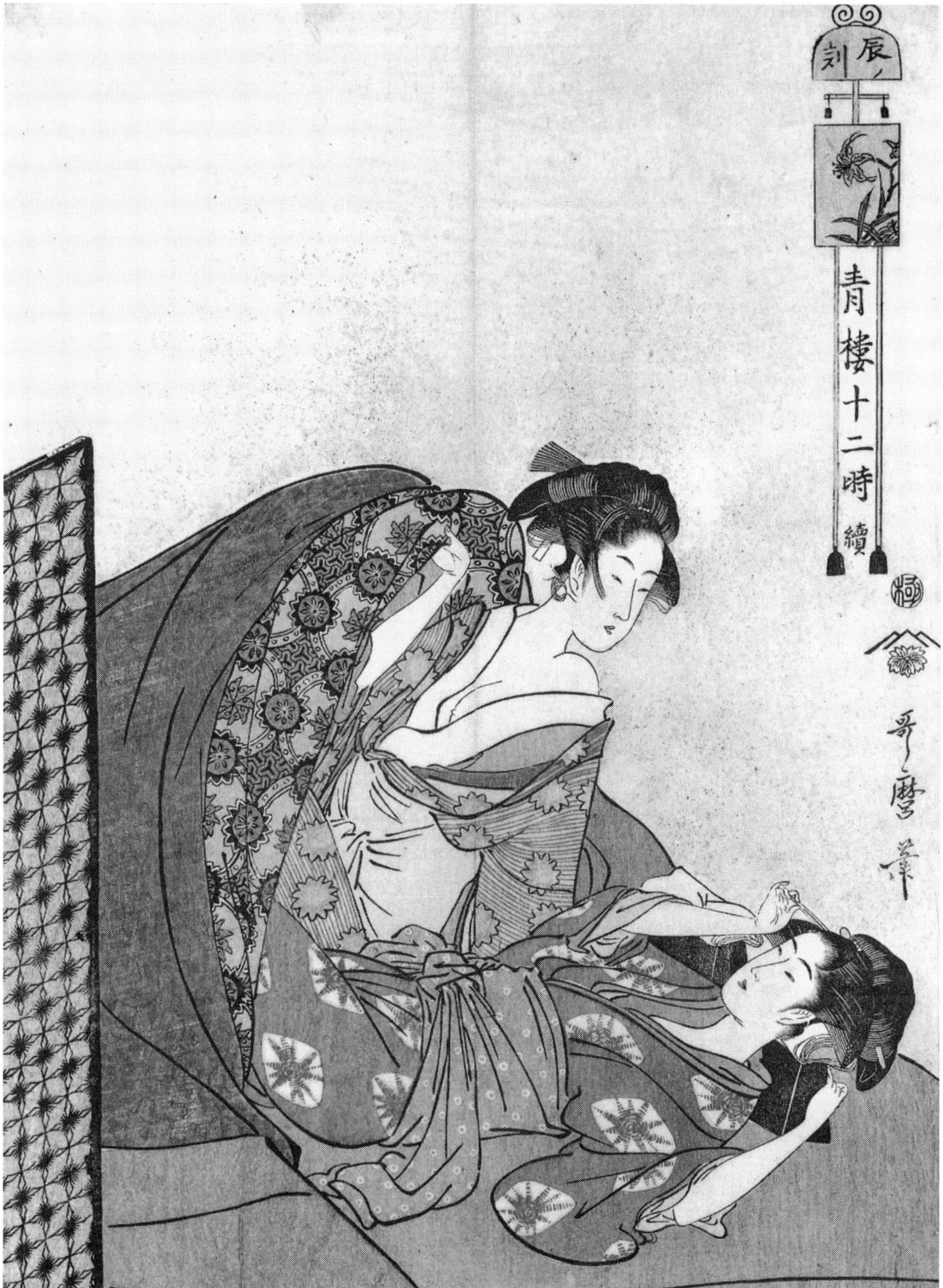

Figure 6.10 Utamaro. *The Twelve Hours of the "Blue Towers" Series: The Hour of the Dragon* (*Seirō jūni toki tsuzuki: Tatsu no koku*), ca. 1796. Woodblock print, 24.7 cm x 38.8 cm. Clarence L. Buckingham Collection, 1925.3054. Photograph courtesy of the Art Institute of Chicago.

Utamaro's images, by contrast, never attempt to strip away the glamor of the quarters. The differences between these representations may have to do with specific protocols unique to the respective medium. In Utamaro's prints from *The Twelve Hours*, the women retain their beauty even when they are weary. The disagreeable facts of everyday life in the pleasure districts remain concealed behind the brocade curtain of ukiyo-e codes of representation. For example, in Figure 6.9 a courtesan emerges from behind a screen at the hour of the ox (from about two to four A.M.), holding a lighted taper in one hand and tissues in the other. The tilt of her head and bedraggled state of her hair indicate her exhaustion. Her robes appear to have slipped open, better to expose two parts of the female form highly appreciated in Japan, the nape of her neck and the inner side of her long, slender white leg.[55] This is meant to suggest a natural moment, as though she goes about her usual activities without noticing that she is being observed. The image is constructed to imply firsthand observation of the scene. It seems doubtful that most viewers of the print would have been familiar with the view of a courtesan on her way presumably to the toilet. It is worth noting, too, that even though the image may be read as a sympathetic portrayal of an exhausted woman, the figure is rendered as an elegant form in a scene designed for the male gaze.

In another image from *The Twelve Hours* (Figure 6.10), two courtesans are retiring to bed at the hour of the dragon (about eight to ten A.M.). Weariness is here signified by their rumpled garments and hair, and in the hour, while the image still maintains the Utamaro style of beauty and sophistication. Some men may have enjoyed the intimate relations suggested in the previous scene, but it is not as likely that a customer would have been privileged to view an early morning scene such as this.[56] Utamaro again reveals for the viewer these captured moments as though he had observed them in life.

By contrast, Kyōden stripped away the veneer of glamor to disclose the banal concerns of day-to-day life in the pleasure quarters. He even describes in humorous, albeit realistic, prose the abject state of one of the brothels in the early morning:

> The scene one morning there on the second floor: drink-stands all over the place, and tea-bowls piled on top of small trays on the lacquered tables in the corridor. It's just like the pile of stools on which a pedlar might make a show of drawing a sword in order to sell his wares! To one side, under rings of orange peel, two broken chopsticks lie where they were thrown—how's that for a misty moon? There are as many bits of paper lying around as there would be on the offertory table in the bathroom on a festival day, as many straw slippers lined up as you would expect at the way into Nyōgo Island, and vomit is scattered around the lavatory like fallen flowers. With only a few glowing embers left, the brazier in the Supervisor's room is almost out. Rows of letters wait at the bottom of the stairs, and there is a heap of salt by the door. The trinkets in

> the juniors' hair are all awry, and the apprentices' forelocks have all slipped sideways in disarray: they have slept long, but have been on their backs a while as well. Last night's devastating beauty is this morning's unrivalled hag. All is revealed at dawn: slight pock marks on the nose, scars on the neck, and to Katsuragi's sorrow, receding hair.[57]

Although colored with parodic humor in typical Kyōden fashion, the text also contains features that serve to make the scene more convincing, producing the "effect of the real."[58] To embrace Kyōden-style realism in pictorial form, however, would have been detrimental to the Utamaro persona, not to mention being unseemly in visual representation. The effects of disarray and debauchery might well be parodied in word, but the pictorialization of the abject would disrupt the seamless identification between what is shown in picture and the image of Utamaro.[59] It might also be asked whether the portrayal of courtesans in the Kyōden mode would have been good for the business of a publisher whose primary enterprise had long been the peddling of the glitter of the quarter in question.

THE FICTION OF THE "SELF-PORTRAIT"

The delineation of Utamaro as an artist/sophisticate is reinforced in a diptych from about 1794–95, part of the series *The Story of the Chūshingura Parodied by Famous Beauties: A Set of Twelve Prints* (*Kōmei bijin mitate Chūshingura-jūni tsuzuki*), published by Ōmiya Gonkurō (Figures 6.11a and 6.11b). The twelve sheets in the series, composed of ten single-sheet prints and this final diptych, illustrate the true story of the famous Akō vendetta, in 1703, of the forty-six loyal retainers. The story is transformed through the kind of parodic inversion typical of a practice known as *mitate*.[60] Although the story itself was based on a historical event, it was better known through its Kabuki and jōruri presentations, the *Kanadehon Chūshingura*, where the names of the historical figures were changed to obviate censorship regulations. In Utamaro's series, the story is retold with the roles of the loyal retainers played by local celebrities. The substitution of the known "beautiful people" of Edo, including teahouse girls, courtesans, and even a few male entertainers of the day, used the kind of gender transformation that was popular in ukiyo-e, while paying homage to these cultural icons of the day.

Utamaro's diptych parodies the final scene of the Kabuki play, where the villain, Ko no Moronao, is captured by the retainers when they storm his mansion. Moronao, who had been amusing himself that evening with a party, was completely unprepared for their attack. Being a notorious coward, he hid in the storehouse, seen in the darkened garden in the middle left of the print. Once in the custody of the retainers, Moronao was taken up to their leader,

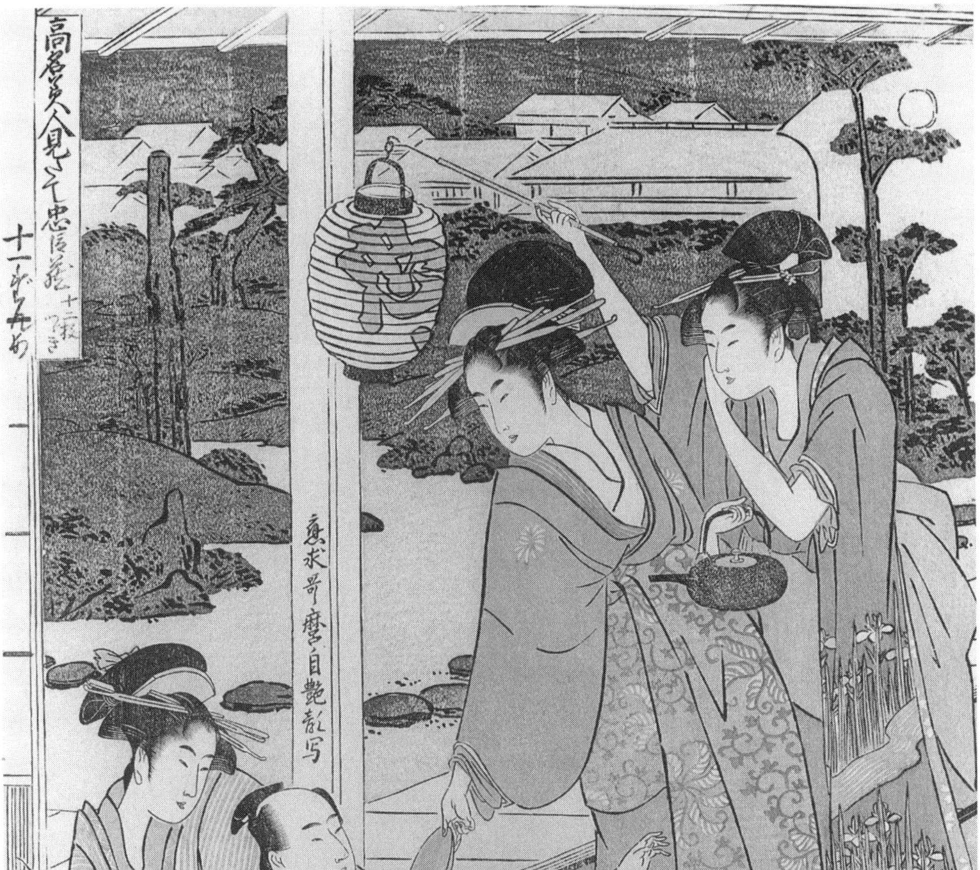

Figure 6.11 Utamaro. *The Story of the Chūshingura Parodied by Famous Beauties: A Set of Twelve Prints, Scene Eleven* (*Kōmei bijin mitate Chūshingura-jūni tsuzuki*), 1794–1795. Nishiki-e, ōban format diptych. Photograph courtesy of the Fitzwilliam Museum, University of Cambridge.

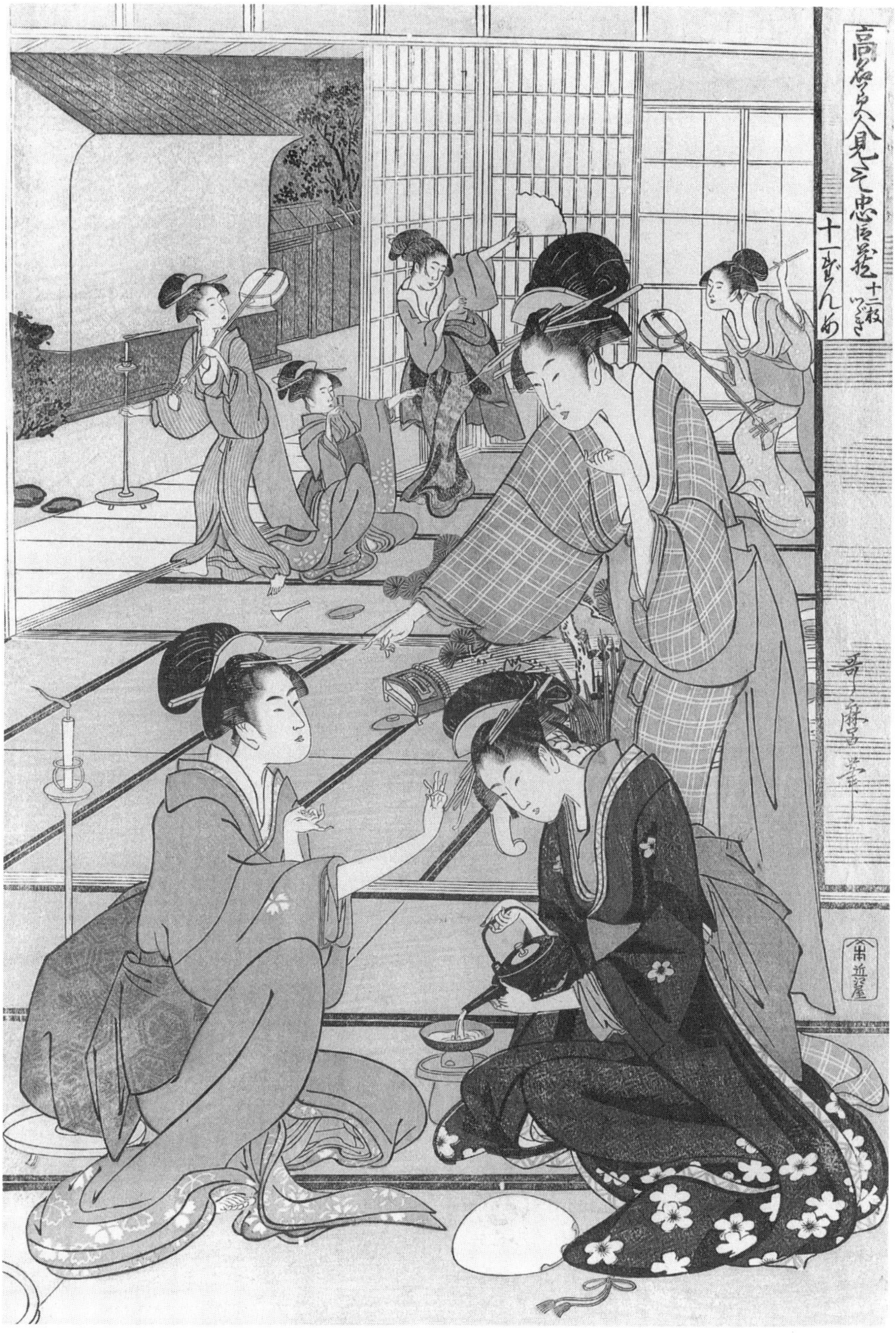
高名美人見立忠臣蔵 十二枚つゞき
十一だんめ
哥麿筆
近江屋

Ōboshi Yūranosuke. Yūranosuke offered Moronao the same dagger used by their master for his ritual suicide and thus the possibility of taking his life with honor. Moronao refused and Yūranosuke was forced to complete the revenge by putting Moronao to death.

In Utamaro's print, a dashing male figure is seated to the left, almost at the point where the perspectival lines of the room converge. He is clad in elegant robes, with the *kasuri* pattern of the uppermost robe similar to that worn by the male figure in *The Poem of the Pillow* (see Figure 6.6). A high-ranking courtesan and her associates lavish attention upon him, as though he were an honored Yoshiwara guest. The crests on his robe read "Uta" and "Maro," and the inscription above his head declares "By Request Utamaro Draws His Own Ravishing Features."[61] The image proclaims this to be the very image of Utamaro. It is remarkable, though perhaps not surprising, how much the image of this man accords with the ideals of male elegance that were the archetype for the refined sophisticate (*tsū*). This is, indeed, exactly what the Utamaro persona would lead us to expect Utamaro to look like.[62]

Utamaro's depiction retains important details that accord with the moment as described in the Kabuki dramatization, but it is also transformed into the sort of extravagant party that would have been held in the Yoshiwara. In the right background, several women act out the roles of the retainers in battle, using their musical instruments as weapons. In the right foreground, two women compete in a drinking game of fox and hunter (which resembled the game of scissors, rock, paper); a third woman pours out the sake for the loser. The battle in the *mitate* form has been stripped of the danger experienced in the actual scene and choreographed for cosmopolitan entertainment. The role of the valiant warrior has thus been pressed into the service of the world of pleasure.

In the left foreground, a high-ranking Yoshiwara courtesan, and the most important woman in the scene, plays the part of the leader Yūranosuke. She hands Utamaro a ceremonial sake cup in lieu of the dagger offered to Moronao. To Utamaro's right is a courtesan in training (*furisode shinzō*) who assists, as these women often did, in attending a distinguished guest. Her long sleeves (*furisode*), hairstyle, and sash tied at the back indicate that she has not yet made her full debut as a courtesan. The woman holding the lantern is another attendant from the district, not a courtesan. The lantern she holds is emblazoned with the character "chū" from "Chūshingura," representing loyalty, likely a prop derived from the Kabuki theater.

Why has the figure of Utamaro been placed in the role of the villain Moronao at the moment he was captured by the retainers, who are now played by Yoshiwara women? Why has he not, for example, been given the more honorable role of Yūranosuke? In each of the ten other scenes, the roles of retainers are played by celebrated beauties of the day, and it may not have suited the logic of *mitate* for Utamaro to assume the role of the retainers' leader. Instead, placing Utamaro in the role of villain proposes that he is the object of desire for these "beauties of Edo." Perhaps, one narrative suggests, they are fed up with his making money off their images, and the "retainers" thus seek their retribution from Utamaro. Indeed, this is the point of the joke: Utamaro is their villain. Certainly, they, like the retainers, would not have been celebrated if they had not had their villain; they are constructed, as the retainers were, by their relationship to their target. But for Utamaro to be loved so well as to be their object fits easily into the persona traced throughout this chapter and is predicated upon the many features of his "personality" that the discursive operations of the images proclaim.

One might also ask, If not Utamaro, then who should play the part of Moronao? This would certainly have been a dilemma in light of the self-censorship system carried out by publishers at the time. Clearly, no real villain or political figure could be put in the role. Placing a Kabuki actor, and one famed for his portrayal of Moronao, for example, at the climax dulls the point of the parody. Answering the question of "Why Utamaro?" is also made more difficult by the ambiguity that surrounded the actions of the retainers and continuing period debates about whether or not they should be heroized. The figure of Utamaro shown in the so-called self-portrait neatly matches his persona. Unfortunately, we are still left with little or no insight into the man himself.

Utamaro's portrayal as Moronao also stands in for one of the ideal masculine archetypes of the day. This archetypal construction was established and reinforced by him in the many images of ideal femininity, in those prints of courtesans, tea girls, wives, mothers, and daughters that are such a prominent part of his corpus. As Utamaro described their appearance, their representations reflexively inscribed his own as one who knew them as they were. Drawing his own face along those lines reinforced the image of Utamaro as a naturalist and *tsū*. But that spectacle also served in the commodification of his own public image. Thus, Utamaro—his image, and by extension, his represented body—is made available to the transformative gaze of commodification. Utamaro's public image here assumes a status equivalent to that of Hanaōgi, and other "beauties," made accessible to the public eye as an object of desire.

RHETORICAL FLOURISHES

Much of the rest of Utamaro's career may be demarcated with an awareness of how these powerful signifiers of artistic merit continued to be used. They were occasionally modified to respond to changes in the ukiyo-e market, as though they were retrofitted to meet shifts in demand. The contours of the Utamaro persona were vigorously defended.

In the period around 1796–98, Utamaro designed three prints that include texts deriding the current state of ukiyo-e (Figure 6.12). The series, *New Patterns of Brocade Woven in Utamaro Style* (*Nishiki-ori Utamaro-gata shin moyō*), published by Tsuruya Kiemon, is well known. The title suggests that the Utamaro name carried some weight as a style designation, or that it was worthwhile for the publisher to promote the name as though it had. In either case, it implies a certain degree of name-brand marketing.

The texts included in the prints claim that Utamaro's brilliance should be recognized in what is purportedly an age of declining quality in ukiyo-e prints. It may have well been the case that there was a noticeable decline in print quality following Tsutaya Jūzaburō's death in 1797.[63] Tsutaya's death was the loss of a reliable supporter and publisher. More important, these writings suggest that the Utamaro style was being encroached upon by others, and these artists, in Utamaro's opinion, were less worthy of admiration than he. Exactly who is the object of his critique is not known, but perhaps it could have been one of his contemporaries. Without knowing the actual target of the critique, it is difficult to ascertain how much this has to do with the actual situation at the time. It is significant, however, that the Utamaro style is being portrayed as under attack.

This presents the opportunity for the texts to reassert the characteristics for Utamaro that have already been noted. In their slightly pedagogical tone, they suggest that the strategy has become less effective than it may have been in the past. It is as if Utamaro must remind the audience that his qualities are still what they should value. The text on one of the prints claims that there are two things meaningful in determining beauty in women, a comely figure and a pretty face; it refers to the conformation of a beautiful figure as though it were an established, and empirical, practice that must be followed in painting. The proper presentation of a beautiful figure will have an effect on the viewer, and those of "poor tools" (as the text calls Utamaro's rivals) should not be mistaken for those composed by a true master.[64] The oft-quoted statements on another of the three prints include the phrase that Utamaro's fees are "as high as my nose," but that the value of commissioning Utamaro over an inferior artist is comparable to the difference between hiring a high-ranked courtesan "costing a thousand gold coins" and that of engaging a street-walker.[65]

The comments on Figure 6.12 are contemptuous toward a public deceived by inferior work. The text at the upper left of this image, written on the unfurled scroll, includes this passage:

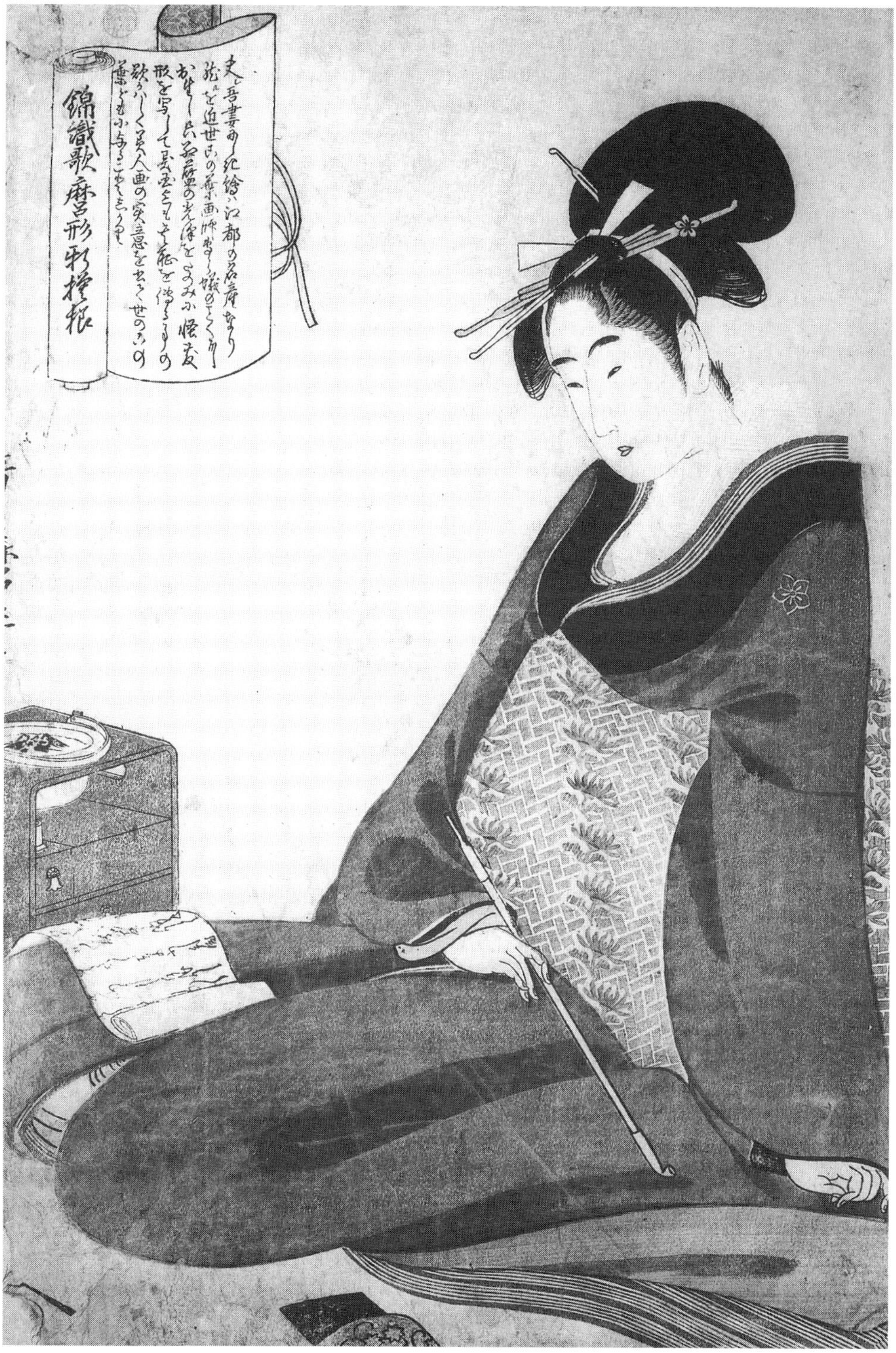

Figure 6.12 Utamaro. *New Patterns of Brocade Woven in Utamaro Style: Summer Robe* (*Nishiki-ori Utamaro-gata shin moyō*), ca. 1797. Nishiki-e, ōban format. Woodblock print, ink and color on paper, 33.9 cm x 25.3 cm. Clarence L. Buckingham Collection, 1925.3049. Photograph courtesy of the Art Institute of Chicago.

> Now Azuma brocade prints are a famous product of Edo, but recently minor painters have sprung forth in this district just like ants. Relying on the lusters of red and blue [color], drawing on clumsy forms, it is deplorable that such shameful things make their way even as far as other provinces. Thus do I draw the true form of the picture of a beautiful figure (*bijinga*) and bestow it on these unworthies.[66]

Consequently, those who employ brilliant color should not be compared with the true form of beauty as it would be rendered through the brush of Utamaro. Connoisseurship as an act of distinction, in prints as in women, is rhetorically expressed as being on the wane in Edo culture. Perhaps these are genuine expressions of regret for standards now gone by, in an era of "ants," "poor tools," and miserly publishers. On the other hand, they ring as the familiar refrain of one who is himself hanging on to the vestiges of celebrity. It may well have been the case that these comments were written by Utamaro and represented his feelings about the then current state of ukiyo-e. Yet one wonders if, in a market as competitive as ukiyo-e, it may not have been useful to manufacture a controversy whereby the famous Utamaro weighed in on the state of ukiyo-e to the benefit of the Edo public. Indeed, the prints *have* fulfilled their mission: we turn our attention back again to what Utamaro has to tell us about artistic standards.

CONCLUSION

Once we understand how the strategies for constructing the artist's image followed particular paradigms, we become aware of how they are employed repeatedly in prints bearing Utamaro's signature. Later series on female types reiterate Utamaro as an expert on feminine behavior, using a similar discursive strategy as in *The Ten Types* series discussed earlier. His many prints of daughters, wives, and mothers with children restate his apparent assurance and intimacy with the private, domestic realm of women in the home. Like *The Poem of the Pillow*, texts and images in other erotic albums describe an Utamaro who was a master of that realm as well. Consequently, the Utamaro persona continued to be reasserted, while the modes in which that identity was enunciated were adjusted to make them appear new and engaging.

In the sophisticated economy of ukiyo-e production and consumption, it is striking to realize how much these prints partook in the cultural construction of the "artist," his subjects, and his audiences. The self-perpetuating effect of such discourse is apparent in how we today think about Utamaro, and other ukiyo-e figures. As I have suggested here, Utamaro-signed prints participated in the formation of a public identity for an Utamaro who may not have been identical with his historical identity. To what end was that identity constructed? Was it simply to sell more prints? It may have been for so simple a reason that such a persona was formulated for Utamaro. But what is so persuasive about this public identity is its multifarious associations, and the conscious way age-old art historical and cultural paradigms were brought to bear upon it. Such associations with natural talent, cultural sophistication, and genius are familiar devices in the history of art, both in East Asian and Western contexts. To this, the Utamaro construction successfully added period distinctions of an idealized masculinity and other gendered identities.

If we return to the print of Hanaōgi of the Ōgiya that introduced this chapter, it is apparent how much the image is structured to suggest that Utamaro drew it from life, as though it were an actual portrait of this woman at a particular moment (see Figure 6.1). Her attitude of absorption allows us to look at her without the fear of her challenging our gaze. Set up through formal elements to create this particular response, the image persuades us that this is indeed a portrait of Hanaōgi. Yet this is a mirage. There is nothing beyond the visual discourses at work in the image itself to conclude that this view of Hanaōgi was based on direct observation. She is as much an Utamaro type as any other. It is thanks to the manipulation of the codes of replicating reality that the woman depicted has been furnished with a name, and thus the image assumes the *status* of portraiture (rather than being an actual portrait).

Acknowledging these associations surrounding the name of Utamaro as a strategy of promotion indicates that there was an advantage to a public identity for which a range of meanings and intentions could be given. It is possible that the Utamaro represented in the dialogue of text and image may have been a close match with the historical figure. But this cannot be assumed from extant documents or statements from his lifetime. Such a reading is possible only if the prints are understood as a form of objective documentation delivered directly from the designer himself. I propose, instead, that the tropes of naturalism, talent, and sophistication were used as metaphors for genius and constructed him as a man with a special talent for seeing into the very being of his subject. The "artist" described in the discourse of the prints was a public persona rhetorically constructed to serve, create, and delight its audience.

Chapter Seven

Takamura Kōun and Takamura Kōtarō: On Being a Sculptor

CHRISTINE M. E. GUTH

Takamura Kōun (1852–1934) and his son Kōtarō (1883–1956) participated in the dramatic transformations that reshaped the artistic profession over the course of the Meiji and Taishō eras (1868–1926). Their careers framed the shift in the function of three-dimensional images, from contextualized devotional icons to decorative objects for domestic and international consumption and then to fine art sculpture. They embodied the changing social status of the maker of such objects, from nonliterate craftsman to intellectual artiste. The dynamics of their intergenerational conflicts mirrored and shaped the battles being fought during the late nineteenth and early twentieth centuries on many cultural fronts in Japan and Europe.

Kōun began his career as a craftsman specialized in carving Buddhist icons, *busshi*, when he was apprenticed at the age of twelve to the head of a family workshop in the shogunal city of Edo. He capped it by participating in the creation of a monumental bronze equestrian figure of Kusunoki Masashige, which still stands before the Imperial Palace in Tokyo. His son Kōtarō began his career at age fourteen when he entered the government sponsored Tokyo School of Fine Arts (Tokyo Bijutsu Gakkō, later Tokyo Geijutsu Daigaku). After graduating from its department of sculpture, he continued his studies abroad. Shortly after his return, he galvanized the avant-garde in Japan by the publication of "Green Sun," in which he declared, "I am in search of absolute freedom in the artistic world."[1] This and other provocative essays, poetry, and sculpture would make him a leading artistic spokesman for his generation.[2]

Although Japan had a long and rich tradition of wood carving, the term for sculpture, *chōkoku*, was coined only in 1876 and embraced a new and broader range of media, techniques, forms, and styles than had traditionally been practiced in Japan. *Chōkoku* was first used to characterize the training in the Western plastic arts offered by the Sicilian sculptor Vincente Ragusa (1841–1927) at the newly established Technical Arts School, Kōbu Bijutsu Gakkō.[3] There, under Ragusa's tutelage, Japanese students were introduced to clay, plaster, and marble, as well as new techniques of bronze casting.

Kōtarō's aspiration to become a sculptor entailed radically different ideas about his professional identity than had been true of his father. Satō Dōshin has remarked that *chōkoku*, formed as it was from two characters denoting carving and chiseling, slipped more easily into Japanese usage than many of the more abstract art terms coined in the Meiji era to bring the classification of Japanese art into line with that prevailing in the West.[4] This apparent ease, however, masks the crisis of personal and professional identity many Edo craftsmen experienced as they sought to overcome deeply ingrained habits of mind to negotiate the new modes of artistic training, production, and consumption implicit in this new vocabulary. Words alone also fail to convey the anguish aspiring young sculptors of Kōtarō's generation experienced as they struggled to come to terms with the gap between the rhetoric and the reality of their new professional ideal. This chapter mines a rare combination of visual and verbal testimony left by father and son to explore their divergent visions of what it meant to be a sculptor.

"WRITING IS UNNECESSARY FOR A CRAFTSMAN"

Although Kōtarō considered his father old-fashioned and declassé, Kōun in fact personifies the stunning adaptations Edo craftsmen made in order to become successful in the Meiji era. Kōun's rapid acculturation to the realities of his changing profession is dramatically revealed in his memoirs. First published in 1929, they constitute a richly informative, entertaining, vignette-filled account of an extraordinary seventy-year career spanning the Edo (1615–1868), Meiji, Taishō, and early Shōwa (1926–88) eras.[5]

Such extensive personal records are rare in the history of Japanese sculpture. Information about the professional life of the *busshi* before the late nineteenth century must be gleaned from a formal analysis of surviving works, dedicatory inscriptions, and references in the diaries of their patrons. Such testimony, moreover, is available only in the relatively rare instances when the carver's identity is known. *Busshi* had little need to write or reflect on the nature of their profession until the Meiji era, when the time-honored values and practices they took for granted were challenged by the introduction of European ideas about sculpture. Kōun is the only *busshi* to have left such an extensive record of his career. Written in an unpretentious colloquial style, it vividly conveys his down-to-earth attitude toward life, sense of humor, and nostalgia for the lost world of the "man of Edo," *Edokko*. Tamura Shōgyō, the novelist who recorded the elderly Kōun's recollections, no doubt played a significant role in shaping this lively narrative.

Kōun's professional roots were in the world of the craftsman, *shokunin*. In the Edo period, *busshi* were identified as craftsmen along with carpenters, dyers, and barrel makers, all skilled professionals who made products of use to society. In the official Edo social hierarchy, *shokunin* constituted a recognized social class that ranked third, after the *samurai* and farmer. Though skilled with their hands, *busshi* did not generally have the same level of literacy customary among painters.

The son of Nakajima Kanemitsu, a perfumer (*kogushi*) and petty gangster in the Shitamachi district of Edo, Kōun was apprenticed at the age of twelve (by Japanese count) to the *busshi* Takamura Tōun (1826–79), the head of a hereditary workshop located at Moritamachi in the vicinity of the Asakusa Kannon temple (Asakusa Kuramae). There Tōun was ideally situated to capitalize on commissions from this religious complex and the large number of devotees it attracted. His personal and professional life was also closely entwined with that of the surrounding community. Nakajima Kanemitsu's influence in the area probably contributed to Kōun's acceptance as Tōun's disciple, marriage to his teacher's daughter, and assumption of the workshop's direction.

This is how Kōun recalled his introduction to Takamura Tōun and acceptance as his disciple:

> Then the master asked "Have you learned to read and write?" I had learned a little from my mother, but it didn't count for much, so I answered, "I haven't." Upon which he responded, "I see. It's just as well. Writing is unnecessary for a craftsman." To his next question, "Have you learned how to use an abacus?" I answered that I didn't know that either. "The abacus is also unnecessary. It's not good for a craftsman to calculate money. If you become a master sculptor, you can hire other people to write and calculate. All you have to do is work as hard as you can at carving," he said. And, with that brief oral exam, I became his apprentice.[6]

Kōun's training began immediately. To master the art of carving in wood, the *busshi*'s primary medium, he was given a flat board into which he learned to chisel the decorative patterns common in the transom work of Buddhist temples and shrines. This was repeated time and again "until the tools broke."[7]

Once this task was satisfactorily completed he moved on to the next stage: carving a three-dimensional figure of Daikokuten. Statues of this deity, one of the seven gods of good fortune, were followed by those of Ebisu, another popular member of this group. Daikoku's auspicious connotations may underlie his selection as the apprentice's first sculptural project, but Kōun's comments about the third exercise—statues of Fudō Myōō and his two attendants—suggest that there may have been shrewd, more practical reasons as well.

Daikoku, Ebisu, and Fudō were all the objects of widespread popular devotion. A good supply of images of the fierce Fudō Myōō, however, was especially important to the workshop's economic success since a statue of this deity was the principal icon at the Narita Shinshōji, a temple just north of Edo. Because of the temple's proximity to the shogunal city, the Narita Fudō had become the object of particular veneration among Edoites, including, most notably, the seventeenth-century Kabuki actor Ichikawa Danjūrō and his successors. The first Danjūrō had become a devotee after his prayers to this deity were rewarded by the birth of a son in 1688.[8]

Only when these three basic iconographic types had been thoroughly mastered was the apprentice allowed to proceed to statues of other deities in the Buddhist pantheon, beginning with the various Buddhas—Amida, Shaka, and Yakushi—then the Bodhisattvas, and finally the multitudinous lesser deities. Kōun recalled that, as part of their training, apprentices also had to learn how to fashion the haloes, daises, and shrine boxes required to adorn and house the finished icons. There were seven types of shrine box alone. Learning to recognize and decorate statues using the various modes of painting and gilding was also important. Lastly, the apprentice had to learn how to measure wood (*kiyose*) accurately. Because of the difficult calculations involved in the assembled-wood technique (*yosegi-zukuri*) used for large images, sculptors who specialized in this task were often called in during the initial stages of production.

It is curious that Kōun does not discuss how he achieved the iconographic accuracy and fidelity to the style of his master that were required of a young apprentice in such a workshop. He no doubt relied on the woodblock printed iconographic model books that were widely available at the time for information about the principal Buddhist and Shinto deities and the various poses and attributes appropriate to each.[9] He must have learned the studio style, however, by directly copying his master's work.

Tōun bestowed on his disciple the professional name Kōun after a typical ten-year apprenticeship. In many cases, this "gift" was followed by a year during which, as an expression of gratitude for his training, the sculptor worked without pay. Kōun, exceptionally, continued to live with his master yet was treated as a salaried employee. At a time when a daily salary of twelve *sen* was the norm, his salary of twenty-five *sen* was also unusual.[10] This may have reflected both Kōun's skill as well as Tōun's desire to remain in Nakajima Kanemitsu's good graces.

"CARVING FROM LIFE"

In 1877 Kōun submitted in Tōun's name a statue of a White-robed Kannon to the first Domestic Industrial Exposition, Naikoku Kangyō Hakurankai, sponsored by the Ministry of Agriculture and Commerce, an event that marked a turning point in the younger *busshi*'s career. The purpose of such industrial shows was to promote the production of high-quality goods, including arts and crafts, which had become a critical part of the Japanese export economy. Kōun's statue was made of sandalwood (*byakudan*), a hard wood that can be carved with a degree of precision and complexity not possible in the softer cryptomeria wood (*hinoki*) customarily used for Buddhist imagery. Since technical skill was a chief criterion in determining artistic merit at the time, it is likely that Kōun's display of technical virtuosity contributed to his being awarded first prize (*ryūmon*) in the sculpture division. The statue was subsequently purchased by a Yokohama merchant for seventy yen, a substantial sum at the time. In the years that followed, and especially after his master's death, Kōun would strive to adapt his sculpture to suit the changing tastes at home and abroad.

In the early Meiji era, such exhibitions became the chief route for artistic recognition and economic success. Presided over by judges associated with the various art schools or by government officials, these events were intended primarily to promote the creation of works with international commercial value. Award winners at such domestic exhibitions were assured of commissions, invitations to contribute to international expositions, and, in some cases, imperial recognition.

The shift from images designed for a specific function and site to those designed for temporary display at domestic and international exhibitions led to profound changes throughout the Japanese artistic profession. Exhibitions artificially stimulated and redirected supply and demand. By encouraging novelty and virtuosity, they also accelerated the pace of change in materials, styles, and subjects. Until the 1850s and 1860s, for instance, ivory had been used chiefly for carving small functional articles such as *netsuke*, but recognition that there was a large foreign market for decorative carvings made of this exotic, precious material prompted sculptors to expand its use. By 1890, when the third Domestic Industrial Exposition was held in Ueno Park, ivory carvers had increased the size of their carvings from under ten centimeters to over fifty, to attract attention in the vast, crowded exhibition hall.[11] They had also expanded their repertory to include figures drawn from Japanese myths, subject matter designed to appeal to the Western taste for historicism and exoticism while at the same time satisfying the growing movement within Japan to glorify its national heritage.

The advent of domestic and international exhibitions also transformed the viewing experience. Previously, images had been created primarily as objects of religious devotion in temples and shrines or as decorative accessories (*okimono*) for the *tokonoma*. The multitude of works displayed in exhibition halls, however, often bore no meaningful relationship to one another or to their surroundings, giving even Japanese viewers no context for their comprehension or appreciation. This estrangement between the work of art and its setting contributed to the advent of the professional art critic, in which capacity Kōun's son Kōtarō would later make his reputation.

Kōun did not take up ivory carving, a matter of considerable pride to him as a *busshi*. During the 1880s, he made a living fabricating wooden models for bronze statues designed for export. In Japan, unlike the West, wood rather than clay was traditionally used for the model. Members of the Takamura studio had apparently engaged in this kind of work since the Edo period. Takamura Tōun's master, Takahashi Hōun, is thought to have carved the wooden models for the bronze statues of Shaka, two attendants, and a set of five hundred *lohan* made by Kurihara Teishū for Kenchōji temple in Kamakura.[12]

Kōun created the wooden model for an unusually large and ornate bronze grouping made for the foreign market (Figure 7.1). It depicts an emissary of the dragon king of the sea presenting a magic jewel to Takeuchi no Sukune, a subject in keeping with the mythological narratives in favor during the early Meiji era. The inscription on its base reads, "Started at the beginning of the 9th month of Meiji 12 and finished in the first month of Meiji 14 (1881). Artist Oshima Jōun assisted by Takamura Kōun and Hasegawa Shu'un."[13] This collaborative work, submitted by the Sanseisha Company to the 1881 Domestic Industrial Exposition, testifies to the technical skills and professional collaboration between Edo craftsmen of different regions, backgrounds, and workshops as they sought to meet the challenging conditions of their rapidly expanding world.

Several of Kōun's most celebrated works were made for international exhibitions. His first opportunity to carve a wooden statue for display abroad came when he was approached by Wakai Kenzaburō (1834–1908) to carve an image of a bird for the 1889 Paris Universal Exposition. Wakai was the chief purchasing agent for Kiritsu Kōshō Kaisha, a company founded with government support for the express purpose of promoting arts and crafts for

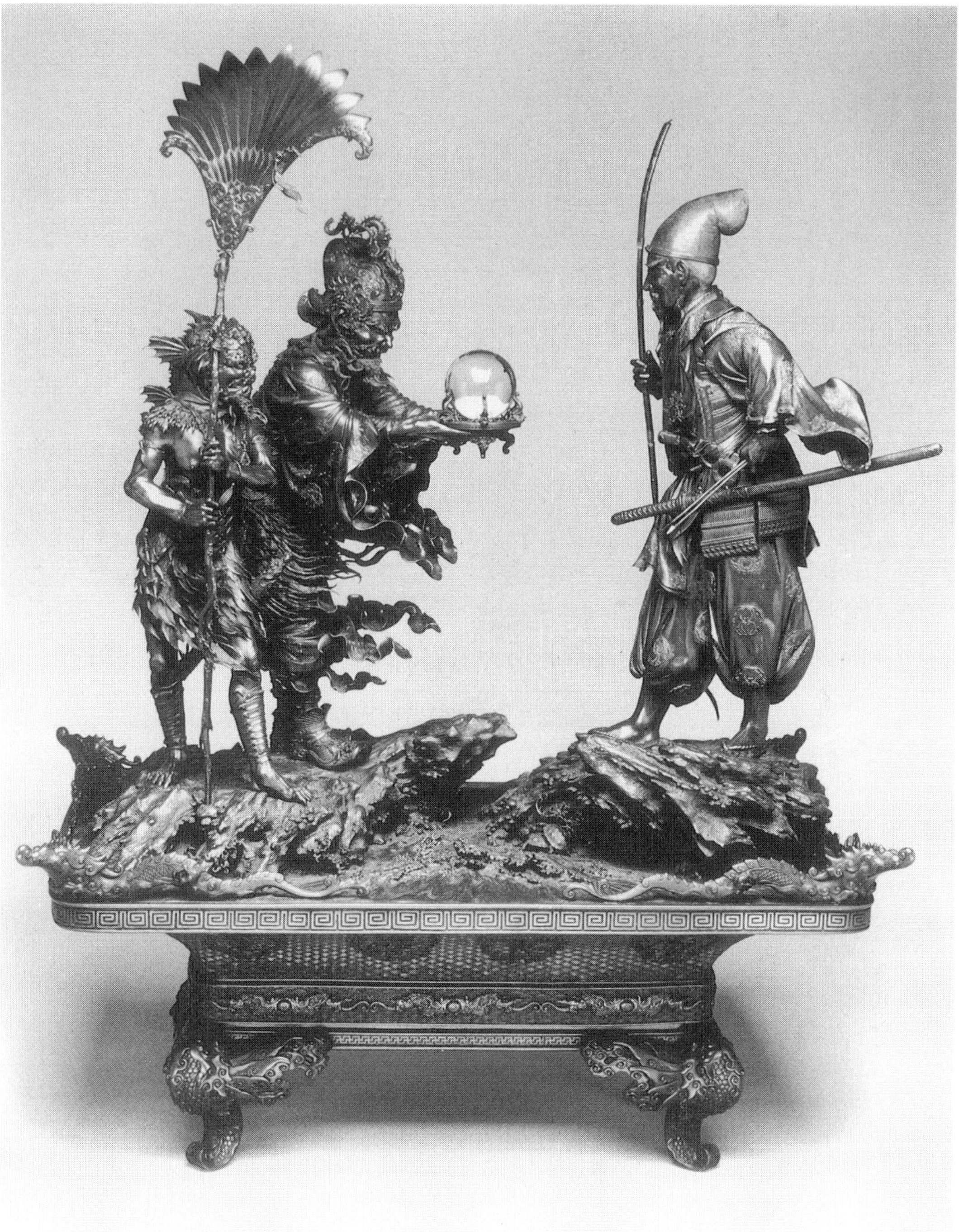

Figure 7.1 The Dragon King of the Sea. Signed by Sanseisha, Tokyo, 1879–1881. Bronze, height 135 cm, width 101.5 cm. Dallas Art Museum; gift of John Young.

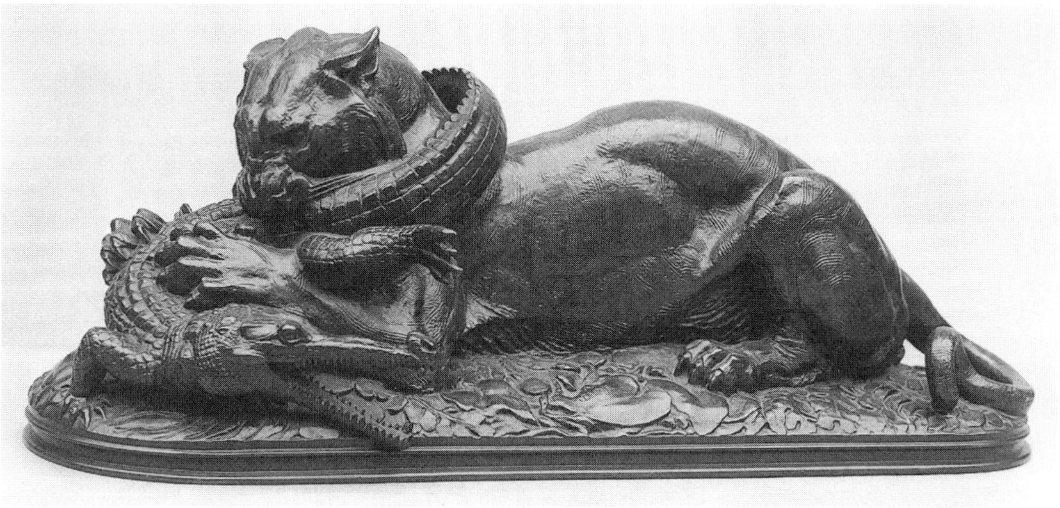

Figure 7.2 Antoine-Louis Barye. Tiger Devouring a Gavial, 1831. Bronze, height 50.8 cm. The Metropolitan Museum of Art, Rogers Fund, 1910.

the international market. After some discussion about what species of bird Kōun would carve, the two men settled on a Japanese bantam (*chabo*).

Wakai's guidance was crucial since Kōun had no sense of his prospective clientele's tastes. Wakai had learned through hard experience the necessity of knowing his market, when the ceramics he had selected for display at the 1878 Paris Exposition were severely criticized by French reviewers and remained unsold.[14] His directives to Kōun were no doubt based on his awareness of European and American Orientalist expectations. It was widely held in the West that Japanese artists excelled in representing flora and fauna because they were somehow closer to nature than their more "civilized" European counterparts. Kōun's use of unpainted wood was allied to this image.

Wakai may also have sought to capitalize on the enormous popularity the sculptor Antoine-Louis Barye (1796–1875) enjoyed in France at the time.[15] Barye specialized in bronze figures of exotic animals in mortal combat, made on a scale suitable for display on tabletops in the bourgeois home. Although Barye's *animalier* statuary was based on direct observational studies at the Paris zoo, his pairings, such as a "Tiger Devouring a Gavial" (Figure 7.2), were entirely imaginary.

Kōun's preparations for this commission reveal his determination to create realistic sculptures on the basis of careful observation of living animals (*jitsumono shasei*). Painters of the Edo period had made realistic sketches from nature (*shasei*), but this was not a common practice among *busshi*. In the early Meiji era, however, photographic realism was emblematic of high

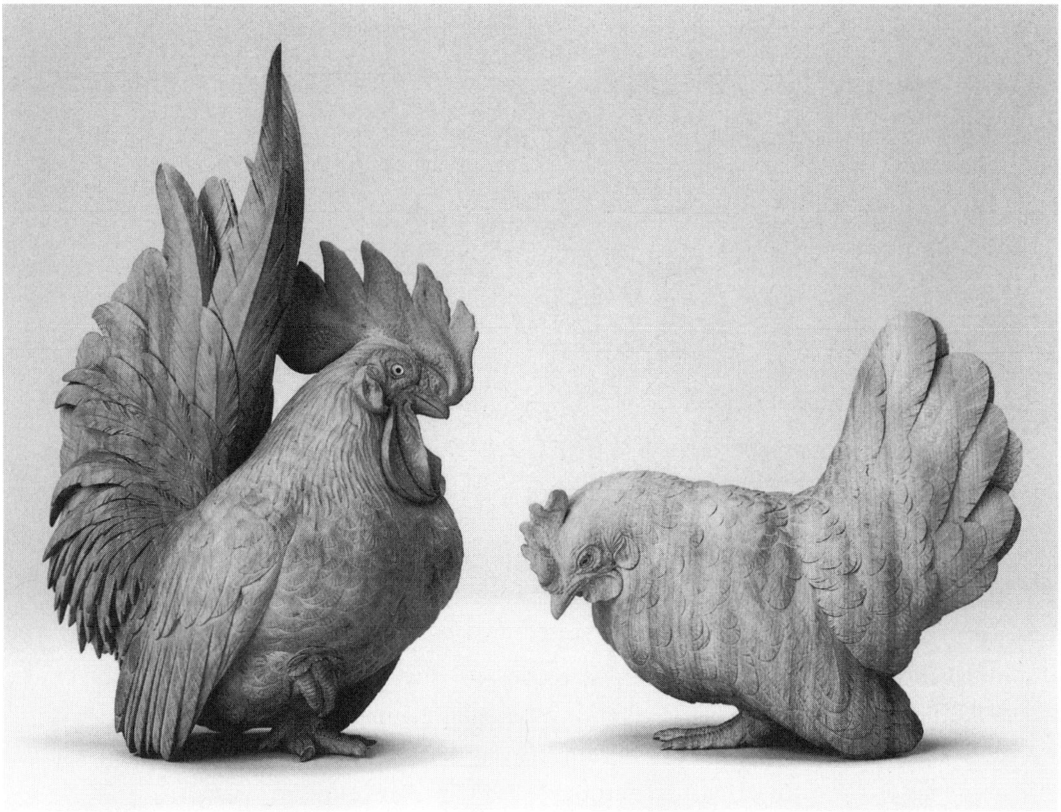

Figure 7.3 Takamura Kōun. Domestic Fowl, 1889. Cherry wood, rooster, height 31.6 cm; hen, height 22.5 cm. Imperial Household Collection, Sannomaru Museum, Tokyo.

culture and modernity.[16] Carving a bantam with veristic accuracy, he believed, would require careful study of its anatomy, movements, and distinctive feathering. This meant procuring a live bird. Kōun's quest, eventual acquisition, and intense observation of the bantam took so long, however, that the statue was not completed in time to be sent to Paris.

With Wakai's permission, Kōun instead submitted the work to the 1888 exhibition sponsored by the Japanese Art Association, Nihon Bijutsu Kyōkai, where it caught the eye of the Dowager Empress. Since the carving had been commissioned by Wakai, Kōun could not sell it, so he offered to carve a more elaborate male and female pair (Figure 7.3), which the Imperial Household Office purchased the following year for one hundred yen.[17] In October 1890, he became one of the first two sculptors appointed Imperial Household Artists, Teishitsu Gigei'in.

Barye's sculptures drew attention to the drama and conflict in the animal world, a theme no doubt influenced by Darwinism, but Kōun's generally were informed by a more peaceable vision. Unlike Barye also, Kōun chose to celebrate the familiar rather than the exotic, although his Western viewers may not have been aware that his subjects—monkeys among them—were native to Japan. "Old Monkey" (Figure 7.4), however, stands out among Kōun's wood carvings because of its unusually large size and anthropomorphic character. Seated on a massive rock, clutching the tail feathers of an eagle that has just escaped its grasp, this monkey has an almost brooding facial expression. Kōun left both figure and rock unpainted, thus drawing attention to the natural grain and glow of the wood.

In his memoirs, Kōun says nothing about the reasons for his choice of this subject or its anthropomorphism, recalling only the unusual difficulty and cost entailed in acquiring such a large block of chestnut, and his intense study of live monkeys before putting hand to wood. Okakura Kakuzō (1862–1913), the director of the Tokyo School of Fine Arts, where Kōun was teaching at the time, may have given him some guidance. Okakura would have been aware of the prevailing Western fascination with the evolution of species from his travels in Europe and the United States. In 1872, for instance, Barye had presented at the Paris Salon a work entitled "Man of the Stone Age," and in 1887 the sculptor Emmanuel Frémiet had caused a sensation with his "Gorilla Carrying off a Woman."[18] In any event, both its large scale and treatment suggest that Kōun was aware that "Old Monkey," unlike his entries in earlier expositions, would be exhibited in the Palace of Fine Arts rather than in the Palace of Arts and Industry. Chicago was the first International Exposition where Japanese painting and sculpture were awarded such recognition.

"Old Monkey" was enthusiastically reviewed by the American press.[19] The coverage it received, however, was eclipsed by the scandal surrounding the removal from public display of several nudes by Rodin on account of American prudishness.[20] The availability of photographs of these and other works soon made Rodin an international celebrity.

KŌUN AS PROFESSOR AT TOKYO SCHOOL OF FINE ARTS

The choice of Takamura Kōun to represent Japan at the 1893 Chicago Columbian Exposition was due in large part to his stature as a master sculptor in wood and as a professor at the Tokyo School of Fine Arts. He was among the first group of appointments to its Sculpture Department when the school opened in 1889, seven years after the Technical Arts School (Kōbu Bijutsu Gakkō) closed. The older school had been established primarily to train Japanese painters and sculptors to decorate the Imperial Palace. The initial aim of this newer institution, however, was to foster the development of national

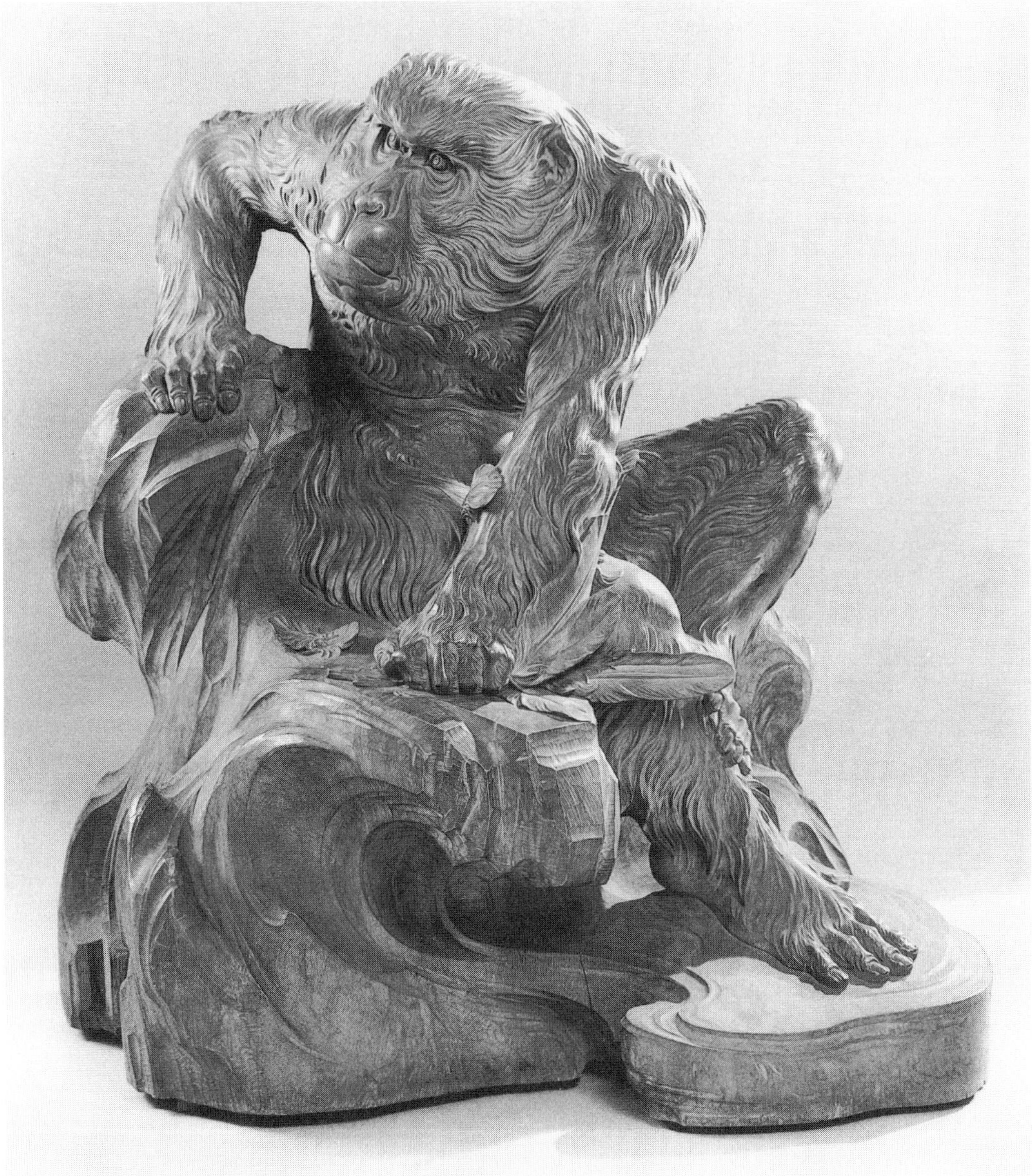

Figure 7.4 Takamura Kōun. Old Monkey, 1893. Chestnut wood, height 110 cm. Tokyo National Museum.

themes, forms, and styles. This emphasis helps to explain the selection of Ishikawa Kōmei (1852–1913), a specialist in ivory carving noted for his historical and mythological themes; Takeuchi Kyūichi (1857–1916), an ivory carver who had shifted to wood sculpture; and Takamura Kōun, a master carver of Buddhist images.

By appointing Kōun, Okakura Kakuzō (director of the school from its founding until 1898) hoped to revitalize the tradition of carving in wood. A wooden statue of Shō Kannon Kōun (Figure 7.5) completed in 1892, which is now part of the school's art collection, testifies to Kōun's mastery of this medium. Inspired by an eighth-century standing figure of Jūichimen Kannon in Hokkeji, it also expresses the strong retrospective orientation in sculpture at the time. Although its lack of polychromy is in keeping with the new natural wood style of the day, this statue was not in fact intended as a finished work, but as the model for a bronze version later cast by Okazaki Sessei (1854–1921) for Kyoto's Chion'in temple.[21]

Accepting a post on the faculty at the Tokyo School of Fine Arts was not an easy step for Kōun. He was self-conscious about his lack of formal education and reluctant to leave his own workshop, with its familiar professional hierarchy and working methods. Kōun's transition from *busshi* to professor of sculpture also required new ways of thinking about and practicing his craft.

Although he had been trained to copy and repair Buddhist icons, Kōun never visited the temples and shrines of Nara and Kyoto to study the ancient works they housed. Shortly after his appointment, he made his first trip with Okakura Kakuzō. Afterward, Kōun and his students undertook the study, restoration, and copying of many now-celebrated images in Hōryūji and other temples in the Kansai region. In keeping with the training prevailing in European academies, Okakura advocated copying as a means of familiarizing students with the nation's historical styles of painting and sculpture.[22] The images they replicated were not viewed as Buddhist icons, however, but as part of Japan's artistic heritage.

Kōun and his students were also commissioned to create monumental public statuary, a new genre of imagery outside the range of the Edo *busshi*. This development was a part of the Meiji government's efforts to transform Tokyo into a modern European-style capital. Ōkuma Ujihiro (1856–1934), who had trained under Ragusa at the Tokyo Technical School and completed his studies in Italy, was a pioneer of Western bronze casting. His commemorative portrait of Ōmura Masujirō (1825–69), a vice-minister of the army assassinated in 1869, was unveiled in 1893. Occupying a commanding position atop a column at the entrance to Tokyo's Yasukuni Shrine, its novelty quickly made it one of Meiji Tokyo's new scenic sites.[23]

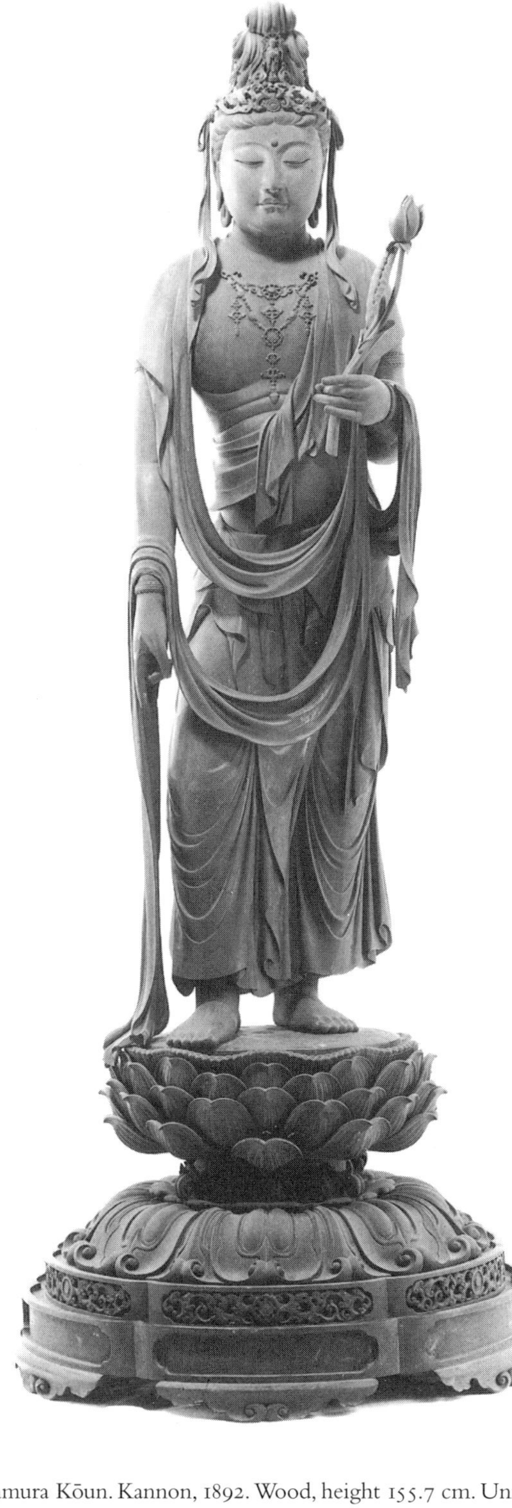

Figure 7.5 · Takamura Kōun. Kannon, 1892. Wood, height 155.7 cm. University Art Museum, Tokyo National University of Fine Arts and Music.

The awe-inspiring bronze statue (Figure 7.6) of Kusunoki Masashige (1294–1336) astride a prancing horse that stands before Nijūbashi Bridge was installed seven years later. As the most politically loaded commission undertaken by Kōun and his associates at the school, the circumstances of its design and execution are exceptionally well documented. These bring into sharp focus the new artistic, technical, and ideological challenges Kōun and his team had to overcome in carrying out their commission.[24]

The statue of Kusunoki Masashige was commissioned by the Sumitomo family as a self-interested expression of patriotic devotion to the Emperor. They chose the year 1890 to make this gift to the Imperial family because it marked the two hundredth anniversary of the Besshi Copper Mines, the source of their enormous wealth and the copper to be used for the colossal bronze statue.

A legendary warrior, popularly known as Nankō, who joined Emperor Godaigo in his unsuccessful effort to challenge the power of the Kamakura military establishment, Masashige was venerated as the embodiment of loyalty to the emperor. Although he was a popular subject in nineteenth-century painting, finding a suitably realistic model for the statue proved to be very difficult. The decision to portray Masashige astride his horse, a guise in which he had not been previously shown, may have been prompted by admiration for Donatello's statue of Gattamelata in Padua or Verrocchio's Bartolomeo Colleoni in Venice. These fifteenth-century commemorative portraits of professional soldiers (*condottieri*) were among the most influential Renaissance monuments of their kind, and inspired many similar works throughout Europe. The sculptor Naganuma Moriyoshi, who had recently returned from studies in Italy, may have played a role in the decision to portray Nankō in this manner.

To arrive at a suitable model, a competition was held among members of the school, a practice without precedent in the pre-Meiji art world. A sketch by Okakura Shūsei showing Masashige going to meet Godaigo as he returned from his exile on Oki Island was selected. To ensure that the image was historically accurate, Kurokawa Mayori, a respected antiquarian, and Imaizumi Yūsaku, a young art historian, were consulted on matters of costume. Kawasaki Chitora led a survey of temples and shrines claiming to have armor and other articles that had belonged to the hero. Kanō Natsuo, a specialist in metalwork, and Imamura Chōga examined ancient swords to discover suitable models. Okakura also agreed to hire Gotō Sadayuki as a consultant in equine anatomy. The final task of casting the bronze statue, approximately four meters high, was entrusted to Okazaki Sessei, with whom Kōun had collaborated earlier in the creation of the statue of Kannon.

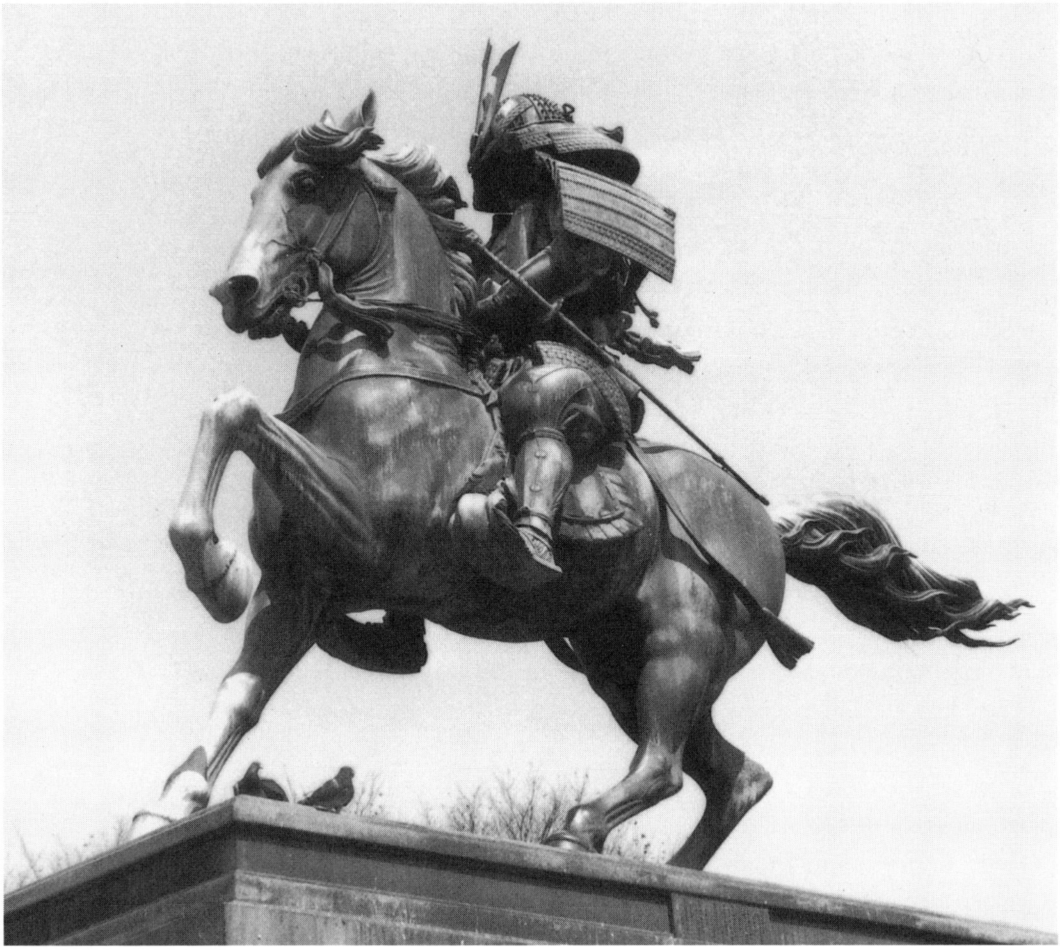

Figure 7.6 Takamura Kōun. Kusunoki Masashige, 1900. Bronze, height 4 m. Nijūbashi, Tokyo.

Sessei, like Kōun, was among the craftsmen who adapted with unusual success to the new conditions of the Meiji era. He began his career casting kettles for the tea ceremony but after 1868 devoted his talents primarily to bronze statuary. Because of the scale, complexity, and political import of the task, Sessei traveled at his own expense to the United States to study the latest bronze casting techniques.[25]

Kōun's contribution to this patriotic monument was the carving of the wooden model, a task he carried out with three assistants. The young Meiji emperor, Mutsuhito, himself examined and approved this work in 1893. Thereafter, Kōun served primarily in a supervisory capacity. Because of his stature in the Japanese sculptural world at that time, however, he is generally identified as the sculptor of the Nankō statue.

"I AM IN SEARCH OF ARTISTIC FREEDOM"

Kōun's son Kōtarō entered the Tokyo School of Fine Arts in 1897, a year after a new curriculum was implemented. When the school was founded in 1889, its three departments—painting, sculpture, and crafts—were all devoted to the revitalization of "traditional" Japanese arts. In 1896, however, the curriculum was expanded to include Western-style oil painting and sculpture. Young artists who had just returned from their studies in Europe were hired to teach these courses. Among them was Kuroda Seiki (1866–1924), a charismatic painter who spent ten years in Paris. Kuroda introduced a new course on Western-style painting, *yōga*. He was followed in Western sculpture by Naganuma Moriyoshi (1857–1942), who had trained in Italy, and later by Shirai Uzan (1864–1928), who had spent a year in Paris. Kōun himself remained on the faculty until 1926.

Young Kōtarō's education could not have been more different from his father's. As a child, he took lessons in English and in the violin, and when he entered the Tokyo School of Fine Arts his curriculum included courses in the liberal arts as well as training in painting and sculpture. His teachers included some of the intellectual luminaries of the day. Imaizumi Yūsaku, later the director of the museum that the industrialist Okura Kihachirō founded, taught Asian art history and archeology; Kume Keiichirō, recently returned from his painting studies in France, taught Western painting, theory, and archeology; Ōmura Seigai, a pioneer in the study of Chinese cave temples, taught the history of sculpture; and for a year the eminent writer Mori Ōgai taught aesthetics.[26]

The bronze statue of the thirteenth-century monk Nichiren (Figure 7.7) that Kōtarō submitted as his graduation project in 1902 testifies to his father's influence, even as it reveals a more expressive approach to the portrayal of a historic personality. Though cast in bronze, the broad rigid folds of the monk's garment show the kind of stiffness associated with wood carving rather than modeling in clay.[27] The bold movement and intensity in the facial expression, however, show Kōtarō's efforts to move beyond his father's vision.

When Kōtarō began the more specialized phase of his studies, he wanted to major in oil painting rather than sculpture. This decision, motivated by his desire to study under Kuroda Seiki, must have been painful to Kōun, who had given his son a set of chisels at the young age of five, with the expectation that he would follow in his footsteps.[28] Kōun himself did not touch on this subject in his memoirs, but Kōtarō, writing many years later, leaves no doubt that his desire to become a painter wasn't due to a lack of interest in sculpture, but embarrassment about his father's humble background and craftsmanlike vision.

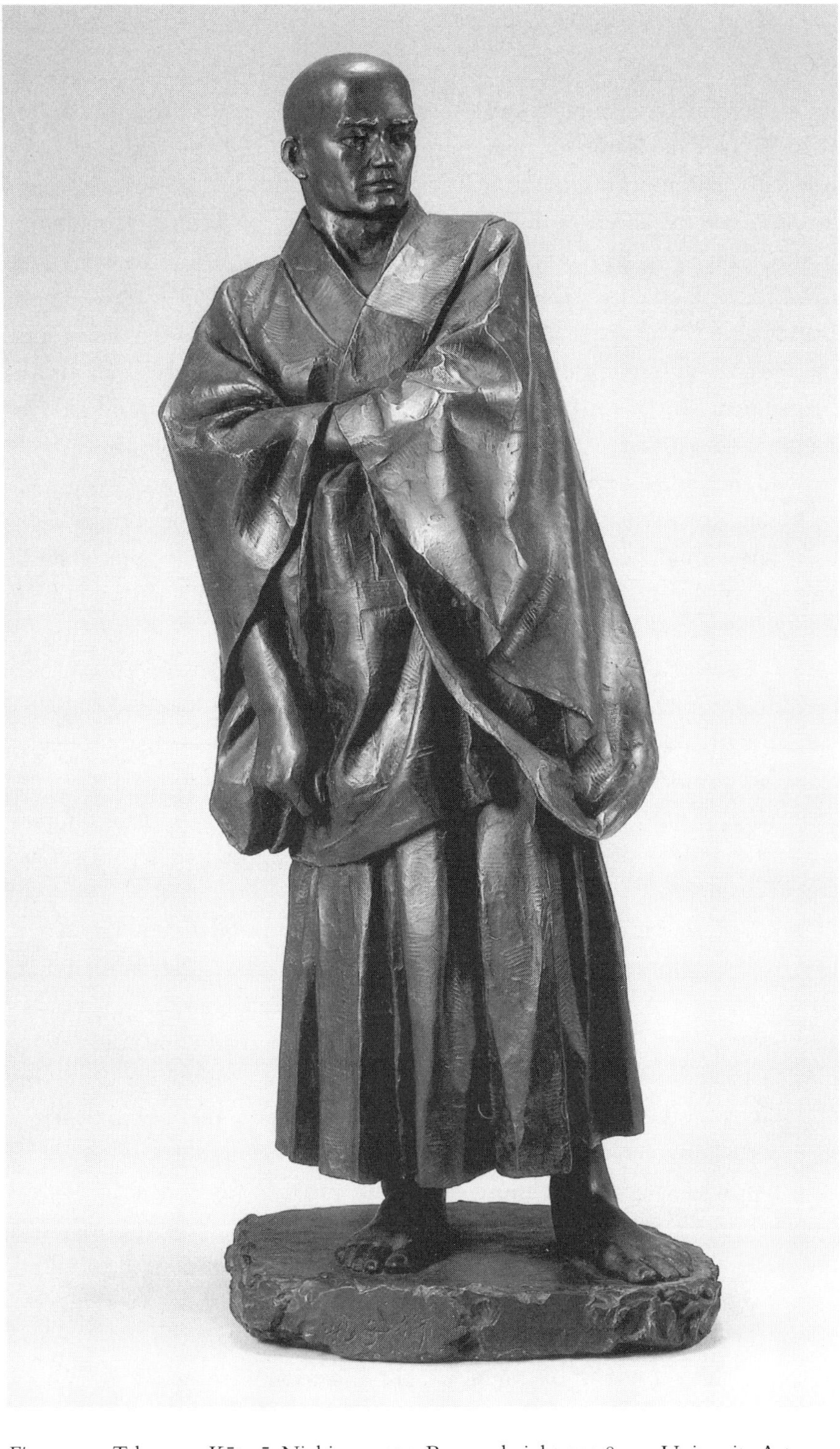

Figure 7.7 Takamura Kōtarō. Nichiren, 1902. Bronze, height 105.8 cm. University Art Museum, Tokyo National University of Fine Arts and Music.

Kōtarō's effort to distance himself from his father was not an isolated phenomenon, but an instance of the generation gap that manifested itself among many young professionals who came of age around the time of the Russo-Japanese war (1904–5). As Oka Yoshitake has written, both the older and the younger generations aspired to worldly success, but getting ahead in the world (*risshin shusse*) meant different things to them. For the older generation, it implied helping one's family and attaining a high government post; for the younger one, it assumed more individualistic connotations.[29]

Although the precise meaning of individuality (*kojinshugi*) in the context of Japan is a subject of much debate, there is no doubt that many members of the cultural elite during the late Meiji and early Taishō eras embraced the Romantic rhetoric of artistic freedom and individuality.[30] This trend was especially conspicuous among the well-educated and pampered sons of successful men of the early Meiji era. Casting off the bonds of tradition often took the form of alienation from their fathers. Kōtarō himself expressed this view when he declared in 1911, "Father and son indeed have to carry on a war from which no truce is possible. If the father is strong, he degrades his son and ends up making a so-called filial son out of him. If the son is strong, he ends up devouring his father like the bell-insect."[31]

Hirakawa Sukehiro has noted that estrangement between fathers and sons was also a recurrent theme in many novels written in the first decade of the twentieth century.[32] He has further suggested that the fictional father in "After the Death of Ransai, Master of Metal Carving" (Ransai botsugo), a short story by Kōtarō's contemporary and friend Shiga Naoya (1883–1917), may have been modeled on Kōun. The son in this story is angered not only by the fact that he has no identity except as the son of a famous carver but also by his father's duplicity: Ransai had written certificates authenticating works of art knowing full well that the articles in question were not genuine.

The relationship between art and commerce central to the story of Ransai was in fact a thorny issue between Kōtarō and his father. Even though it was by no means a new topic of debate in the Japanese art world, European Romanticism invested it with new connotations and heightened intensity. In Kōtarō's eyes, the true artist did not seek commercial success—an outlook that prompted him to reject his father's offer to open a workshop to produce bronze portrait sculpture.

When economic dictates later forced Kōtarō to undertake such work, he displaced his resentment about engaging in such enterprises to his poetry. Among Kōtarō's commissions was a portrait of the industrialist collector and patron of the arts, Ōkura Kihachirō (1837–1928). In the concluding lines of "Portrait" ("Nigao"), a poem evoking the artist's emotions during its creation, the industrialist becomes the embodiment of the materialism he ostensibly rejects:

> Measuring this lump of avarice which is never off guard
> I draw, taking care not to miss a single arc,
> Record the whole history, incised on the grotesque mask,
> Of the capitalist development of Imperial Japan.
> Ninety-one year old catfish,
> Don't you see what I want is the sort of cruel likeness
> You don't want?[33]

Kōtarō's travels abroad in 1906–9 expanded the professional gulf between father and son. Kōun used his long association with Okakura Kakuzō to help arrange for his son to study in the United States.[34] At the time, however, Paris was the Mecca for Japanese artists, so Kōtarō was disappointed. In New York, he managed to find work in the studio of John Gutzon Borglum (1867–1941). Borglum's bronze "Mares of Diomedes" had the distinction of being the first example of American sculpture purchased by the Metropolitan Museum of Art, where Kōtarō himself saw it.[35] Despite his admiration for Borglum's work, Kōtarō's experiences as a Japanese in his studio were unsettling. After declining a scholarship to the New York School of Art, Kōtarō used the money he received from Borglum to travel to London, Italy, and Paris.

Kōtarō's engagement with American and European sculpture forced him to confront many artistic issues, but none more fundamental than his desire to identify himself as a sculptor rather than a craftsman. During the Meiji era, American and European viewers admired Japanese art for its craftsmanship, and painters and sculptors whose work departed from what Western viewers understood to be "traditional" media, themes, and styles met with little success. For Kōtarō, determined to become a sculptor, this realization was intensely painful.

In "The Country of Netsuke" ("Netsuke no kuni"), written not long after his return from Europe, Kōtarō expressed the sense of personal and artistic inadequacy he felt as a Japanese abroad in his identification with a *netsuke*. The craftsman Sangorō may also be a foil for his father, whose values he sought to transcend.

> Cheekbones protruding, lips thick, eyes triangular,
> with a face like a netsuke carved by the master Sangorō
>   blank, as if stripped of his soul
>   not knowing himself, fidgety
>   life-cheap
>   vainglorious
>   small and frigid, incredibly smug

monkey-like, fox-like, flying squirrel-like, mudskipper-like,
minnow-like, gargoyle-like, chip-from-a-cup-like
Japanese[36]

"RODIN IS THE ARTIST AND HUMAN BEING I REVERE THE MOST"

Kōtarō's vision of himself as a sculptor was shaped by his discovery of Auguste Rodin. This momentous event, of which he later gave varying accounts, seems to have occurred around 1903 or 1904, just after the sculptor Shirai Uzan's return from Paris. By this time, Rodin had become an international celebrity. Uzan, however, described Rodin as an "eccentric" (*kijin*) and his sculpture as bizarre (*kikyō*). Since he had brought back photographs only of the work of the Academic sculptors Paul-Albert Bartholome (1848–1929), Jean-Baptiste Carpeaux (1827–75), and Jules Dalou (1838–1902), it wasn't until Kōtarō saw a photograph of Rodin's celebrated "Thinker" in *Studio International* that he was able to form his own judgment: "The 'Thinker' made a profound impression on me. None of the Western sculpture I had seen before had so moved me, there was something so unpretentious, so vital about it. I showed the photograph to my father, but he did not feel the same way; nevertheless, I immediately determined that I wanted to meet this sculptor."[37]

Kōtarō had his first opportunity to see Rodin's sculpture in the United States, but it was while in Paris that he really began to appreciate Rodin's artistic scope. Rodin's drawings of female nudes, he later wrote, moved him "in a manner I won't be able to describe completely in simple words. . . . These women are made up of dreamy swirls of mysterious, live, slender lines that smoke. Looking at these drawings I feel that special kind of fragrance and heat that comes out of the human skin."[38] His response to Rodin's work was so visceral that upon his return he claimed he could never look at art in the same way again: "Having sent me to foreign countries was the biggest mistake in the old man's life. . . . Rodin is the artist and human being I revere the most. But suppose I was *his* son. When I think of this, I tremble with fear of the sin of having eaten the apple."[39]

By the time Kōtarō returned from Europe, Rodin had already acquired a devoted following among other avant-garde writers and artists in Japan. At the second Ministry of Education Exhibition (Bunten) in 1909, the sculptor Ogiwara Morie (1879–1910), an artist who had reputedly switched from painting to sculpture after seeing Rodin's "Thinker," displayed two bronzes in the Rodin style, one of which was awarded third prize. A bronze nude (Figure 7.8) Kōtarō later made is deeply indebted to Ogiwara's 1910 interpretation of the same subject.[40]

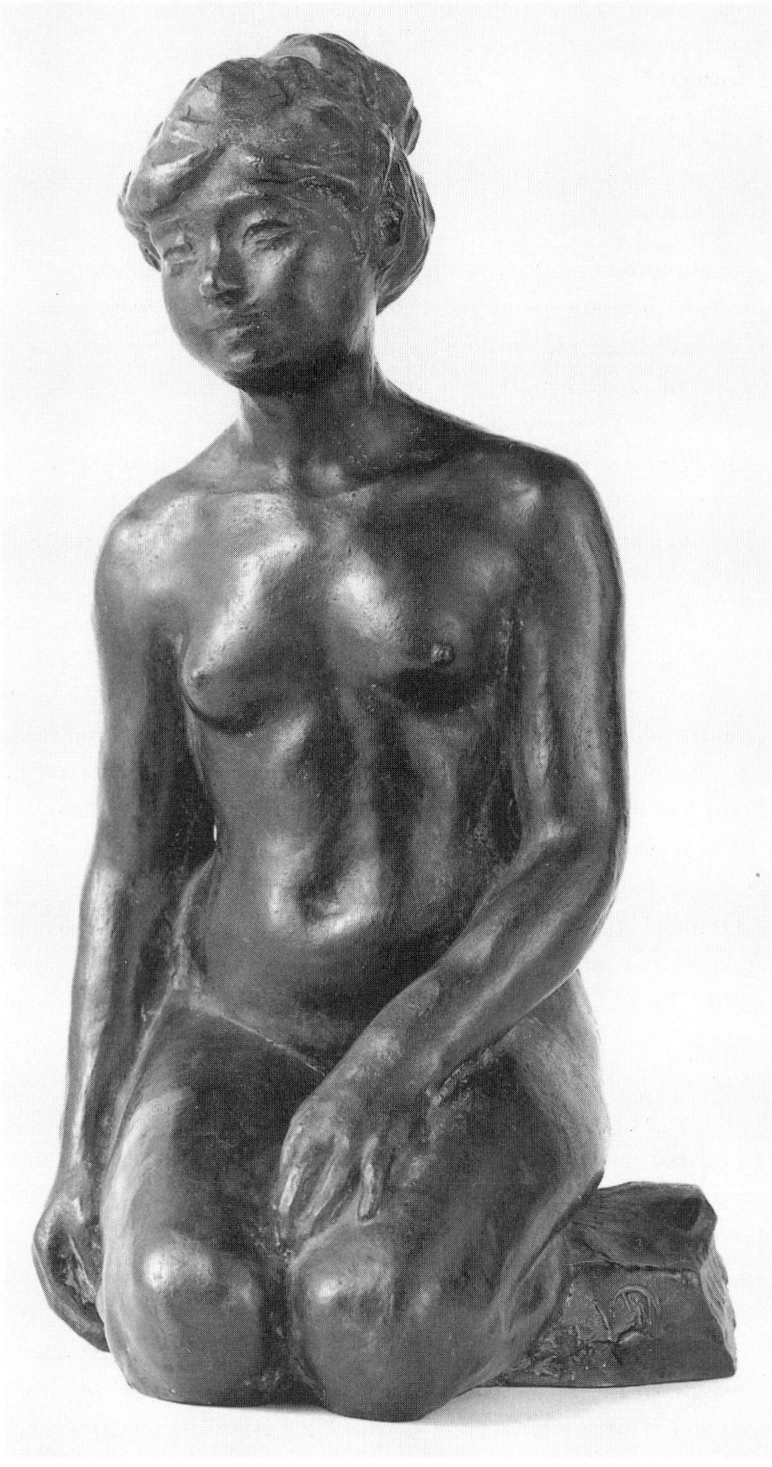

Figure 7.8 Takamura Kōtarō. Kneeling Nude, 1917. Bronze, height 28 cm. National Museum of Modern Art, Kyoto.

The following year saw the publication of Mori Ōgai's "Hanako," a short story about an acclaimed Japanese dancer who modeled for Rodin. Also in 1910, *Shirakaba*, a monthly magazine published by a group of avant-garde writers and artists, devoted an entire issue to Rodin. Kōtarō's self-conscious, awkwardly written contribution, entitled, "Méditations sur le Maître," was the first of his many paeans to Rodin and his sculpture. In honor of his seventieth birthday, the members of the Shirakaba group even sent Rodin a selection of thirty-odd woodblock prints, and he in return sent three of his own statues. Their display was the first time Rodin's works were ever shown in Japan.[41]

Kōtarō's effort to fashion himself in Rodin's image is evident in a photographic portrait taken in 1911, showing him standing next to the clay model of a bust portrait of his father he had just completed (Figure 7.9). Kōtarō reveals the distance he has traveled from Kōun's world, both in his Rodinesque handling of his medium and in his recognition of photography as the currency of artistic celebrity. He presents himself to the viewer as a worldly young *artiste*, equally at home in the realms of the mind and the hand. His wavy hair is perfectly coiffed, his immaculate cover-all, its collar stylishly upturned, is thrown over his shoulders. He establishes his connection with the bust of his father almost casually, by resting two fingers on the table supporting it. Yet even as he declared his autonomy as a sculptor, in creating this portrait he was also fulfilling his filial duty as his father's successor. As he wrote that same year, in "My Father's Face:"

> When I make my father's face with clay,
> Below the window in twilight
> The mysterious lineage of the blood whispers.[42]

Over the following decades, Rodin continued to exert a profound influence on Kōtarō's efforts to construct his professional identity, as well as on his belief in the ennobling power of art. He expressed his admiration directly, by closely emulating Rodin's sculptural style and subjects, as in his interpretation of the human hand (Figures 7.10 and 7.11). He expressed it also in his views about the artist and his relationship to society. As the translator and author of many books and articles on Rodin's artistic career, Kōtarō was familiar with Rodin's declaration that his genius had remained unrecognized until late in life[43]: "I suffered for my sculpture. If I had not been stubborn I would never have done what I have done. . . . Until I was fifty, I had all the aggravations of poverty, I had always lived like a laborer, but the joy of work made me bear everything."[44] In Kōtarō's eyes, this assertion of the priority of art over life made Rodin a true artist.

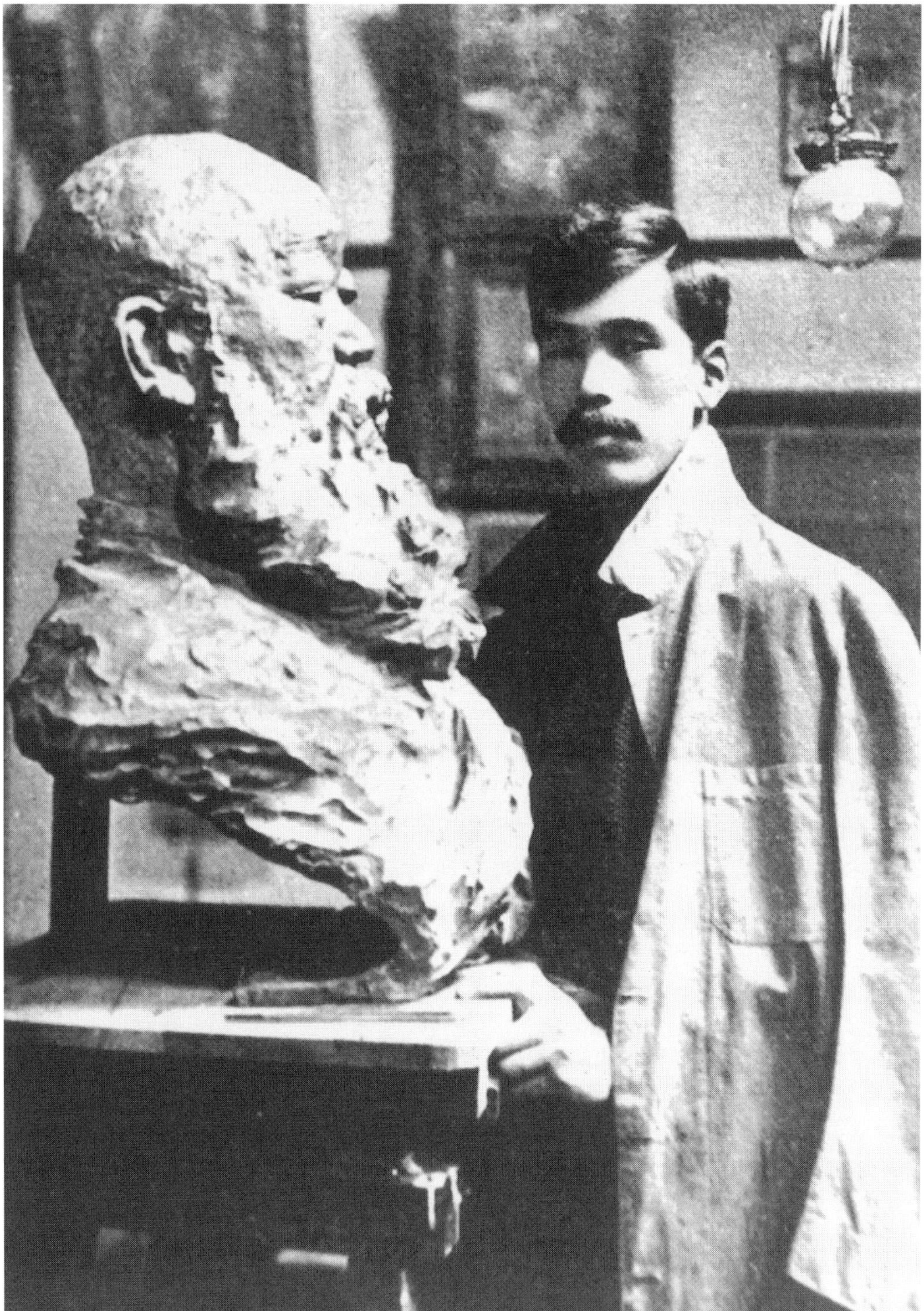

Figure 7.9 Photograph of Takamura Kōtarō with bust of his father, 1911. Photo courtesy of Takamura Tadashi.

Rodin's artistic struggles no doubt resonated deeply with Kōtarō because of the trouble he had in establishing himself as a sculptor. During the Taishō era, there was as yet little market in Japan for Western-style sculpture since it was seen primarily as a public art form. As the commission of Ōkura's portrait reveals, the realities of the sculptor's life often forced Kōtarō to compromise the high ideals he professed. He did, however, refuse to participate, either by submitting his work or by serving as a judge, in government-sponsored competitive exhibitions, whose role he saw as being comparable to the French Salons.

"THE SUN IS GREEN"

"Green Sun" (1910), one of Kōtarō's most influential and oft-cited essays, was a profession of the Romantic aesthetic principles he held until the onset of the Pacific War. Written in a self-conscious, almost confessional style, studded with German and French terms that were unfamiliar, but no doubt impressive, to his readers, it propelled him into the artistic limelight at the unusually young age of twenty-eight (by Japanese count). Its success led him to devote himself increasingly to art criticism, a relatively new genre of writing in Japan, and an unusual one for a practicing sculptor. These articles, which appeared in avant-garde art magazines, supplemented the income he made from the sale of his sculpture.

In "Green Sun," Kōtarō championed artistic autonomy. Art, he held, is universal, transcending time and place:

> I was born a Japanese; and as a fish cannot leave the water to make his life, I will always be a Japanese whether I acknowledge that fact to myself or not. And, by the same token, just as a fish has no consciousness that it is wet with water, there are times when I take no notice that I am Japanese. . . . At such times, I never think of Japan. I proceed without hesitation, in terms of what I think and feel. Seen later, perhaps the work I have created may have something "Japanese" about it, for all I know. Or then again, perhaps not. To me, as an artist, it makes no difference at all.[45]

He also urged viewers to look beyond surface appearances and respond emotively to the work of art.

> If another man paints a picture of a green sun, I have no intention to say that I will deny him. For it may be that I will see it that way myself. Nor can I merely continue on, missing the value of the painting just because "the sun is green." For the quality of the work will not depend on whether the sun depicted is either green or red. What I wish to experience, to savor, as I said before, is the flavor of the work in which the sun is green.[46]

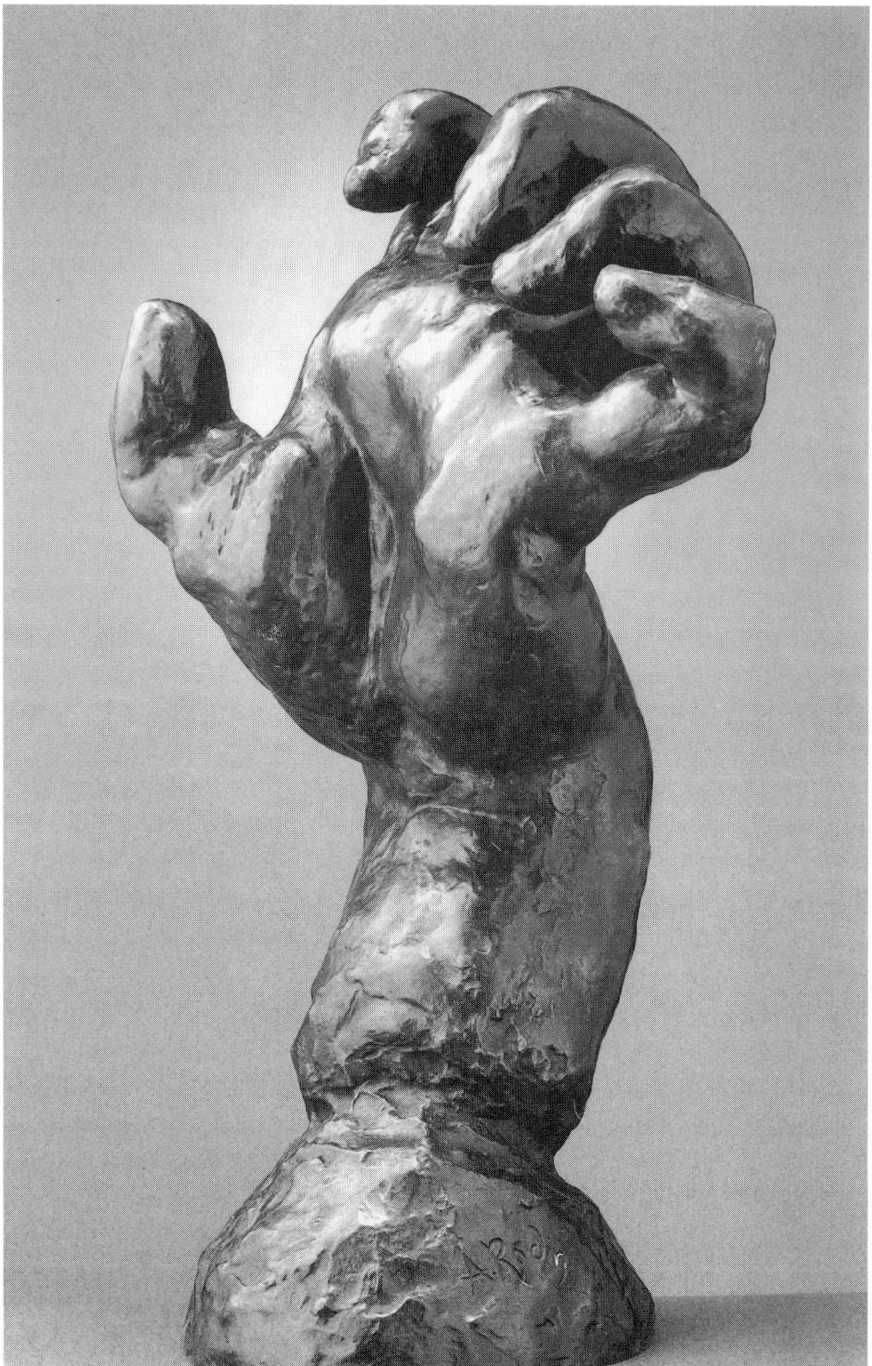

Figure 7.10 Auguste Rodin. Large Clenched Left Hand, ca. 1885; cast 1974. Bronze, height 47 cm. The Metropolitan Museum of Art; gift of B. Gerald Cantor Art Foundation, 1984.

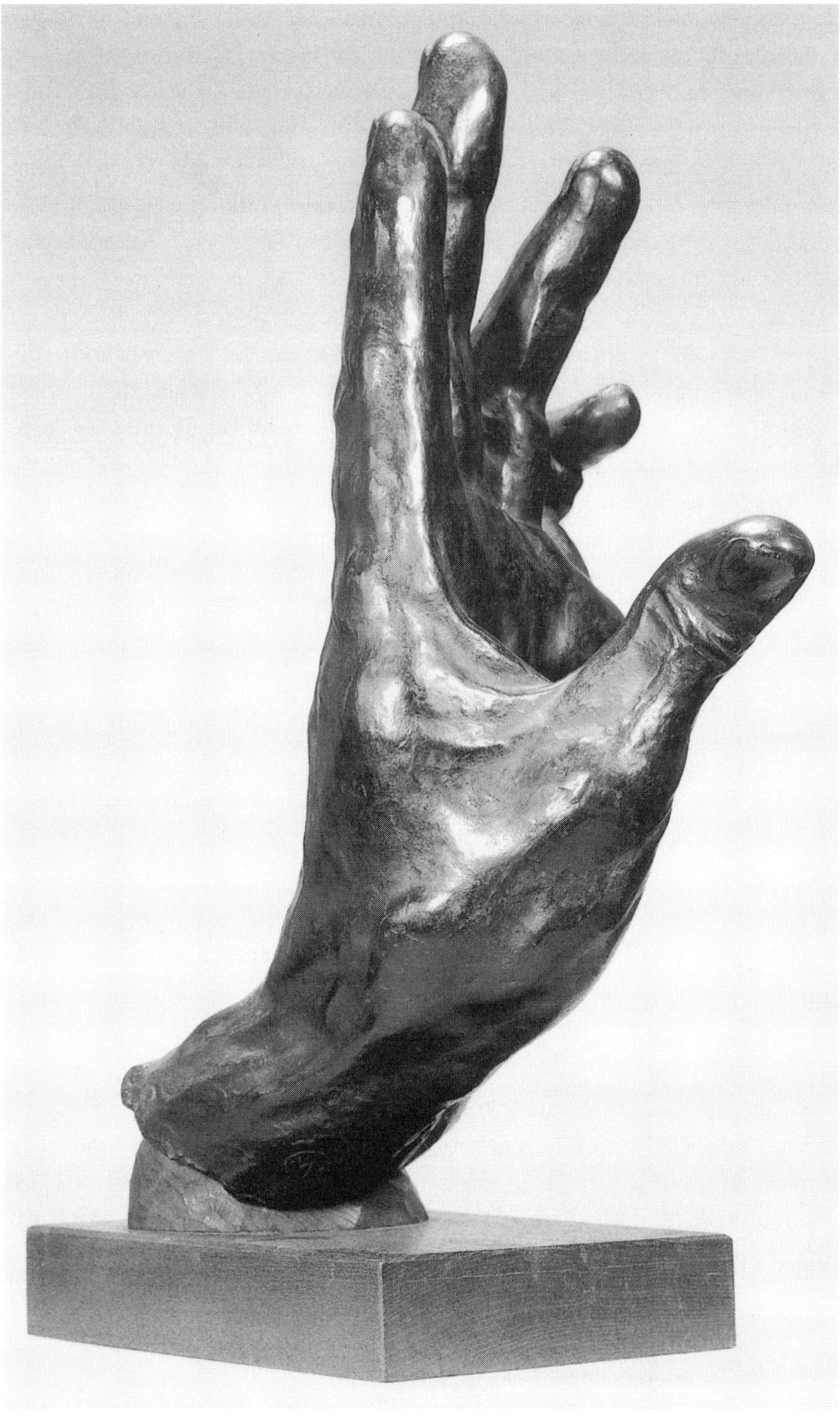

Figure 7.11 Takamura Kōtarō. Hand, 1923. Bronze, height 38 cm. Collection of the National Museum of Modern Art, Tokyo.

Empathy was the key to artistic appreciation. In criticizing the work of a contemporary sculptor exhibited at the Third Bunten exhibition of 1910, he put it quite bluntly: "Art isn't interesting unless it makes you feel something without fuss, directly."[47] This view is strikingly similar to Baudelaire's definition of Romanticism: "Le romantisme n'est précisément ni dans le choix des sujets, ni dans la vérité exacte, mais dans la manière de sentir"[48] (Romanticism is neither precisely in the choice of subjects nor in veristic accuracy but in the manner of feeling).

Kōtarō wrote often about sculpture. This focus reflected both his personal experiences as a sculptor and his conviction that this art form was more difficult than painting for the Japanese viewer to appreciate. From the very beginning of his career as a writer, his coverage was unusually broad, ranging from Japanese and European to Egyptian sculpture. Time and again, he stressed the importance of capturing the essence of the subject rather than merely its outward likeness. In "The Appeal of Sculpture" (Chōkoku no omoshiromi), published in 1910, he proclaimed that those works that move us do so "not because they reproduce nature, but because they enable our eyes to see a vision of nature's soul—because they enable our ears to listen directly to nature's breathing, enable our fingers to touch nature's pulse."[49] The ability to do so, he believed, was what separated the sculptor from the craftsman.

He returned to this theme many years later in "Two Aspects of Realism," a lecture that he gave in 1937. Commenting on the shallow reproduction of reality (*shasei*) typical of crafts such as *netsuke*, he declared:

> These things are interesting in a certain way, but they are in the end, not sculptures. Those who make them have no sculptural grasp of nature and objects. Where a round thing is simply presented as round, a thin thing as thin, there's no sculpture. A sculptor has, as part of his being, the knack—or the plastic sensibility—of making something thick but making it look thin, making something square but making it look round.[50]

Kōun served as an aesthetic foil in many of Kōtarō's writings. Although the son respected his father's devotion to his craft, he considered the traditional values and artistic practices he embodied to be antithetical to modern sculpture. As he explained near the end of his own life in "My Relationship with My Father," Kōun was a craftsman, not a sculptor:

> When I think about it calmly, after all, my father Kōun was a typical *shokunin* of the late Edo and early Meiji eras. He was what was called a woodcarver (*kibori-shi*) or more precisely a Buddhist sculptor (*bushiya*). Although he created a variety of works that seem to transcend the range of the Buddhist sculptor—the bronze statues of Nankō or Saigo Takamori, for example—even these are informed by the outlook of a Buddhist sculptor. And yet, the craftsman's

strengths and weaknesses can be attributed to this ethical outlook and personal temperament. This craftsman's way of looking at things continued until the end of his life. Even as he displayed in all his work a stubborn craftsman ethic that wouldn't yield to human feelings or authority, he was extremely susceptible to worldly success, and had a *chōnin*'s tendency to attribute great importance to his title of Imperial Craftsman Third Rank, Second Level, which he carefully inscribed on the boxes for his sculptures.[51]

CONCLUSION

The struggles between Kōun and Kōtarō to come to terms with themselves and each other offer a rare personal vantage point from which to appreciate the contradictory voices and heterogeneous claims in the intense debates about the nature of the artistic profession that began in the Meiji era. Both men were equally dedicated professionals, separated by differing views about what a sculptor was, wasn't, or should be. Their professional self-definition called into question the meaning of sculpture, the relationship between arts and crafts, and the distinction between the fine and commercial arts, thorny issues with no easy resolution even today.

The international expansion of the art market and introduction of European sculptural forms, media, and styles broadened the professional opportunities for both Kōun and his son. Japan's engagement with European art also spurred and legitimated Kōtarō's efforts to fashion himself, not merely as a professional possessed of technical skills but also as a cultural arbiter, with the intellectual authority to guide the public's appreciation of art. Cultural interaction with Europe and America, however, also set in place professional stereotypes that denied or demeaned both Kōun and Kōtarō's legitimacy as Japanese sculptors.

Even as father and son, each in his own way, responded to the manifold changes in their profession, they were also reshaping it. Kōun was hardly the rigid reactionary his son claimed him to be. On the contrary, he vividly testifies to the successful strategies of accommodation and invention that many Edo *shokunin* adopted to survive economically and professionally. Nor was Kōtarō the rebellious, bohemian *artiste* he professed himself to be. Together, Kōun and Kōtarō throw light on the formation of two modern myths: the craftsman, stubbornly dedicated to his traditional craft; and the sculptor, possessed of a transcendent genius that enables him to grasp the essence of life and transmit it through his art.

Chapter Eight

The Formation of a Japanese Architectural Profession

JONATHAN M. REYNOLDS

One popular opinion survey from the 1970s identified the architect Kurokawa Kishō as the third most popular man in Japan.[1] Today Kurokawa continues to maintain a high profile as a designer of prominent public projects and as an advisor to government. Architects have gained a special place in the public imagination in Japan; they are often perceived as dynamic leaders who can effectively combine highly esteemed technical prowess with a sweeping social vision and personal style. Yet the creation of the "architect" as an occupational category is a relatively recent phenomenon in Japan. It was only during the Meiji period (1868–1912) that the institutions that characterize the architect as a modern professional, as distinct from other older building craftsmen, were formed. This chapter examines the establishment of some of these critical institutions and analyzes efforts by several of Japan's first architects to define their profession and its role in society.

The master carpenter (*daiku tōryō*), the craftsman in premodern construction who most closely resembles the modern architect, combined carpentry skills with knowledge of planning and design. He supervised every aspect of a building project. But as William Coaldrake has argued, the master carpenter was distinct from the modern architect in several significant ways:

> The carpenter, therefore, must be seen as both artisan and artist, architect and builder. Like the medieval mason of Europe, the Japanese carpenter designed and built in a single, organic process. . . . It is important to note here that this process is very different from architectural practice today. The modern architectural profession makes a doctrinaire distinction between design and execution. This is reinforced by separate training for architects and builders, making it difficult to appreciate the role of the traditional master carpenter who did both.[2]

Even the master carpenters from the elite carpentry families who managed the major construction projects of the Edo period (1615–1868) were rigorously trained in the craft of construction. Architects usually had far less experience with nitty-gritty building techniques. In terms of this kind of experience, the Japanese architects who carved out a place for themselves during the Meiji period had more in common with their European colleagues than they did with these building craftsmen.

In the West, the distinction between architects and other building craftsmen became increasingly important from the Renaissance onward. There was, undoubtedly, some justification for increased specialization on account of the increased complexity of major building projects. However, this process also had profound social implications independent of "rational" benefits of this emerging division of labor. Magali Sarfatti Larson has observed: "The first architects were not only freed from the stigma of manual work, they gained prestige from the complexity, the civic importance, and the ancient aesthetic lineage claimed for the new style of building."[3] As intellectual workers, architects assumed higher social status than carpenters or masons. The professional organizations and centers for architectural education formed in Europe and the United States in the late eighteenth and nineteenth centuries reinforced the role of the architect as a technologist and artist apart from the builder.[4]

In Japan, the rapid introduction of new building technology and architecture styles from the West beginning in the middle of the nineteenth century led to a dramatic shift in the division of labor in the building trades. During the early stages of this process, Japanese carpenters played a creative role in the adoption of Western building practices. Over time, however, as the first Japanese architects entered the field, a new professional hierarchy began to emerge. Architects eventually seized many of the responsibilities that had once been the prerogative of master carpenters in key segments of the building industry.

THE FIRST IMPACT OF WESTERN ARCHITECTURE ON BUILDING IN JAPAN

Western building technology breached Japan's wall of seclusion even before the arrival of Commodore Perry's black ships in 1853.[5] Perry's threatening presence only intensified the pressure to modernize. As early as 1850, the Saga domain employed Western technology to construct a brick reverberating furnace for iron smelting to improve that province's weapons production. The domain probably acquired the technology directly from texts such as

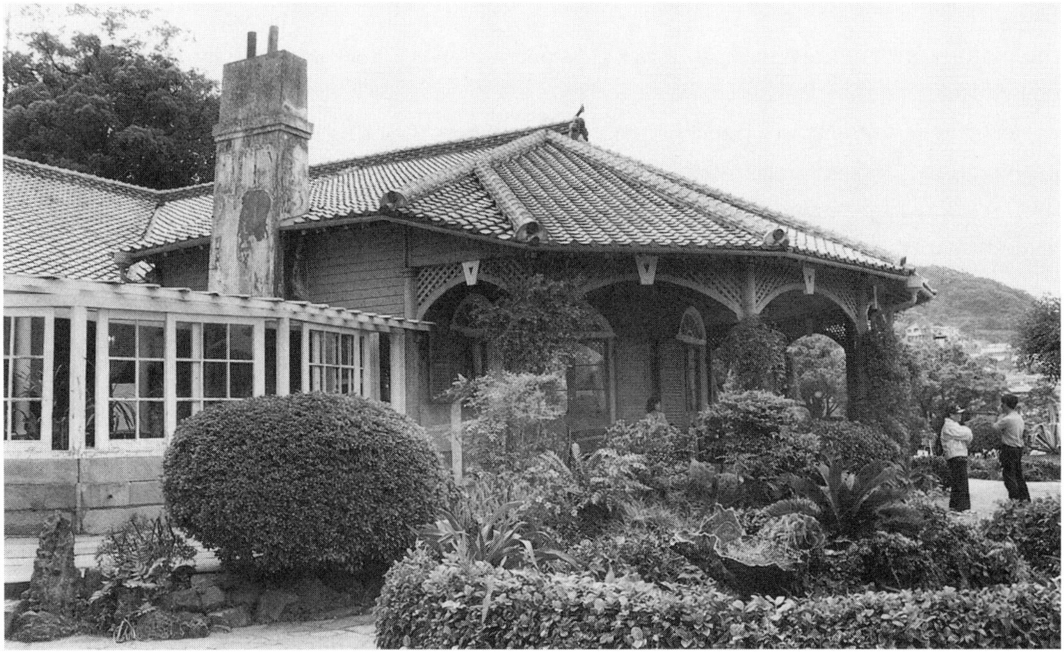

Figure 8.1 Koyama Hidenoshin. Glover Residence, Nagasaki, 1863. Jonathan M. Reynolds photograph.

Ulrich Huguenin's military treatise of 1826.[6] The feudal domains grasped at Western technology to address the threat of both foreign powers and domestic rivals. The shogunate and other provinces quickly followed Saga's lead, employing Western methods to build foundries, weaving mills, and shipyards.[7] This process of technological transfer accelerated after the fall of the shogun to imperial forces in the Meiji Restoration of 1868.

During this transitional period, Western architectural styles were also introduced into Japan. Japanese workmen constructed warehouses, churches, and residences for foreigners in the treaty ports in the late 1850s and 1860s. For these clients, they produced architectural forms based on Western models, though in most cases they continued to rely on familiar building techniques and materials. One of the best-preserved examples of this type of structure is the Glover Residence (Figure 8.1), which was completed in Nagasaki in 1863. The master carpenter Koyama Hidenoshin (1828–98) constructed the building as a guesthouse for the English merchant Thomas Glover (1838–1911).[8] The design combined Western elements such as glass windows having painted sashes, French doors, and a stone-floored veranda with Japanese techniques for framing the structure and tiling the roof. Exterior walls were covered in clapboard siding, a method of construction used in both traditions, but behind the clapboards the Japanese workmen employed an indigenous traditional earthen wall-building technique known as *komaikabe*.[9]

The master carpenter Shimizu Kisuke II (1815–81) was especially successful at adapting to the tremendous changes in building during the transition from the Edo period to the Meiji. He was born Fujisawa Seishichi, the third son of a merchant in Tōyama. He became a carpenter and traveled to Edo in search of work. In Edo, he married into the family of the master carpenter Shimizu Kisuke, who had worked on various projects for the shogunate. The son-in-law recognized the potential for opportunities in the newly established treaty port of Yokohama and set up shop there. He soon inherited the business and, in 1861, won the appointment of the shogunate to handle public construction at the port. At this time, Shimizu began to collaborate with the American R. P. Bridgens (1819–91).[10] As Fujimori Terunobu has argued, this partnership was decisive; through Bridgens Shimizu learned many of the Western architectural features that characterized Shimizu's later work.[11] He was so successful that his company, Shimizu Construction, has survived to become one of the largest construction firms in Japan, with offices worldwide.

Shimizu Kisuke II is associated with some of the most dynamic structures erected during the Edo-Meiji transition, including the Tsukiji Hotel (1868), which he built in collaboration with Bridgens, and the Mitsui House (First National Bank, 1872; Figure 8.2). The Mitsui House was built by the rapidly growing Mitsui Company to house its new national bank. Before the building was completed, the government announced that it would run the national bank and appropriate the building for that purpose.[12]

The Mitsui House must have appeared predominantly "Western" to many Japanese viewers when it was first completed, at Kaiun Bridge in the heart of Tokyo's business district. It was a wood-framed structure but had masonry-faced walls and an elaborate two-story balcony across the full width of the façade. On the ground floor, shuttered windows alternated with two sets of French doors surmounted with glass fanlights. Along the second floor, five shuttered French doors opened out onto the balcony. A central multistoried tower and two smaller flanking towers rose above the main block of the building. Shimizu employed lavish building materials in this showcase.[13] The columns of the balcony, various details, and even the roof tiles were made of bronze. Although the inclusion of masonry, balconies, and towers suggest Bridgens's influence, there was still strong evidence of Shimizu's Japanese carpenter's training.[14] Above the extravagant bronze columns along the balconies, he placed polychrome transoms carved with the auspicious theme of the

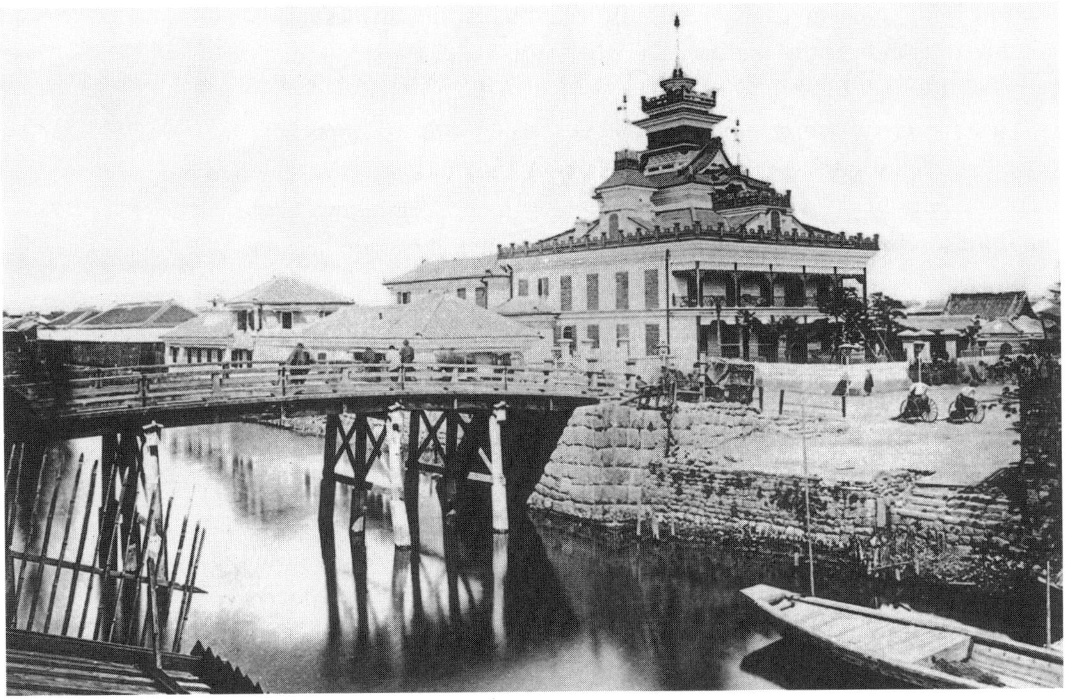

Figure 8.2 Shimizu Kisuke II. Mitsui House (First National Bank), Tokyo, 1872. Archives of the Architectural Institute of Japan.

turtle and crane. Shimizu articulated the towers with "Chinese-style gables" (*karahafu*) and "plover gables" (*chidori hafu*), transforming the "Western-style" central tower into a Japanese castle keep.

The hybrid nature of the Mitsui House is an apt reflection of the dynamic cultural milieu in which it was constructed. The design should not be viewed as a failed attempt at "authentic" reproduction of either Japanese or Western models. The modern materials and Western architectural elements could act as free-floating signs of modernity, which, when combined with high-status features drawn from Japanese architectural traditions, created a distinguished and progressive appearance reflective of the importance of this central new financial institution.

The Western concessions attracted widespread interest. Prints illustrating the exotic manners, clothing, and architecture of the treaty ports became extremely popular.[15] In the late 1860s and 1870s, Western architectural forms began to spread beyond the confines of the treaty ports. Carpenters, inspired by the Western-style buildings and their representations in the popular press, created structures clothed in extravagant assemblage of Japanese and Western decorative motifs.

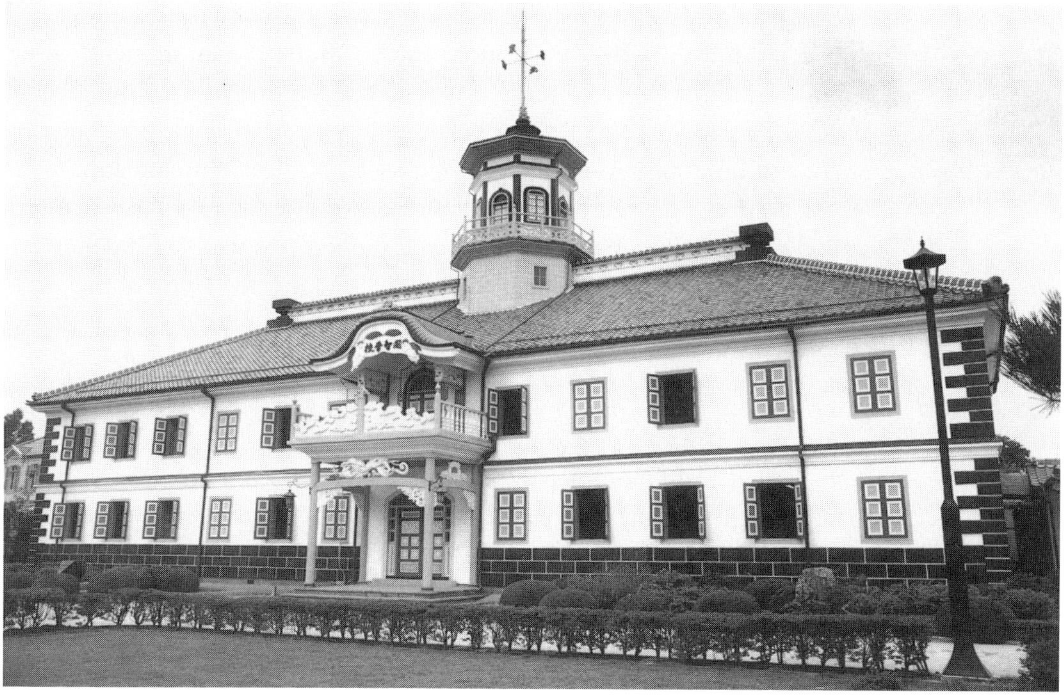

Figure 8.3 Tateishi Seijū. Kai'chi Primary School, Matsumoto, 1876. Jonathan M. Reynolds photograph.

One dramatic example of this eclectic approach is the Kai'chi Primary School (Figure 8.3) in Matsumoto, completed in 1876. The school was constructed by the master carpenter Tateishi Seijū (1829–94). The tiled roof and "Chinese style" gable (*karahafu*) over the main entrance are characteristic of certain pre-Meiji public buildings and of ruling-class residential structures. But Tateishi also appropriated a number of prominent Western features in the structure, drawing on buildings by Shimizu and others as models. He traveled to Tokyo twice in 1875 and sketched many of the Western-style buildings that he visited.[16]

The school is a two-story structure with classrooms and offices arranged on either side of central hallways in the Western manner. The building incorporates modern materials such as imported glass. The school façade is framed with quoining and an apron of paint and plaster that reproduce the appearance of Western masonry construction. Baroque *putti* suspended from the "Chinese-style" gable unravel a banderole proclaiming the school's name.[17] The cultural identity of some of the structure's features is ambiguous. Although in this particular case the plaster at the base of the façade was designed to resemble Western masonry, the effect was not entirely foreign; the lower portion of the exterior of building façades was often marked off in a similar fashion in wood in Japanese construction. The prominent tower, reminiscent of the Mitsui House, can be traced to both Western models and Japanese precedents. The Kai'chi Primary School is the result of a complex process of appropriation and recombination of diverse architectural elements. Western architectural forms were appealing even though the materials and methods that originally generated those forms were not being used. The school vividly demonstrates the degree to which the allure of the modern was being felt outside of the capital and the treaty ports.

SOUND BUILDING FOR A STRONG NATION

The intellectual and politician Nishi Amane (1829–97) published an article in 1874 in the journal *Meiroku zasshi* in which he used Western brick construction as a metaphor to frame his defense of good government and people's rights. Nishi described brick walls that he encountered in Europe as "so firm and strong that they cannot be rocked or bent."[18] Nishi acknowledged that similar construction was being used to build the new Ginza "brick town" north of Shinbashi, but he felt that those buildings did "not compare in strength and firmness with those of Europe."[19] For Nishi, the Japanese political structure did not measure up to its Western counterparts any more than contemporary Japanese architecture did. Just as a building could be strong only if each brick were intact and set square and upright, the state could only be strong if individual rights were protected from the arbitrary oppression of officials. He concluded: "The builder and the statesman, therefore, will be successful if the former does not trifle with the character of a single brick and if the latter does not make light of the rights of the common people. Especially is this the case in a country such as ours in which the bricks are basically fragile and the rights of the people are especially weak."[20] Some officials in the newly formed Meiji government might not have been sympathetic toward Nishi's admonitions about good government based on people's rights, but many would have responded positively to Nishi's metaphor equating the firmness of Western architecture with a stable modern government. Indeed, Western architecture became one of the preferred media through which the government attempted to present a strong and progressive face to the world.

The Meiji government drew heavily on Western architecture to meet its changing needs. Interest in Western architecture was pragmatic; the West could, for example, offer efficient prototypes for modern office buildings to house the country's burgeoning bureaucracy. The choice of Western archi-

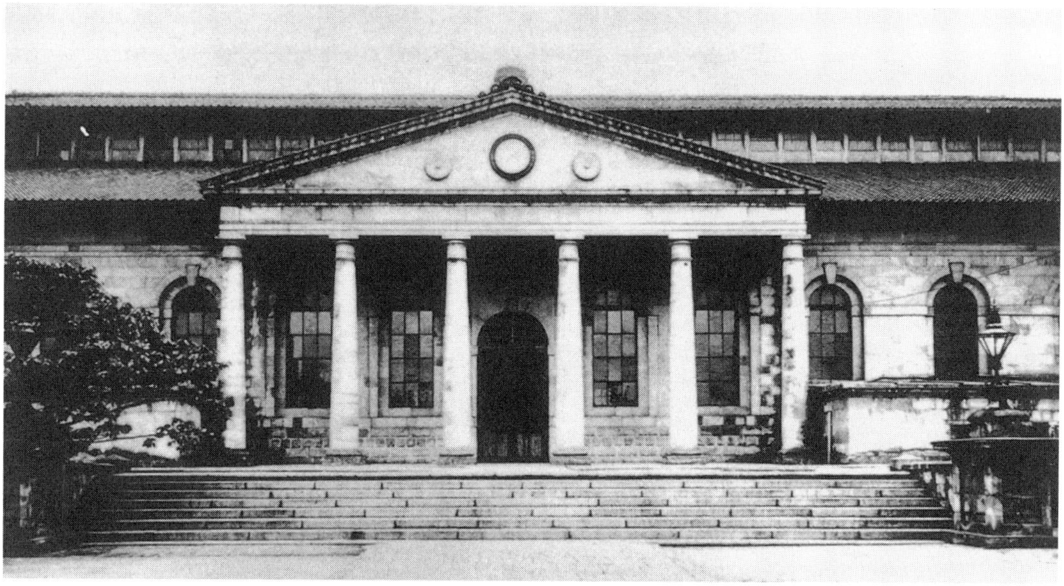

Figure 8.4 Thomas Waters. Osaka Mint Foundry Building, Osaka, 1868. Archives of the Architectural Institute of Japan.

tectural *styles* also had profound ideological implications. Designs based on the West's monumental public architecture could project power in a manner appropriate to the imperial government's aspirations. The patronage of these forms was a direct outgrowth of the commitment to the modernization efforts at the heart of the new regime's policies. Western-style architecture served as a tangible expression of the government's determination to transform Japan into a modern nation capable of interacting with the Western powers on equal terms.

The government looked to foreign technicians for some of its earliest construction projects, such as the Osaka Mint (Figure 8.4). In 1868, the year the new regime took power, it purchased from the British minting equipment and materials used in a mint in Hong Kong. The Irishman Thomas James Waters (1842–?) was hired to design the foundry for the mint. The enormous masonry structure (the largest factory in Asia at the time) featured a prominent pedimented portico supported by six stone Tuscan columns on the main riverfront façade. The foundry was by no means graceful, but it projected an image of confidence and stability that was essential for this key financial institution of the as-yet-untested government.

Waters completed a number of projects for the government, including the Reception Building (Senpukan) for the Osaka Mint (1871), the Takebashi Army Barracks in Tokyo (1871), and the Ginza "brick-town" (1872–77), a

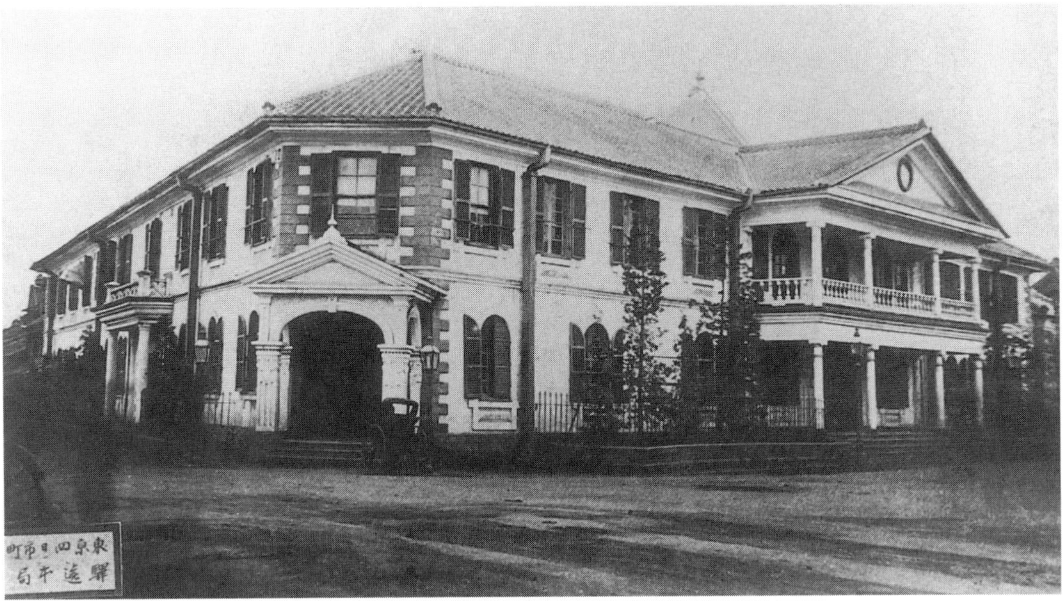

Figure 8.5 Hayashi Tadahiro. Postal Service, Tokyo, 1874. Archives of the Architectural Institute of Japan.

partially executed project to rebuild a section of downtown Tokyo in brick after the devastating fire of 1872. Waters's work in Japan encompassed a range of skills, among them surveying, architecture, and engineering. He described himself as a "surveyor general."[21] This kind of generalist was just what was needed at this early stage of the incorporation of Western methods to Japan. Over time, however, government expectations rose. The generalists could not produce complex designs on a par with academically trained architects. The government did hire a few such architects from Europe and the United States as consultants. The English architect Josiah Conder (1852–1920) and the German firm of Ende and Böckmann are the most significant examples. By the 1890s, however, Japanese architects educated in Japan and abroad were able to meet the government's demands without relying on continued foreign assistance.

Many of the Meiji government's projects were constructed under the direction of the offices in the Treasury Ministry and the Ministry of Public Works. In 1880, there were twenty-three technicians affiliated with the latter ministry.[22] Most of the technicians, including some who had worked as master carpenters under the shogunal government, were trained along traditional lines but able to adapt to the government's orders for Western-style buildings. Hayashi Tadahiro (1835–93) was the best known of these government technicians. He worked as a blacksmith before he pursued carpentry.

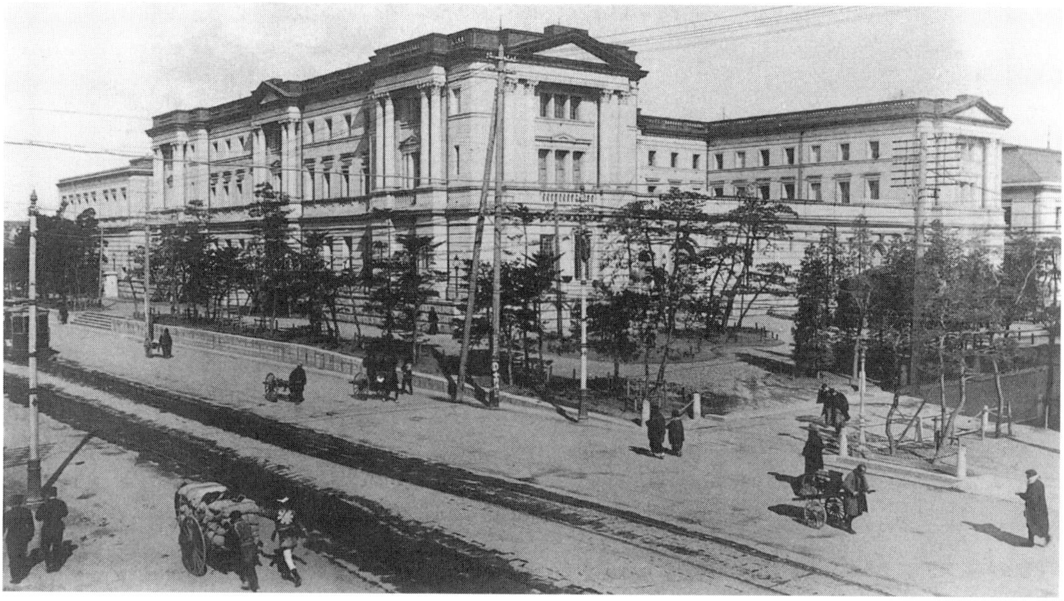

Figure *8.6* Tatsuno Kingo. Bank of Japan, Tokyo, 1896. Archives of the Architectural Institute of Japan.

After a period in Yokohama in Bridgens's employ, he joined the Treasury Ministry and produced designs such as the Home Ministry (1874) and an office for the Postal Service (1874). In his design for the Postal Service (Figure 8.5), Hayashi signaled the modernity of this government agency with a two-story pedimented portico, prominent quoins, and wood shutters on the windows. This work was typical of many government structures of the period.

Tatsuno Kingo (1854–1919) was one of Japan's first modern architects. He graduated from the first class of the government's College of Engineering in 1879 (more on this later) and then studied in England for three years. Tatsuno taught architecture for many years and also completed numerous important commissions for the government and for private clients. The Bank of Japan was completed in 1896, one year after the Japanese defeated the Chinese in the Sino-Japanese war. The bank offers vivid evidence of the speed with which the radically different Western approach to design and construction matured in Japan. This gray edifice located in Tokyo's business district was constructed of iron-reinforced brick faced with stone (Figure 8.6). Tatsuno took an exhaustive study tour of Europe to ensure that the design was in accordance with the standards of the time. The grand, neo-Baroque Banque National de Belgique (1874) in Brussels is thought to have been one of Tatsuno's most important models, although his ornamentation is somewhat more subdued than that of the earlier work.[23] The imposing façade of the Bank of Japan eloquently communicates the imperial ambition and sobriety of the later part of the Meiji era.

PROFESSIONAL INSTITUTIONS

During the first fifteen years of Meiji, Japan relied heavily on Western advisors in technical fields, including architecture and civil engineering. To reduce this dependence, the Ministry of Public Works (Kōbushō) established the College of Engineering in 1871; instruction began there in 1873.[24] The College of Engineering began to offer a full-time program in architecture under the tutelage of the English architect Josiah Conder in 1877 and graduated its first class of four students in 1879.[25] Conder was the principal instructor for the program until 1884 and lectured there until 1888. He played a central role in the establishment of rigorous academic training in architecture in Japan. Conder and other foreign advisors were expensive, however, and the College of Engineering replaced the foreigners with Japanese instructors as quickly as possible. Sone Tatsuzō (1852–1937), a student in Conder's first graduating class, became an assistant professor in the College of Engineering in 1881. Kojima Noriyuki (1857–1918), who trained at Cornell, began to teach engineering in the program in the same year. Tatsuno Kingo, who was a classmate of Sone's and had recently returned from postgraduate training in England, became a professor in the program in 1884. By the time the College of Engineering became absorbed into the Imperial University in 1886, the responsibility for education in Western-style architecture in Japan was primarily in Japanese hands.

The establishment of a university-level program in architecture marked a dramatic break with Japanese practices of the past. Carpenters in Japan usually inherited their occupation from their fathers or were adopted into established carpentry families. They were trained from an early age through apprenticeship and learned about building materials and the use of tools, rules of proportion, stylistic conventions, and planning guidelines through hands-on experience.[26] The university-based training process was radically different from the patterns of occupational access and methods of education in the building trades.[27] Students of architecture in the College of Engineering were often from backgrounds unrelated to architecture.[28] They gained the opportunity to study at the college on the basis of successful entrance exams that tested academic knowledge rather than practical building experience. Once they were admitted, the students were educated for six years at the expense of the state and were then required to work for the government for a period of seven years after graduation. The program was divided into three two-year phases. During the first two years, the students studied liberal arts and general classes in science and engineering. During the second two years, they began to concentrate on their primary field (architecture, mechanical engineering, and so on) and divided their time between class work and field experience. At this stage, classes included architecture, architectural drawing, general drawing, surveying, applied measurement, materials, geology, construction inspection, and design inspection.[29] Students increasingly concentrated on practical experience in the field in the final two-year phase of their training.[30] They visited building sites to have a better understanding of the construction process, but they were not expected to acquire the building skills required for actual construction work. Their architectural training at the Imperial University prepared them for quite another role; they were trained to be "executives" who could design projects in Western style and could serve as intermediaries between patrons and builders.[31]

In her study *The Rise of Professionalism*, Larson has observed that "for professions, the most significant 'modern' dimensions are the advance of science and cognitive rationality, and the related rationalization and growing differentiation in the division of labor."[32] In this system, the university played a crucial role in the transmission of scientific knowledge and served as a center for research. In addition, by providing institutionalized certification of this training, the university contributed to the rationalization process resulting in the division of labor that distinguishes modern professionals from craftsmen or laborers. The formation of a university-level program for architects was therefore essential to the emergence of architecture as a modern profession in Japan.

In the 1880s, several other important milestones were reached in the process of professionalization. The first professional organization for architects was founded in 1886. It was named the Zōka Gakkai, or "Building Institute," or literally "House Building Institute," a title that aptly reflected the emphasis on building within the Japanese architectural community at this time. A professional organization for engineers, the Kō Gakkai, had been formed seven years before, and the founders of the Zōka Gakkai assembled their new group to gain autonomy from the older organization.[33]

The Zōka Gakkai was modeled to a great extent on the Royal Institute of British Architects (RIBA), which had been very successful at advancing architectural standards and improving the standing of its members since its founding in 1834.[34] The members hoped that they too would be able to improve their position and the profession as a whole. As declared in the group's initial statement of principles, the "organization's aim is to measure the improvement and progress of the building industry through the exchange of knowledge."[35] To that end, the Zōka Gakkai met regularly, sponsored lectures, and published an architectural journal. The emphasis on "progress" through "the exchange of knowledge" is a reflection of the founders' acknowledgment of the link between the production of a specialized field of knowledge and the profession's future.

The year it was founded, the Zōka Gakkai established an architectural journal, *Kenchiku zasshi*, which went to press the following January. Here too the organization was following the precedents of the Kō Gakkai and the RIBA, which had publications of their own.[36] *Kenchiku zasshi* recorded the activities of the Zōka Gakkai and published articles on various topics relevant to the profession. In its second year of publication, for example, the journal included reports on architecture around the world, such as a travel log of a member's visits to various European sites, discussions of architects in suburban Chicago, and plans for the water supply for the city of Paris. In this the journal was acting as an "imaginary museum of world architecture," providing access to buildings scattered around the globe and serving to select and install certain works within the canon of architecture "worthy" of emulation.[37] The journal reflected interest in architectural history through an analysis of the Hiunkaku, a residential structure at the Buddhist temple Nishi Honganji dating to the seventeenth century. Technical articles were the most numerous. There were pieces on the handling of mortar in cold weather, the manufacture of cement and bricks in Japan, and the problem of fires in theaters in Europe and the United States.

Writing had been an important medium for the building trades in Japan long before the Meiji Restoration. Carpenters' manuals, known as *hidensho* ("secret hereditary writings"), *hinagatabon* ("pattern books"), or *gijutsusho* ("technique books"), date back at least to the fourteenth century.[38] These manuals were jealously guarded within carpenters' families and were handed down from generation to generation. At the beginning of the Edo period, the demand for carpenters outstripped the supply provided through traditional channels of training, and the strictures of secret transmission began to break down. Some manuscripts of manuals were reproduced as woodblock printed books; through this medium architectural knowledge was distributed to a much wider audience.[39]

Even though the dissemination of architectural information through print was not new in the Meiji period, there are significant differences between the earlier carpenters' manuals and the later architectural journals such as *Kenchiku zasshi*. The value of the former—their legitimacy—rested on the belief that they accurately transmitted appropriate architectural forms from the past (the character *den* for the term *hidensho* means to transmit or bequeath). *Kenchiku zasshi* and later journals certainly dealt with architectural history and with contemporary architecture employing historicizing architectural detail, but the transmission of past architectural forms per se was not their primary goal. The weight of coverage focused squarely on contemporary practice as contemporary practice, and the greatest attention was directed toward newly developed technology. This is not to say that carpentry before the Meiji restoration was unchanging; carpenters had often proven to be resilient and innovative in the face of constantly changing conditions. Nonetheless, the ideological force of carpenters' manuals was rooted in the concept of continuity, whereas the ideological justification for the architectural journals was the dissemination of technology in the name of "progress."

Both the Zōka Gakkai and the journal *Kenchiku zasshi* contributed to the improvement of professional standards, facilitated the flow of information, and gave architects a forum for debating major issues in architecture.

ARTIST OR ENGINEER?

A heated debate arose within the Japanese architectural community at the end of the nineteenth century as architects trained in recently imported Western architectural methods and styles struggled to define the parameters of their profession. At issue was the appropriate balance of technology and artistic expression in architectural practice.[40] Should the architect concentrate primarily on structural problems and on the development of new technology (was the architect, in effect, a special type of engineer), or should the architect view himself first and foremost as an artist? The profession of architecture had emerged as but one part of a broad program of modernization initiated in response to a national crisis. Therefore architects approached the question of their professional identity with a sense of urgency, hoping to shape their new profession so that it could best serve their country's needs.

In the early years, most architects recognized that aesthetics had an important role in their profession, but at the same time they viewed architecture as a field within engineering. This engineering bias is reflected in the fact that the first academic training ground for architects was established within an engineering program. Kawai Kōzō (1856–1934) reflected this conception of architecture when he wrote:

> First of all, aspects of our field of building studies (*zōkagaku*) fall within the sphere of engineering (*kōgaku*). Yet, while our field shares important features with the field of engineering in general, there are also major differences. What the field of building studies has in common with engineering is that it expresses the laws of physics [in meeting structural requirements]; it differs from engineering in that it also expresses the artistic.[41]

Kawai's view that architecture was both a science and an art was representative of the position of many architects of his generation.

After decades of extraordinarily rapid change, the profession entered a process of intense self-examination. During this period, architects' views of their profession began to coalesce into two factions. A young graduate from the Imperial University named Itō Chūta (1867–1954) was instrumental in the formation of one of these factions. In 1894, just two years after graduation, Itō published an essay in *Kenchiku zasshi* firmly asserting that architecture in Japan should be one of the fine arts (*bijutsu*).[42] Itō pointed out that in the West "architecture"—and here he used the English loan-word "*akitekuchūru*" written in *katakana* syllabary—had been grouped with fine arts of the highest order since antiquity. He argued that in Japan, just as in the West, architecture should be viewed as one of the fine arts, not as an industrial art (*kōgei*).

Itō criticized the use of the word *zōka*, or "house building," as a translation for the English word *architecture*, because the English term covered a far wider range of design activities than just house building. He advocated the substitution of the word *kenchiku* for *zōka* arguing that although *kenchiku* was still not ideal, its meaning was ambiguous enough that it could be stretched to cover the full scope of the profession. Itō also objected to the use of the characters *gaku* ("studies"), as in *zōkagaku* ("architectural studies"); and *gakkai* ("institute"), as in "Zōka Gakkai" in an architectural context, because these characters could impart a scientific or technical tone that was inappropriate for a fine art. Itō proposed that the Zōka Gakkai be renamed Kenchiku Kyōkai, or Architectural Association, arguing that the new name would more effectively convey the artistic nature of architectural practice. Three years later, the Zōka Gakkai partially followed Itō's suggestions by changing its name to Kenchiku Gakkai (Architectural Institute).[43]

Itō's effort to assert the primacy of aesthetics in architecture was inextricably linked with his growing appreciation for Japan's architectural past. Until the middle of the Meiji period, most Japanese architects working with Western styles and building technology ignored Japan's own architectural traditions.[44] The architectural historian Inagaki Eizō has even suggested that these traditions represented a psychological burden for early Western-style architects.[45] One reflection of the degree to which the newly emerging architectural community initially turned its back on Japanese tradition is that the Architecture Department of the Imperial University did not offer courses focusing primarily on Japanese architecture until 1889, thirteen years after instruction began there. Before this, Japanese architectural history was taught, but only in the context of general surveys of world architecture. In 1889, the master carpenter Kigo Kiyoyoshi (1845–1907) was invited to teach at the Imperial University. His classes concentrated on the traditional proportional design method known as *kiwarihō*.[46] Although this introduction to the Japanese carpentry tradition was still limited, the symbolic value of its inclusion in the Imperial University program was high. Itō was among the first to benefit from these additions to the curriculum.

The introduction of this material into the curriculum of the Imperial University was just one sign of a significant shift in the intellectual climate of Japan that began to take shape in the late 1880s and early 1890s. Growing impatience with the West over such issues as extraterritoriality soured some Japanese who had long been advocates of Westernization. At the same time, many Japanese experienced a new self-confidence in the wake of the country's many achievements in the twenty years since the Restoration, a self-confidence that stimulated greater interest in asserting a cultural identity distinct from the West.[47]

Itō is one of the best representatives within the architectural community of this new development. He primarily studied Western architecture at the Imperial University. His graduation project of 1892 was a Gothic cathedral richly ornamented with carefully rendered architectural details. During his long career, Itō completed designs in a number of Western historical styles, notably the Italian Romanesque-style Kanematsu lecture hall at Hitotsubashi University (formerly Tokyo Shōka Daigaku), completed in reinforced concrete in 1927. The column capitals and walls of the lecture hall were animated by a bestiary of pelicans, lions, and other creatures inspired by medieval European architecture.

As immersed as Itō was in Western architecture, he benefited from courses on the history of Japanese architecture and acquired a deep appreciation for Japan's architectural traditions. Itō's campaign to assert the primacy of aesthetics in architecture became intimately bound up with a commitment to Japan's architectural heritage. Itō made numerous contributions to the study of the history of Japan's premodern architecture, beginning with a groundbreaking work on the seventh-century Buddhist temple complex at Hōryūji published in 1893. He participated in the restoration and reconstruction of historic buildings. Collaborating with his former teacher Kigo Kiyoyoshi, Itō designed the Heian Shrine (Figure 8.7), a replica of the ninth-century Hall of State completed in 1895.

Throughout his career, Itō incorporated architectural elements from Japanese and other Asian architectural traditions into new designs for temples, museums, memorials, and private homes. He also produced a number of buildings based on premodern architectural forms, but constructed with

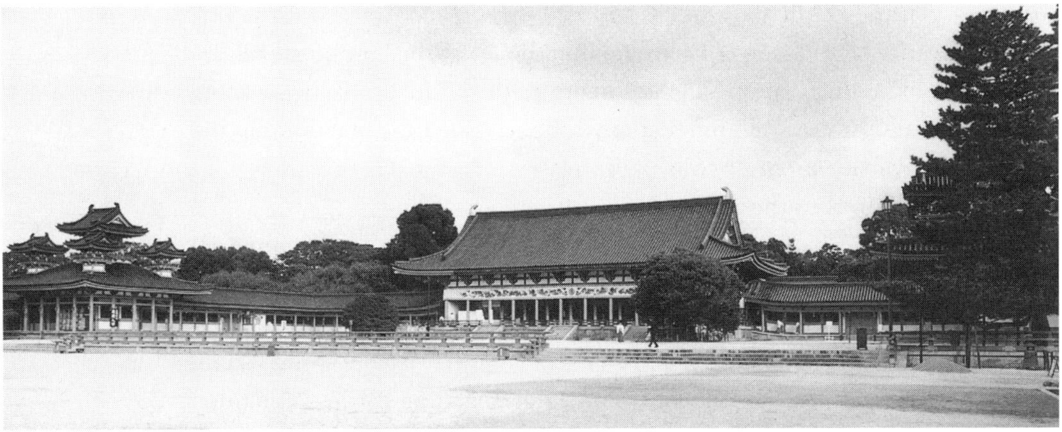

Figure 8.7 Itō Chūta and Kigo Kiyoyoshi. Heian Shrine, Kyoto, 1895. Jonathan M. Reynolds photograph.

modern materials. His memorial to the victims of the Great Kantō Earthquake of 1923 (Figure 8.8), completed in 1930, was erected on a site in Tokyo where tens of thousands of people were killed by the fires that ravaged the city after the earthquake. The Memorial Hall is constructed of steel and reinforced concrete, materials that are particularly appropriate in this case, being relatively resistant to earthquake and fire damage. The design is a complex fusion of Japanese and Western architectural sources.

The plan of the entire hall resembles the cross-shaped plan of a Christian church. At the west end of the hall stands a pagodalike tower forty-one meters high. At the base of the tower is an ossiary for the ashes of thousands of the victims of the earthquake. The use of the pagoda form is appropriate in this context in that pagodas were used as reliquaries or memorial structures in Buddhist temples. Usually, however, pagodas were free-standing buildings in Buddhist temple complexes. Itō made the pagoda an integral element in the main memorial building (it is placed at the apse of the plan), making it a visual focus for the entire design in much the same way that a tower or dome over the crossing would in a Christian church. This is probably an outgrowth of Itō's Western-style academic training (the cathedral he designed as a graduation project had a prominent crossing tower) rather than a continuation of Buddhist precedents. Although he had a more sophisticated knowledge of his Western sources than Shimizu or Tateishi, his hybrid design for the Memorial Hall is still reminiscent of the eclecticism seen at the Mitsui House and the Kai'chi Primary School.

Just as Western historical styles were an appropriate expression in the modern world of those countries' cultural heritage, traditional Japanese architectural forms were in Itō's view relevant in contemporary Japanese architectural practices as a reflection of Japan's unique culture. Itō argued that Japan could not move forward until it got back in touch with its own artistic and spiritual roots. His intense commitment to the revival of premodern Japanese architectural forms resembles in some ways the nationalistically charged historicism that was widespread among northern European architects in the second half of the nineteenth century.[48] Yet despite the nationalist overtones of this aspect of his work, Itō did not advocate purging Western influence from architectural practice in Japan and returning to an idealized premodern and pre-Western past. To the contrary, he shared with many Meiji intellectuals a faith in the idea of technological "progress" and continued to employ Western-derived architectural practices throughout his career.

Itō's emphasis on aesthetics and on reestablishing ties with Japan's architectural heritage was compelling for many in the architectural community. However, the profession never lost its basic engineering orientation. The "engineering camp" found an effective spokesman in an architect thirteen years younger than Itō, named Sano Riki (1880–1956).

Sano Riki graduated from Tokyo Imperial University in 1903 just as the

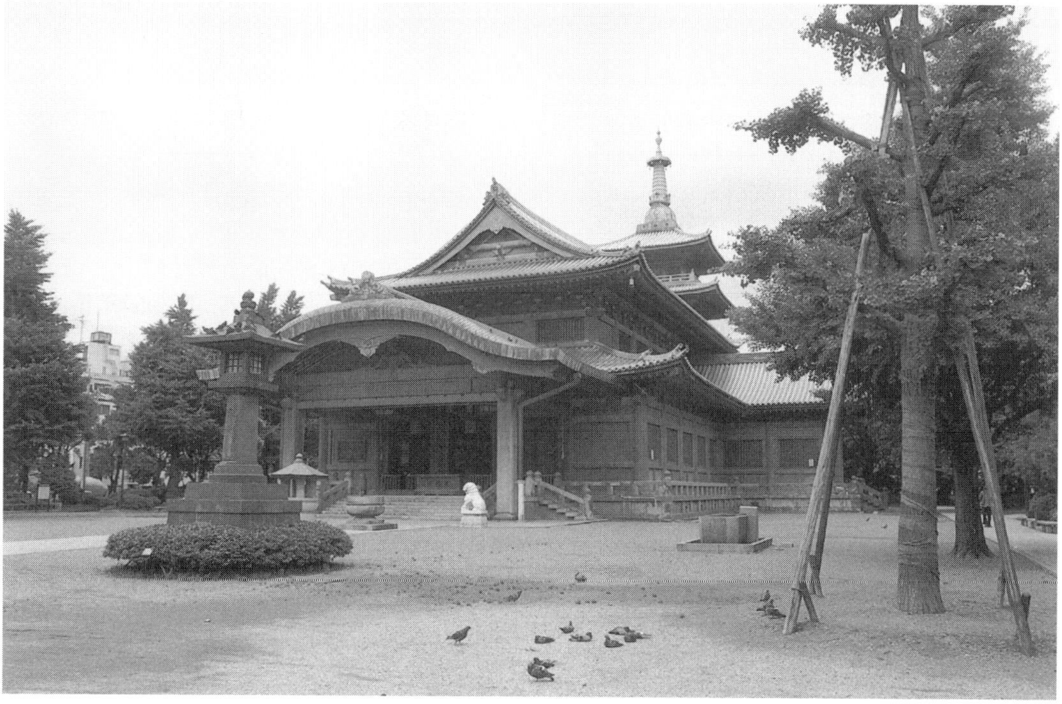

Figure 8.8 Itō Chūta. Great Kantō Earthquake Memorial, Tokyo, 1930. Jonathan M. Reynolds photograph.

"aestheticists" were at their apogee. Sano was inspired by coursework with his professor Tatsuno Kingo to study earthquake-resistant structure, and within a few years he became one of the leading authorities on the subject in Japan. A powerful earthquake that struck Tokyo in 1894 demonstrated that Western-style masonry structures, particularly buildings in unreinforced brick, were extremely vulnerable to earthquake damage. This lesson became even more salient for Sano after he traveled to California in 1906 to inspect the devastation wrought by San Francisco's powerful earthquake of that year. Sano studied alternative structural systems based on steel frame and reinforced concrete. He incorporated these materials into his own building designs, including his Maruzen Bookstore (Figure 8.9), which, when it was completed in 1909, was one of the first steel-frame structures in Japan. The design was dressed with certain Queen Anne features such as the round corner turret, but the innovative steel structure was still evident on the façade because it allowed Sano to give the store an unprecedented expanse of windows across the façade. He also collaborated with his professor, Tatsuno, as a structural engineer on the design of the steel-framed Tokyo Station, completed in 1914.

Sano recognized that Japanese architects faced other special challenges besides earthquakes. In 1911, he published an influential article in *Kenchiku zasshi* entitled "An Architect's Resolve" (*Kenchikuka no kakugo*). In this piece, Sano presented some of his views on the nature of modern architectural practice in general, and on the special problems faced by Japanese architects in particular. He argued that in the past most great architecture was religious or commemorative in nature. The artistic expectations for these buildings were high, but there was little impetus for technical innovation. The architect served primarily as an artist. However, the recent proliferation of new building types had, in Sano's opinion, transformed the architect's function. Many projects presented architects with new technical problems but did not necessarily call upon them to address artistic concerns. He wrote:

> Given the present state of our nation, if we decide that benefiting all of the people of the nation should be our primary consideration, then it is clear that Japanese architects ought to base their work in science and ought to be engineers. . . . [T]he most important responsibility of the Japanese architect is to understand the problem of how to build the strongest and most efficient building at an affordable price.[49]

In Sano's view, the focus of the architect's practice had shifted. On balance, he was more engineer than artist.

Sano directly challenged Itō's essay of 1894, declaring that there was no reason a Japanese architect (*Nihon no kenchikuka*) should be exactly like a

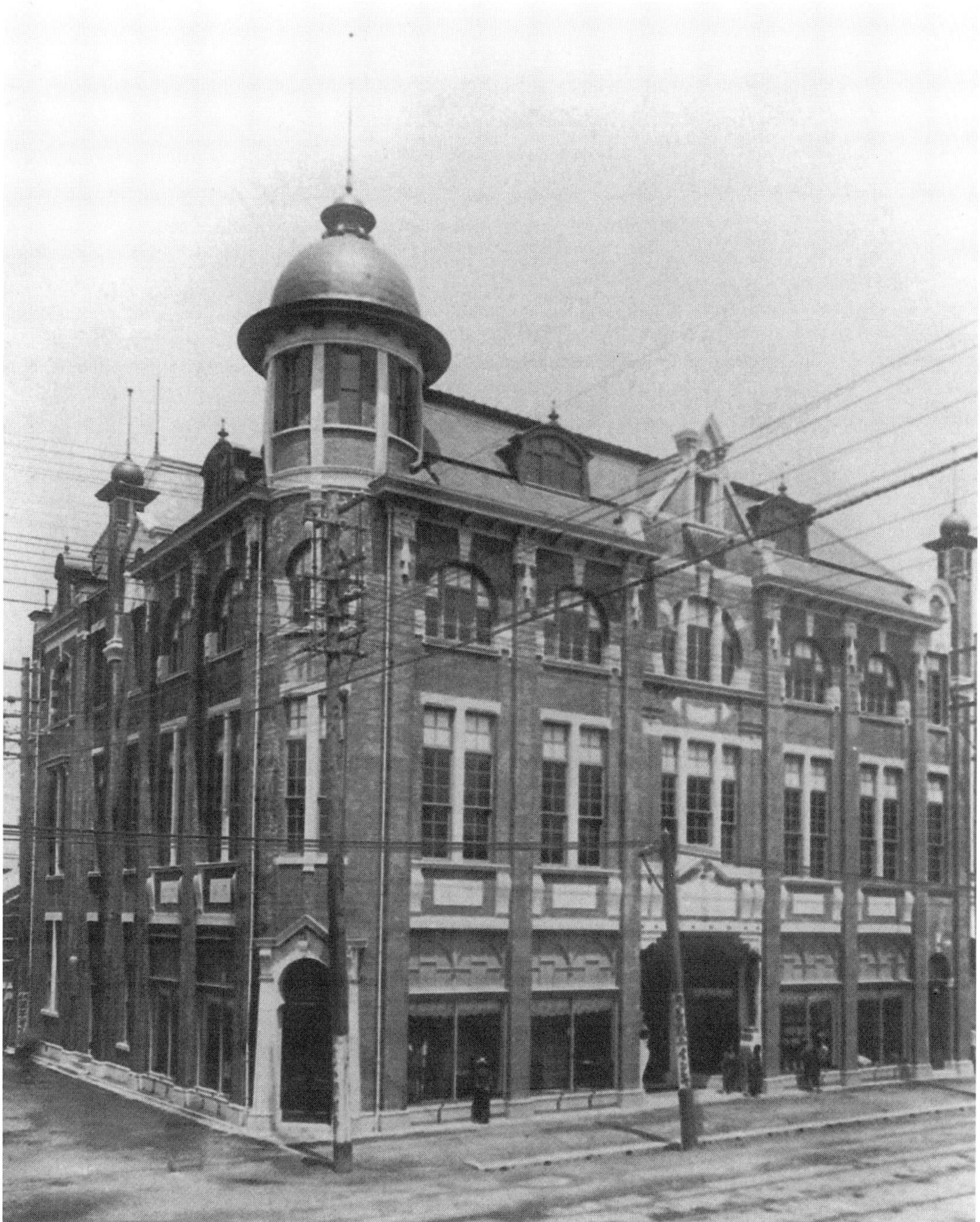

Figure 8.9 Sano Riki. Maruzen Bookstore, Tokyo, 1909. Archives of the Architectural Institute of Japan.

Western architect (*seiyō no ākitekuto*). To the contrary, the architect in contemporary Japan faced unique challenges and had a duty to respond to those challenges appropriately. He pointed out that Japan was a poor country with a high national debt. Echoing arguments that had promoted technology since before the Meiji Restoration, Sano raised the specter of the Great Powers and of their ever-increasing military strength. Faced with the threat of foreign encroachment, Japan must concentrate its limited resources on efficient, no-frills engineering. "In light of this situation," he wrote, "it is natural that the nation's architectural requirements are of a scientific cast that is based in practicality; this is no time to laze about in meaningless luxury."[50] Sano assured his readers that he was not opposed to artistic architecture, but in Japan under the present circumstances utilitarian concerns must come first.

Itō and Sano became powerful figures in the architectural community through their positions as teachers, government advisors, and jurors in major architectural competitions. Nonetheless, their conceptions of the architectural profession did not go unchallenged. As early as the 1920s, a younger generation of architects influenced by European modernism began to question both Itō's and Sano's positions.[51] Many of these architects embraced Itō's vision of architecture as high art but explicitly rejected his historicism. Although they emphasized aesthetics in architecture as forcefully as Itō, at the same time they shared with Sano a commitment to the development of technology in architecture. They sought a new aesthetic, rooted not in historical styles but in the nature of modern materials themselves. The emerging modernist position was therefore to a large extent a fusion of these two earlier opposing arguments. So, even though they were attacked by the modernists, the older architects succeeded in exerting an indirect influence over the ongoing debate within the architectural community.

Although their strategies differed, both Itō and Sano were participating in a process whereby the body of architectural practices that had been imported en masse could be sorted through and integrated more effectively into the Japanese cultural context. Itō and Sano both viewed the architect not as an isolated individual pursuing self-expression but as a public figure with a responsibility to society. They shared with their contemporaries in other spheres of public life a sense of national purpose that was inexorably linked to the stability of the established Meiji political and social order. From this perspective, the formation of the architectural profession was viewed as contribution to a much broader social project; the architect could claim his role as a key figure in the building of a nation.

Reference Matter

Notes

CHAPTER ONE

Mimi Yiengpruksawan, as usual, changed the entire configuration of this text with the smart-bomb conceptual skills for which she is famous; she and Christine Guth gave it such a close reading that perhaps they deserve credit as coauthors. I also thank Helen Nagata, Jonathan Reynolds, and Karen Brock for their attention, criticism, and advice.

1. See Satō Dōshin, *Meiji kokka to kindai bijutsu—bi no seijigaku* (The Meiji state and modern art: The politics of the beautiful; Tokyo: Yoshikawa kōbunkan, 1999), especially pp. 43–75. After I had written several drafts of this introduction and the deadline for submitting it had passed, Mimi Yiengpruksawan sent me her copy of Satō's book. With the valiant help of Helen Nagata, I have tried to integrate his discussion herein.

2. Satō (p. 55) suggests that *bijutsu* and *geijutsu* at different times encompassed the literary and visual arts respectively. He believes that the former term later came to designate the visual arts, while *geijutsu*, a wider category, included music, literature, and the visual arts. In the Edo period, *gei* certainly encompassed music and the performing arts, as seen by the term *geisha*, someone skilled at song and dance. Scroll two of *Assemblage of Edo Shokunin* (*Edo shokunin zukushi*) by Kuwagata Keisai (1764–1824) includes a whimsical passage considering the relative rankings of the four *gei*—music, *shōgi* (a chesslike game), calligraphy, and painting—with the board game coming out on top. The text is reproduced and transcribed in Asakura Haruhiko, *Edo shokunin zukushi* (Assemblage of Edo shokunin; Tokyo: Iwasaki bjutsusha, 1980), unpaged, description for scroll 2, section 15.

3. Lothar Ledderose, *Ten Thousand Things: Module and Mass Production in Chinese Art* (Princeton, N.J.: Princeton University Press, 2000), p. 189, states that "no general term for art existed in traditional China. The current word *meishu* is a late-nineteenth-century translation of the Japanese word *bijutsu*, which, in turn, is a translation of the French *beaux-arts*."

4. See, for example, such books as Kobayashi Tadashi, *Edo no e o yomu* (Reading Edo art; Tokyo: Perikansha, 1989).

5. Brenda G. Jordan, "Education in the Kanō School in Nineteenth-Century Japan: Questions About the Copybook Method," in John Singleton (ed.), *Learning in Likely Places: Varieties of Apprenticeship in Japan* (Cambridge, England: Cambridge University Press, 1998), pp. 45–67, gives a good case history of nineteenth-century Kano studio protocol. (According to Carolyn Wheelwright, "Although modern Japanese sources give the reading of the Kano family name with a long o [Kanō], primary documents write it with a short o. The modern pronunciation is an exceptional rendering of the second character. In this study, the Kano family name will be written as it was pronounced in the sixteenth century." Carolyn Wheelwright, "Kano Painters of the Sixteenth Century A.D.: The Development of Motonobu's Daisen-in Style," *Archives of Asian Art*, 1981, *34*, pp. 6–31, note 1.)

6. Ōnishi Hiroshi, on the other hand, was beset by the opposite problem when he set about translating Ernst Kris and Otto Kurtz's classic *Legend, Myth, and Magic in the Image of the Artist* (New Haven and London: Yale University Press, 1979) into Japanese. He settled for the word *geijutsuka* to designate "artist."

7. See Alison Burford, *Craftsmen in Greek and Roman Society* (Ithaca, N.Y.: Cornell University Press, 1972)..

8. Calvin L. French, *Shiba Kōkan: Artist, Innovator, and Pioneer in the Westernization of Japan* (New York and Tokyo: Weatherhill, 1974), p. 173. The translation is French's, except for the last two words, "painting methods" (*gahō*), which he rendered as "art." This shows how easy it is to slip contemporary concepts of art anachronistically into a translation. The original text appears in Sakazaki Tan, *Nihon kaigaron taikei* (Overview of Japanese painting treatises; Tokyo: Meicho fukyūsha, 1979), vol. 1, p. 159.

9. Sakazaki, *Nihon kaigaron taikei*, vol. 1, p. 158.

10. See French, *Kōkan*, plate 66, and its prototype, plate 67.

11. The painting combines two copperplate engravings from a book by Jan Luiken (1649–1712) and his son Caspar (1672–1708). The book, *Het Menselyk Bedryf*, was published in Amsterdam in 1694 (Naruse Fujio, personal communication). For reproductions see Naruse's *Shiba Kōkan: shōgai to gagyō* (Shiba Kōkan: His life and painting career; Tokyo: Yasaka shobō, 1995). Plate 154 reproduces Kōkan's painting, and the unnumbered figures on p. 181 show the pages from the artists the Japanese called simply *Rauken*.

12. Satō, in addition, points out the elite origins of the majority of the new-style artists and relates their activities to the ideological program of nationhood (see his extensive charts on pp. 58–62).

13. *Nihongi: Chronicles of Japan from the Earliest Times to A.D. 697*, W. G. Aston (trans.) (Rutland, Vt., and Tokyo: Charles E. Tuttle, 1985), p. 41.

14. Ibid., pp. 47 and 49.

15. Ibid., p. 81.

16. Ibid., p. 20.

17. According to popular belief, this fire, which killed one hundred thousand people and destroyed most of the city of Edo in 1657, was ignited from an exorcism ceremony burning a kimono that belonged to a woman consumed by passion.

18. *Nihongi*, p. 53.

19. See John M. Rosenfield, Fumiko E. Cranston, and Edwin A. Cranston, *The Courtly Tradition in Japanese Art and Literature* (Cambridge, Mass.: Fogg Art Museum, Harvard University, 1973), pp. 26–29.

20. This is as opposed to the donor supplying the artist's name in an inscription. The earliest surviving signed sword dates to 1159 and was made by a smith named Yukimasa. For a concise history of the Japanese sword, see Walter Compton, "Swords," in *Kodansha Encyclopedia of Japan* (Tokyo: Kodansha, 1983), vol. 7, pp. 285–88.

21. The familial structure of the Japanese workshop is discussed in Yoshiaki Shimizu, "Workshop Management of the Early Kano Painters, ca. A.D. 1530–1600," *Archives of Asian Art*, 1981, *34*, pp. 32–44; and in John Rosenfield, "Japanese Studio Practice: The Tosa Family and the Imperial Painting Office in the Seventeenth Century," in Peter Lukehart (ed.), *The Artist's Workshop*. (Studies in the History of Art, no. 38.) Washington, D.C.: Center for Advanced Studies in the Visual Arts, 1993, pp. 79–101.

22. On occasion, surprisingly, they spoke out forcefully. Quitman E. Phillips (*Practices of Painting*, Stanford: Stanford University Press, 2000, pp. 105–6) cites excerpts

from a late-fifteenth-century diary revealing that Kano Masanobu (1434–1530), a Nichiren Buddhist, balked at depicting the *Ten Pleasures of the Pure Land* for the shogun Yoshimasa's Tōgūdō (a building on the grounds of his temple Jishōji) because they were associated with teachings from a rival sect that he despised. Occasionally, skilled people refused to act as subordinates. Kamo no Chōmei (1153 or 1155–1216) included a story in his *Hosshinshū* (A collection to rouse the mind) about a pair of court musicians who were so absorbed in humming a classical *gagaku* tune while playing *go* that they refused to respond to an order from a palace messenger to appear before the emperor. Instead of being livid, as the messenger expected, the emperor proclaimed his admiration of the pair's intense devotion to their métier. See Thomas Blenman Hare, "Reading Kamo no Chōmei," *Harvard Journal of Asiatic Studies*, June 1989, *49*(1), p. 217. This is a revision of a tale about a court painter related by Zhuangzi.

23. This is the *Rites of Zhou* (*Zhou li*); see Morohashi Tetsuji, *Dai kanwa jiten* (Tokyo: Taishukan shoten, 1955–60), vol. 9, p. 232.

24. Ōe's work, *Zoku honchō ōjō den* (Lives of Japanese Buddhist saints, continued) is cited in Amino Yoshihiko, "Chūsei no 'shokunin' o megutte (A consideration of medieval 'shokunin')," in Amino Yoshihiko and Ishida Hisatoyo (eds.), *Shokunin* (Tradespeople), vol. 12 of *Kinsei fūzoku zufu* (Picture compendium of early modern manners and customs; Tokyo: Shogakukan, 1983), p. 63. Satō also has a discussion of the differing trades incorporated in the spectrum of *shokunin*; he sees a progression from skills that are not linked to tangible products (those of a doctor, for example) to the notion of *shokunin* as a person connected with things (*mono*) (*Meiji kokka*, pp. 49–54).

25. See, for example, Kozo Yamamura, "The Development of Za in Medieval Japan," *Business History Review*, Winter 1973, *47*, p. 463.

26. This is reproduced in *Ise shinmeishoe utaawase, Tōhokuin shokunin utaawase emaki, Tsurugaoka hōjōe shokunin utaawase emaki, Sanjūni-ban shokunin utaawase emaki* (Poetry competition for new famous places of Ise, picture scroll of the poetry competition among workers at Tōhokuin, picture scroll among workers at the ceremony to release living beings at Tsurugaoka, picture scroll of workers in thirty-one rounds), vol. 28 of *Shinshū Nihon emakimono zenshū* (Complete compendium of Japanese handscroll paintings, new ed.; Tokyo: Kadokawa shoten, 1979).

27. This is discussed in Asakura, *Edo shokunin zukushi*, p. 1.

28. Women also took part in divination, prostitution, mochi vending, sake making, cord making, and various kinds of dancing (kusemai and shirabyōshi), as well as selling fish, beans, rice, noodles, tofu, malt (*kōji*), lamp wicks, undyed rolls of cotton cloth, and incense. This partial list comes from the seventy-one-round *shokunin* poetry contest reproduced in *Gunsho ruijū*.

29. Amino, "Chūsei no 'shokunin' o megutte," p. 62.

30. These included, in ascending order, "Bridge of the Law" (*hokkyō*), "Eye of the Law" (*hōgen*), and "Seal of the Law" (*hōin*). See Rosenfield, "Japanese Studio Practice," p. 82.

CHAPTER TWO

1. Excellent photographs, and detailed discussion, can be found in Tazawa Yutaka et al. (eds.), *Hōryūji shiryō chōkoku hen 1, Hōryūji Kondō Shaka sanzon zō* (Tokyo: Iwanami shoten, 1949, hereafter abbreviated to *HSC*). More recent is Nara Rokudaiji

Taikan Kankokai (ed.), *Nara rokudaiji taikan* 2 (Tokyo: Iwanami shoten, 1968, 11–29, plates 1–10, 37–63, hereafter abbreviated to *NRT*). For a newer version of this work, see Mizuno Keizaburō, *Hōryūji: Kondō Shaka sanzon zō*, vol. 3 of *Nara no tera* (Tokyo: Iwanami shoten, 1992).

2. All of the books in the previous note have illustrations and discussions of the inscription. A fierce controversy has raged between Kasai Masaaki and Ōhashi Katsuaki over the interpretation of the inscription, and the status of the triad itself. For a summary of the issues, with full bibliography, see Saitō Rieko, "Hōryūji Kondō Shaka sanzon zō no seisaku nendai: Kasai-Ōhashi ronsō," in Ōhashi Katsuaki (ed.), *Ronsō: Nara bijutsu* (Tokyo: Heibonsha, 1994), pp. 41–66.

3. See Kuno Takeshi, "Asuka Daibutsu ron," *Bijutsu kenkyū*, 1975, *300*, 37–49, and 1975, *301*, 89–98, with full bibliography. See also Kawamura Chigyō, "*Gangōji engi* to Asuka Daibutsu," in Ōhashi Katsuaki (ed.), *Nara bijutsu no sōten* (Tokyo: Gurafusha, 1984), 97–138.

4. *NRT* 2, 29–38, plates 11–14, 64–75.

5. *NRT* 4, 7–13, plates 1–13, 61–73. This image has been extensively discussed in English; see Sherwood F. Moran, "The Yumedono Kannon of Hōryūji," *Archives of the Chinese Art Society of America*, 1957, *11*, 59–68; Lucie R. Weinstein, "The Yumedono Kannon: Problems in Seventh-Century Sculpture," *Archives of Asian Art*, 1989, *42*, 25–48; and Jonathan W. Best, "Early Korea's Role in the Stylistic Formation of the Yumedono Kannon, a Major Monument of Seventh-Century Japanese Buddhist Sculpture," *Korea Journal*, 1990, *30*(10), 13–26.

6. *HSC* 2 (*Hōryūji hōzō shō Kondō butsu*, 1954), 14–27, plates 11–19, English summary, pp. 14–17; *NRT* 2, 55–59, plates 22–33, 98–101. The most complete publication of this monument is Nara Kokuritsu Bunkazai Kenkyūjo, Asuka Shiryōkan (ed.), *Asuka/Hakuhō no zaimei Kondō butsu* (1st ed.), Nara, plates on pp. 17–23 and text on pp. 75–76, 99–101; in the second edition, plates on pp. 16–19, 61–66, text on pp. 151–52, 175–77. For a reconstruction of the image, see Tanaka Yoshiyasu, "Boshi nenmei Shaka sanzon zō no fukugen," in *Agaruma: Sawayanagi sensei koki kinen bijutsushi ronbunshū* (Tokyo: Dōhōsha, 1982), 289–302.

7. *HSC* 2, 9–14, plates 1–10; *NRT* 2, 54–55, plates 21, 94–97.

8. Tokyo Kokuritsu Hakubutsukan (ed.), *Hōryūji kennō hōmotsu tokubetsu chōsa gaihō* (Tokyo, 1985–90), 1, 22–24 (hereafter abbreviated to *Chōsa*); Tokyo Kokuritsu Hakubutsukan (ed.), *Hōryūji kennō hōbutsu: Kondō butsu* I (Tokyo, 1996), 438, 470–72, plates 23–25, 100–103 (hereafter abbreviated to *Kondō butsu*).

9. *Chōsa* 2 (1986), 10–13; *Kondō butsu* I, 440–41, 480–82, plates 34–36, 121–23.

10. *Chōsa* 2 (1986), 4–7; *Kondō butsu* I, 442, 489–92, plates 46–48, 136–39.

11. I have attempted a general account of Asuka sculpture in Jane Turner (ed.), *The Dictionary of Art* (London: Macmillan, 1996), "Asuka Period," vol. 17, pp. 106–10; and "Tori Busshi," vol. 31, p. 167.

12. See Ōhashi Katsuaki, "Shaka zō to Yakushi zō wa dochira ga saki ka: Hōryūji Shaka-Yakushizō no meibun to yoshiki," in Ōhashi, *Nara bijutsu no sōten*, 43–95. See also Kawase Yoshiteru, "Kondō Shaka sanzon zō to Yakushi zō," in Ōhashi Katsuaki (ed.), *Hōryūji bijutsu ronsō no shiten* (Tokyo: Gurafusha, 1998), 79–100.

13. Donald F. McCallum, "The Buddhist Triad in Three Kingdoms Sculpture," *Korean Culture*, 1995, *16*(4), 18–25.

14. For standing Buddha figures, see Tokyo Kokuritsu Hakubutsukan (ed.), *Tokubetsuten zuroku—Kondō butsu: Chūgoku, Chōsen, Nihon* (Tokyo, 1988), Standing Buddha, Myōjōin, Nagasaki, plate 27, p. 110; Standing Buddha, Dainichibō, Yamagata, plate 28, p. 111; and Standing Buddha no. 150 (48 Buddhist Deities, Tokyo National Museum), plate 29, p. 112.

15. There are very few other standing bodhisattvas dating from the earliest period of icons in Japan. One controversial piece is the Sekiyamajinja standing bodhisattva (ibid., plate 57, pp. 149–50). I have discussed this piece and related images in "The Earliest Buddhist Statues in Japan," *Artibus Asiae*, 2001, *61*(2), 149–88.

16. Excellent illustrations, transcriptions, and translations into modern Japanese of the inscription can be found in *HSC* 1, 46–57, figure 27 (actual size rubbing), plates 54–55, English summary, pp. 10–11; and *NRT* 2, 22–25, plate 59. See also Nabunken, Asuka Shiryōkan (1st ed.), Nara, 1976, 116, plates 56–57; in second edition, Nara, 1979, 192–93, plates 27–40.

17. There is considerable confusion as to the death date of Prince Shōtoku. The mandorla inscription and several other sources give the date as here, but *Nihon shoki* (hereafter, *NS*) states that he died on the date corresponding to the fifth day of the second month of the year Suiko 29, or 621. See *NS*, Suiko 29/2/5 (621), in Aston 2, 148; and Sakamoto Tarō et al., *NS* 1 and 2, vols. 67 and 68 of *Nihon koten bungaku taikei* (Tokyo: Iwanami shoten, 1980; hereafter, Sakamoto), 2, 204–5. Chari Pradel deals with this issue in detail in her forthcoming monograph on the *Tenjukoku Shūchō Mandara*.

18. See Tanaka Tsuguhito, *Nihon kodai busshi no kenkyū* (Tokyo: Yoshikawa kōbunkan, 1983). For Tori, see chapter 1 of that work, "Busshi-bukkō no seiritsu to Tori-busshi," pp. 21–87.

19. The so-called immigrants, now usually referred to as *toraijin*, were previously designated by the pejorative term *kikajin*. An example of the latter is Seki Akira, *Kikajin: Kodai no seiji, keizai, bunka o kataru* (Tokyo: Shibundō, 1966). For the *be* system, see Takemitsu Makoto, *Kenkyūshi: Bemin sei* (Tokyo: Yoshikawa kōbunkan, 1981).

20. See Gari Ledyard, "Galloping Along with the Horse-Riders: Looking for the Founders of Japan," *Journal of Japanese Studies*, 1975, *1*, 217–54, for a discussion of the theory. For a critique, see Walter Edwards, "Event and Process in the Founding of Japan: The Horse-Rider Theory in Archaeological Perspective," *Journal of Japanese Studies*, 1983, *9*, 265–95.

21. A magnificent gilt-bronze saddle back was recently excavated from the Fujinoki tomb, directly adjacent to Hōryūji. For a monochrome illustration, see Penelope Mason, *History of Japanese Art* (New York: Prentice Hall, 1993), figure 36.

22. *NS*, Yūryaku seventh year (463?), in Aston 1, 350; Sakamoto 1, 476.

23. For a general discussion of the work of the saddlemakers, see Katsube Mitsuo and Suzuki Tsutomu, *Kodai no gi: Fujinoki kofun no bagu o hakaru* (Tokyo: Yoshikawa kōbunkan, 1998).

24. For a discussion in English of changing dynastic lines, see Cornelius J. Kiley, "State and Dynasty in Archaic Yamato," *Journal of Asian Studies*, 1973, *33*(1), 25–49.

25. See *Gangōji garan engi* in Sakurai Tokutarō et al. (eds.), *Jisha engi*, vol. 20 of *Nihon shisō taikei* (Tokyo: Iwanami shoten, 1975), 20.

26. For Fukuri's appointment as interpreter on the first mission, see *NS*, Suiko 15/7/3 (607), Aston 2, 136; and in Sakamoto 2, 189, p. 148 note 7 and p. 555 note 20.4. For Fukuri's participation in the second mission, see *NS*, Suiko 16/9/11 (608), Aston 2, 139; and Sakamoto 2, 192. In an entry of the next year, the text states: "Only the interpreter Fukuri did not return." See *NS*, Suiko 17/9 (609), Aston 2, 140; and Sakamoto 2, 194.

27. *NS*, Suiko 31/4/3 (624), Aston 2, 152–53; and Sakamoto 2, 208–11. (Sakamoto gives this entry under the thirty-second year of Suiko.)

28. For the organization of the Buddhist order, see Naobayashi Futai, *Nihon kodai bukkyō seido shi kenkyū* (Kyoto: Nagata bunshōdō, 1988), especially section I, "Suiko chō no sōjō, sōzū, hōzu sei," pp. 19–83; Nakai Shinkō, *Nihon kodai bukkyō*

seido shi no kenkyū (Kyoto: Hōzōkan, 1991), especially section I.1, "Suiko chō no sōjō-sōzu to hōzu," pp. 27–48. (Despite the close similarities in these book and section titles, they are as cited.)

29. *NS*, Kōgyoku 4/4/1 (645), Aston 2, 190; Sakamoto 2, 260–61. Mizutani Chiaki has tried to place this story in an appropriate historical context in "Kuratsukuri no Tokushi no kijutsu: *Kōgyoku ki* no kisai ni tsuite," *Ryūkoku daigaku bukkyō bunka Kenkyūjo kiyō*, 1989, *27*, 44–47.

30. For the complex historiography of this period, see Kasai Wajin, *Kenkyūshi: Wa no goō* (Tokyo: Yoshikawa kōbunkan, 1973). A good general discussion of the issues is Ueda Masaaki, *Ōkimi no seiki*, vol. 2 of *Nihon no rekishi* (Tokyo: Shōgakkan, 1973), 254–79. Some material in English is available in Hirano Kunio, "The Yamato State and Korea in the Fourth and Fifth Centuries," *Acta Asiatica*, 1977, *31*, 51–56.

31. For Shiba Sōtatsu, see Sakamoto Yoshitane, "Wa no goō no gaiko—Shiba Sōtatsu o chūshin ni," in *Akamatsu Toshihide kyōju taikan kinen kokushi ronshū* (Tokyo: Akamatsu Toshihide kyōju taikan kinen jigyō kaihen, 1972), 57–72; and Fujima Seita, *Wa no goō* (Tokyo: Iwanami shoten, 1968), 85.

32. Machida Kōichi, "Kuratsukuri-be no shusshin to Asuka jidai in okeru 'Tori shiki butsuzō' no kōbō ni tsuite," in *Jōdai chōkoku shi no kenkyū* (Tokyo: Yoshikawa kōbunkan, 1977), 120–21.

33. Since the history of the title and name Sima is extraordinarily complicated as it moves from China to Korea and then to Japan, only a brief discussion is possible here. Originally a military title in the Zhou Dynasty, it was subsequently adopted as a surname. Perhaps the most famous bearer of the name was Sima Qian, the compiler of *Shih Ji*, the first Chinese dynastic history. For the Chinese background, see Mu Liusen (ed.), *Bai jia xing ci Dian* (Hong Kong: Yi wen yin shu kuan, 1977), 553–54. Significantly, the title also appears in Three Kingdoms Korea; see *Han'guk minjok munhwa taebaekkwa sajŏn* (Seoul, 1991), vol. 19, p. 188. The entries for Koguryŏ and Paekche are by Yi To-hak, and that for Silla is by Yi Ki-dong.

34. There are a variety of positions as to the possibility of Tatto arriving in 522: Mōri Hisashi, "Asuka daibutsu no shuhen," in *Nihon bukkyō chōkokushi no kenkyū* (Kyoto: Hōzōkan, 1970), 18, accepts this early date, while Kobayashi Takeshi, "Shiba Kuratsukuri obito Tori-busshi," in *Nihon chōkoku sakka kenkyū* (Yokohama: Yurindō, 1978), 8–9, argues against it, convincingly in my opinion.

35. Tatto is discussed in *NS*, Bidatsu 13/9 (584), Aston 2, 101; Sakamoto 2, 148–49 (Sakamoto reads "Kuratsukuri Suguri . . . ," rendering *be* as *tsukuri*; it is not clear to me what the basis is for this reading); and in *Gangōji engi*, 11. The later texts are *Fusō ryakki* and *Genkō shakusho*.

36. *NS*, Bidatsu 13/9 (584), Aston 2, 101; Sakamoto 2, 148–49. For discussions of this image, see Fujisawa Kazuo, "Kafuka no omi Kudara shorai Miroku seki zō setsu," *Shiseki to bijutsu*, 1947, *177*, 81–93; Tanaka Shigehisa, "Kudara denrai to shosuru saisho no Miroku seki zō utagau," ibid., 1961, *318*, 290–96; Fujisawa Kazuo, "Kafuku no omi Kudara shorai Miroku seki zō setsu hoi," ibid., 1962, *323*, 97–105; Hino Akira, "Bidatsu ki Miroku seki zō to sono shuhen," in Tamura Enchō sensei koki kinenkai (eds.), *Higashi ajia to Nihon 2, Shukyō-bungaku hen* (Tokyo: Yoshikawa kōbunkan, 1987), 19–43.

37. Hino Akira, "Kuratsukuri-be Tasuna no shukke ni tsuite," *Ryūkoku shidan*, 1973, *66/67*, 62–73. One can be suspicious about such a formal name at this early stage in the development of Buddhism in Japan.

38. *NS*, Yōmei 2/4/2 (587), Aston 2, 111; Sakamoto 2, 160–61. Surprisingly, there is a second *Nihon shoki* reference three years later, in 590 (Sushun 3), which states it was in that year that Tasuna entered the Buddhist order along with a number of

other people. I am unable to explain why this important event is recorded twice. See *NS*, Sushun 3/10 (590), Aston 2, 118; Sakamoto 2, 168–69.

39. *Jō roku* is a canonical height for Buddhist statues. For a standing figure, it would correspond to approximately sixteen feet; for a seated image it is half the size. That this is a contemporaneous usage is highly doubtful.

40. A good source for Sakatadera is Nabunken, Asuka Shiryōkan (ed.), *Toraijin no tera: Hinokumadera to Sakatadera* (Nara, 1985). For the most recent excavations of Sakatadera, see Nabunken, Asuka Shiryōkan (ed.), *Nenpō*, 1997, no. 2, 75–77.

41. It is difficult to form an opinion on this matter; I suggest that the Paekche references are related in some way to an awareness of the Kuratsukuri connection with Paekche.

42. As with the name of Tokusai-hosshi already mentioned, Zenshin seems unlikely for this early period.

43. A good source for the three generations of the Soga clan is Nabunken, Asuka Shiryōkan (ed.), *Soga sandai* (Nara, 1995).

44. For the flogging, see *NS*, Bidatsu 14/3/30 (585), Aston 2, 103; and Sakamoto 2, 150–51. The flogging incident seems as if it were borrowed from somewhere else. For the building of the temple for the three nuns, see *NS*, Bidatsu 14/6 (585), Aston 2, 104; and Sakamoto 2, 151–53.

45. For their trip to Paekche, see *NS*, Sushun 1 (588), Aston 2, 118; and Sakamoto 2, 168–69. For their return, see *NS*, Sushun 3/3 (590), Aston 2, 118; and Sakamoto 2, 168–69.

46. *NS*, Suiko 13/4/1 (605), Aston 2, 134; Sakamoto 2, 186–87.

47. *NS*, Suiko 14/4/8 (606), Aston 2, 134; Sakamoto 2, 186–87.

48. *NS*, Suiko 14/5/5 (606), Aston 2, 134–35; Sakamoto 2, 187–89.

49. For the ranking system, see Richard J. Miller, *Ancient Japanese Nobility: The Kabane Ranking System* (Berkeley and Los Angeles: University of California Press, 1974).

50. Ōhashi Katsuaki, "Kuratsukuri Tori no zōbutsu gihō no Shōtoku ni tsuite," in *Nihon kodai sōkō* (Tokyo: Takatori Masato sensei koki shukuga ronbunshū kankōkai, 1994), 23–49.

51. Recorded in *NS*, Bidatsu 6/11/1 (577), Aston 2, 96; Sakamoto 2, 140–41.

52. See Ōhashi Katsuaki, *Asuka no bunmei kaika* (Tokyo: Yoshikawa kōbunkan, 1997), 1–2.

53. The volume of publication on Shōtoku Taishi is extensive. For a large group of essays and an extensive bibliography through 1970, see Shōtoku Taishi kenkyūkai (eds.), *Shōtoku Taishi ronshū* (Kyoto: Heiryaku shoten, 1971). Standard biographies include Tamura Enchō's *Shōtoku Taishi: Ikaruga miya no arasoi* (Tokyo: Chūō kōronsha, 1964); Sakamoto Tarō's *Shōtoku Taishi* (Tokyo: Yoshikawa kōbunkan, 1979); Takemitsu Makoto's *Shōtoku Taishi: Nihon shisō no genryū* (Tokyo, Dōseisha, 1984); and Tōyama Mitsuo's *Shōtoku Taishi: Mikan no ō-kimi* (Tokyo: Nihon hōsō shuppan kyōkai, 1997).

54. The literature on Hōryūji is enormous. An interesting treatment of the rebuilding, with many references, is Ōhashi Katsuaki, "Saikon Hōryūji to Shaka sanzon zō: Taishi shinkō no seiritsu," *Bukkyō geijutsu*, 1996, *224*, 15–31.

55. See Tanaka Tsuguhito, *Shōtoku Taishi shinkō no kenkyū* (Tokyo: Yoshikawa kōbunkan, 1983); Takeda Sachiko, "*Shinkō no ōken: Shōtoku Taishi*" (Tokyo: Chūō kōronsha, 1993). A radical, revisionist analysis of Prince Shōtoku is Ōyama Seiichi's *Shōtoku Taishi no tanjō* (Tokyo: Yoshikawa kōbunkan, 1999).

56. Publication on the Soga clan in recent years has been considerable. My thought has been influenced strongly by Kadowaki Teiji, *Asuka: Sono kodaishi to fūdo* (Tokyo: Nihon hōsō shuppan kyōkai, 1977). See also, by the same author, *Soga Emishi-Iruka* (Tokyo: Yoshikawa kōbunkan, 1977). A general account is Takemitsu Makoto,

Soga sandai (Tokyo: Mainichi shinbunsha, 1993). An excellent source for illustrations of monuments associated with the Soga clan is Nabunken, Asuka Shiryōkan (ed.), *Soga sandai* (Nara, 1995). More specialized are Katō Kenkichi, *Soga shi to Yamato ōken* (Tokyo: Yoshikawa kōbunkan, 1983), and a collection of essays edited by Mayuzumi Hiromichi, *Kodai o kangaeru: Soga shi to kodai kokka* (Tokyo: Yoshikawa kōbunkan, 1991). Popular accounts include Ishiwatari Shin'ichirō, *Soga Umako wa tennō datta* (Tokyo: San'ichi shobō, 1992), which claims that Shōtoku Taishi did not exist and, as the title states, Umako was the "emperor"!

57. A paper that takes a different approach from that used here is Konno Toshifumi, "Shōrai 'hon'yō' no utsushi to busshi (I)—Asuka butsu no tanjō to Tori-busshi," *Bukkyō geijutsu*, 2000, *248*, 69–98. I have discussed some of his ideas in "The Earliest Buddhist Statues in Japan," pp. 182–87 (see note 15 for this chapter).

CHAPTER THREE

Research for this study was supported by a Japan Foundation Professional Fellowship in 1995–96. The author thanks Ogawa Chie of Kōzanji and Okuda Isao for their unfailing support; Wakasugi Junji and Izumi Takeo of Kyoto National Museum; Robert L. Thorp, Christine M. E. Guth, Melinda Takeuchi, and Sylvan Barnet. Portions of this chapter were presented at workshops in Buddhist studies at MacMaster University (fall 1997) and Yale University (fall 1998). This chapter is dedicated to John M. Rosenfield, who long ago urged me to look more closely at the issue of Jōnin's artistic identity.

1. Chuck and Jan Rosenak, *The Saint Makers: Contemporary Santeras y Santeros* (Flagstaff, Ariz.: Northland, 1998), p. 96.

2. Hirata Yutaka, Preface to *Ebusshi no jidai* (The age of painted-buddha masters), 2 vols. (Tokyo: Chūōkōron, 1994), vol. 1, p. i.

3. Ibid.

4. The earliest painters' seals appear on works by Takuma Chōga (active ca. 1253–ca. 1265). See Tanaka Ichimatsu, "Ebusshi Chōga to sono sakuhin" (The painted-buddha master Chōga and his works) in *Nihon kaigashi ronshū* (Collected essays on Japanese painting history; Tokyo: Chūōkōron, 1966), pp. 134–47; and Hirata, *Ebusshi no jidai*, vol. 1, pp. 44, 160–62.

5. *Ebusshi no jidai*, volume one, collects Hirata's articles from 1966 through 1993; volume two consists of documentary references to painters from 808 to 1395. This study deservedly won the prestigious Shimada Price in 1995. Hirata's companion volume is *Ebusshi no sakuhin* (The works of painted-buddha masters; Tokyo: Chūōkōron, 1998).

6. "Canon" refers here to registered objects ("national treasure" and "important cultural property"). On the national registry and the creation of the "canon," see Christine M. E. Guth, "Kokuhō: From Dynastic to Monastic Treasure," *Cahiers d'Extrême-Asie*, 1996–97, *9*, 313–22; Tokyo National Research Institute of Cultural Properties (ed.), *Katoru genzai, katorareru kakko: Nihon no bijutsu shigaku hyaku-nen* (In speaking of the present, the past has spoken: one hundred years in the history of Japanese art; Tokyo: Heibonsha, 1999); John M. Rosenfield, "Japanese Art Studies in America Since 1945," in Helen Hardacre (ed.), *The Postwar Developments of Japanese Studies in the United States* (Leiden, Netherlands: Brill, 1998), pp. 161–94; Mimi Hall Yiengpruksawan, "Japanese Art History 2001: The State and Stakes of Research," *Art Bulletin*, Mar. 2001, pp. 105–22; and Yoshiaki Shimizu, "Japan in American Museums—But Which Japan?" *Art Bulletin*, Mar. 2001, pp. 123–34.

7. *Kegon Origin Tales* (*Kegon engi emaki*) and *Illustrated Lives of Kegon Patriarchs* (*Kegonshū soshi eden*) are relatively recent titles for *Tales of Gishō and Gangyō* (*Gishō Gangyō e*). Kegon refers to the teachings of the *Flower Garland Sutra* (Skt. Avatamsaka, Ch. Huayan). On these names, see Karen L. Brock, "The Case of the Missing Scroll: A History and Reconstruction of *Tales of Gishō and Gangyō*," *Archives of Asian Art*, 1988, *41*, 6–31. From 1991 through 1996, *Kegon Origin Tales* underwent restoration at Kyoto National Museum; see Oka Bokkōdō, *Shūfuku* (Conservation), 1997, *4*, 6–29. For color photographs before restoration, see Komatsu Shigemi (ed.), *Kegonshū soshi eden*, Nihon emaki taisei, vol. 17 (Tokyo: Chūōkōron, 1978). For the restored set, see Wakasugi Junji, *Emaki: Kegonshū soshi eden*, Nihon no bijutsu 413 (Tokyo: Shibundō, 2000). The most extensive publication of Kōzanji's collection of objects and manuscripts is Kyoto National Museum (ed.), *Kōzanji-ten* (Kyoto, 1981); *Saint Myōe Seated in Meditation in a Tree* is no. 84.

8. Mori Tōru, *Kamakura jidai no shōzōga* (Portraiture of the Kamakura period; Tokyo: Misuzu shobō, 1971), pp. 49–83.

9. Early references to the portraits and picture scrolls include Sumiyoshi Hiroyuki and Shibano Ritsuzan, *Jisha ten'etsu hōmotsu mokuroku* (Catalogue of viewings of shrine and temple treasures, 1792), in Zoku zoku gunsho ruijū, vol. 16 (Tokyo: Kokusho kangyōkai, 1910), pp. 174–75; Kurokawa Harumura (et al.), *Kōko gafu* (Painting manual of antiquities, 1882–1902), reprinted as *Chōtei zōho kōko gafu* (Tokyo: Hirotani Kokusho kangyōkai, 1925), part 1, pp. 148–49 and part 2, p. 252. *Kegon Origin Tales* appeared in *Kokka*, 1891, *27*, 49–51, attributed to Fujiwara Nobuzane, but the attribution was discarded in *Kokka*, 1903, *152*, 143–44. Ernest F. Fenollosa published *Kegon Origin Tales* (mislabeled *Kitano tenjin engi*) as painted by Nobuzane, whose "style is most individual," in *Epochs of Chinese and Japanese Art*, vol. 1, (New York: Frederick A. Stokes, 1912), between pages 84 and 85.

10. *Honchō gashi* (History of painting in this realm, 1678), as reprinted in Kasai Masaaki, Suzuki Susumu, and Takei Akio (eds.), *Yakuchū honchō gashi* (Kyoto: Dōhōsha, 1985), pp. 117–23 and 128. Jōnin (p. 123) is listed among six painters named Takuma: Tametō, Tamehisa, Tameyuki, Chōga, Shōga, and Eiga. Einō does not identify Takuma *hōgen*; see pp. 11, 15, and 166. Einō's friend, the physician Kurokawa Dōyū (d. 1691) stated that Takuma *hōgen* was Shōga, in *Yōshū fushi* (Gazetteer of Yamashiro province, 1684), Zoku zoku gunsho ruijū, vol. 8 (Tokyo: Kokusho kangyōkai, 1970), pp. 130–32 and 312. His information may have come from an inscribed stele commemorating Takuma Shōga, erected in 1673; see Takaoka Gikai, *Umegahata-mura shi* (Gazetteer of Umegahata village; Kyoto: Takao Elementary School, 1931), pp. 215–16. For the Takuma lineage, see Hirata, *Ebusshi no jidai*, vol. 1, pp. 154–83 and *passim*.

11. The practice of bestowing Buddhist ranks on artisans began in the late tenth century; Hirata, *Ebusshi no jidai*, vol. 1, pp. 26–40.

12. Discussion of the term *Yamato-e* in premodern and recent contexts would require a volume of its own; see my essay on *yamato-e* in *The Dictionary of Art* (London: Macmillan, 1996), vol. 17, pp. 153–68. For studies of Kanō Einō's rhetoric and conception of Japanese painting, see Quitman E. Phillips, "*Honchō gashi* and the Kano Myth," *Archives of Asian Art*, 1994, *47*, 46–57; Sakakibara Satoru, "'Honchō gashi' zaikō" (A reconsideration of *Honchō gashi*), in four parts: *Kokka*, 1997, *1220*, 31–33; *1221*, 32–34; *1223*, 25–29; and *1224*, 32–35.

13. *Dai Nihon shiryō*, vol. 5 part 7 (Tokyo: Tokyo daigaku shuppankai, 1930), pp. 248–705, compiles primary sources under Myōe's death date of Kangi 4/1/19 (1232); several of Kōzanji's primary sources first appeared in *Dainihon bukkyō zensho* (Tokyo: Bussho kankōkai, 1912–22) and Okuda Shōzō, *Myōe shōnin yōshū*, 5 vols. (Tokyo: 1931–33).

14. Murakami Sōdō, *Toganoosan Kōzanji Myōe Shōnin* (Kyoto, Kōzanji, 1929), pp. 76, 99, 100, 102, 138, and 324. His information came from inscriptions on extant sutras in the Kōzanji storehouse and from *Kōzanji Origin Tales* (1253), discussed in detail later in this chapter. Later biographies of Myōe are Tanaka Hisao, *Myōe*, Jinbutsu sōsho, vol. 60 (Tokyo: Yoshikawa kōbunkan, 1961); Okuda Isao, *Myōe: henreki to yume* (Saint Myōe: pilgrimages and dreams; Tokyo: Tokyo daigaku shuppan, 1978; Frédéric Girard, *Un Moine de la sect Kegon à l'époque de Kamakura, Myōe (1173–1232) et le "Journal de ses Rêves"* (Paris, École Française d'Extrême-Orient, 1990); and George J. Tanabe, *Myōe the Dreamkeeper: Fantasy and Knowledge in Early Kamakura Buddhism* (Cambridge, Mass.: Harvard University Press, 1992). For numerous previously published articles, see Hagami Shōchō et al. (eds.), *Myōe shōnin to Kōzanji* (Tokyo: Dōhōsha, 1981).

15. Murakami, *Toganoosan*, 187–88. Shunga's name never appeared in lineages of Takuma painters, although he was included in Asaoka Okisada, Ota Kin, et al., *Zōtei Koga bikō* (Expanded research on ancient painting, 1905; reprinted Kyoto: Shibunkaku, 1970), vol. 2, pp. 530–31.

16. Minamoto Toyomune, "Myōe Shōnin no gazō to sono hissha ni tsuite" (The portraits of Saint Myōe and their painters, 1931), in Hagami, *Myōe Shōnin to Kōzanji*, pp. 263–71; Fukui Rikichirō, "Emakimono gaisetsu" (Explanations of picture scrolls), in *Iwanami kōza Nihon bungaku*, vol. 13 (1933), pp. 13–19.

17. Shimomise Shizuichi, "*Kegon engi* zakkō" (Notes on *Kegon Origin Tales*), *Shiseki to bijutsu*, 1937, *75*, 9–24; idem, *Yamato-e to Kara-e* (1944), reprinted in *Shimomise Shizuichi chosakushū*, vol. 7 (Tokyo: Kōdansha, 1986), pp. 320–30; and idem, *Yamato-e*, Kyoto sōsho, vol. 4 (Kyoto: Kōtō shoin, 1946), pp. 173–78.

18. Umezu Jirō, "Gishō-Gangyō-e no seiritsu" (The establishment of *Tales of Gishō and Gangyō*), *Bijutsu kenkyū*, 1947, *149*, 170–81, and idem, *Kegon engi*, Nihon no meiga (Tokyo: Heibonsha, 1957); Kameda Tsutomu, "*Kegon engi* ni tsuite," in Tanaka Ichimatsu (ed.), *Kegon engi emaki*, Nihon emakimono zenshū, vol. 7 (Tokyo: Kadokawa shoten, 1959), pp. 3–15; Nakashima Hiroshi, "'Myōe Shōnin jujō zazen zō' no shudai" (Principal subject of *Saint Myōe Seated in Meditation in a Tree*), *Museum*, 1978, *329*, 20–29; Hiruma Noriko, "Kōzanji ni okeru 'Gishōe' no seisaku to E'nichibō Jōnin—karabon rakanzu no sesshu to sono imi" (The production of the *Gishō* scrolls at Kōzanji and E'nichibō Jōnin: the implication of the reception of Chinese versions of rakan paintings), *Bijutsushi*, 1995, *135*, 50–65.

19. Hirata, "Myōe no shūhen—E'nichibō Jōnin to Shunga no baai" (Myōe's circle, the case of E'nichibō Jōnin and Shunga; 1975), in *Ebusshi no jidai*, vol. 1, pp. 183–99; the quotation is on p. 185.

20. John M. Rosenfield and Shūjirō Shimada, *Traditions of Japanese Art: Selections from the Kimiko and John Powers Collection* (Cambridge, Mass.: Fogg Art Museum, 1970), p. 388; John M. Rosenfield and Elizabeth ten Grotenhuis, *Journey of the Three Jewels: Japanese Buddhist Paintings from Western Collections* (New York: Asia Society, 1979), p. 170; Helmut Brinker, "Ch'an Portraits in a Landscape," *Archives of Asian Art*, 1973–74, *27*, 11; and Helmut Brinker and Hiroshi Kanazawa, *Zen Masters of Meditation in Images and Writings* (Zurich: Artibus Asiae 1996), p. 135.

21. Tanaka Ichimatsu, *Suibokuga*, Genshoku Nihon no bijutsu, vol. 11 (Tokyo: Shogakukan, 1970), pp. 163–69; and idem, *Japanese Ink Painting: Shubun to Sesshu*, Bruce Darling (trans.), Heibonsha Survey of Japanese Art (New York and Tokyo: Weatherhill/Heibonsha, 1972), pp. 30–58. The earliest tale of the tea encounter dates to the late thirteenth century; see Murakami, *Toganoosan*, pp. 222–30 and 259–63, and Tanaka, *Myōe*, pp. 205–10.

22. Ebine Toshio, "Kan no sekai no seiritsu to tenkai" (The establishment and

development of the Chinese world), in Toda Teisuke, Ebine Toshio, and Chino Kaori (eds.), *Suibokuga to chūsei emaki* (Ink painting and medieval picture scrolls), Nihon bijutsu zenshū, vol. 12 (Tokyo: Kōdansha, 1992), pp. 146–48. Hirata later attacked the myth of the early Takuma school association with the "new movement" in "Takuma-ha ni okeru dentō sei" (The traditionalism of the Takuma school), *Kokka*, 1985, *1085*, 11–26.

23. Karen L. Brock, "'Tales of Gishō and Gangyō': Editor, Artist, and Audience in Japanese Picture Scrolls" (Ph.D. dissertation, Princeton University, 1984), pp. 6–13. My initial interest in collaboration was sparked by a comment from Hayashiya Tatsuburō in *Chūsei bunka no kichō* (Tokyo: Tokyo daigaku shuppankai, 1959), p. 31.

24. I published this conclusion in "*Gangyōe* ni Myōezō o miru" (Seeing Myōe in *Tale of Gangyō*) in Tsuji Nobuo sensei kanreki kinen kai (ed.), *Nihon bijutsushi no suimyaku* (Currents of Japanese art history; Tokyo: Perikan, 1993), p. 386, note 8.

25. Hiruma, "Kōzanji ni okeru *Gishōe*," pp. 61–62 and p. 65, note 38; Itoh Daisuke, "Kōzanji zō 'Myōe shōnin jujō zazen zō' kō—omo ni sono kōzuhō ni okeru sōga to no kankei ni tsuite" (Kōzanji's *Saint Myōe Seated in Meditation in a Tree*: The relationship of its composition to Song painting," *Bijutsushi*, 1996, *140*, 174–88; Wakasugi, *Emaki*, pp. 74–75.

26. The Kōzanji archive is now better known and published than ever before. See Kōzanji tenseki komonjo sōgō chōsadan (Comprehensive investigative team for Kōzanji books and documents, eds.), *Kōzanji shiryō sōsho* (Compendium of Kōzanji source materials, hereafter *KSS*), 21 vols. (Tokyo: Tokyo University Press, 1968–present); the journal *Myōe sangyō* (In praise of Myōe), published by Semuiji in Yuasa since 1969; and the yearly *Kenkyū hōkoku ronshū* (Research report), published by the Kōzanji Team since 1981. Other than Okuda Isao, Miyazawa Toshimasa, and Sueki Fumihiko, few members work specifically on Myōe or Kōzanji. Their work as a whole has enormous potential for understanding the activities of Kōzanji monks throughout the temple's entire history.

27. *Yume no ki*, in *KSS*, vol. 7, pp. 1–503; translated by Tanabe in *Myōe the Dreamkeeper*, pp. 159–209; and Girard, *Un Moine*, pp. 109–200. Several fragments are illustrated in *Kōzanji-ten*, nos. 41–43.

28. *Yume no ki*, in *KSS*, vol. 7, p. 130. Both Girard, *Un Moine*, p. 132, and Tanabe, *Myōe the Dreamkeeper*, p. 169, recognize Satsuma as Shunga, but Tanabe calls him a sculptor. I discuss Myōe's commissions of Shunga extensively in "'My Reflection Should Be Your Keepsake': Myōe's Vision of the Kasuga Deity," in Robert H. Sharf and Elizabeth Horton Sharf (eds.), *Living Images: Japanese Buddhist Icons in Context* (Stanford: Stanford University Press, 2001), pp. 49–113.

29. Tanaka Hisao, "Myōe shōnin no okibumi" (Saint Myōe's directives; 1970), reprinted in idem, *Kamakura bukkyō zakkō* (Miscellaneous research on Kamakura Buddhism; Kyoto: Shibunkaku shuppan, 1982), pp. 343–66; Okuda, *Myōe*, pp. 106–9; illustrated in *Kōzanji-ten*, nos. 64–65.

30. In addition to the texts introduced later in this chapter, see the several recollections of Myōe published in *KSS*, vol. 16; Yanagida Seiji, "Myōe no kōgi to sono oboegaki" (Myōe's lectures and recollections of them), in *KSS*, bekkan (separate volume), pp. 181–97.

31. Buddhist dictionaries define *shōnin* as pertaining to the buddha, an enlightened being, an extraordinary person, a follower of the buddha, and an eminent monk with extraordinary knowledge; Nakamura Hajime, *Bukkyōgo daijiten shukusaiban* (Reduced-size printing, great dictionary of Buddhist terms; Tokyo: Tokyo shoseki, 1981), pp. 693 and 728; Mochizuki Shinkō, *Mochizuki bukkyō daijiten*, 10 vols. (Tokyo: Sekai seiten kankō kyōkai, 1933–36), vol. 3, pp. 2748–49.

32. Okuda Isao, "Myōe shōnin kankei shikigo shū" (Collection of inscriptions by Saint Myōe), in *KSS*, vol. 7, pp. 1103–20.

33. In thinking about Myōe as "saint," I have been inspired by James C. Dobbins, "The Biography of Shinran: Apotheosis of a Japanese Buddhist Visionary," *History of Religions*, Nov. 1990, *30*(2), 175–96; and idem, "Envisioning Kamakura Buddhism," in Richard K. Payne, *Re-Visioning "Kamakura" Buddhism* (Honolulu: University of Hawai'i Press, 1998), pp. 24–42, especially pp. 32–36.On Buddhist saints and sacred biography more broadly, see Frank E. Reynolds and Donald Capps (eds.), *The Biographical Process* (The Hague: Mouton, 1976); Stanley Jeyaraga Tambiah, *The Buddhist Saints of the Forest and the Cult of Amulets* (Cambridge, England: Cambridge University Press, 1984); Richard Kieckhefer and George D. Bond (eds.), *Sainthood: Its Manifestations in World Religions* (Berkeley: University of California Press, 1988); Thomas Head, *Hagiography and the Cult of the Saints* (Cambridge, England: Cambridge University Press, 1990); Aviad M. Kleinberg, *Prophets in Their Own Country: Living Saints and the Making of Sainthood in the Later Middle Ages* (Chicago: Chicago University Press, 1992); Reginald Ray, *Buddhist Saints in India* (Oxford, England: Oxford University Press, 1994); and Juliane Schober, *Sacred Biography in the Buddhist Traditions of South and Southeast Asia* (Honolulu: University of Hawai'i Press, 1997).

34. *Kōzanji komonjo* (Kōzanji documents), in *KSS*, vol. 4; *Kōzanji kyōzō tenseki monjo mokuroku* (Catalogue of books and documents in the Kōzanji storehouse, hereafter *Catalogue*), 5 vols., in *KSS*, vols. 3, 5, 8, 10, and 11.

35. Myōe was trained in both Kegon (Avatamsaka) and Shingon doctrines and practices; hence his followers are found in both circles; Okuda Isao and Ishizuki Harumichi, "Myōe shōnin kankei ketsumyaku shū" (Collection of lineage charts related to Saint Myōe), in *KSS*, vol. 7, p. 1167; *Kōzanji-ten*, nos. 10 and 16; Brock, "The Case of the Missing Scroll," pp. 24–26.

36. On Gyōji, see Nakamura Ken, "Jingoji Jōgakubō Gyōji to sono shūhen" (The circle of Jōgakubō Gyōji at Jingoji), *Bunka Shigaku*, 1963, *17*, 100–112; Yamada Shōzen, "Jingoji shōnin Jōgakubō Gyōji denkō" (Research on Jōgakubō Gyōji's biography), in *Kushida Hakushi jōju kinen kōsō den no kenkyū* (Tokyo: Sangibō, 1973), pp. 359–78. For Jōshin, see Okuda, *Myōe*, pp. 183–84; an example of Jōshin's calligraphy appears in *Kōzanji-ten*, no. 36.

37. At Kōzanji, Jōshin founded the Hōbenchiin subtemple, where he was succeeded by Ninshin (1218–1303). Many important manuscripts related to Myōe were kept in Hōbenchiin, as evidenced by Hōbenchiin seals; Kinsui Satoshi, "Hōbenchiin shōkyō mokuroku" (Catalogue of sacred texts in Hōbenchiin), in *KSS*, vol. 18, pp. 387–473.

38. *Saigo rinjū gyōgi no koto* (Record of events of His passing), in *KSS*, vol. 1, pp. 563–71 and 729–30; *Shōnin no koto* (Saintly matters), in *KSS*, vol. 1, pp. 591–601 and 731–33.

39. Jōshin, *Saigo rinjū*, in *KSS*, vol. 1, p. 572.

40. For Zenzai and the "good friends" (J. Zenchishiki, S. Kalyanamitra), see Jan Fontein, *The Pilgrimage of Sudhana: A study of Gandavyuha illustrations in China, Japan and Java* (The Hague and Paris: Mouton, 1967), pp. 78–115; Ishida Hisatoyo, *Kegon-kyō e* (Paintings of the flower garland sutra), Nihon no bijutsu 270 (Tokyo: Shibundō, 1998); Thomas Cleary (trans.), *Entry into the Realm of Reality: The Gandavyuha, the Final Book of the Avatamsaka Sutra* (Boston: Shambhala, 1987).

41. Tanaka Hisao, "Girinbō Kikai no shōgai" (The life of Girinbō Kikai), 1975, reprinted in *Kamakura bukkyō zakkō*, pp. 581–639. For Kikai's calligraphy, see *Kōzanji-ten*, nos. 103 and 114.

42. Kikai wrote the three-volume *Kōzanji Myōe shōnin gyōjō* in Japanese in 1232.

In 1255 Ryūchō translated the text into Chinese and Kōshin made corrections. Neither original survives. The Semuiji version (in Japanese) of *Kana gyōjō* lacks volume 2, in *KSS*, vol. 1, 13–80; the Ueyama version (in Chinese) of *Kanbun gyōjō* is complete in three volumes, in *KSS*, vol. 1, 79–145.

43. *Kana gyōjō*, in *KSS*, vol. 1, pp. 76–80. The five monks must have been five of the elders mentioned in Myōe's directive.

44. Okuda, *Myōe*, pp. 175–79.

45. *Kōzanji shōgyō mokuroku*, in *KSS*, vol. 14 (1985), pp. 3–76 and 278–99. Since Kikai was in charge of scholarship after Myōe's death, I suspect that he had begun the project before his death.

46. Brock, "The Case of the Missing Scroll," pp. 7–9.

47. Hirata, *Ebusshi no jidai*, vol. 1, pp. 188 and 196–97.

48. Okuda, *Myōe*, pp. 74–76. Details about all of these volumes are found in *Catalogue*, in *KSS*, vol. 3, pp. 376–77 and vol. 5, pp. 92–98; and in Kōzanji Team (eds.), *Kōzanji zenbon mokuroku* (Catalogue of Kōzanji rare books; Tokyo: Tokyo daigaku shuppan, 1988), pp. 25–26.

49. *Kegonshū matsugaku shamon Jōnin.*

50. *Kegonshū gakusha shamon Jōnin*; in *KSS*, vol. 3, p. 376.

51. *Guhō shamon Jōnin.*

52. Shōhan (1183–1249), who signed himself "The Kegon Monk Shōhan," wrote the remainder of the volume "at Kōzanji"; in *KSS*, vol. 5, pp. 92–93. According to Kikai, during this period Myōe and he were both involved in a large copying project of their own; *Kanbun gyōjō*, in *KSS*, vol. 1, p. 125.

53. Shibazaki Terukazu, "Myōe to bukkō sanmai kan (1): jissenkan kara mita sono juyō no riyu oyobi haikei" (Myōe's meditation on Buddha's light: background and reception as seen from practice), *Nantō Bukkyō*, Mar. 1991, *65*, 44–70, especially pp. 48–50. Hiruma, "Kōzanji ni okeru," pp. 51–53, cites Shibazaki to make her case for the existence of imported Song paintings at Kōzanji.

54. Tanaka, *Kamakura bukkyō zakkō*, pp. 344–45.

55. This complete version of the Tripitaka would eventually be housed in the Western Sutra Repository at Kōzanji.

56. By contrast, Myōe entered Jingoji at age nine, studied with a variety of Shingon and Kegon teachers, and was fully ordained at age sixteen.

57. *Jūji rongi ki*; the only other signature in this project is "Shingyō, who as yet has no lineage in Kegon doctrine"; in *KSS*, vol. 3, p. 121.

58. Okuda, *Myōe*, pp. 91–95; *Kana gyōjō*, in *KSS*, vol. 1, pp. 52–53 and 56. A headnote to a poem in Myōe's poetry collection explains the move; Yoshihara Shikeko, *Myōe shōnin kashū no kenkyū* (Research on Saint Myōe's poetry collection; Tokyo: Obūsha, 1976), pp. 123–24 and 180–81. Retired emperor Gotoba appointed the new superintendent, Chōgon (1152–1228), on Kenpō 6/2/11; *Dainihon shiryō*, vol. 4, part 14, pp. 651–53. Six months later, on Kenpō 6/8/22, Gotoba directed Nobuhisa to build the Kamo retreat for Myōe.

59. Brock, "'Tales of Gishō and Gangyō,'" pp. 374–79; William H. McCullough (trans.), "Shōkyūki, An Account of the Shōkyū War of 1221," *Monumenta Nipponica*, 1964, *19*(1), 103–215; idem (trans.), "The *Azuma kagami* Account of the Shōkyū War," *Monumenta Nipponica*, 1968, *23*(1–2), 102–55.

60. Fascicles 4, 14, 24, and 34, in *KSS*, vol. 3, pp. 24–28. See also *Kōzanji-ten*, no. 115; and *Kōzanji zenbon moku roku*, no. 19, p. 20.

61. *KSS*, vol. 3, pp. 27–28.

62. For "prescribed method" (*nyohō*), see Willa Jane Tanabe, *Paintings of the Lotus Sutra* (New York: Weatherhill, 1988), pp. 43–45.

63. Two younger sisters of Nobuhisa, both nuns, later sponsored memorial ceremonies for Myōe at Kōzanji.

64. *Kana gyōjō*, in *KSS*, vol. 1, p. 56.

65. The characters for "lion," *shishi*, could indicate Jōnin's status as head of the project; for *shishi*, see Nakamura, *Bukkyōgo*, pp. 544–45.

66. Okuda, *Myōe*, p. 98.

67. The two elders are listed as Girinbō and Gienbō; *Toganoo sekkai nikki*, in *KSS*, vol. 16, pp. 631 and 757–61; and also in Tanaka Hisao, "Toganoo sekkai nikki ni tsuite," 1964, reprinted in Tanaka, *Kamakura bukkyō zakkō*, pp. 512–24. This text is thought to have been written by Chōen (dates unknown), a follower of Jōshin.

68. *Meigetsuki*, Kangi 1/5/15; Imagawa Fumio (ed.), *Kundoku Meigetsuki* (Tokyo: Kawade shobō, 1977–78), vol. 5, pp. 27–28.

69. *Kana gyōjō*, in *KSS*, vol. 1, pp. 58–60.

70. Tanaka, *Kamakura bukkyō zakkō*, p. 346.

71. *Kōzanji engi*, in *KSS*, vol. 1, pp. 629–66.

72. For Kōshin, see Okuda Isao, "Junshōbō Kōshin Shōnin o megutte—Myōe Shōnin kōdai oboegakisho yori" (Concerning Junshōbō Kōshin: from the recollections of Saint Myōe's senior followers), *Myōe sangyō*, 1973–74, *15*, 1–4; Kōshin's calligraphy appears in *Kōzanji-ten*, nos. 44 and 67.

73. For the term *engi*, see Sakurai Tokutarō, "Engi no ruikei to tenkai" (Variety and development in origin tales), in Sakurai Tokutarō (ed.), *Jisha engi*, Nihon shisō taikei, vol. 20 (Tokyo: Iwanami shoten, 1975), pp. 445–78.

74. *Kōzanji engi*, in *KSS*, vol. 1, pp. 644–49.

75. A chronology of Nagafusa's activities appears in Okuda Isao, "Myōe to Jishinbō Kakushin," *Myōe sangyō*, 1994, *22*, 3–11; I discuss Nagafusa's role in the founding of Kōzanji in "My Reflection Should Be Your Keepsake," pp. 87–91.

76. Myōe's funeral is described in *On sōhō sakuhō* (Method for his burial), a document owned by Ninnaji; *Dainihon shiryō* part 5, no. 7, pp. 281–84.

77. *Kōzanji engi*, in *KSS*, vol. 1, p. 645.

78. *Shōjō zazen zō*, first published in Mori, *Kamakura jidai no shōzōga*, pp. 53–56; *Kōzanji-ten*, no. 128.

79. Throughout *Kōzanji Origin Tales* Kōshin consistently makes a clear distinction between walls and screens.

80. Tanabe, *Myōe the Dreamkeeper*, pp. 123–24.

81. The rhetoric of *katami* appears frequently in the Kōzanji documents; see Brock, "My Reflection Should Be Your Keepsake," pp. 64–66.

82. The memorial function of portraits is discussed by Yonekura Michio, *Minamoto Yoritomo zo, chinmoku no shōzōga* (The portrait of Minamoto Yoritomo, the silent portrait painting), E wa kataru, vol. 4 (Tokyo: Heibonsha, 1995), pp. 12–32.

83. On this group of paintings, see Brock, "My Reflection Should Be Your Keepsake," pp. 49, 101, 109, 213, and 229.

84. *Kōzanji engi*, in *KSS*, vol. 1, pp. 646–47.

85. Mori, *Kamakura jidai no shōzōga*, pp. 60–63; *Kōzanji-ten*, no. 26.

86. For instance, Jingoji's portrait of Mongaku (ca. 1137–ca. 1204); Mori, *Kamakura jidai no shōzōga*, pp. 25–47; *Kōzanji-ten*, no. 25.

87. *Kana gyōjō*, in *KSS*, vol. 1, pp. 75–80.

88. Ibid.

89. The Five Saints formed a devotional grouping conceived by Myōe late in life: Rushana, Kannon, Miroku, Monju, and Fugen; Ishida, *Kegon kyō-e*, pp. 41–46; *Kōzanji-ten*, no. 108. A standing image of Miroku bodhisattva is traditionally said to be the very image described by Kikai, *Kōzanji-ten*, no. 81.

90. See note 8.
91. See the cover image and color plates in Wakasugi, *Emaki.*
92. Tanabe, *Myōe the Dreamkeeper*, p. 124.
93. The character *sha*, meaning copy, appears in numerous copyist inscriptions on Kōzanji manuscripts.
94. *Saigo rinjū*, in *KSS*, vol. 1, pp. 574–75.
95. Tenpuku 2/10/19 (1234); *Kōzanji engi*, in *KSS*, vol. 1, pp. 655–56.
96. Takaoka, *Umegahata-mura shi*, p. 23, suggests that in 1931 Morikane's old stone stupa was still located on the site of Kangien, and that it was mistakenly identified as a stupa dedicated to Myōe's mother. If Takaoka's reference is to the stupa now in front of Myōe's tomb, perhaps it was moved there during Myōe's seven-hundred-year memorial activities in that same year.
97. *Kanbun gyōjō*, in *KSS*, vol. 1, pp. 119–20; *Kōzanji Origin Tales*, in *KSS*, vol. 1, pp. 651–52.
98. Dated Karoku 2/8/9; Yoshihara, *Myōe shōnin kashū*, pp. 85–87.
99. *Meigetsuki*, Kangi 1/5/15. Fujiwara Sadataka (1197–1238) was either the brother or the son of Fujiwara Nagafusa.
100. *Kōzanji komonjo*, no. 40, in *KSS*, vol. 4, p. 48.
101. Several of Myōe's followers, including Jōshin, Kikai, and Kōshin, all wrote in a hand very similar to Myōe's.
102. Hirata, *Ebusshi no jidai*, vol. 1, pp. 42–43. In addition to Kaneyasu's image of Bishamon in Myōe's buddha chapel, a sketchbook (*ehon*) said to be in the Meditation Hall Precinct is listed in *Kōzanji shōgyō mokuroku*, in *KSS*, vol. 14, p. 48.
103. Hirata, *Ebusshi no jidai*, vol. 1, pp. 240–51. Several preparatory drawings are associated with Kōzanji. A full-scale portrait drawing of Konoe Kanetsune (1210–59) is illustrated in *Kōzanji-ten*, no. 70, and a preparatory drawing for a devotional icon of Miroku is in *Selected Masterpieces of Asian Art* (Boston, Museum of Fine Arts, 1992), p. 38.
104. See Hamada Takashi, *Zuzō*, Nihon no bijutsu 55 (Tokyo: Shibundō, 1970) and Hisatoyo Ishida, *Esoteric Buddhist Painting*, E. Dale Saunders (trans. and adapt.), Japanese Arts Library, vol. 15 (New York and Tokyo: Kodansha International, 1987), pp. 82–88.
105. *Kanbun gyōjō*, in *KSS*, vol. 1, p. 110.
106. *Kana gyōjō*, in *KSS*, vol. 1, p. 31.
107. *Kōzanji engi*, in *KSS*, vol. 1, pp. 639–40 and 657.
108. *Kana gyōjō*, in *KSS*, vol. 1, p. 52.
109. The woman was Lady Sanmi, an imperial wetnurse and important patron of Myōe from 1216 to 1221, and my candidate for the patron of the *Gishō* scrolls. See Karen L. Brock, "Chinese Maiden, Silla Monk: Zenmyō and Her Thirteenth-century Japanese Audience," in Marsha Weidner (ed.), *Women in the History of Chinese and Japanese Painting* (Honolulu: University of Hawai'i Press, 1990), pp. 205–11.
110. *Kōzanji komonjo*, in *KSS*, vol. 4, p. 52. In addition to a painting of Bishamon, there was also a colored sketch of Taishaku drawn by Myōe and a painting of Taishaku.
111. Brock, "My Reflection Should Be Your Keepsake."

CHAPTER FOUR

I owe a debt of gratitude to many people who read and commented on versions of this manuscript: Christine Guth, Julia Meech, Susan Matisoff, Richard Vinograd,

Karen Brock, Elizabeth Lillehoj, and Sumie Jones. Laura Allen shared a great deal of material from her own research, both published and unpublished, with a generosity of spirit that went far beyond the call of duty. Mimi Yiengpruksawan took it apart and put it back together with a degree of "tough love" that merits special thanks.

1. Pierre Bourdieu, *The Field of Cultural Production: Essays on Art and Literature* (New York: Columbia University Press, 1993), p. 81.

2. Jacques Derrida, *On the Name* (Stanford, Calif.: Stanford University Press, 1995), p. 84.

3. Further delving revealed that the screens constitute the tip of a large iceberg. Mitsunobu's name is also linked to an enormous variety of other formats as well, but that problem is beyond the scope of this chapter.

4. Discussed in Taizō Kuroda, Melinda Takeuchi, and Yamane Yūzō, *Worlds Seen and Imagined: Japanese Screens from the Idemitsu Museum of Art* (New York: Asia Society, 1995), no. 2.

5. See ibid., no. 3. The translator transcribed "Shōgen" as "Shōkan."

6. Discussed in Tokyo National Museum (ed.), *Screen Painting of the Muromachi Period (Muromachi jidai no byōbu-e*; Tokyo: Tokyo National Museum, 1989), no. 11. Mitsuoki's inscription reads "Tosa Gyōbu Tayū Mitsunobu hitsu" ([by the] brush of Tosa Mitsunobu, Senior Assistant Head of the Punishments Ministry).

7. Discussed in *Worlds Seen and Imagined*, no. 9. This inscription simply says "Tosa Mitsunobu hitsu" ([By] the brush of Tosa Mitsunobu).

8. For a good discussion of the problematic nature of these terms, see Karen Brock, "Yamatoe," *Dictionary of Art* (London: Macmillan, 1996), vol. 17, pp. 153–62, and "Karae," ibid., p. 162.

9. This was the work entitled *Painting Catalog of the Xuanhe Period (Xuanhe huapu)*. Quoted in Alexander C. Soper, "The Rise of Yamatoe," *Art Bulletin*, Dec. 1942, *24*(4), p. 374.

10. This contrasts with the Suiboku lineage, where painters such as Sesshū Tōyō (1460–1506) and others copied signed Chinese paintings (including their signature) and then added their own name to the finished copy. Signatures first start appearing in abundance in the fourteenth century, in a Buddhist and ink-painting context: Ryōzen (fl. 1348–55); Gyoku'en Bonpō (ca. 1348–ca. 1420); Kitsuzan Minchō (1352–1431); and Ue Gukei (1361–75) all have signatures reproduced in Kanazawa Hiroshi, *Kaō, Minchō* (*Nihon bijutsu kaiga zenshū*), vol. 1 (Tokyo: Shūeisha, 1977), pp. 124–26. A votive plaque of a horse (*ema*) at the Itsukushima shrine with Mitsunobu's name on it (the signature "Mitsunobu painted this, Eishō 17 [1520]" is given in *Koga bikō*, vol. 33, p. 1489, but this does not seem to be accepted as part of his oeuvre; most authors ignore it.

11. Suggested by Herbert Plutschow in the discussion following presentation of this chapter as a paper at Nichibunken. The Edo-period Tosa painters seem to have signed their works routinely, even those painted for members of the imperial court.

12. They are (1) *Portrait of Momoi Naoakira*, 1480; (2) *Legends of Seikō-ji*, 1487, Tokyo National Museum; (3) *Ten Kings*, 1489, Jōfuku-ji; (4) *Portrait of Goen'yū*, 1492, Reiun-in; (5) *Legends of Tsukimine-dera*, Freer; (6) *The Tongue-cut Sparrow*, private collection, Japan; (7) sketch for a portrait of Sanjōnishi Sanetaka; (8) *Legends of the Kitano Shrine*, 1503, Kitano Shrine; and (9) *Legends of Kiyomizu-dera*, 1517, Tokyo National Museum (see Yoshida Yūji, *Tosa Mitsunobu*; Tokyo: Shūeisha, 1979, p. 146). The list constantly changes, however. See Karen Brock, "Tosa Mitsunobu," *Dictionary of Art* (London: Macmillan, 1996), vol. 31, pp. 197–98, for a more expanded list.

13. For basic information on Mitsunobu, see Yoshida Yūji, *Tosa Mitsunobu*; Yoshida

Yūji, "Shihai monjo no eshi Mitsunobu—'Tosa Mitsunobu' hī 1" (Background documents on the painter Mitsunobu—Tosa Mitsunobu, supplement 1), in *Teizukayama Gakuin daigaku kenkyū ronshū*, Apr. 1979, *15*, 1711–1821; Tani Shin'ichi, "Tosa Mitsunobu kō: Tosa-ha kenkyū no issetsu," *Bijutsu kenkyū*, 1940, *100*, *101*, *103*, 115–28, 159–69, 207–21, and reprinted in his *Muromachi judai bijutsushi ron* (Tokyo: Tōkyōdō, 1942), pp. 418–514 (page numbers in this article refer to the reprint); and Miyajima Shin'ichi, "Tosa Mitsunobu to Tosaha no kefu," *Nihon no bijutsu*, Dec. 1986, *247*. Not much on Mitsunobu is published in English. See Brock, "Mitsunobu"; and Melissa McCormick, "Tosa Mitsunobu's *Ko-e*: Forms and Functions of Small-Format Handscrolls in the Muromachi Period (1333–1573)," Ph.D. dissertation, Princeton University, 2000. Quitman E. Phillips covers Mitsunobu among the other artists treated in *The Practices of Painting in Japan, 1475–1500* (Stanford, Calif.: Stanford University Press, 2000), *passim*.

14. See Tani Shin'ichi, "A Consideration of Tosa Yukihiro" (*Tosa Yukihiro kō*), 1 and 2, *Bijutsu kenkyū*, Nov. 1942, *127*, 275–84; and *Bijutsu kenkyū*, Jan. 1943, *128*, 8–14.

15. See Kimura Tokue, *Explanation to the Tosa Documents* (*Tosa monjo kaisetsu*; Tokyo: Iwai Kameijirō, 1935), p. 1. Kimura transcribes the documents and appends explanations. My limited exposure to the original *Tosa monjo*, now mounted as a handscroll, consists of seeing a section of it on display at the Tokyo National Museum in November 1997. There is no way to verify the authenticity of any or all of the contents, and before embarking on the art historian's love affair with such material one would do well to remember that forging documents was a widespread practice from the Kamakura period onward. See Hitomi Tonomura, "Forging the Past: Medieval Counterfeit Documents," *Monumenta Nipponica*, Spring 1985, *40*(1), 70–96.

16. He is listed as one of the artists of the *Tale of the Circulating Homage to Amida* (*Yūzū nenbutsu engi*), in Seiryōji, dated 1414, as "Tosa no Kami Yukihiro."

17. This is in the list of painters contributing scenes to the *Tale of the Circulating Homage to Amida*. See Tani, "Tosa Yukihiro kō," 1, p. 277; and Yoshida, *Tosa Mitsunobu*, p. 108. *Gakō* is sometimes glossed as "*edakumi*."

18. Kimura, *Explanation of the Tosa Documents*, pp. 5–6.

19. Sanjōnishi Sanetaka, *Record of Lord Sanetaka* (*Sanetaka kō ki*), entry for 1489, regarding a set of paintings of the "Ten Kings of Hell." See Yoshida, *Tosa Mitsunobu*, p. 105. It is possible that the Kasuga workshop might be the same as the Tosa workshop; it takes its name from Kasuga-kōji, the former name of Kyoto's Marutamachi-dōri, near what would become the location of the Tosa studio.

20. See Herbert Plutschow, *Japan's Name Culture: The Significance of Names in a Religious, Political, and Social Context* (Kent, England: Japan Library, 1995), esp. pp. 106–10.

21. Laurance P. Roberts, *Dictionary of Japanese Artists* (New York and Tokyo: Weatherhill, 1976), lists at least fifty-five. These include unexpected people such as Okamoto Shūki, a samurai-painter of Odawara; and Fujiwara Gyōkō, an ukiyo-e printmaker.

22. See Yoshida, *Tosa Mitsunobu*, p. 105.

23. Sakakibara Yoshio and Matsuo Yoshiki, *Tosake no shozō funpon* (The Tosa house portrait sketches; Kyoto: Kyoto shoin, 1998), reproduced 190 such sketches from the Tosa archive at Tokyo University of Fine Arts. Images of Hitomaro are found in plates 126–53.

24. Tani, "Tosa Mitsunobu," p. 422. The information comes from various courtiers' diaries.

25. Indeed, the medieval word for craftsperson, *shokunin*, which literally means "person" (*nin*) of "skill" (*shoku*), may well derive from employment at the palace

(*kanshoku*). This material comes from Amino Yoshihiko, "Chūsei no 'shokunin' o megutte" (A consideration of medieval "shokunin"), in Amino Yoshihiko and Ishida Hisatoyo (eds.), *Kinsei fūzoku zufu*, vol. 12 (Tokyo: Shogakukan, 1983), pp. 62–63.

26. See Yoshiaki Shimizu, "Workshop Management of the Early Kano Painters, ca. A.D. 1530–1600," *Archives of Asian Art*, 1981, *34*, 32–44; John M. Rosenfield, "Japanese Studio Practice: The Tosa Family and the Imperial Painting Office in the Seventeenth Century," in Peter Lukehart (ed.), *The Artist's Workshop* (Studies in the History of Art, no. 38), Washington, D.C.: Center for Advanced Studies in the Visual Arts, 1993, pp. 79–102; John M. Rosenfield, "Japanese Painting Workshops and the Gardner Museum Collections," *Fenway Court*, 1992, pp. 9–13; Kozo Yamamura, "The Growth of Commerce in Medieval Japan," in Kozo Yamamura (ed.), *Medieval Japan*, vol. 3 of *The Cambridge History of Japan* (Cambridge, England: Cambridge University Press), p. 352. Donald Keene, "The *Iemoto* System (Nō and Kyōgen)," *Fenway Court*, 1992, p. 31, thinks that the notion of guarding the secrets of the house may be connected to the practice of secret transmission within the esoteric sects of Buddhism. See also Amino, "Chūsei no 'shokunin,'" p. 64. On p. 70 Amino describes the establishment of the post of "Director of Prostitutes" (Yūjō bettō) by Minamoto Yoritomo in 1193 to handle lawsuits by prostitutes. One Satomi Yoshinari was appointed to this position. The source cited is *Azuma kagami*.

27. Jōfuku-ji's *Ten Kings*, for example, was recorded by Sanetaka as being a *shinzu*, "new picture," by Mitsunobu for Emperor Gotsuchimikado. See Tani, "Tosa Mitsunobu," p. 487; and Yoshida, *Tosa Mitsunobu*, p. 105 and plates 61–63. But paradoxically, *shinzu* entail older models. Mitsunobu painted many *shinzu*, which are pictures, often religious, made as replacements or supplements for old pictures. In the case of the *Ten Kings*, Mitsunobu copied models that he and Sanetaka claimed were by Mitsunobu's "ancestor," Kasuga Edokoro Yukimitsu (act. ca. 1339–49). The models for these paintings, still extant, are in Nison'in. (There is no reason, however, to think these pictures were executed by Yukimitsu.) Paintings of the Ten Kings of Hell would be used at memorial services. There is little room for artistic license in such pictures. Sanetaka's role as a go-between and project coordinator between extremely high-born individuals (including the emperor) and Tosa artists is discussed in Karen Brock, "Sanetaka and the Making of a Japanese Picture Scroll," paper presented at "The Triumph of Japanese Style: 16th Century Art in Japan" (Cleveland Museum of Art, 1993); see also Phillips, *Practices of Painting*, pp. 110–17.

28. This presented the occasional problem. For example, there is the reference to Mitsunobu's painting a picture of a generic body for a portrait of Emperor Gotsuchimikado, which the emperor then completed by sketching his own face in a mirror. The coloring was completed by the courtier Tachibana Mochikazu; Yoshida, *Tosa Mitsunobu*, p. 103.

29. See Earl Miner, Hiroko Odagiri, and Robert E. Morrell, *The Princeton Companion to Classical Japanese Literature* (Princeton, N.J.: Princeton University Press, 1985), pp. 443–60, esp. pp. 446–47. See also William H. and Helen Craig McCullough (trans.), *A Tale of Flowering Fortunes: Annals of Japanese Aristocratic Life in the Heian Period*, 2 vols. (Stanford, Calif.: Stanford University Press: 1980), pp. 790–831. These two works describe the court structure as it existed during the Heian period. The meaning of the various ranks had deflated considerably by medieval times, but they exerted a powerful inclusive-exclusive structure nonetheless.

30. Phillips, *Practices of Painting*, pp. 122–23, touches on the differing modes of address in medieval society.

31. See Miyajima Shin'ichi, "Jūyonseiki no edokoro azukari no kefu" (The lin-

eage of the fourteenth-century Painting Bureau directorship), *Bijutsushi* 88, Mar. 1973, *22*(4), 87–102. Mitsunobu's directorship spanned the reigns of two emperors: Gotsuchimikado (r. 1465–1500) and Gokashiwabara (r. 1521–26).

32. Kamei Wakana, "A Re-Evaluation of 'The Head of the Painting bureau, Tosa Mitsunobu'" (*Edokoro azukari Tosa Mitsunobu' no saikentō*), *Kokka*, Aug. 1997, *1222*, 15–17.

33. See, for example, the famous diary entry of Daijōin Jinson, abbot of a subtemple of Kōfukuji in Nara. The entry, dated 1472, lists, somewhat cryptically: Kubota at Yanagihara; Kano (Tosa pupil) at Oshiage; Awataguchi Oki (Etchū); Mizokui (Awataguchi pupil in Nara); the "Tenka" or Imperial Workshop at Reizei Higashi-no-tōin; Rokkaku Takakura; Shijō Horikawa; Tosa Shōgen (Ōtaki), Takakura; and Awataguchi Minbu. See Mushakōji Minoru, *Eshi (Painters). Mono to ningen no bunkashi* 63 (Tokyo: Hōsei daigaku, 1990), p. 108 (Mushanokōji talks about the devalued position of palace painters); and Yoshida, *Tosa Mitsunobu*, p. 109.

34. For example, the fief in Tanba, the traditional land grant awarded to the Director of the Palace Painting Bureau, was plagued by plunder in 1484; the problem was resolved in 1485. Then again in 1501, and in 1506–7, there were conflicts having to do with taxation by the military government. In 1508, Mitsunobu received an imperial directive restoring his prerogatives, but even in his successor's tenancy there continued to be conflicts over property rights and income. In 1509, a three-way dispute arose over Tosa properties in Kokubunji, which involved Buddhist sculptors' claims to the income. Another dispute occurred between 1511 and 1514. See Kimura, "Tosa monjo kaisetsu," p. 55; and Tani, "Tosa Mitsunobu," pp. 432–33 and 436.

35. Minamoto Toyomune, "Tōhaku on Painting" (Tōhaku gasetsu), *Bijutsu kenkyū*, Jan. 1932, no. 1, p. 27. Tōhaku mentions that Kubota participated in the execution of a twenty-eight-volume edition of the *Lotus*. According to Minamoto, Kubota appears in documents from 1441 to 1536 and painted for the shogun Yoshimasa. Although no mention is made of Tōbei, there is a brief entry for a Kubota Tōtai, a slightly later figure, in Tani Shin'ichi and Noma Seiroku (eds.), *Nihon bijutsu jiten* (Dictionary of Japanese art; Tokyo: Tōkyōdō, 1952), p. 229: "an edokoro painter for Kyoto's temples, active during the Tenmon era, 1523–54." They add that there were a number of painters with the Kubota surname, constituting a sort of lineage running from early Muromachi to the Momoyama period. Scattered references to Tōbei are found in Phillips, *Practices of Painting*, pp. 5, 53, 63, 124, 145, 149, 157–59, 183, 189, 191, and 196–98.

36. Laura Allen, personal communication, June 2, 1998.

37. Reproduced in Ishida Hisatoyo, Naitō Akira, and Moriya Kastuhisa (comps.), *Rakuchū Rakugaizu taikan*, vol. 1 (Tokyo: Shōgakukan, 1987).

38. See Tani and Noma, *Nihon bijutsu jiten*, p. 280.

39. Jurgis Elisonas, "Notorious Places: A Brief Excursion into the Narrative Topography of Early Edo," in James L. McClain et al. (eds.), *Edo and Paris: Urban Life and the State in the Early Modern Era* (Ithaca, N.Y.: Cornell University Press, 1994), p. 284. *Edo kanoko* was published between December 1687 and January 1688. It included such headings as "Master Craftsmen and Merchants," "The Professions and the Arts" (the latter boasting forty-two entries), and twenty kinds of wholesaler.

40. See Karen M. Gerhart, *The Eyes of Power: Art and Early Tokugawa Authority* (Honolulu: University of Hawai'i Press, 1999), chapter 4, "*The Tōshō Daigongen engi* as Political Propaganda," pp. 107–40.

41. For a translation of the passage, see Quitman E. Phillips, "*Honchō gashi* and the Kano Myth," p. 47. The original text is given in Sakazaki Tan, *Nihon kaigaron taikei*, vol. 2 (Tokyo: Meicho fukyūsha, 1979), pp. 366–466.

42. This text is reproduced in Sakazaki, *Nihon kaigaron taikei*, vol.5, pp. 27–59.

43. Yoshida, *Tosa Mitsunobu*, p. 98. For a brief biography of Dōyū, see Sugimura Kendō (ed.), *The Ocean of Confucianism—Speculum of Eminent Confucianists* (*Jukai—jusha meikan*; Sendai: Ōkubo shoin, 1975), p. 164.

44. This pleasant pastime appears under the heading of "Delightful Things" in the early-seventeenth-century printed book *The Dog Pillow* (*Inu makura*), a satire on Sei Shonagon's famous *Pillow Book*. See Edward Putzar (trans.), "*Inu Makura: The Dog Pillow*," *Harvard Journal of Asiatic Studies*, 1968, *28*, 101. Putzar simply lists "A real bargain at a shop." The brackets suggesting that the shop should be an antique shop come from Donald Shively, "Popular Culture," in John Whitney Hall (ed.), *The Cambridge History of Japan*, vol. 4, *Early Modern Japan* (Cambridge, England: Cambridge University Press, 1991), p. 734. For the talismanic properties of ancient Chinese collections, see Lothar Ledderose, "Some Observations on the Imperial Art Collections of China," *Transactions of the Oriental Ceramic Society*, 1978–79, *43*, 33–46.

45. An example of the former notion (that paintings could help one's family flourish) may be seen in an inscription on a box containing a painting by Ike Taiga (1723–76): "These paintings are the treasures of the realm; . . . they will surely protect and preserve the very household itself!" For more on this, see Melinda Takeuchi, "Individualism in Perpetuity: Ike Taiga and the Tale of the Taigadō lineage," in John M. Rosenfield (ed.), *Competition and Collaboration: Hereditary Schools in Japanese Culture* (*Fenway Court*, 1992), p. 98. How widely held was the belief that erotic prints protected the house from fire has been disputed by Timon Screech, *Sex and the Floating World* (London: Reaktion, 1999), p. 34. Screech does, however, cite as evidence an eighteenth- and nineteenth-century source, thus undercutting his own argument. One of Screech's sources, *Stories of Famous Painters and Calligraphers of Recent Times* (*Kinsei meika shogadan*), is cited also in Onishi Hiroshi, *Geijutsuka denka* (Legends about artists; Tokyo: Perikansha, 1989), p. 218, as an example of belief in the magical powers of objects. This is a Japanese version of Ernst Kris and Otto Kurz, *Legend, Myth, and Magic in the Image of the Artist: A Historical Experiment* (New Haven, Conn., and London: Yale University Press, 1979).

46. Kris and Kurz.

47. For the section on Motonobu in *Honchō gashi*, see Sakazaki, *Nihon kaigaron taikei*, vol. 2, pp. 408–9.

48. Tani Shin'ichi, "Tosa Mitsunobu," p. 468. Tani cites a late Edo work, *Gadensho*, attributing forty-five works to Mitsunobu; to this number he adds an estimate of all the Kano and Tosa copies of old works bearing attributions to Mitsunobu. (He adds, "Most of these are not by Mitsunobu.") Nakabayashi Chikutō (1747–1806) cited the dearth of Muromachi Tosa painting; see Yoshida, *Tosa Mitsunobu*, p. 98.

49. Michel Foucault, "What Is an Author?" in Paul Rabinow (ed.), *The Foucault Reader* (New York: Pantheon Books, 1984), p. 107.

CHAPTER FIVE

1. The text of the diary was first published as Ono Kan'ichirō (ed.), *Morita Kyūemon nikki* (The Morita Kyūemon diary), Tōki zenshū, vol. 10 (Tokyo: Tōki zenshū hankōkai, 1932). More recently, a corrected transcription was published, together with photographs of the original manuscript, in Maruyama Kazuo (trans.), "Morita Kyūemon Edo Nikki" (Morita Kyūemon's Edo diary), *Tōyō tōji* (*Oriental ceramics*), vol. 5 (Tokyo: Tōyō Tōji Gakkai, 1978), not paginated. My translation into English, based on the latter, was supported by a National Endowment for the Hu-

manities translation grant during a sabbatical leave in 1987–88. Research in Japan was funded by a Japan Foundation short-term professional fellowship. I am grateful for the encouragement of the late Marius Jansen in providing introductions to his Kōchi colleagues and for the ongoing help of Luke Roberts in passing along discoveries made in the course of his research on Tosa economic policy. In Kōchi, I benefited especially from the generous cooperation of the late Maruyama Kazuo; Moriguchi Kōji of the Kōchi Prefectural Library; and Matsuyama Kokutarō of the Yamauchi Shrine Archive. Above all, I am thankful for the generous cooperation and friendship of the Morita family, descendants of Kyūemon and keepers of his diary. This chapter was first presented as a paper at the panel "Tosa and Edo," organized by Constantine Vaporis for the Association for Asian Studies forty-fourth annual meeting in Washington, D.C., Apr. 3, 1992.

2. Pioneering scholarship on the marketing of ceramics in Kyoto has been conducted by Oka Yoshiko: "*Kakumeiki* ni miru karamonoyatachi: kinsei shoto no tōjiki ryūtsū" (Antique dealers as seen in the *Kakumeiki*: Distribution of ceramics at the start of the early modern period), *Shisō* (Journal of the History Association of Kyoto Women's University), Mar. 1991, 48, 245–62; and "Karamonoya oboegaki—Ōhira Gohei to Katsuyama Chōji" (Memo on antique dealers—Ōhira Gohei and Katsuyama Chōji), in *Kan'ei bunka no nettowaaku: "Kakumeiki" no sekai* (Networks of Kan'ei era culture: The world of the *Kakumeiki*), ed. by Oka Yoshiko and Iwama Kaori (Kyoto: Shibunkaku shuppan, 1998), pp. 199–208. A notable series of exhibitions of recent archaeological finds of ceramics in Kyoto and Osaka was organized by the Toki Municipal History Museum of Mino Ceramics: *Rakuchū shutsudō no Mino Momoyama tō* (Momoyama-period Mino ceramics excavated in Kyoto; Toki City, Gifu Prefecture: Toki-shi Mino Tōji Rekishikan, 1990); *Rakuchū shutsudō no Momoyama tōki* (Momoyama-period ceramics excavated in Kyoto; Toki City, Gifu Prefecture: Toki-shi Mino Tōji Rekishikan, 1991); *Utsuwa: Momoyama no bi* (Vessels: Momoyama beauty; Toki City, Gifu Prefecture: Toki-shi Mino Tōji Rekishikan, 1992); and *Momoyama no hana: Osaka shutsudō no Momoyama tōji* (Flowering of Momoyama: Momoyama ceramics excavated in Osaka; Toki City, Gifu Prefecture: Toki-shi Mino Tōji Rekishikan, 1993). The implications of recent archaeological findings are presented in Louise Allison Cort, "Shopping for Pots in Momoyama Japan," in *Japanese Tea Culture: Art, History, and Practice*, ed. by Morgan Pitelka (London and New York: Routledge Curzon, 2003), pp. 61–85.

3. *Tadayoshi-kō ki*, 1653, ninth month (vol. 1, pp. 261–62).

4. According to the Morita family genealogy, Kyūemon's father, Morita Gembei Mitsuuji, served for twenty-six years as a bailiff with responsibilities for the foothill region of the domain lands. He died while his son was still a minor and had not yet succeeded to the position, with the result that the position was transferred elsewhere. This circumstance—the lack of an obvious role within the domain administration—more than any inherent skill probably made Kyūemon a likely candidate for training in the new occupation of pottery production. After completing his apprenticeship in ceramics and taking on responsibility for the Odo pottery in 1658, after Kuno Shōhaku returned to Osaka, Kyūemon was granted the right to a New Year's audience with the Yamauchi lord (*omemie*). In 1678 he began receiving an annual rice stipend of *sannin fuchi*, the lowest basic stipend for a Tosa warrior.

5. *Tadayoshi-kō ki*, 1653, ninth month (vol. 1, p. 261).

6. *Tadatoyo-kō ki*, 1657, third month, thirtieth day (vol. 1, p. 135).

7. Takahara ware, consisting chiefly of tea bowls whose use is recorded in *chanoyu* diaries of Kyoto nobles, seems to have developed as an offshoot of rooftile production in the locale by that name within Osaka; nearby Naniwa ware was a similar en-

terprise (Funaki Kayoko, "Osaka-Nara no yakimono" [Ceramics of Osaka and Nara], in Mitsuoka Tadanari et al., eds., *Kinki II* [Kinki region II], Nihon yakimono shūsei, vol. 7 [Tokyo: Heibonsha, 1981], 106–7). Both seemed to have ceased operation sometime in the eighteenth century. Asahi ware, still active as a single-family enterprise in Uji, is associated with the taste of warrior and influential tea master Kobori Enshū (1579–1647); see Nakanodō Kazunobu, "Minami Yamashiro to Tango no yakimono" (Ceramics of southern Yamashiro and Tango provinces), in Mitsuoka Tadanari et al., eds., *Kyoto* (Kyoto), Nihon yakimono shūsei, vol. 5 (Tokyo: Heibonsha, 1981), p. 103. Little is known about the financial basis for the establishment and early operation of any of these kilns.

8. At the time of Kyūemon's visit, the Zeze domain in Ōmi province, from which the ware took its name, was controlled by Honda Yasumasa, a *fudai daimyo* or hereditary vassal of the Tokugawa house (Fujii Sadafumi and Hayashi Rikurō, eds., *Hanshi jiten* [Dictionary of domainal history; Tokyo: Akita shoten, 1976], p. 314). Kuwana ware was supported by the Matsudaira house based in Kuwana in Ise province, an important port on Ise Bay (ibid., pp. 347–48). Shigaraki in Ōmi province, governed by a bailiff who reported to Tokugawa government agents in Kyoto, produced glazed tea-leaf storage jars in which Uji tea was packed for government use (Louise Allison Cort, *Shigaraki, Potters' Valley*, 2nd ed. [New York and Tokyo: Weatherhill, 2000], pp. 193–206).

9. The carefully cultivated pedigree of Edo-period Seto tea ceramics is discussed in Louise Allison Cort, *Seto and Mino Ceramics* (Washington, D.C.: Freer Gallery of Art, 1992), pp. 118–19.

10. According to Oka Yoshiko, precedent for potters' demonstrations before distinguished patrons and advisors can be found in records of Nonomura Ninsei's activities at the imperially associated monastery of Ninnaji (personal communication). Thus the Tosa domain officials may have been following established practice in arranging Kyūemon's activities in Edo.

11. The operation of the Ofuke pottery is discussed in Cort, *Seto and Mino Ceramics*, pp. 143–47. The related phenomenon of amateur pottery production by warriors associated with the Owari Tokugawa domain is presented in ibid., p. 166.

12. Both the Imado pottery and the Edo Takahara kiln operated within the commercial discrict associated with the Asakusa Honganji temple (Naitō Katsuo and Masui Kunio, "Minami Kantō no yakimono" [Ceramics of the southern Kantō region], in Mitsuoka Tadanari et al., eds., *Hokkaidō-Tōhoku-Kantō* [Hokkaidō, Tōhoku, and Kantō regions], Nihon yakimono shūsei, vol. 1 [Tokyo: Heibonsha, 1981], p. 148).

13. Known as Rakurakuen after the name of the garden in which it was located, the kiln is believed to have been fired for the first time in 1673 (Naitō and Masui, p. 154).

CHAPTER SIX

1. I would like to express my gratitude to Melinda Takeuchi for her unerring editorial advice, to Amy Newland for her generous assistance with the final version, to the Office of the Dean of Arts and Sciences, Oberlin College, for its financial support, and to my family, as always.

2. Asano Shūgō sets the current total for Utamaro's oeuvre as thirty paintings, including drawings and sketches; single-sheet color prints, about two thousand distinct designs (counting diptychs and triptychs as a single design); surimono, more than twenty; illustrated books and poetry anthologies, twenty-one; other kinds of

illustrated books (*kibyōshi, sharebon, hanashi-bon, ehon banzuke*), more than forty titles; erotic books and albums, twenty to thirty titles; and a range of miscellaneous objects, such as libretti covers, illustrations for haikai anthologies, and the like. See Asano Shūgō, "A Brief Factual Biography of Utamaro and an Overview of His Artistic Achievements," in Asano Shūgō and Timothy Clark, *The Passionate Art of Kitagawa Utamaro* (Tokyo and London: Asahi Shinbun and the British Museum, 1995), pp. 67–68.

3. Masanobu achieved his "name" in part from being his own publisher; his signatures also make claim to artistic merit following patterns established in painting traditions. Harunobu's collaboration with poetry groups, particularly with Kikurensha Kyōsen (1722–77), was instrumental in his success. Both also manipulated codes of "high culture" in ways that appealed to specific markets and likely guaranteed return on investment. Masanobu and Harunobu are important precedents in the manipulation of concepts of the figure of the "artist" in ukiyo-e.

4. The similar marketing of an authorial persona has also been considered by Adam Kern in "Blowing Smoke, Tobacco Pouches, and Authorial Puffery in the Pictorial Comic Fiction (Kibyōshi) of Santō Kyōden" (Ph.D. dissertation, Harvard University, 1997); Kyōden's authorial voice is also discussed by Sumie Amikura Jones, "Comic Fiction in Japan During the Later Edo Period" (Ph.D. dissertation, University of Washington, 1979); and the literary world in which he lived is considered by Haruko Iwasaki, "The World of 'Gesaku': Playful Writers of Late Eighteenth Century Japan" (Ph.D. dissertation, Harvard University, 1984).

5. Henry D. Smith II offers a useful critique of the commonly discussed "four classes" of Tokugawa society in "Five Myths About Early Modern Japan," in Ainslie Thomas Embree and Carol Gluck (eds.), *Asia in Western and World History: A Guide for Teaching* (Armonk, N.Y.: M. E. Sharpe, 1997), pp. 514–22.

6. Kyōden wrote in an illustrated book of 1805 that one could buy a large full-color print for about 20 *mon*, a price equivalent to a bowl of noodles or a haircut; cited in Akai Tatsurō, "The Common People and Painting," Timothy Clark (trans.), in Nakane Chie and Ōishi Shinzaburō (eds.), *Tokugawa Japan: The Social and Economic Antecedents of Modern Japan* (Tokyo: University of Tokyo Press, 1990), p. 184. Because carpenters in Edo were paid a daily wage of about 200 *mon*, this price for a print may be relatively inexpensive, although 20 *mon* also seems too little for a finely produced image with special effects such as embossing, mica background, sumptuous pigments, and the like.

7. Various population counts have been reported. Yazaki Takeo, *Social Change and the City in Japan*, in a translation by David L. Swain (Tokyo: Japan Publications, 1968), p. 134, reported that the population of Edo in the 1720s has been estimated at 1.3 million, while the 1801 populations for London and Paris were 864,000 and 547,000, respectively. Hanley and Yamamura write that the 1720 population high of one million in Edo declined in the eighteenth century, reaching a low during the Tenmei famine but regaining steadily into the early nineteenth century. They note that since officials did not count transients, such as rōnin, who were known to live in high numbers in the major cities, an exact population count is hard to garner from the city records; Susan B. Hanley and Kozo Yamamura, *Economic and Demographic Change in Preindustrial Japan 1600–1868* (Princeton, N.J.: Princeton University Press, 1977), p. 351. The population of Peking reached eight hundred thousand to nine hundred thousand in the eighteenth century; Nakamura Satoru, "The Development of a Rural Industry," in Nakane and Ōishi, p. 84.

8. *Nishiki-e no tanjō—Edo chomin bunka no kaika*, edited by Kobayashi Tadashi (Tokyo: Tokyo Metropolitan Edo-Tokyo Museum, 1996).

9. One fictional account that may suggest how well known the names of print designers had become is in Shikitei Sanba's 1809 *Bathhouse of the Floating World* (*Ukiyoburo*). The mothers described there complain about how well informed their children are about prints; they even go so far as to learn the names of the designers—but we should not ignore the fact that the designers named therein are also often listed as illustrators for Sanba's texts. For a translation of *Ukiyoburo*, see Robert Leutner, *Shikitei Sanba and the Comic Tradition in Edo Fiction* (Cambridge, Mass., and London: Council on East Asian Studies, Harvard University, and the Harvard-Yenching Institute, distributed by Harvard University Press, 1985); the mothers' remarks are on pp. 174–75.

10. For more discussion of names and authorial function, see Michel Foucault, "What Is an Author?" in *The Foucault Reader*, edited by P. Rabinow (New York: Pantheon, 1984); and Roland Barthes, "The Death of the Author," in *Image, Music, Text* (New York: Hill and Wang, 1977).

11. The remaining documents used to reconstruct a "biography" for Utamaro are included in Asano, "A Brief Factual Biography of Utamaro," pp. 67–68, and Suzuki Jūzō, "Shiryō ni tadoru Utamaro no gagyō to shōgai," in *Ehon to ukiyo-e* (Tokyo: Bijutsu shuppansha, 1979), pp. 433–62. Aspects of Utamaro's biography are also discussed in Hayashi Yoshikazu, "Utamaro no saikekkon," *Ukiyo-e geijutsu*, 1964, *8*, 39–41; Sugimoto Ryūichi, "Utamaro kaimei izen—Toyoaki ki no shomondai," *Museum*, 1987, *435*, pp. 20–28; Ōta Kinen Bijutsukan, *Utamaro geijutsu no saihakken* (Tokyo: Ōta Kinen Bijutsukan, 1993). Suzuki Jūzō's discussion of the documents is the most thorough; see also Julie Nelson Davis, "'Drawing His Own Ravishing Features': Kitagawa Utamaro and the Construction of a Public Identity in Ukiyo-e Prints" (Ph.D. dissertation, University of Washington, 1997), pp. 39–80.

12. The stele currently standing at Senkōji was given to the temple in 1917 by a group of Utamaro appreciators. The inscription on the 1917 stele that gives the date of Utamaro's death as the twentieth day of the ninth month of the year Bunka 3 (1806) was derived from temple records that were then extant. The stele also bears inscriptions for a woman who died in Kansei 2 (1790), a child who died in Bunsei 7 (1824) at age eleven, and a woman who died at age fifty-four in Bunsei 8 (1825). The identities of these others are unconfirmed. The first woman may have been a member of Utamaro's family, and it is possible that the child and second woman were the son and wife of Utamaro II. The stele and temple records are discussed by a member of the group of Utamaro aficionados who donated the stele to the temple named Hoshino Chōyō in "Utamaro no bosho oyobi kako-chō hakken no yurai," in *Ukiyo-e*, 1917–18, *1*, 27–37. Senkōji, along with its records, was destroyed in the fires following the 1923 Great Kantō earthquake and subsequently relocated from Asakusa to the Kitakarasuyama district of Setagaya ward, Tokyo.

The Utamaro II just referred to may have been formerly known as Koikawa Harumachi II and taken the name Utamaro II after the death of Utamaro I. However, there were two who called themselves Utamaro II, so the identity of Utamaro II is a matter of some complexity; see Ishida Yasuhiro, "Futari no nidai Kitagawa Utamaro," *Museum*, 1992, *492*, 13–27. The relationship between Utamaro I and Utamaro II is further complicated by a woodblock printed book from 1917 written by one "Beibei Sanjin" (a pseudonym) that lists images and assigns them to Utamaro I or Utamaro II; see *Utamaro hanga nishiki-e narabi ehon mokuroku* (Tokyo: Tanaka Shigenobu, 1917). Comparisons between Beibei Sanjin's list and accepted catalogues of Utamaro images (such as the Ōta Kinen Bijutsukan list in *Utamaro geijutsu no saihakken*, Tokyo: Ota Kinen Bijutsukan, 1994) reveal differences of opinion on the authorship of several images. Who Beibei Sanjin was or how he compiled his listing is unknown (and his conclusions may prove to be unsubstantiated). Nevertheless, his list feeds nagging doubts about the accuracy of current estimations of the distinguishing characteristics of "Utamaro I" and "Utamaro II," bringing to mind the problems still remaining in the oeuvres of such ukiyo-e figures as Harunobu, Hokusai, Hiroshige, and others.

13. Davis, 49–57.

14. This manuscript copy was one of a group of documents compiled by Kitakōji Ken, including the *zuihitsu* essay titled *A Record of Things Just as I Heard Them* (*Kiku mama no ki*) by Kimura Mokurō (1774–1856); Hamada Giichirō (ed.), *Ōta Nanpo zenshū*, vol. 18 (Tokyo: Iwanami shoten, 1988), p. 436. Sasaya's additions date to about 1800, while those of Santō Kyōden may be dated to 1802. Sanba edited the *Ukiyo-e ruiko* between the years 1804 and 1808. Keisei Eisen brought these earlier editions together with his own comments in an 1833 version, the *Mumei-ō zuihitsu* (also titled *Zoku Ukiyo-e ruikō*). Saitō Gesshin edited the *Zōho Ukiyo-e ruikō* in 1844; this will be republished in Kobayashi Tadashi and Kōno Motoaki, *Teihon Nihon kaigaron taisei* (Tokyo: Perikansha, forthcoming). See also Nakada Katsunosuke, *Ukiyo-e ruikō* (Tokyo: Iwanami shoten, 1982).

15. Bracketed words indicate either my additions to the text or the closest English word. See also the translation in Tadashi Kobayashi, *Utamaro: Portraits from the Floating World*, Mark A. Harbison (trans.) (Tokyo: Kodansha, 1993), p. 71.

16. See Suzuki, op. cit.; Sugimura, op. cit.; and Asano Shūgō, "The Chronology of Utamaro's Woodblock Prints," in Asano and Clark, pp. 55–64, among others.

17. Michael Ann Holly, *Past Looking: Historical Imagination and the Rhetoric of the Image* (Ithaca, N.Y.: Cornell University Press, 1996), pp. 1–28.

18. Barthes, p. 143.

19. See Mieke Bal and Norman Bryson, "Semiotics and Art History," *Art Bulletin*, June 1991, 174–208.

20. Jerome Silbergeld, *Chinese Painting Style: Media, Methods, and Principles of Form* (Seattle and London: University of Washington Press, 1981), p. 19.

21. *Ōta Nanpo zenshū*, vol. 18, pp. 338–39.

22. Ibid., p. 343.

23. Ōta Kinen Bijutsukan, *Utagawa Toyoharu to sono jidai* (Tokyo: Ōta Kinen Bijutsukan, 1994), pp. 21 and 109.

24. Shimada Tsukuba, "Sekien no Bashō zu," *Ukiyo-e geijutsu*, 1935, *4*(10), 1–3, Yamada Kakuzō, *Nihon no ukiyoeshi* (Tokyo: Daiichishobō, 1930), pp. 268–70; Sugimoto, 22; Ōta Kinen Bijutsukan, *Utagawa Toyoharu to sono jidai*, p. 109; and Hillier, *The Art of the Japanese Book*, vol. I, pp. 394–403.

25. Matsuki Hiroshi, *Tsutaya Jūzaburō* (Tokyo: Nihon Keizai Shinbunsha, 1974), pp. 49–51.

26. The recent biographical study of Tsutaya by Suzuki Toshiyuki, *Kinsei bungaku kenkyū sosho 9: Tsutaya Jūzaburō* (Tokyo: Wakakusa shobo, 1998), gives the most thorough account of Tsutaya Jūzaburō's career and associations.

27. *Ōta Nanpo zenshū*, vol. 7 (1986), pp. 234–35.

28. Takahashi Yasuo, "Tsutaya Jūzaburō," *Rekishi dokukon*, 1997, *42*(6), 72.

29. Hayashi Yoshikazu, *Kitagawa Utamaro* (Tokyo: Kawaide shoten, 1993), vol. 2, p. 72. The *Seirō bijin awase sugata kagami*, as a large color-printed book with sumptuous double-page illustrations, is preceded in size and publishing quality by the *Sekien gafu* of 1774.

30. See Hamada Giichirō, "Shokusanjin hantei-chō," *Ohtsuma Women's University Annual Report* (1970), *2*, 99–113; Suzuki Toshiyuki, *Tsutaya Jūzaburō*, pp. 61–62; and Timothy Clark, "Utamaro and Yoshiwara: The 'Painter of the Blue Towers' Reconsidered," in Asano and Clark, text vol., pp. 39–40.

31. They are listed by their *kyōka* names in Fuguri Tsurikata, *Kyōka shittari furi* (Edo: Manmandō, 1783), n.p.

32. See also Clark, "Utamaro and Yoshiwara," pp. 37–41.

33. Bracketed words are additions to Sekien's text; unless otherwise noted, all translations are my own, in consultation with others, including Clark, in Asano and Clark, text vol., catalogue entry 463, pp. 256–57; Jack Hillier, *Utamaro: Color Prints and Paintings*, 2nd ed. (Oxford, England: Phaidon, 1979), pp. 38–39; and Kobayashi, *Utamaro*, p. 72; among others.

34. For similar textual associations in Chinese painting, see Susan Bush and Hsio-yen Shih (eds.), *Early Chinese Texts on Painting* (Cambridge, Mass.: published for the Harvard-Yenching Institute by Harvard University Press, 1985), among others; for Japanese and Chinese legends of the artist, see Ōnishi Hiroshi, "Nihon Chūgoku no geijutsuka densetsu," in *Geijutsuka densetsu*, edited by Ōnishi Hiroshi (Tokyo: Perikansha, 1989), among others.

35. On aspects of Kano rhetoric and representation, see Quitman E. Phillips, "Honchō gashi and the Kano Myth," *Archives of Asian Art*, 1994, *47*, 46–57; for Tosa, see Takeuchi's Chapter Four in this volume, as well as John Rosenfield, "Japanese Studio Practice: The Tosa Family and the Imperial Painting Office in the Seventeenth Century," in Peter M. Lukehart (ed.), *The Artist's Workshop*, Studies in the History of Art 38 (Washington, D.C.: National Gallery of Art, 1993), pp. 79–102; and Makoto Ueda, "In Search of the Lifelike: Mitsuoki on the Art of Painting," in *Literary and Art Theories in Japan* (reprinted, Ann Arbor: Center for Japanese Studies, 1991; 1st ed., Cleveland: Press of Western Reserve, 1967), pp. 128–44; among others.

36. This was the name used by *kyōka* poet Ishikawa Masamochi. Like many other poetry names, this one has humorous overtones. It may be literally translated along the lines of "the specialty of the house," but it also puns off the term used to describe "meshimori" women at wayside inns, who served up their bodies for the entertainment of the male guests.

37. My translation, adapted from Timothy Clark, "Utamaro's Erotic Album Utamakura," *Ukiyo-e hizō meihinshū: Utamakura* (Tokyo: Gakken, 1991), p. iii.

38. Peter F. Kornicki, "Nishiki no Ura: An Instance of Censorship and the Structure of a Sharebon," *Monumenta Nipponica*, 1977, *32*(2), 156.

39. Nakano Mitsutoshi, "Bunka-men in okeru Kansei kaikaku," in *Nihon no Kinsei 12: Bungaku to bijutsu no seijuku* (Tokyo: Chūō Kōronsha, 1993), p. 70; see also Suzuki Toshiyuki, pp. 159–205.

40. Nakano, pp. 69–70.

41. Nakano, p. 70.

42. See Kornicki, p. 157, for the relevant passage.

43. See Suzuki Toshikyuki, *Tsutaya Jūzaburō*, pp. 159–70; it is also discussed in, among others, Matsuki, pp. 103–4; Ōkubo Jun'ichi, "Utamaro no 'Seirō jūnitoki' to sono shuhen," *Museum*, 1989, *462*, 21–22; Kornicki, "Nishiki no Ura," pp. 153–88; Jones, "Comic Fiction in Japan During the Later Edo Period," pp. 55–56.

44. Clark proposed another apt translation for this type as "fancy-free," in Asano and Clark, text vol., p. 103.

45. Following Utamaro's signature are two other marks that were important in the wake of the Kansei reforms. They are the *kiwame* seal, which guaranteed the approval of the publishers' guild representative, and the Tsutaya shop trademark, the ivy leaf crest under the triple peaks of Mount Fuji. All three—artist, guild representative, and publisher—would have been held responsible if the print had violated the edicts.

46. Sasaki Jōhei and Sasaki Masako, *Maruyama Ōkyo kenkyū* (Tokyo: Chūō Kōron Bijutsu Shuppan, 1997), p. 255.

47. Richard Vinograd, *Boundaries of the Self: Chinese Portraits, 1600–1900* (Cambridge, England: Cambridge University press, 1992), pp. 5–6. See also the remarks by Chinese painter Wang I (active ca. 1360) in Susan Bush and Hsio-yen Shih, *Early Chinese Texts on Painting*, pp. 271–72.

48. Satō Yasuhiro, "Ōkubi-e to iu mōdo, ōkubi-e made, Utamaro," in *Nihon no bijutsu* 9 (365, 1996), p. 32.

49. See, for example, "Seven Amorous Types According to Their Physiognomies" (Irogoto ninsō nana iro no kangai), in Fusen Sanjin, *Revelation of Secret Truths (Hiji matsuge)*, published in 1757; reprinted in *Sharebon taikei*, edited by Takagi Kōji, vol. 9 (Tokyo: Rokugōkan, 1931), pp. 19–30.

50. For example, people speaking of women's physiognomies during a tea ceremony, as portrayed in the *sharebon Sequel to the Fashionable Sophisticates (Kōhen fūzoku tsū)*; see Kano Hiroyuki, *Meiho nihon no bijutsu 28—Utamaro*, vol. 28 (Tokyo: Shogakkan, 1991), p. 65. The *sharebon* is reprinted in Takagi Kōji et al. (eds.), *Sharebon taikei*, vol. 2 (Tokyo: Rokugōkan, 1931).

51. Satō, p. 33.

52. Ōkubo Jun'ichi, "Utamaro no 'Seirō jūnitoki' to sono shuhen," *Museum*, 1989, *462*, pp. 19–22.

53. The actual length of the "hours" varied according to the season. See Timon Screech, "Clock Metaphors in Edo Period Japan," *Japan Quarterly*, 1996, *43*(4), 66–75.

54. Cecilia Segawa Seigle, *Yoshiwara: The Glittering World of the Japanese Courtesan* (Honolulu: University of Hawai'i Press, 1993), p. 113.

55. That the nape of the neck was an erogenous zone is well known, but how much slim "bow-shaped" legs were also highly fetishized is discussed by Sugiura Hinako, *Burari Edo gaku, Yōnaka no gakkō* 5 (Tokyo: Madora, 1992), pp. 19–20.

56. Seigle also notes that the cost of staying late accumulated at a rapid rate; the payment structure for the highest-ranking courtesans was arranged so that the day was divided into an afternoon and an evening segment, and the privilege of staying overnight added on a charge for the following day. The price for staying from noon to the next morning was higher than the total for the periods of time if they had been calculated separately, but the value of the display seems to have been worth more than the irregular accounting; Seigle, p. 113.

57. Translation by Kornicki, p. 170. He notes explanatory information for this section of the text: the second floor was the courtesans' living and working quarters while the staff worked on the first floor. The sandals lined up appear as though they are on the beach of Nyōgo Island, the mythic island of women, where men were claimed as they came ashore. "Katsuragi" refers to the legendary god of Mt. Katsuragi, who was apparently so ugly that he was ashamed to be seen by daylight (p. 170, notes 88–92).

58. Barthes, *S/Z*, pp. 54–56.

59. The signifying associations of the abject is particularly suggestive in Utamaro's series *The Five Shades of Ink in the Northern Quarter* (*Hokkoku goshiki-zumi*) of 1794–95, published by Ise-Mago. The depictions of the lowest-ranking prostitutes, the *kashi* ("riverbank") and the *teppō* ("shotgun"), are abject by Utamaro and Tsutaya standards, but they are not quite as low as Kyōden's figures revealed by the harsh morning light as pockmarked hags. See Davis, pp. 246–58.

60. For writings on *mitate-e* in English, see Timothy Clark, "*Mitate-e*: Some Thoughts, and a Summary of Recent Writings"; and David Waterhouse, "Some Confucian, Buddhist, and Taoist *Mitate-e* by Harunobu," *Impressions: The Journal of the Ukiyo-e Society of America*, 1997, *19*, 6–27 and 28–47, respectively; Kobayashi Tadashi, "*Mitate-e* in the Art of the Ukiyo-e Artist Suzuki Harunobu"; and Haruko Iwasaki,

"The Literature of Wit and Humor in Late Eighteenth-Century Edo," in Donald Jenkins (ed.), *The Floating World Revisited* (Portland, Ore.: Portland Art Museum, 1993), pp. 85–92 and 47–62, respectively.

61. The Japanese reads: "motome ni ōjite Utamaro mizukara engan o utsusu." My translation agrees with Clark's.

62. It is worth comparing the "self-portrait" to two paintings long held to be memorial portraits of Utamaro. Timothy Clark's analysis of the British Museum painting attributed to Eishi suggests that this is *not* in fact a portrait of Utamaro; see Timothy Clark, *Ukiyo-e Painting in the British Museum* (London: British Museum Press, 1992), p. 131. The second possible portrait of Utamaro is currently missing; see Clark, p. 131.

63. From beri-beri after a lengthy illness; Matsuki, p. 210.

64. The text on the print depicting a woman wearing a summer kimono reads:

> As a rule, there are two things to "take the measure of the body" in painting a beautiful figure—simply, a lovely form and a beautiful face—and if the drawing of the face is beautiful, and one mixes affection with coquetry, naturally the heart of the viewer will be stirred. And, too, when elegance is combined with a figure that is stunningly gorgeous, then human feeling will be communicated. I entreat that you compare the charms of my brush to the pictures rendered by those poor tools, gentlemen, awaiting your esteemed assessment.

My translation, adapted from Clark, in Asano and Clark, text vol., catalogue entry 275, page 186.

65. In Clark's translation:

> Providing the "looks" of the brushwork are beautiful and the "visage" of ink and color is graceful, even if I'm painting the "tattered rags" of a rough sketch or the "stark naked" of a painting in abbreviated style—my lively brush is like the fabled beauty Xi Shi. Then again, you can wrap them in multi-coloured brocades and disguise those unattractive courtesans with applications of powder and paint. But as the days go by the more wretched the mediocre drawing, the more the deformity of the body parts is revealed, and you end up losing all affection for them. So my fee is as high as my nose and I put it to publishers who buy cheap—thinking that compared to a high-ranked courtesan costing a thousand gold coins, a street-walker is a good deal—that their noses will be squashed.

Clark, in Asano and Clark, text vol., catalogue entry 274, p. 185.

66. My translation. This passage has been previously published in translation; see Clark, in Asano and Clark, text vol., catalogue entry 273, page 185; and Harbison in Kobayashi, *Utamaro*, p. 64, among others.

CHAPTER SEVEN

I would like to express my gratitude to the many colleagues who offered insightful critiques of various versions of this manuscript, most notably Ellen Conant, Brenda Jordan, Melinda Takeuchi, and especially Gennifer Weisenfeld.

1. Takamura Kōtarō, *Takamura Kōtarō zenshū* (Complete works of Takamura Kōtarō). 18 vols. Tokyo: Chikuma shobō, 1957–58, vol. 4, p. 23 (hereafter, *TKZ*).

2. Today Kōtarō is best known as the author of *Chieko shō* (Writings about Chieko), a collection of poetry published in 1941 that broke new ground in its unusually direct treatment of his troubled relationship with his lover (and later his wife) Chieko, who was institutionalized following a mental breakdown. This and other

works written during and after the Pacific War are beyond the period under review in this study. For discussion of how these have contributed to Kōtarō's reputation, see the introduction to Steve Rabson, *Righteous Cause or Tragic Folly: Changing Views of War in Modern Japanese Poetry* (Ann Arbor: Center for Japanese Studies, University of Michigan, 1998), pp. 191–99 and Makoto Ueda, *Modern Japanese Poets and the Nature of Literature* (Stanford, Calif.: Stanford University Press, 1983), pp. 232–83.

3. Satō Doshin, *Nihon bijutsu tanjō* (The birth of "art" in Japan). Tokyo: Kōdansha, 1996, p. 51.

4. Ibid., p. 51.

5. It was so popular that it was published under various titles: in 1929 as *Kōun kaikodan* (Kōun's reminiscences) and in 1967 as *Mokuchō shichijūnen* (Seventy years of wood sculpture). The publication used here is *Bakumatsu isshin kaikodan* (Reminiscences from the Bakumatsu and early Meiji eras), Tokyo: Iwanami bunko, 1995. Unless otherwise noted, all information about Kōun in this chapter comes from this source, hereafter abbreviated as *BIK*.

6. *BIK*, p. 33.

7. Ibid., p. 34.

8. Actors of this line were also famous for their embodiment of Fudō in the popular Kabuki play of the same name; Timothy Clark and Osamu Ueda, *The Actor's Image: Print Makers of the Katsukawa School* (Art Institute of Chicago and Princeton University Press, 1994), p. 162.

9. *Zōho shōshū butsuzō* (Illustrated compendium of Buddhist deities of all sects, rev. ed.) was printed in 1783, 1796, 1832, and 1886. For illustrations, see Bernard Frank, *Le panthéon bouddhique au Japon: les collections d'Emile Guimet* (Paris: Réunions des musées nationaux, 1991), pp. 19–20.

10. Yoshida Mitsukuni, *Nihon no shokunin* (Japanese craftsmen). Kadokawa sensho 86 (Tokyo: Kadokawa shoten, 1976), p.293.

11. Naoteru Uyeno (ed.), *Japanese Arts and Crafts of the Meiji Era* (Tokyo: Pan-Pacific Press, 1958), pp. 87–88.

12. Tsuji Nobuo (ed.), *Edo no shūkyō bijutsu* (Religious art of the Edo period), in *Nihon bijutsu zenshū* (A compendium of Japanese art), vol. 23 (Tokyo: Gakken, 1975), p. 149.

13. Oliver Impey and Malcolm Fairley, *The Dragon King of the Sea* (Oxford, England: Ashmolean Museum, 1991), p. 32.

14. Christine M. E. Guth, *Art, Tea, and Industry: Masuda Takashi and the Mitsui Circle* (Princeton, N.J.: Princeton University Press, 1993), pp. 36–37.

15. Horst W. Janson, *Nineteenth Century Sculpture* (New York: Harry Abrams, 1986), pp. 115–18.

16. On the varied and changing definitions of realism (*shajitsu*, *shashin*, and *shasei*) during the Meiji era, see Satō Dōshin, *Meiji kokka to kindai bijutsu* (The Meiji state and modern art; Tokyo: Yoshikawa kōbunkan, 1999), pp. 209–32.

17. Kunaichō (comp.), *Kōshitsu no shihō: chōkoku, kōgei* (Treasures from the Imperial Household Collection: Sculpture, crafts), 13 vols. (Tokyo: Mainichi shinbunsha, 1991), vol. 4, p. 186.

18. See Janson, *Nineteenth Century Sculpture*, pp. 184–85.

19. Shimura Shōko, "Takamura Kōun saku 'Rōen' o meguru chōkoku to kōgei" (Sculpture and crafts from the perspective of Takamura Kōun's "Old Monkey"), *Bigaku*, 1996, *3*, 26–28.

20. Ruth Butler, *Rodin: The Shape of Genius* (New York and New Haven, Conn.: Yale University Press, 1993), p. 400.

21. Manabe Shunshō (ed.), *Meiji, Taishō, Shōwa no butsuga butsuzō* (Buddhist paint-

ing and sculpture of the Meiji, Taishō, and Shōwa eras). 3 vols. Tokyo: Shōgakkan, 1986, vol. 1, p. 116.

22. Ellen P. Conant, in collaboration with Steven D. Owyoung and J. Thomas Rimer, *Nihonga: Transcending the Past* (St. Louis: St. Louis Art Museum, 1995), pp. 26–27.

23. Yōsai Enichi issued a series of prints of the shrine, including one in 1893 featuring the statue and its fashionable viewers.

24. In addition to Kōun's own account, these sources were consulted: Suga Toshio, "Nankō dōzō seisaku no yurai" (Genesis of the bronze statue of Nankō), *Bijutsu kenkyū*, Jan. 1938, *73*, 28–40; Tanabe Saburōsuke, "Takamura Kōun saku Nankō dōzō" (The Bronze Statue of Nankō by Kōun), *Kokka*, 1991, *1153*, 33–35; and Sukehiro Hirakawa, "Loyalty Incarnated: the Equestrian Statue of Kusunoki Masashige" (unpublished manuscript).

25. Nakagawa Chisaki, *Meiji no kōgei* (Meiji era crafts), *Nihon no bijutsu* no. 41. Tokyo: Shibundō, 1969, pp. 71–73.

26. Horitsu Shōji, *Shiryō Takamura Kōtarō no dokusho: shonenki, bijutsugakkō jidai* (A Takamura Kōtarō reader: Sources on childhood and school days; Tokyo: Hokutokai, 1992), pp. 25–28.

27. Tokyo Geijutsu Daigaku (comp.), *Geidai bijutsukan shozō meihinten* (Selected masterpieces from the University Art Museum; Tokyo: Tokyo Geijutsu Daigaku, 1999), pp. 136–37.

28. *TKZ*, vol. 10, p. 232.

29. Yoshitake Oka, "Generational Conflict After the Russo-Japanese War," in *Conflict in Modern Japanese History: The Neglected Tradition*, Tetsuo Najita and J. Victor Koschmann (eds.). Princeton, N.J.: Princeton University Press, 1982, pp. 197–98.

30. Sharon Hamilton Nolte, "Individualism in Taishō Japan," *Journal of Asian Studies*, 1984, *43*(4), 667–84.

31. Hiroaki Sato (trans.), *A Brief History of Imbecility: Poetry and Prose of Takamura Kōtarō* (Honolulu: University of Hawai'i Press, 1992), p. 153. For original text see *TKZ*, vol. 9, p. 52.

32. Sukehiro Hirakawa, "Takamura Kōtarō's Love Hate Relationship with the West," *Comparative Literature Studies*, 1989, *26*(3), 216.

33. Sato (trans.), *A Brief History of Imbecility*, p. 71; *TKZ*, vol. 2, pp. 162–63.

34. Kakuzō Okakura, *Collected English Writings*. 3 vols. (Tokyo: Heibonsha, 1984) vol. 3, p. 74.

35. Robin Borglum Carter, *Gutzon Borglum: His Life and Work* (Austin, Tex.: Eakin Press, 1998), p. 26; and Sato (trans.), *A Brief History of Imbecility*, p. 189.

36. Sato (trans.), *A Brief History of Imbecility*, p. 3; and *TKZ*, vol. 1, p. 41.

37. *TKZ*, vol. 7, p. 137.

38. Sato (trans.), *A Brief History of Imbecility*, pp. 159–60; *TKZ*, vol. 9, pp. 62–63.

39. Sato (trans.), *A Brief History of Imbecility*, pp. 153–54; *TKZ*, vol. 9, pp. 52–53.

40. Kōtarō also expressed his admiration in a tribute written after Ogiwara's premature death. See Sato (trans.), *A Brief History of Imbecility*, pp. 174–79.

41. Nakamura Densaburō, "Meiji maki ni okeru Rodin" (Rodin in the late Meiji era), *Bijutsu kenkyū*, 1951, *163*(2), 63–67.

42. Sato (trans.), *A Brief History of Imbecility*, p. 7; *TKZ*, vol. 1, p. 111.

43. Kikuchi Kazuo, "Takamura Kōtarō to Rodin" (Kōtarō and Rodin), in Yoshida Seiichi (ed.), *Takamura Kōtarō no ningen to geijutsu* (Takamura Kōtarō: The man and his art; Tokyo: Kyōiku shuppan senta, 1972), pp. 256–71.

44. Albert Elsen, *Auguste Rodin: Reading on His Life and Work* (Englewood Cliffs, N.J.: Prentice Hall, 1961), pp. 177, 179.

45. Thomas Rimer, *Paris in Japan: The Japanese Encounter with European Painting* (St. Louis: Washington University 1987), p. 60; *TKZ*, vol. 4, pp. 24–25.

46. Rimer, ibid., p. 60; *TKZ*, vol. 4, pp. 25–26.

47. Sato (trans.), *A Brief History of Imbecility*, p. 167; *TKZ*, vol. 6, p. 13.

48. Nina Athanassoglou-Kallmyer, "Romanticism: Breaking the Canon," *Art Journal*, Summer 1993, 52(2), 18.

49. Ueda, *Modern Japanese Poets and the Nature of Literature*, p. 260; *TKZ*, vol. 4, p. 45.

50. Sato (trans.), *A Brief History of Imbecility*, p. 203.

51. *TKZ*, vol. 10, pp. 225–26.

CHAPTER EIGHT

Portions of this chapter first appeared in my *Maekawa Kunio and the Emergence of Japanese Modernist Architecture* (University of California Press, 2001).

1. Kurokawa trailed behind only the emperor and the then Prime Minister Tanaka Kakue. This survey is cited by Charles Jencks in his introduction to Kurokawa Kishō's *Metabolism in Architecture* (Boulder, Colo.: Westview Press, 1977), p. 8. Few architects have enjoyed this level of recognition in the United States in recent years.

2. William H. Coaldrake, *The Way of the Carpenter: Tools and Japanese Architecture* (New York: Weatherhill, 1990), p. 14.

3. Magali Sarfatti Larson, *Behind the Postmodern Facade: Architectural Change in Late Twentieth-Century America* (Berkeley: University of California Press, 1993), pp. 3–4.

4. In the twentieth century, some institutions, such as the Bauhaus, began to challenge the insulation of the architect from manual labor by introducing crafts training into architectural education. Yet even at the Bauhaus there were those who were reluctant to surrender the elite position of the architect. In 1919, just months before he became the director of the Bauhaus, Walter Gropius stated in a lecture: "To be an architect means to be a leader in art. The architect alone can raise himself up again to this leadership in art, to the position of being its highest servant, the superhuman guardian and steward of its complete and indivisible existence." Cited in Andrew Saint, *The Image of the Architect* (New Haven, Conn.: Yale University Press, 1983), p. 120.

5. The Tokugawa regime outlawed Japanese travel abroad in 1635, expelled the Portuguese from Japan in 1639, and in 1641 proscribed all interaction with the outside world except for highly restricted contacts with Korea and the Ryūkyū Islands and limited trade with Dutch and Chinese merchants at the port of Nagasaki. Commodore Perry was sent by the U.S. government to Japan in 1853 to demand that the Japanese open their ports to the West.

6. Dallas Finn, *Meiji Revisited: The Sites of Victorian Japan* (New York: Weatherhill, 1995), p. 7.

7. Inagaki Eizō, *Nihon no kindai kenchiku: Sono seiritsu katei* (Japan's modern architecture: The process of its formation; Tokyo: Kajima shuppankai, 1979), vol. 1, p. 29.

8. Koshino Takeshi, *Kaika no katachi* (The form of enlightenment), vol. 1 of Muramatsu Teijirō (ed.), *Nihon no kenchiku: Meiji, Taishō, Shōwa* (Architecture of Japan: Meiji, Taishō, Shōwa; Tokyo: Sanseidō, 1979), p. 100.

9. Muramatsu, *Nihon kindai kenchiku gijutsushi* (The history of modern architectural technology in Japan; Tokyo: Shōkokusha, 1976), pp. 25–27.

10. Bridgens came to Japan from San Francisco. Nothing is known about his training, but while he was in Japan he designed a number of major buildings, in-

cluding the British Consulate in Yokohama (1866); Fujimori Terunobu, *Nihon no kindai kenchiku* (Modern Japanese architecture), vol. 1 (Tokyo: Iwanami shinsho, 1993), pp. 48–50.

11. Ibid., pp. 92–96.

12. Julia Meech-Pekarik, *The World of the Meiji Print: Impressions of a New Civilization* (New York: Weatherhill, 1986), pp. 80–82.

13. The building cost 47,601 *ryō*, whereas the Tsukiji Hotel that Shimizu completed with Bridgens was four times as large and yet cost only 30,000 *ryō*; Suzuki Hiroyuki and Yamaguchi Hiroshi (eds.), *Kindai gendai kenchikushi* (Modern and contemporary Japanese architecture), vol. 5 of Uchida Yoshichika (ed.), *Shin kenchikugaku taikei* (The new compendium of architecture studies; Tokyo: Shōkokusha, 1993), p. 237. In 1871, numerous older currencies were abandoned and the yen currency was established. The *ryō* was converted to yen at a rate of 1 to 1.

14. Fujimori suggests this link with Bridgens's designs in *Nihon no kindai kenchiku*, pp. 94–96.

15. For an especially rich treatment of this phenomenon, see Meech-Pekarik, *The World of the Meiji Print*.

16. Fujimori, *Nihon kindai kenchiku*, vol. 1, pp. 112–13.

17. Although the ultimate source for the *putti* was undoubtedly a European print, a more immediate source was the bannerlike masthead of the newspaper *Tokyo nichi nichi shinbun* (Tokyo Daily Newspaper); Fujimori, *Nihon kindai kenchiku*, vol. 1, p. 114.

18. Nishi Amane, "An Essay on Brick Construction," in William Reynolds Braisted (trans.), *Meiroku zasshi: Journal of the Japanese Enlightenment* (Cambridge, Mass.: Harvard University Press, 1976), p. 52.

19. Ibid., p. 53.

20. Ibid., p. 54.

21. Fujimori, *Nihon no kindai kenchiku*, vol. 1, p. 80.

22. Cited in Onogi Shigekatsu, *Yōshiki no ishizue* (The cornerstone of style), vol. 2 of Muramatsu, *Nihon no kenchiku*, p. 144.

23. Suzuki and Yamaguchi, *Kindai gendai kenchikushi*, p. 257.

24. The College of Engineering was at first named the Kōburyō and in 1877 was renamed the Kōbudaigakkō. For a discussion of the formation on the engineering college, see Inagaki, *Nihon no kindaikenchiku*, vol. 1, pp. 38–43.

25. The engineering college also offered programs in civil engineering, mechanical engineering, electrical engineering, chemistry, mining, metallurgy, and nautical engineering (added in 1882).

26. Coaldrake, *Way of the Carpenter*, pp. 13–19, 150–66.

27. The great center for architectural training in France, the École des Beaux-Arts, was established in 1797 (classes in the arts dated back to the seventeenth century). In England, architectural education and testing remained unsystematized until the 1880s; see John Wilton-Ely, "The Rise of the Professional Architect in England," in Spiro Kostof (ed.), *The Architect: Chapters in the History of the Profession* (New York: Oxford University Press, 1977), pp. 197–204. The Massachusetts Institute of Technology formed the first program in the United States in 1865.

28. The first five students in the architecture program were all of samurai origin.

29. These courses were a part of the curriculum as of 1885; Inagaki, *Nihon no kindaikenchiku*, vol. 1, p. 41.

30. In the early years of the development of the architecture program, the field opportunities were considered so limited that the students remained at the college and continued to work directly with Conder in Tokyo. This is according to Tatsuno

Kingo, one of the students in Conder's first class; Shirotori Seigo (ed.), *Kōgaku hakushi Tatsuno Kingo den* (The life of Tatsuno Kingo, doctor of engineering; Tokyo: Tatsuno kasai jimusho, 1926), p. 25.

31. For a more detailed discussion of the architecture program at the College of Engineering and the educational philosophy guiding the program, see Don Choi, "Educating the Architect in Meiji Japan," presented at the symposium Architecture and Modern Japan, Columbia University, Oct. 2000.

32. Magali Sarfatti Larson, *The Rise of Professionalism: A Sociological Analysis* (Berkeley: University of California Press, 1977), p. xvi.

33. This objective was articulated in the organization's initial statement of principles. A list of these principles is reproduced in Suzuki and Yamaguchi, *Kindai gendai kenchikushi*, p. 263.

34. The RIBA was well known to one of the founders of Zōka Gakkai, Tatsuno Kingo, who had studied in England for three years. See Fujimori, *Nihon no kindai kenchiku*, vol. 1, p. 220–21. The first major professional organization in the United States, the American Institute of Architects, was organized in 1857.

35. Suzuki and Yamaguchi, *Kindai gendai kenchikushi*, p. 263.

36. The *Transactions of the Institute of British Architects of London* (forerunner of today's *Journal of the Royal Institute of British Architects*) was first published in 1836. The Kō Gakkai's *Kōgaku sōshi* (Periodical of engineering studies) was first published in 1881.

37. The term "imaginary museum of world architecture" was coined by Larson, who, in turn, was paraphrasing André Malraux; Larson, *Behind the Postmodern Facade*, p. 11.

38. Coaldrake, *Way of the Carpenter*, p. 38.

39. Ibid., pp. 139–40.

40. At this time, a similar debate was raging in England, where the issue was linked to conflicts over proposed systems of examination and registration of architectural professionals. See Saint, *The Image of the Architect*, pp. 62–68; Barrington Kaye, *The Development of the Architectural Profession in Britain: A Sociological Study* (London: George Allen and Unwin, 1960), pp. 135–41.

41. Kawai Kōzō, "Bijutsu no setsu," *Kenchiku zasshi* (Architecture Journal), Sept. 1888, *2*(21), 152; cited in Yamamoto Gakuji, et al. (eds.), *Kindai kenchiku shi* (History of modern architecture), vol. 6 of *Kenchikugaku taikei henshū iinkai* (eds.), *Kenchikugaku taikei* (Compendium of architecture studies; Tokyo: Shōkokusha, 1958), p. 266. Kawai graduated from the College of Engineering in 1882, was employed by the Ministry of Public Works, and was one of the founding members of the Zōka Gakkai.

42. Itō Chūta, "Akitekuchūru no hongi" (The true meaning of the word "architecture"), *Kenchiku zasshi*, 1894, *90*, 195–97; reprinted in Fujii Shōichirō and Yamaguchi Hiroshi (eds.), *Nihon kenchiku sengen bunshū* (Collected Japanese architectural manifestos; Tokyo: Shōkokusha, 1973), pp. 4–9.

43. The organization was renamed Nihon Kenchiku Gakkai (Architectural Institute of Japan) after World War II.

44. Christine Guth's Chapter Seven documents some of the difficulties faced by traditionally trained sculptors as a result of similar attitudes related to the rapid Westernization during the early Meiji period.

45. Inagaki, *Nihon no kindai kenchiku*, vol. 1, p. 169.

46. Ōta Hirotarō, *Kenchikushi no sendatsutachi* (Pioneers in architectural history; Tokyo: Shōkokusha, 1983), p. 9. I would like to thank Cherie Wendelken for this reference.

47. See, for example, Kenneth Pyle's study of the shift in thinking among intel-

lectuals such as Tokutomi Sohō during this period, *The New Generation in Meiji Japan* (Stanford, Calif.: Stanford University Press, 1969).

48. See Peter Collins, *Changing Ideas in Modern Architecture, 1750–1950* (Montreal: McGill-Queen's University Press, 1995), pp. 100–105.

49. Sano Riki, "Kenchikuka no kakugo," *Kenchiku zasshi*, May 1911, 25(295), 363; cited in Fujii and Yamaguchi, *Nihon kenchiku sengen*, p. 54.

50. Sano, "*Kenchikuka no kakugo*," p. 363; Fujii and Yamaguchi, p. 55.

51. The architectural group known as the Bunriha (Secession Group), which was formed by former students of Sano and Itō in 1920, is representative of this stream of modernist thought in Japan. See my "The Bunri-ha and the Problem of 'Tradition' for Modernist Architecture in Japan, 1920–1928," in Sharon A. Minichiello (ed.), *Japan's Competing Modernities: Issues in Culture and Democracy, 1900–1930* (Honolulu: University of Hawaii Press, 1998), pp. 228–46.

Glossary

Akera Kankō　朱楽管江
ākitekuchūru　アーキテクチュール
Anahobe no Hashihito　穴穂部間人
Arita　有田
Asahi　朝日
ason　朝臣
Asuka　飛鳥
Asuka Daibutsu　飛鳥大仏
Asukadera　飛鳥寺
Awataguchi　粟田口
Azuma nishiki-e　吾妻錦絵
Bank of Japan (Nippon Ginkō)　日本銀行
be　部
bijinga　美人画
bijutsu　美術
Bishamon　毘沙門
bun　文
busshi　仏師
butsuzō　仏像
chanoyu　茶湯
Chidori hafu　千鳥破風
Chiyo no haru　ちよのはる
Chōsokabe　長宗我部
daibu　大夫
daiku tōryō　大工棟梁
dainin　大仁
dōbō　同法
dōbōshū　同朋衆
ebusshi　絵仏師
Edo shokunin zukushi　江戸職人尽
edokoro　絵所
Ehon mushi erabi　絵本虫選
Eisai　栄西

engi 縁起
E'nichibō Jōnin 恵日房成忍
eshi 絵師
Fujin sōgaku juttai 婦人相学十体
Fujiwara Morikane 藤原盛兼
Fujiwara Nagafusa 藤原長房
Fujiwara Nobuzane 藤原信実
Fujiwara Teika 藤原定家
Fujiwara Yukimitsu 藤原行光
Fusō ryakki 扶桑略記
gakō 画工
gakumonsho 学問所
Gangōji engi 元興寺縁起
Gangyō 元暁
gei 芸
geijutsu 芸術
gesō 下僧
gijutsusho 技術書
Ginza "Brick Town" Plan 銀座煉瓦街計画
(Ginza rengagai keikaku)
Gishō 義湘
Glover House グラバー邸
Gohimitsu 五秘密
Gomizuno'o 後水尾
Gotoba 後鳥羽
goyō 御用
Great Kantō Earthquake Memorial 関東大震災記念堂
(Kantō daijishin ki'nendō)
Gyōben 行弁
gyōbu 刑部
Gyōji 行慈
Hagi 萩
Hanaōgi of the Ōgiya 扇屋の花扇
(Ōgiya no Hanaogi)
Hasegawa Tōhaku 長谷川等伯
Hayashi Tadahiro 林忠恕
Heian Shrine 平安神宮
(Heian jingū)
heki 壁
hidensho 秘伝所

hinagata bon 雛形本
Hirata Yutaka 平田寛
Hishikawa Moronobu 菱川師宣
Hizen 肥前
hōgen 法眼
Hōkō gan sanjūichi nen 法興元三十一年
hokkyō 法橋
honzon 本尊
Hōryūji 法隆寺
Hōseidō Kisanji 朋誠堂喜三二
ifū 以風
Imado 今戸
Itō Chūta 伊東忠太
Izutsuya Han'emon 井筒屋半衛門
jibutsudō 持仏堂
jija 侍者
Jingoji 神護寺
Jōshin 定真
jōshin seki 定心石
Jōshōju 縄床樹
Jōkyū 承久
Jū'ninbō 十忍房
jushi ige 従四位下
Kafuka no omi 鹿深臣
kagyō 家業
Kai'chi Primary School 開智学校
(Kai'chi Gakkō)
Kakuyū 覚猷
kami 神
kami 守
(governor)
Kamigata 上方
Kamitsumiya hōō 上宮法王
Kamo 鴨
Kanematsu Lecture Hall 兼松講堂
(Kanematsu kōdō)
Kaneyasu 兼康
Kangien 観喜園
Kannon 観音
Kano (Kanō) Einō 狩野永納

Kano Gyokuen 狩野玉燕
Kano Ikkei 狩野一渓
Kano Tan'yū 狩野探幽
Karahafu 唐破風
karamonoya 唐物屋
Karatsu 唐津
Kasuga 春日
katami 形見
Katsukawa Shunshō 勝川春章
Kawai Kōzō 河合浩蔵
Kegon 華厳
Kegon engi emaki 華厳縁起絵巻
kenchiku 建築
Kenchiku gakkai 建築学会
Kenchiku kyōkai 建築協会
Kenchiku zasshi 建築雑誌
kibyōshi 黄表紙
Kigo Kiyoyoshi 木子清敬
Kikai 喜海
Kinbutsu 近仏
Kitagawa Utamaro 喜多川歌麿
Kitao Shigemasa 北尾重政
kiwame 極め
kiwarihō 木割法
kō 工
Kō gakkai 工学会
Kōben 高弁
Kōbushō 工部省
Kōchi 高知
Kofun 古墳
kōgaku 工学
kōgei 工芸
Koguryŏ 高句麗
Koikawa Harumachi 恋川春町
Kojima Noriyuki 小島憲之
Komai kabe 小舞壁
Kōmei bijin mitate Chūshingura-jūnimai tsuzuki 高名美人見立て忠臣蔵十二枚続
Kondō 金堂
Kōshin 高信

Koyama Hidenoshin 小山秀之進
Kōzanji 高山寺
Kōzen 高然
Kubota 窪田
Kudara Kannon 百済観音
Kujō Michiie 九条道家
Kuno Shōhaku 久野正伯
kura 鞍
Kuratsukuri-be 鞍作部
Kuratsukuri Kenkui 鞍作堅貴
Kuratsukuri no Fukuri 鞍作福利
Kuratsukuri no Obito Karami 鞍作首加羅爾
Kuratsukuri no Tokushaku 鞍作徳積
Kuratsukuri no Tokushi 鞍作得志
Kurokawa Kishō 黒川紀章
Kusanagi no tsurugi 草薙剣
Kuwana 桑名
kyōka 狂歌
kyōkabon 狂歌本
Liang 梁
machi eshi 町絵師
Maruyama Ōkyo 円山応挙
Maruzen Bookstore 丸善書店
(Maruzen shoten)
Meiroku zasshi 明六雑誌
mekiki 目利
Minabuchi 南淵
Miroku 弥勒
mitate 見立て
Mitsui House 三井ハウス (第一国立銀行)
(Daiichi Kokusai Ginkō)
Momokawa Chōki 百川長喜
Mononobe no Okoshi 物部尾輿
Mori Tōru 森暢
Morita Kyūemon 森田久右衛門
Myōe 明恵
Nabeshima 鍋島
Naeshirogawa 苗代川
Nakamura 中村
Nakatomi no Kamako 中臣鎌子

Naniwa 難波
nengō 年号
New Yoshiwara pleasure district 新吉原
(Shin Yoshiwara)
Nihon no kenchikuka 日本の建築家
Nihon shoki 日本書記
Nishi Amane 西周
Nishikawa Shuntei 西川春貞
nishiki-e 錦絵
Nishiki-ori Utamaro-gata shin moyō 錦織歌麿形新模様
Nishiki no ura 錦の裏
(The Other Side of the Brocade)
Nishimuraya Yōhachi 西村屋与八
niwayaki 庭焼
Nobuhisa 信久
Nonomura Ninsei 野々村仁清
nyohō 如法
Obito 首
Odo 尾戸
Ōe Masafusa 大江匡房
Ofuke 御深井
okibumi 置文
ōkubi-e 大首絵
Okumura Masanobu 奥村政信
Ōmiya Gonkurō 近江屋権九部
Omuro 御室
Ono no Imoko 小野妹子
Osaka Mint 大阪造幣寮
(Osaka zōheiryō)
Ōta Nanpo 大田南畝
Paekche 百済
Postal Service Offices 駅停寮
(Eki teiryō)
Rakan 羅漢
Rokkaku 六角
rōsō 老僧
ryō 両
Ryōga 楞伽
Ryōten 霊典
sadō 茶頭

Saga 佐賀
Saionji Kintsune 西園寺公経
Sakai Uta-no-kami Tadakiyo 酒井雅楽頭忠清
Sakata 坂田
Sakatadera 坂田寺
sakon 左近
san 讃
Sano Riki 佐野利器
Santō Kyōden 山東京伝
Satō Dōshin 佐藤道信
Satsuma 薩摩
Sei Shōnagon 清少納言
Seirō bijin awase sugata 青楼美人合姿
Seirō jūni toki 青楼十二時
Seiyō no ākitekuto 西洋のアーキテクト
Seiyōga dan 西洋画談
Sekien gafū 石燕画風
Sen no Rikyū 千利休
sengoku jidai 戦国時代
Seto 瀬戸
sha 写
Shaka Triad 釈迦三尊
(Shaka sanzon)
sharebon 洒落本
shi 師
Shiba 司馬
Shiba Kōkan 司馬江漢
Shiba Kuratsukuri Obito Tori-busshi 司馬鞍作部止利仏師
Shiba Sōtatsu 司馬曹達
Shiba Tatto 司馬達等
Shigaraki 信楽
Shijūhattai butsu 四十八体仏
Shikitei Sanba 式亭三馬
Shima 嶋
Shimizu Kisuke II 第二清水喜助
Shinkei 信慶
shōgen 将監
shōji 障子
Shōjitsu 性実
Shōjō 證定

shokunin 職人
Shōnin 上人
Shōnin Eidokoro 上人影所
shōnin shin'ei 上人真影
Shōtoku Taishi 聖徳太子
shōyū 小輔
Shūgakuin 修学院
Shunga 俊賀
shuppitsu biku 執筆比丘
shuppitsu sō 執筆僧
Silla 新羅
Sima 司馬
Soba-ishi 蘇婆石
Soga no Emishi 蘇我蝦夷
Soga no Iname 蘇我稲目
Soga no Iruka 蘇我入鹿
Soga no Umako 蘇我馬子
Soga-Tori 蘇我止利
Sone Tatsuzō 曽禰達蔵
Sui 隋
Suiko tennō 推古天皇
Sumiyoshi 住吉
Suzuki Harunobu 鈴木春信
tairō 大老
Takahara 高原
Takebashi Army Barracks 竹橋陣営
(Takebashi jin'ei)
Takizawa Bakin 滝沢馬琴
Takuma Chōga 詫間長賀
Takuma Chōga 詫間澄賀
Takuma Hōgen 詫間法眼
Takuma Shōga 詫間勝賀
takumi 工
Tanaka Ichimatsu 田中一松
Tani Bunchō 谷文晁
Tasuna 多須奈
Tateishi Seijū 立石清重
Tatsuno Kingo 辰野金吾
tayū 大輔
ten 天

Toba Sōjō 鳥羽僧正
Toganoo 栂尾
Tokugawa Ieyasu 徳川家康
Tokugawa Tadayoshi 徳川忠義
Tokugawa Toyomasa 徳川豊昌
Tokugawa Tsunayoshi 徳川綱吉
Tokutomi Sohō 徳富蘇峰
Tokusai-hosshi 徳済法師
Tori-busshi 止利仏師
Torii Kiyonaga 鳥居清長
Toriyama Sekien 鳥山石燕
Tosa 土佐
Tosa Mitsumochi/Mitsushige 土佐光茂
Tosa Mitsumoto 土佐光元
Tosa Mitsunari 土佐光成
Tosa Mitsunobu 土佐光信
Tosa Mitsuoki 土佐光起
Tosa Yukihiro 土佐行広
Toyama 戸山
tsū 通
Tsukiji Hotel 築地ホテル館
(Tsukiji hoteru kan)
Tsuruya Kiemon 鶴屋喜右衛門
Tsutaya Jūzaburō 蔦屋重三郎
Uji 宇治
Ukiyo-e kōshō 浮世絵考証
Ukiyo-e ruikō 浮世絵類考
ukon 右近
Umayado no Ōji 馬屋王子
Utagawa Toyoharu 歌川豊春
utai 謡い
Utamakura うたまくら
Wa 倭
Yakushi 薬師
Yamato-e やまと絵
Yamauchi 山内
Yamauchi Tadatoyo 山内忠豊
Yamauchi Tadayoshi 山内忠義
Yamauchi Toyomasa 山内豊昌
Yoshiwara saiken 吉原細見

yūjo 遊女
Yumechigai Kannon 夢違観音
Yumedono Kannon 夢殿観音
Zendōin 禅堂院
Zenmyōji 禅妙寺
Zenshin-ni 善信尼
Zenzai 善財
Zeze 膳所
Zōka gakkai 造家学会

Works Frequently Cited

Amino Yoshihiko. "Chūsei no 'shokunin' o megutte" (A consideration of medieval 'shokunin'). In Amino Yoshihiko and Ishida Hisatoyo (eds.), *Shokunin* (Tradespeople), vol. 12 of *Kinsei fūzoku zufu* (Picture compendium of early modern manners and customs). Tokyo: Shogakukan, 1983, pp. 62–73.

———. "Some Problems Concerning the History of Popular Life in Medieval Japan," *Acta Asiatica*, Mar. 1983, *44*, 77–97.

Asakura Haruhiko. *Edo shokunin zukushi* (Assemblage of Edo shokunin). Tokyo: Iwasaki bijutsusha, 1987.

Asano Shūgō and Timothy Clark. *The Passionate Art of Kitagawa Utamaro*. Tokyo and London: Asahi Shinbun and British Museum, 1995.

Aston, W. G. *Nihongi: Chronicles of Japan from the Earliest Times to 697*. Rutland, Vt., and Tokyo: Tuttle, 1972.

Barthes, Roland. "The Death of the Author." In *Image, Music, Text*. New York: Hill and Wang, 1977.

Brock, Karen L. "'My Reflection Should Be Your Keepsake': Myōe's Vision of the Kasuga Deity." In Robert H. Sharf and Elizabeth Horton Sharf (eds.), *Living Images: Japanese Buddhist Icons in Their Monastic Contexts*. Stanford, Calif.: Stanford University Press, 2001, pp. 49–113.

Coaldrake, William H. *The Way of the Carpenter: Tools and Japanese Architecture*. New York: Weatherhill, 1990.

Cort, Louise Allison. *Seto and Mino Ceramics*. Washington, D.C.: Freer Gallery of Art, 1992.

———. *Shigaraki, Potters' Valley* (2nd ed.). New York and Tokyo: Weatherhill, 2000 [1979].

———. "Shopping for Pots in Momoyama Japan." In Morgan Pitelka (ed.), *Japanese Tea Culture: Art, History, and Practice*. London and New York: Routledge Curzon, 2003, pp. 61–85.

Foucault, Michel. "What Is an Author?" In P. Rabinow (ed.), *The Foucault Reader*. New York: Pantheon Books, 1984.

Fujii Sadafumi and Hayashi Rikurō (eds.). *Hanshi jiten* (Dictionary of domainal history). Tokyo: Akita shoten, 1976.

Fujii Shōichirō and Yamaguchi Hiroshi (eds.). *Nihon kenchiku sengen bunshū* (Collected Japanese architectural manifestos). Tokyo: Shōkokusha, 1973.

Fujimori Terunobu. *Nihon no kindai kenchiku* (Modern Japanese architecture), vols. 1 and 2. Tokyo: Iwanami shinsho, 1993.

Funaki Kayoko. "Osaka-Nara no yakimono" (Ceramics of Osaka and Nara). In Mitsuoka Tadanari et al. (eds.), *Kinki II* (Kinki region II), pp. 106–11. Nihon yakimono shūsei, vol. 7. Tokyo: Heibonsha, 1981.

Hagami Shōchō et al. (eds.). *Myōe shōnin to Kōzanji*. Tokyo: Dōhōsha, 1981.

Hamada Giichirō (ed.).. *Ōta Nanpo zenshū* (Collected works of Ōta Nanpo), vol. 18. Tokyo: Iwanami shoten, 1988.

Hirata Yutaka. *Ebusshi no jidai* (The age of painted-buddha masters), 2 vols. Tokyo: Chūōkōron, 1994.

Inagaki Eizō. *Nihon no kindai kenchiku: Sono seiritsu katei* (Japan's modern architecture: The process of its formation), vols. 1 and 2. Tokyo: Kajima shuppankai, 1979.

Kimura Tokue. *Tosa monjo kaisetsu* (Explanation of the Tosa archive). Tokyo: Iwai Kameijirō, 1935.

Kornicki, Peter F. "Nishiki no Ura: An Instance of Censorship and the Structure of a Sharebon." *Monumenta Nipponica*, 1977, *32*(2), 153–88.

Kōzanji tenseki komonjo sōgō chōsadan (Comprehensive investigative team for Kōzanji books and documents, ed.). *Kōzanji shiryōō sōshō* (Compendium of Kōzanji source materials), 21 vols. Tokyo: Tokyo University Press, 1968–present.

Kris, Ernst, and Otto Kurz. *Legend, Myth, and Magic in the Image of the Artist.* New Haven, Conn., and London: Yale University Press, 1979.

Kyoto National Museum (ed.). *Kōzanji-ten.* Kyoto, 1981.

Machida Kōichi. "Kuratsukuri-be no shusshin to Asuka jidai ni okeru 'Tori shiki butsuzō' no kōbō ni tsuite." In *Jōdai chōkoku shi no kenkyū.* Tokyo: Yoshikawa kōbunkan, 1977.

Maruyama Kazuo (trans.). "Morita Kyūemon Edo nikki" (Morita Kyūemon's Edo diary). In *Tōyō tōji* (Oriental ceramics), vol. 5 (unpaginated). Tokyo: Tōyō Tōji Gakkai, 1978.

Matsuki Hiroshi. *Tsutaya Jūzaburō.* Tokyo: Nihon Keizai Shinbunsha, 1974.

McCallum, Donald F. "The Buddhist Triad in Three Kingdoms Sculpture." *Korean Culture*, 1995, *16*(4), 18–25.

Meech-Pekarik, Julia. *The World of the Meiji Print: Impressions of a New Civilization.* New York: Weatherhill, 1986.

Miyajima Shin'ichi. *Tosa Mitsunobu to Tosaha no kefu* (Tosa Mitsunobu and the lineage of the Tosa School). Nihon no bijutsu, no. 247. Tokyo: Shibundō, Dec. 1986.

Mizuno Keizaburō. *Hōryūji: Kondō Shaka sanzon zō* (The Shaka Triad of the Golden Hall of Hōryūji). In *Nara no tera* (Temples of Nara), vol. 3. Tokyo: Iwanami shoten, 1992.

Mizutani Chiaki. "Kuratsukuri no Tokushi no kijutsu: *Kōgyoku ki* no kisai ni tsuite" (The conjuring of Kuratsukuri no Tokushi: The entry in the Kōgyoku Chronicles). *Ryūkoku daigaku bukkyō bunka kenkyūjo kiyō*, 1989, *27*, 44–47.

Mori Tōru, *Kamakura jidai no shōzōga* (Portraiture of the Kamakura period). Tokyo: Misuzu shobō, 1971.

Murakami Sōdō. *Toganoosan Kōzanji Myōe Shōnin.* Kyoto, Kōzanji, 1929.

Mushakōji Minoru. "Eshi" (Painters). In *Mono to ningen no bunkashi* (The cultural history of things and people), no. 63. Tokyo: Hōsei daigaku, 1990.

Naitō Katsuo and Masui Kunio. "Minami Kantō no yakimono" (Ceramics of the southern Kantō region). In Mitsuoka Tadanari et al. (eds.), *Hokkaidō-Tōhoku-Kantō* (Hokkaidō, Tōhoku, and Kantō regions), pp. 145–56. Nihon yakimono shūsei, vol. 1. Tokyo: Heibonsha, 1981.

Nakano Mitsutoshi. "Bunka-men in okeru Kansei kaikaku" ("The cultural field of the Kansei Reforms"). In *Nihon no kinsei 12: Bungaku to bijutsu no seijuku* (Early modern Japan 12: The maturation of literature and art). Tokyo: Chūō kōronsha, 1993.

Nakanodō Kazunobu. "Minami Yamashiro to Tango no yakimono" (Ceramics of southern Yamashiro and Tango provinces). In Mitsuoka Tadanari et al. (eds.),

Kyoto (Kyoto), pp. 131–34. Nihon yakimono shūsei, vol. 5. Tokyo: Heibonsha, 1981.

Nara Kokuritsu Bunkazai Kenkyūjo, Asuka Shiryōkan (ed.). *Asuka/Hakuhō no zaimei kondō butsu* (Inscribed gilt-bronze images of the Asuka and Hakuhō periods, 1st ed.). Nara: Nara Kokuritsu Bunkazai Kenkyūjo, Asuka Shiryōkan, 1976. (2nd ed.), 1979.

Nara Rokudaiji Taikan Kankokai (ed.). *Nara rokudaiji taikan* (Overview of the six great temples of Nara), vol. 2. Tokyo: Iwanami shoten, 1968.

Nishi Amane. "An Essay on Brick Construction." In William Reynolds Braisted (trans.), *Meiroku zasshi: Journal of the Japanese Enlightenment*. Cambridge, Mass.: Harvard University Press, 1976, pp. 52–54.

Ōhashi Katsuaki (ed.). *Hōryūji bijutsu ronsō no shiten* (The art of Hōryūji: viewpoints on controversies). Tokyo: Gurafusha, 1998.

———. "Kuratsukuri Tori no zōbutsu gihō no shūtoku ni tsuite" (Concerning the mastery of sculptural techniques by Kuratsukuri Tori). In Takatori Masato sensei koki shukuga ronbunshū kankōkai (ed.), *Kodai shi sōkō* (Collection of research on ancient Japanese history). Tokyo: Takatori Masato sensei koki shukuga ronbunshū kankōkai, 1994, pp. 23–49.

———. *Nara bijutsu no sōten* (Controversial points in Nara art). Tokyo: Gurafusha, 1984.

Oka Yoshiko. "*Kakumeiki* ni miru karamonoyatachi: kinsei shoto no tōjiki ryūtsū" (Antique dealers as seen in the *Kakumeiki*: Distribution of ceramics at the start of the early modern period). *Shisō* (Journal of the History Association of Kyoto Women's University), Mar. 1991, *48*, 245–62.

———. "Karamonoya oboegaki—Ōhira Gohei to Katsuyama Chōji" (Memo on antique dealers—Ōhira Gohei and Katsuyama Chōji). In *Kan'ei bunka no nettowaaku: "Kakumeiki" no sekai* (Networks of Kan'ei era culture: The world of the Kakumeiki), ed. by Oka Yoshiko and Iwama Kaori. Kyoto: Shibunkaku shuppan, 1998, pp. 199–208.

Ōkubo Jun'ichi. "Utamaro no 'Seirō jūnitoki' to sono shuhen (Utamaro's *Twelve Hours of the Blue Towers* and its context)." *Museum*, 1989, vol. 462.

Okuda Isao, *Myōe: henreki to yume* (Saint Myōe: pilgrimages and dreams). Tokyo: Tokyo daigaku shuppan, 1978.

Ōnishi Hiroshi (ed.). *Geijutsuka densetsu* (Legends about artists). Tokyo: Perikansha, 1989.

Ono Kan'ichirō (ed.). *Morita Kyūemon nikki* (The Morita Kyūemon diary). Tōki zenshū, vol. 10. Tokyo: Tōki zenshū hankōkai, 1932.

Ōta Kinen Hakubutsukan. *Utamaro geijutsu no saihakken* (Rediscovering the art of Utamaro). Tokyo: Ōta Kinen Bijutsukan, 1993.

Phillips, Quitman E. *The Practices of Painting in Japan, 1475–1500*. Stanford, Calif.: Stanford University Press, 2000.

Rosenfield, John (ed.). *Competition and Collaboration: Hereditary Schools in Japanese Culture (Fenway Court)*. Boston: Isabella Stewart Gardner Museum, 1992.

———. "Japanese Studio Practice: The Tosa Family and the Imperial Painting Office in the Seventeenth Century." In Peter Lukehart (ed.), *The Artist's Workshop*. Studies in the History of Art, no. 38. Washington, D.C.: Center for Advanced Studies in the Visual Arts, 1993, pp. 79–102.

Saint, Andrew. *The Image of the Architect*. New Haven, Conn.: Yale University Press, 1983.

Saitō Rieko. "Hōryūji Kondō Shaka sanzonzō no seisaku nendai: Kasai-Ōhashi ronsō," in Ōhashi Katsuaki (ed.), *Ronsō: Nara bijutsu*. Tokyo: Heibonsha, 1994, pp. 41–66.

Sakazaki Tan. *Nihon kaigaron taikei* (Overview of Japanese painting treatises). Tokyo: Meicho fukyūsha, 1979.

Sakurai Tokutarō, Hagiwara Tatsuo, and Miyata Noboru. *Jisha engi* (Founding legends of shrines and temples). Vol. 20 of *Nihon shisō taikei* (Overview of Japanese thought). Tokyo: Iwanami shoten, 1975.

Satō Dōshin. *Meiji kokka to kindai bijutsu—bi no seijigaku* (The Meiji State and modern art: The politics of the beautiful). Tokyo: Yoshikawa kobunkan, 1999.

Sato, Hiroaki (trans.). *A Brief History of Imbecility: Poetry and Prose of Takamura Kōtarō*. Honolulu: University of Hawaii Press, 1992.

Seigle, Cecilia Segawa. *Yoshiwara: The Glittering World of the Japanese Courtesan*. Honolulu: University of Hawai'i Press, 1993.

Shimizu, Yoshiaki. "Workshop Management of the Early Kano Painters, ca. A.D. 1530–1600," *Archives of Asian Art*, 1981, *34*, 32–44.

Suzuki Hiroyuki and Yamaguchi Hiroshi (eds.). *Kindai gendai kenchikushi* (Modern and contemporary Japanese architecture). Vol. 5 of Uchida Yoshichika (ed.), *Shin kenchikugaku taikei* (The new compendium of architecture studies). Tokyo: Shōkokusha, 1993.

Suzuki Jūzō. "Shiryō ni tadoru Utamaro no gagyō to shōgai" (Pursuing the documents: Utamaro's biography and artistic career) in *Ehon to ukiyoe* (Illustrated books and ukiyo-e). Tokyo: Bijutsu shuppansha, 1979.

Suzuki Toshiyuki. *Kinsei bungaku kenkyū sosho 9: Tsutaya Jūzaburō* (Studies in early modern literature 9: Tsutaya Jūzaburō). Tokyo: Wakakusa shobo, 1998.

Tadatoyo-kō ki (Record of Lord Tadatoyo), vol. 1. (Unpublished holograph manuscript). Yamauchi Jinja Shiryōkan (Yamauchi Shrine Archives), Kōchi.

Tadayoshi-kō ki (Record of Lord Tadayoshi), vol. 1. (Unpublished holograph manuscript). Yamauchi Jinja Shiryōkan (Yamauchi Shrine Archives), Kōchi.

Takamura Kōtarō. *Takamura Kōtarō zenshū* (Complete works of Takamura Kōtarō). 18 vols. Tokyo: Chikuma shobō, 1957–58.

Takamura Kōun. *Bakumatsu isshin kaikodan* (Reminiscences from the Bakumatsu and early Meiji periods). Tokyo: Iwanami bunko, 1995.

Takemitsu Makoto. *Kenkyūshi: Bemin sei* (Historiography: The guild system). Tokyo: Yoshikawa kōbunkan, 1981.

Tanabe, George J. *Myōe the Dreamkeeper: Fantasy and Knowledge in Early Kamakura Buddhism*. Cambridge, Mass.: Harvard University Press, 1992.

Tanaka Tsuguhito. *Nihon kodai busshi no kenkyū* (Research on the Buddhist sculptors of ancient Japan). Tokyo: Yoshikawa kōbunkan, 1983.

Tanaka Hisao, *Kamakura bukkyō zakkō* (Miscellaneous research on Kamakura Buddhism). Kyoto: Shibunkaku shuppan, 1982.

Tani Shin'ichi. "Tosa Mitsunobu kō: Tosa-ha kenkyū no issetsu" (Study on Tosa Mitsunobu: An essay researching the Tosa school), *Bijutsu kenkyū*, 1940, *100*, 115–28; *101*, 159–69; *103*, 207–21.

Tani Shin'ichi. "Tosa Mitsunobu kō" (A consideration of Tosa Mitsunobu). In Tani Shin'ichi, *Muromachi jidai bijutsushi ron* (Discussion of Muromachi period art history). Tokyo: Tōkyōdō, 1942, pp. 418–514.

Tazawa Yutaka, Sawayanagi Daigorō, Kuno Takeshi, and Sakamoto Manshichi. *Hōryūji shiryō chōkuku hen* (Hōryūji research materials: Sculpture series), vol. 1, *Hōryūji Kondō Shaka sanzon zō* (The Shaka Triad of the Golden Hall of Hōryūji). Tokyo: Iwanami shoten, 1949.

Toki-shi Mino Tōji Rekishikan (Toki Municipal History Museum of Mino Ceramics). *Rakuchū shutsudō no Mino Momoyama tō* (Momoyama-period Mino ceramics excavated in Kyoto). Toki City, Gifu Prefecture: Toki-shi Mino Tōji Rekishikan, 1990.

———. *Momoyama no hana: Osaka shutsukō no Momoyama tōji* (Flowering of Momoyama: Momoyama ceramics excavated in Osaka). Toki City, Gifu Prefecture: Toki-shi Mino Tōji Rekishikan, 1993.

———. *Rakuchū shutsudō no Momoyama tōki* (Momoyama-period ceramics excavated in Kyoto). Toki City, Gifu Prefecture: Toki-shi Mino Tōji Rekishikan, 1991.

———. *Utsuwa: Momoyama no bi* (Vessels: Momoyama beauty). Toki City, Gifu Prefecture: Toki-shi Mino Tōji Rekishikan, 1992.

Tōkyō Kokuritsu Hakubutsukan (ed.). *Hōryūji kenno hōbutsu tokubetsu chōsa gaihō* (Report on the special investigation of the treasures donated by Hōryūji). Tokyo: Tōkyō Kokuritsu Hakubutsukan, 1985–90.

———. *Hōryūji kenno hōbutsu: Kondō butsu* I (The treasures donated by Hōryūji: Images in the Golden Hall, I). Tokyo: Tōkyō Kokuritsu Hakubutsukan, 1996.

Yamamura, Kozo. "The Development of Za in Medieval Japan." *Business History Review*, Winter 1973, *47*, 438–65.

———. "The Growth of Commerce in Medieval Japan." In Kozo Yamamura (ed.), *The Cambridge History of Japan*, vol. 3, *Medieval Japan*. Cambridge, England: Cambridge University Press, 1990, pp. 344–95.

Yoshida Yūji. "Shihai monjo no eshi Mitsunobu—'Tosa Mitsunobu' hōi 1" (Background documents on the painter Mitsunobu—'Tosa Mitsunobu' supplement 1). *Teizukayama Gakuin daigaku kenkyū ronshū*, Apr. 1979, *12*, 1711–1821.

———. *Tosa Mitsunobu. Nihon bijutsu kaiga zenshū* (Complete collection of Japanese art painting), no. 5. Tokyo: Shūeisha, 1979.

Index